PUBLISHED FOR
JUDAICA RESEARCH AT YALE UNIVERSITY
on the
LOUIS M. RABINOWITZ FOUNDATION

YALE JUDAICA SERIES

EDITOR

JULIAN OBERMANN

Volume VII

KARAITE ANTHOLOGY

KARAITE ANTHOLOGY

Excerpts from the Early Literature

TRANSLATED FROM ARABIC, ARAMAIC, AND HEBREW SOURCES
WITH NOTES BY

LEON NEMOY
YALE UNIVERSITY

NEW HAVEN
YALE UNIVERSITY PRESS
LONDON · GEOFFREY CUMBERLEGE · OXFORD UNIVERSITY PRESS
1952

Printed in the United States of America

Library of Congress Catalog Card Number: 52-5367

Fratris unici

Simon

(1895–1925)

piam in memoriam

FOREWORD

The purpose of the present anthology is to provide the general reader with a more intimate and authentic glimpse of Karaite literature and thought than might be obtained from popular essays and articles on the Karaites hitherto available.[1] The original texts of the extracts here translated have all been published, and I have advisedly excluded any unpublished material in order to avoid discussion of purely technical problems which such texts invariably involve and which would only prove confusing to the nonspecialist.

For the benefit of those whom this book is primarily meant to serve, I have endeavored to make both the prefatory and the explanatory matter as concise and nontechnical as the subject would permit.[2] As far as possible, too, I have inserted explanatory matter into the text of the extracts in order to make them more readable and to reduce the number of distracting notes.[3] The latter have been limited, for the most part, to factual explanation of the subject matter, and I have purposely avoided detours into the complicated field of comparative law and theology.[4] Where original Karaite texts were available in modern critical editions I have leaned

1. The only other substantial collection of Karaite extracts known to me is the one included in J. Winter and A. Wuensche, *Die juedische Literatur seit Abschluss des Kanons* (Trier, 1894–96), II, 65–118. It is very small, the extracts (translated from Hebrew sources only) are quite short, and the work was published prior to the discovery of several of the most important documents of the early period.

2. For general historical and theological information on Jewish subjects the reader is referred to the *Jewish Encyclopedia*, the *Universal Jewish Encyclopedia*, and the *Encyclopedia Judaica*. The latter, written in German, is the best and most detailed of the three, but has unfortunately been brought up only to the letter L.

3. This explanatory matter is not marked in any way; restorations of textual lacunae, on the other hand, are enclosed within square brackets. Omissions are indicated by ellipses or explained in the notes.

4. This is especially true of the legal texts; the Rabbanite references and parallels supplied for them are meant to be mere hints for the benefit of the reader who may wish to pursue the subject further. They are certainly far from exhaustive, for a full comparative examination of such matters is beyond the scope of this anthology and outside the field of my studies.

heavily upon the annotations of their editors; in other instances I have been obliged to use uncritical editions issued by the Karaites themselves. In the numerous cases where I have found myself compelled to emend the original text or to disagree with an editor's construction of it, I had no choice but to indicate my reasons in a note.

In the choice of texts comprising this anthology, I have endeavored to select specimens which would, on the one hand, make more or less interesting and profitable reading and, on the other, typify as many different branches of Karaite literature as possible. Karaite literature is predominantly theological and for the most part exceedingly technical and dry, but so far as possible, I have chosen texts of historical and literary content, as well as theological and legal texts dealing with subjects not devoid of general interest. Such highly complicated subjects as calendar, ritual cleanness, Hebrew grammar and lexicography have been excluded, even though they are of great importance for the specialist in this field.[5]

The texts here collected belong to the early period of Karaite history, ending, roughly, in A.D. 1500. The only exception is the large extract from the Karaite prayer book, in which the omission of the post-1500 material would have made it difficult to present a fair picture of the unity and charm of the Karaite marriage service.

Since Karaite literature, particularly in the period covered by this anthology, devotes much attention to polemics with Rabbanism, the reader will find in the following pages some passages which were composed in the heat of controversy and employ rather vehement language. Religious conflict is notoriously characterized by disregard of verbal moderation and restraint, and neither the Karaites nor their Rabbanite opponents offer an exception to this

5. It has frequently been found advisable to translate biblical passages occurring in our texts in such a way as to make their wording accord with the interpretation intended by the given Karaite author and thus fit the context of the discussion involved. In instances of this kind, the biblical passages will naturally be found at variance with their wording in the standard translations of the Bible. This is specifically the case in the extracts from Japheth ben Eli (who gives his own Arabic rendering of the Book of Ruth, instead of quoting the Hebrew text) and from Moses of Damascus (where violence has to be done to the biblical quotations to make them fit the context).

rule, each of the two parties being sincerely and profoundly convinced that the other was sunk in grievous error. Yet fairness demands that one bear in mind the fact that this conflict, sharp as it was, remained throughout a war of words and never degenerated into physical violence or armed warfare.

It is a pleasant duty to place on record my profound obligation to Professor Julian J. Obermann of Yale University, who first suggested the plan of this anthology and who has followed my work upon it with kindly interest, constructive assistance, and warm encouragement; and to Professor James T. Babb, Yale Librarian, whose devotion to the development of the Hebrew and Arabic collections in the Sterling Memorial Library of Yale University has made it possible for me to extend the scope of my studies beyond what might have been feasible otherwise. Professors Louis Ginzberg and Harry A. Wolfson have read, respectively, the first four chapters and the Introduction, and have contributed, with their customary generosity, a number of important corrections and suggestions. Dr. Michael Bernstein read the extracts translated from Aramaic and Hebrew originals and supplied many talmudic references and some valuable suggestions for improvement.

L. N.

CONTENTS

INTRODUCTION

I

The Arab conquests of the seventh century, rapidly consolidated into a far-flung empire, brought nearly all Jewish centers of that period under the control and influence of Islam. The most important of these centers of medieval Jewry, the mainspring of Jewish learning, culture, and authority, had long since been anchored in Iraq, the ancient Babylonia. Now this metropolitan Jewish community was to embark upon a new and eventful era of its long history, an era of remarkable accomplishment as well as fateful strife.

The Jewish settlement in Iraq traced its origin as far back as the Babylonian exile (586 B.C.). Under the Persian rule of the Parthian and Sassanid dynasties it developed an autonomous system of self-government, headed by the exilarch (Aramaic *reš galuṯa,* later arabicized as *ra's al-ǧālūt*), who served as the chief representative of Jewry before the king and was responsible for the collection of taxes, the administration of justice, and the maintenance of public order and safety within the Jewish community. To assist him in these administrative functions he had under his control an extensive bureaucracy of officials, whose salaries and expenses, like his own, were paid out of special taxes imposed upon the Jewish population, over and above the regular levies payable to the Persian state. Although some of the exilarchs were competent scholars in theology and law, the exilarchate in itself was essentially a political office and carried no duties and powers in the field of religion and legal theory. This was the province of the rabbinical academies, especially of the two major seats of learning in the cities of Sura and Pumbeditha. During the Persian period these were scholastic institutions pure and simple, whose curriculum covered the Bible, the oral tradition developed in explanation of the biblical legislation and codified in written form about A.D. 200 as the Mishnah, and the auxiliary disciplines necessary in dealing with various special branches of law.

The result of the research and teaching done at these academies was a vast body of new oral tradition built up in exposition and elaboration of the Mishnah and to provide for new conditions and new situations that had not been covered in the biblical and mishnaic legislation. With the progressive decline of the Persian state, it became imperative to re-examine this mass of oral law and custom and eventually reduce it to writing, in order to insure its preservation for the future. Begun in the second half of the fourth century, this sifting was continued, slowly and carefully, for over a hundred years until about A.D. 500, when it culminated in the publication of the encyclopedic thesaurus known as the Babylonian Talmud, which became the mainstay of Jewish life and social order.

This highly developed system of self-government and scholarly activity was based upon a social and economic structure no less complex. The social stratification produced an upper class, represented by the governmental bureaucracy, the upper layer of the intelligentsia, and the wealthy landowners, bankers, and merchants; a middle class, including the lower layer of intellectuals; and the great mass of rural tenant farmers and urban artisans and laborers. The lot of the latter class was far from easy under the heavy burden of double taxation, high land rentals and interest charges, and frequent ravages of foreign and civil wars. The political and economic decay of the Persian Empire during the sixth and seventh centuries intensified the misery of this major component of the Jewish community and produced in many minds a conviction that their situation was desperate and could not be endured very much longer.

The new Arab overlords who replaced the Persian rulers in the middle of the seventh century left Jewish autonomy in Iraq practically undisturbed, and the exilarch continued to function as the chief magistrate of the Jewish community and its representative at the caliph's court. The prestige of the office, however, gradually declined; at the same time the influence of the two major academies increased correspondingly. Their presidents now assumed the title of Gaon (Hebrew *Ga'on,* pl. *Gĕ'onim;* "Eminence" is perhaps as close a rendering of it as is possible), and together with their faculties they became the chief legislative organs and the highest courts of appeal for the Jewish population, thus acquiring a separate corps of public officials, whose salaries added another charge upon the communal treasury. Although few of the Geonim were truly outstanding personalities in the way of creative thought, their imprint upon Jewish life was most profound and lasting, for they applied the finishing touches to the recognition of talmudic law as the guiding rule of Jewish religious and social life.

The transition from Persian to Arab rule again left social and economic conditions practically undisturbed. The social stratification, taxes, and high living costs remained. The consolidation of the Moslem conquests into a world empire stimulated manufacture and commerce, but the lower classes of Iraqi Jewry reaped little of the benefits of increased communication and trade, and their grievances and unsatisfied desires found no new outlets. There was now, however, one new factor of great importance: the conquest and pacification of the sparsely populated provinces in the east and north (Xurāsān, Ğibāl, Aḏārbayğān, Armenia, etc.), and their incorporation into the Arab state opened a vast territory for immigration and made possible an exodus of discontented elements among the Iraqi Jews to new homes on the frontier. Like all such movements this emigration was undoubtedly composed mainly of self-reliant and venturesome individuals, and the mountainous character of their new homelands caused them to acquire quickly the mountaineer's desire to be left alone to live in his own fashion. The remoteness of these frontier settlements from the metropolitan center of Iraq made them practically independent, in both religious and secular matters, from exilarchic and Geonic authority. To the memory of past injustices there was joined in the minds of these Jewish settlers the bitter realization of the futility of the hope that the spectacular collapse of Persian and Byzantine power and the meteoric rise of the Arab Empire might be the herald of the miraculous redemption of Zion and the restoration of Israel to the Holy Land. On the other hand, they could not help but be strongly influenced by the example of their Persian neighbors, who under the religio-political banner of Shiism continued to resist their Arab conquerors and reassert their right to political and economic equality and freedom. For their own religious platform the Jewish frontiersmen had a ready-made example—the ancient and never entirely suppressed opposition (represented in earlier times by the Sadducee faction) to the validity of postbiblical law based on oral tradition and codified in the Talmud, and to the authority of its official administrators and interpreters in Iraq.

All these influences, by their combined action, produced at a very early date the principles common to a large number of schismatic movements which eventually, through a long process of elimination and consolidation, formed the Karaite sect: first, the rejection of the validity of the Talmud, whose adherents were now called Rabbanites, i.e., partisans of the talmudic Rabbis and their successors; second, the disinclination, inspired no doubt by their grievances against the Iraqi religious and secular officials, to recognize the permanent authority of a religious leader, or of a succession of leaders, and the insistence on the freedom of each individual to interpret the Bible—the sole repository of law—in the light of his own understanding and judgment; third, a perfervid messianic nationalism, impatient of the seemingly endless delay in the redemption and restoration of Israel; fourth, a strong flavor of unworldly asceticism; and fifth, an acute sense of social justice and opposition to economic inequality and oppression.

The passage of time and the harsh necessities of reality eventually forced upon Karaism a modification of these principles. While the Talmud remained theoretically outlawed, much talmudic material was quietly incorporated into Karaite practice of law and custom, but a purely Karaite tradition was developed and recognized as well. The anarchy of individual interpretation of the Bible was softened to some extent by partial recognition of the authority of outstanding Karaite scholars. The ascetic tendency was gradually reduced, and the passionate longing for Zion was diverted into the channel of prayer and pious hope. Finally, the distaste for riches and those who possessed them was overcome by the rise of a native Karaite aristocracy and wealthy bourgeoisie.

To distinguish themselves from the Rabbanites the new sectarians assumed the name of Karaites (Hebrew *ḳara'im,* Arabic *ḳarā'iyyūn*), a term which appears first in the ninth century. The most natural rendering of it is "champions of Scripture"—who do not recognize the postbiblical oral tradition—from the Hebrew *ḳara,* "to read," specifically, "to read and study Scripture" (Hebrew *miḳra*). Another explanation derives the term from the alternate meaning of *ḳara,* "to call, to invite"; hence Karaites would signify "callers, missionaries," similar to the Shiite "callers" (Arabic *dā'ī,* pl. *du'āt*), who exhorted Moslems to join their movement. A third interpretation connects the name with the Arabic *ḳarrā'* (pl. *ḳarrā'ūn*), "expert reader in Scripture," alluding to the Karaite preoccupation with biblical exegesis. All these derivations, however, are more or less conjectural and have no documentary evidence to support them.

The Shiite environment in Iraq and Persia in which Karaism was nurtured naturally suggests the inquiry as to whether the early Karaites were influenced not only by the political and social aspirations of their Persian fellow citizens but by their religious views as well. The answer, unfortunately, is beset with considerable difficulties and doubts. Some of the characteristic features of early Karaism seem to have Shiite parallels; for example, the Shiite theoretical rejection of the authority of the oral tradition recording the sayings and customs (Arabic *sunna*) of the Prophet Mohammed, the ascetic practices commemorating the death of 'Alī and his sons, and the passionate longing for the ultimate savior (Arabic *mahdī*). It would be unsafe, however, to assume from this similarity that Karaism borrowed these principles from Shiism, for the basic cause of the split between Sunnism and Shiism, the claim of 'Alī and his descendants to the caliphate, had no interest whatever for the Karaites; and their messianic nationalism, while similar to the Persian national feeling, nevertheless bears the unmistakable stamp of genuine Jewish origin and character. Moreover, the opposition to oral tradition, the tendency to asceticism, and the impatience with the prolonged exile were not totally new elements introduced by the Karaites; they were evident among some groups of Jews several centuries earlier and were merely taken over and developed by the new sectarians. Still, the example of their Shiite neighbors may have had some influence in directing early Karaite thought along these particular lines.

Since the birthplace of Karaism was the northeastern frontier region of the Arab empire, whose culture was essentially Persian, it is no surprise that the earliest known sectarian leader, Obadiah (Arabic Abū ʽĪsā ʽAbd Allāh), hailed from the city of Iṣfahān in the rugged province of al-Ǧibāl. Some time during the reign of the Caliph ʽAbd al-Malik (A.D. 685–705) he organized an armed revolt against the Arab authorities, but was quickly defeated and slain. This unusual attempt to redeem Israel by force of arms found no imitators, and Obadiah's successor and pupil, Yūdġān (presumably a persianized form of the name Judah), who must have lived in the first quarter of the eighth century, turned his attention mainly to rigid asceticism. Neither of these two early schismatics composed any systematic exposition of their teaching in book form, probably because they simply did not have the literary erudition and training for such a task. The honor of supplying a pioneer manual of non-Rabbanite theology fell to a learned and cultured Iraqi of aristocratic Rabbanite descent named Anan ben David who flourished in the seventh decade of the eighth century. How he came to break with the faith of his fathers we do not know, but it seems certain that it was not the result of angry disappointment over the failure of his candidacy for the office of exilarch, as the traditional Rabbanite account would have it. In any case, his secession from Rabbanism marks the first known evidence of Karaite penetration into the metropolitan Jewish center of Iraq, and his code of law is the earliest extant Karaite literary document. It earned for him a hazy sort of prestige among the other sectarians, while later Karaism elevated him to the dignity of the father of its synagogue and honored his lineal descendants with the title of prince. But in actual fact his teaching, permeated by a strong spirit of monastic asceticism, attracted few adherents and was often sharply criticized by other schismatics.

To the sect of Ananites there were added in the ninth century other dissident groups, some in Iraq, some in the provinces to the east and west organized by later schismatic teachers: Ismā'īl al-'Ukbarī, of the town of 'Ukbara in Iraq, a sharp critic of Anan; Benjamin al-Nahāwandī, of the city of Nahāwand (Nihāvend) in Persia, a mild and reasonable individual; and Malik al-Ramlī, a native of al-Ramla in Palestine. Another Iraqi sectarian, Mūsā (Moses), surnamed al-Za'farānī after his native district in the capital city of Bagdad, migrated to Tiflis in Armenia, where he presided over his own group of followers and became known as Abū 'Imrān al-Tiflīsī. In 'Ukbara Ismā'īl's place was taken by Mīšawayh al-'Ukbarī, who appears to have been something of a cynic—a rather unusual trait in early Karaism. With Daniel al-Ḳūmisī, a resident of the city of Dāmaġān in the northern Persian province of Ḳūmis and an able scholar, Karaism reached the tenth century.

The surnames quoted above indicate the territorial expansion of Karaism during the ninth and early in the tenth century into Iraq and Syro-Palestine. In addition to the one in al-Ramla, Karaite colonies were established in Damascus, the capital of Syria, and in Jerusalem, while other Karaite settlers made homes for themselves in Egypt, especially in Cairo. Like other young faiths, Karaism in its early period developed an intense missionary effort, and traveling Karaite preachers went from town to town and from province to province exhorting Rabbanite audiences—Karaism did not seek converts among non-Jews, at least as far as we know—but apparently with little actual success. The Karaite communities remained small and poor compared with their Rabbanite counterparts, and it is significant that with the exception of Anan not a single early Karaite scholar is stated to have been a Rabbanite convert. The reason is not far to seek: the rigorous and ascetic aspect of Karaite practice could have had little attraction for the poverty-stricken Jewish masses, whose life was already full of privation and self-denial, while the Rabbanite intellectuals were repelled by the chaotic condition of Karaism even as late as the second quarter of the tenth century. There was as yet no such thing as a unified Karaite sect, rather a mass of quarreling schismatics among whom, as a contemporary Karaite author (al-Ḳirḳisānī) pointedly expressed it, it was impossible to find two individuals in complete agreement with one another.

The stimulus to put an end to this chaos and introduce some semblance of organized unity was supplied to the Karaites not by one of their own number but by a Rabbanite scholar, the famous Saʻadiah ben Joseph al-Fayyūmī (A.D. 882–942), Gaon of the Academy at Sura in Iraq. Up to this time the Karaites had succeeded in maintaining an amicable relationship with their Rabbanite neighbors, and the failure of the schismatics to gain any appreciable number of converts encouraged the Rabbanite authorities in their belief that the wisest, as well as the easiest, course was to leave them alone. This Fabian policy of his predecessors found no favor at all in the eyes of Saʻadiah. A man of immense learning and pioneering intellect, as well as of profound piety and moral rectitude, he was at the same time human enough to be impatient and strong-willed toward those who disagreed with him. The peaceful intercourse between orthodox Rabbanites and Karaite schismatics appeared to him to be an intolerable and dangerous thing. In a series of polemical tracts Saʻadiah proceeded to attack and refute the doctrine and practice of Karaism, and to demonstrate to his own satisfaction that the Karaites were not just harmless deviators to be mildly chided for their error but complete apostates who should be ostracized from the community of Israel. The suddenness of his attack and its effectiveness, owing to Saʻadiah's great prestige, in bringing about a complete break between Rabbanites and Karaites horrified the latter, since they believed, no doubt quite sincerely, that they had done nothing to provoke so crushing a blow. Moreover, their forced estrangement from the Rabbanite community meant the closing of the only missionary field open to them and the collapse of the hope that their teaching would ultimately be accepted by all of Jewry. It was only natural, therefore, that they came to regard Saʻadiah as their principal enemy and that their writings are full of counter-attacks against him, often phrased in terms surcharged with passionate resentment.

Sa'adiah's attack, however, also had important beneficial consequences for the Karaites. It contributed decisively to the consolidation of the quarreling schismatic groups into a more or less organized sect, and it forced Karaism, for the sake of sheer survival, to purge itself in some measure of the excessive rigorism and pedantry inspired by Anan and others of the same uncompromising attitude. Furthermore, the necessity of meeting Sa'adiah's arguments on his own high level of theological, philosophical, and philological erudition produced a series of very able Karaite scholars, whose works, written in Arabic or Hebrew, mark the golden age of Karaite literary production (*ca.* A.D. 900–1200) and occupy a valuable place in the common treasury of medieval Jewish literature. Nevertheless, the final cleavage between the two camps sealed the fate of Karaism as far as its future expansion was concerned. The historical raison d'être of the sect lay in its role as a corrective to the abuses, theological and practical, produced, on the one hand, by the Rabbanite overemphasis of talmudic studies and, on the other, by the ills of the social and economic order in the Jewish center in Iraq. Sa'adiah's leadership showed that Rabbanism had the seed of reform within itself, and the exclusion of the Karaites from the Jewish community made it impossible for them to participate in this reform, and at the same time, cut them off from the main stream of Jewish thought and social progress.

About the middle of the tenth century Persia and Iraq, the cradle of the schism, gradually lost their dominant position as centers of Karaite population and culture and were superseded in importance by the settlements in Jerusalem and Egypt. At the same time new colonies were established in the Balkans, then still under Byzantine Christian rule, and in Moorish Spain, although the latter colony, which flourished for a short period of time under the leadership of Ibn al-Tarās, a graduate of the Karaite Academy at Jerusalem, soon ceased to exist. The wars of the Crusades, begun in the last decade of the eleventh century, put an end to all Jewish activity in Palestine and much of Syria and forced the Karaites to retreat to their Egyptian and Byzantine settlements. In the former, the rapacious and bigoted rule of the Mameluke dynasty, which held sway over Egypt down to the Turkish conquest in A.D. 1517, created an unfavorable atmosphere for Karaite literary activity. In the Balkan Peninsula, on the other hand, particularly at Constantinople, Karaite learning flourished, and scholars trained at the Academy in Jerusalem produced not only works of their own but also Hebrew translations of Karaite classics originally written in Arabic, thus making accessible to later generations, unfamiliar with the Arabic language, the principal products of the golden age of Karaite literature. The end of the twelfth century saw Karaite immigrants settling on the Crimean Peninsula, and about a century or so later a Karaite colony was established in Lithuania in the town of Troki near Wilno. The gradual conquest of the Balkans by the Ottoman Turks, culminating in their capture of Constantinople in A.D. 1453, brought a measure of stability into the lives of both the Karaite and Rabbanite populations and stimulated scholarly activity which, however, was now mainly devoted to the reformulation of principles and ideas developed by the classical writers whose originality and skill the later scholars could never recapture.

From the sixteenth through the eighteenth century the progressive decline of the Ottoman Empire resulted in the rise in importance of the Russian Karaite colonies at the expense of those in Constantinople and Cairo. The Russian conquest of the Crimea in A.D. 1783 added the Crimean contingent to the Karaite population under the Czar's rule, and some years later the leaders of the Russian Karaites succeeded in securing for their correligionists complete exemption from the crushing disabilities which affected their Rabbanite cousins. The modern history of Karaism is thus chiefly the history of the Russian branch of the sect and beyond the scope of this volume.

II

The chief characteristic of Karaite dogmatic and practical theology is tenacious conservatism; throughout the twelve hundred years of its existence Karaism has remained essentially unchanged. During the tenth century, under the hammer blows of the Sa'adian controversy, it purged itself of the excessive asceticism of Anan and some of the outlandish innovations sponsored by other early schismatics. In the eleventh century the so-called catenary theory of forbidden marriages, which made it increasingly difficult for Karaites to intermarry without laying themselves open to the charge of incest, was modified and made more bearable. Near the end of the thirteenth century the codification of the official Karaite prayer book marked the revocation of the ancient rule that prayer must consist solely of biblical quotations. These three mild reforms constitute the total changes introduced and generally accepted during the entire course of Karaite history. On the other hand, the extreme individualism inherited from the early schismatics, while considerably reduced by the consolidation of Karaism into a more or less cohesive organism, did not cease to plague the Karaites, and a number of religious observances remain to this day subject to individual opinion and custom.

In matters of dogmatic belief there is, aside from the rejection of the authority of the Talmud, no essential difference between Karaite and Rabbanite theology. Moreover, as has been noted above, the Karaites borrowed much from the Talmud and developed a similar oral tradition of their own. Strict monotheism, belief in God's omnipotence, man's responsibility for his actions, the advent of the Messiah, and the prohibition of human sacrifice, homicide, adultery, theft, and perjury are as fundamental in Karaism as they are in Rabbanite Judaism. The formalism and literalism of Karaite teaching, however, have prevented the development of anything like the prolific Rabbanite literature devoted to ethics and mysticism, and the Karaite scholars were much too busy with practical religious law to spend much time on pure metaphysics.

It is in practical theology that Karaism and Rabbanism part company, and even here the general principles are mostly the same, although the particulars differ considerably. As a rule, Karaite regulations are stricter than the Rabbanite. Thus, the law of incest, even after the modification of the catenary theory, remains more restrictive than its Rabbanite counterpart and includes the prohibition of levirate marriage—i.e., the marriage of a childless widow to her husband's brother—so that Karaism has no need of the Rabbanite escape ceremony (Hebrew *ḥăliṣah*), whereby a surviving brother may refuse to marry his sister-in-law. Polygamy is theoretically lawful (a late rabbinic decree recognized by the greater part of Rabbanite Jewry forbids it), but for practical reasons it appears to have been quite rare, even in countries under Moslem rule where it is permitted by the law of the land. The same greater strictness appears in the Karaite regulations affecting the observance of the Sabbath and the preservation of ritual cleanness. On the other hand, Karaite law interprets the biblical prohibition of boiling a kid's flesh in its mother's milk literally and does not extend it, as does Rabbanite dietary law, to apply to all meat and milk foods. Moreover, the Karaite and Rabbanite rules dealing with the slaughter of animals for food differ enough so that devout Karaites consider meat processed by Rabbanites unclean and unfit to be eaten.

The Karaite calendar is based mainly on the actual observation of the moon and is thus not identical with the Rabbanite calendar which employs fixed mathematical calculations. Since the visibility of the moon varies in different localities, there could be no uniformity in the dates of the several annual holidays observed by Karaite communities in various countries. Further confusion was brought about by disagreement among Karaite scholars about particular problems involved in time reckoning. As a result, the Karaite and Rabbanite holidays, including the most sacred day in the Jewish year, the Day of Atonement, do not always coincide, and some Rabbanite fast days, as well as the Feast of Hanukkah (commemorating the victories of the Maccabees, and therefore of postbiblical origin), are not observed by the Karaites at all. Phylacteries (Hebrew *tĕfillin*) and doorpost amulets (*mĕzuzoṯ*) are not used by them either.

In civil and criminal law Karaism is again more stringent than Rabbanism; e.g., in its refusal to accept the Rabbanite substitution of a monetary fine for the biblical principle of *eye for eye*. By the same token, the Karaite law of inheritance allows the husband and wife no share in each other's estate; nor do most Karaite jurists grant the daughter a claim upon her father's property. However, the Karaites, like the Rabbanites, were obliged to submit in civil and criminal matters to the legislation of the country in which they resided, whether Mohammedan or Christian, and both acknowledged it as binding upon themselves.

III

Modern critical study of Karaite history and theology is as yet in its infancy. The Karaites themselves were almost devoid of historical sense and were too absorbed in matters of law and ritual to keep authentic historical records of their past. Their Rabbanite opponents saw no reason to preserve early documents dealing with the schism, so much so that they even let Saʿadiah's anti-Karaite writings lapse into oblivion. Moreover, the writings of the formative period of Karaite history, particularly those antedating the Saʿadian controversy, seemed to later Karaites to be of doubtful worth, especially because their contents were not always in accord with official Karaite theology and because they occasionally referred to Anan in terms of sharp criticism. The greater part of these early writings has consequently been irretrievably lost, and much of the surviving material, mostly handwritten fragments, has yet to be deciphered, published, and properly appraised. The embryonic state of Karaite studies and the difficulties attending them have attracted few students to this field, and the fact that the largest collection of early Karaite manuscripts is under Soviet jurisdiction, in the State Public Library at Leningrad, makes access to it very difficult for Western historians, while their Russian colleagues, with one or two exceptions, prefer other fields of research. Our present knowledge of early Karaism is thus woefully inadequate.

The spirit of sad resignation which permeates Karaite literature after the golden age shows that the Karaites themselves clearly realized the hopelessness of their cause. It will be the task of future research to discover why a movement so promising and fruitful in its youth should have been converted by unyielding resistance to progress into a barren organism, and why Karaism, unlike Rabbanism, proved unable to produce leaders of sufficient vision and foresight to guide the sect toward a more enduring and creative continuity.

ANTHOLOGY

ANAN BEN DAVID

THE oldest information on Anan's life available to date is represented by four short narratives, one Karaite and three Rabbanite. The Karaite account is that of al-Ḳirḳisānī (second quarter of the tenth century) and reads as follows: [1]

Anan's appearance occurred in the days of the Caliph Abū Ǧa'far al-Manṣūr (A.D. 754–775). He was the first to make clear a great deal of the truth about the divine ordinances. He was learned in the lore of the Rabbanites, and not one of them could gainsay his erudition. It is reported that Hay, the president of the Rabbanite Academy,[2] together with his father, translated the book of Anan [3] from the Aramaic into Hebrew and encountered nothing in it of which they could not discover the source in Rabbanite lore . . . The Rabbanites tried their utmost to assassinate Anan, but God prevented them from doing so.

To this the fifteenth-century Karaite chronicler Ibn al-Hītī (who seems to have had access to some early sources) adds [4] that Anan lived at Bagdad; the building of this city, which replaced an older village of the same name, began in 762.

The three Rabbanite accounts are the following:

1. The account of Rab Amram (second half of the ninth century): [5]

The Gaon Natronai [6] said . . . These men who modify the Passover liturgy are heretics and scoffers who hold in contempt the words of scholars, and who are disciples of Anan . . . who had said to those who strayed and were seduced to follow him, "Forsake ye the words of the Mishnah and of the Talmud, and I will compose for you a Talmud of my own." To this day they remain in their error and have become a people unto themselves, while he fabricated an evil and wicked

1. *KA,* I, ii, 14 (see below, pp. 51 f.).
2. Variously identified with Hay ben Nahshon, Gaon at Sura in A.D. 886–896, or, more likely, Hay ben David, Gaon at Pumbeditha in A.D. 890–898.
3. I.e., the *Book of Precepts* (see below, and p. 334).
4. *JQR,* IX (1897), 432, 436.
5. *Siddur Rab 'Amram,* ed. A. L. Frumkin (Jerusalem, 1912), II, 206–207.
6. Flourished about 860.

Talmud for himself. My master Eleazar Alluf[7] has seen this abominable book of his which they call *Book of Precepts;* it contains many heretical deceptions.

2. A more detailed account has been preserved in a tract on the differences between the Karaites and the Rabbanites, written by a Karaite named Elijah ben Abraham who lived probably in the twelfth century.[8] Pinsker, who first published the tract,[9] has assumed that the author of the account was the Gaon Sa'adiah (d. 942). There is, however, no definite internal evidence of Sa'adiah's authorship, nor any proof that the account is much older than Elijah's work, and it may well have been written in the eleventh, or even early in the twelfth, century. It reads as follows:

Anan had a younger brother named Hananiah. Although Anan exceeded this brother in both learning and age, the contemporary Rabbanite scholars refused to appoint him exilarch, because of his great lawlessness[10] and lack of piety. They therefore turned to his brother Hananiah, for the sake of the latter's great modesty, retiring disposition, and fear of Heaven, and they set him up as exilarch. Thereupon Anan was seized with a wicked zeal—he and with him all manner of evil and worthless men from among the remnants of the sect of Zadok and Boethus;[11] they set up a dissident sect—in secret, for fear of the Moslem government which was then in power—and they appointed Anan their own exilarch.

On a certain Sunday, however, the affair was discovered by the government, and the order was given that Anan be imprisoned until the following Friday, when he was to be hanged on the gallows as a political rebel. In prison Anan came upon a Moslem scholar[12] who

7. A Rabbanite scholar who lived about the same time. A resident of Spain, he was, so far as is known, the first European scholar to attend the Babylonian academies.

8. Poznanski, pp. 72–74.

9. *LK,* II, 97–106; this Rabbanite account of Anan is found on p. 103.

10. Or "wickedness" (Hebrew *pĕriṣuṯ*).

11. The two founders of the Sadducee sect who are said to have rejected the oral tradition and the doctrine of the resurrection of the dead on the Day of Judgment.

12. This Moslem scholar is identified in another old Karaite source as Abū Ḥanīfa al-Nu'mān ibn Ṯābit, the founder of the Ḥanafī school of Moslem juris-

was also confined there and was likewise to be hung on the same Friday, as a violator of the Mohammedan faith. This scholar advised Anan, saying, "Are there not in the Law ordinances admitting of two contradictory interpretations?" "Indeed there are," answered Anan. "Observe then," said the Moslem scholar, "the interpretation accepted in the teaching of those who follow your brother, and take the other interpretation for yourself, providing that those who follow you will back you up in it. Then give a bribe to the viceroy,[13] so that you might perchance be permitted to speak in your defense, after which prostrate yourself before the caliph and say: 'O my Lord the King! Did you set up my brother to rule over one religion or over two?' Upon his replying: 'Over one religion only,' say to him further: 'But I and my brother belong to two different religions!' Of a certainty you will save yourself, providing you explain to him the difference [14] between your religion and that of your brother, and providing your followers back you up. Say these things, and when the king hears them he will say nothing further about your execution."

Anan undertook also to deceive his own followers and said to them: "Last night Elijah the Prophet appeared before me in a dream and said to me, 'You deserve to be put to death for violating that which is written in the Law.'" [15] He spoke thus to them in order to entice them with his crafty argumentation and out of fear for his life, so that he might save himself from a cruel death and might perpetuate his name in eternity. He also expended a great sum of money in bribes, until the king gave him permission to speak, whereupon he said, "The religion of my brother employs a calendar based upon calculation of the time of the new moon and intercalation of leap years by cycles, whereas mine depends upon actual observation of the new moon and intercalation regulated by the ripening of new grain." Since the king's religion likewise employed the latter method, Anan thus gained his favor and good will.

---

prudence, who, according to a none too reliable tradition, died in prison in A.D. 767. The passage (quoted in *REJ,* XLIV, 167, n. 2), reads: "Anan lived in the reign of the Caliph al-Manṣūr, and was imprisoned along with Abū Ḥanīfa al-Nuʿmān ibn Ṯābit."

13. I.e., probably the vezier.

14. The following *wĕ-hak-katub* is presumably a scribe's error and should be expunged.

15. Meaning, presumably, for continuing outwardly as a Rabbanite and not breaking openly with the Rabbanite synagogue.

3. In the chronicle of Abraham ibn Dā'ūd, composed in 1161,[16] we come upon the following reference:

In the days of the Gaon Yehudai[17] there lived Anan and his son Saul . . . This Anan was a scion of the family of King David. He was at first an orthodox scholar,[18] but later there became evident in him traces of heresy, for which reason he was not named Gaon, nor was he vouchsafed heaven-inspired help to become exilarch. Moved by envy and hatred, which took hold of his heart, he proceeded to build up a sand hill of heresy and to seduce Israel from the tradition of the Sages . . . He composed books and set up his own disciples, and he invented out of his own heart laws which were not good and judgments by which men could not live in righteousness.

These, then, are the earliest and presumably most reliable bits of information on Anan's life available at present.[19] Later Karaite accounts embellished the pseudo-Sa'adian story with fanciful details, down to and including Anan's alleged assassination by the Rabbanites.[20] These later accretions, however, are obviously worthless, and the solid facts of Anan's biography must therefore be extracted from those earliest sources alone.

The impression conveyed by them is unmistakable. Natronai, scarcely ninety years after Anan's secession, tells us nothing about his aristocratic (Davidic) descent or about the contest for the office of exilarch which allegedly served as the immediate cause of his apostasy. It seems reasonable to assume that Natronai's silence signifies that he knew nothing about it, for it would have been to his advantage, had he knowledge of Anan's disqualification for the high office, to set it forth in detail in order to demonstrate the more convincingly, from his own point of view, Anan's unworthy and ungodly motives. Moreover, Natronai lived in the very center of the scene of Anan's activity and belonged to the

16. A. Neubauer, *Medieval Jewish Chronicles* (Oxford, 1887–95), I, 63–64.

17. Gaon at Sura, A.D. 757–761.

18. Hebrew *talmiḏ ḥaḵam.*

19. The accounts given by several medieval Arab historians are all based on Karaite sources and have no primary value.

20. Cf. Mordecai Sultansky, *Zeḵer ṣaddiḵim,* ed. S. Poznanski (Warsaw, 1920), pp. 38–39.

higher strata of Rabbanite society, where the alleged particulars of Anan's secession should have been known best, had they been true.

The next account, in chronological order, that of al-Ḳirḳisānī, a devout Karaite, though not an Ananite, and an outspoken foe of Rabbanism, likewise contains no reference to Anan's noble lineage and his unsuccessful candidacy for the office of exilarch. It is difficult to believe that al-Ḳirḳisānī would have deliberately suppressed these particulars, for they ought certainly to have appealed to him as choice bits of damning evidence of Rabbanite wickedness. The only statement by al-Ḳirḳisānī reminiscent of the pseudo-Sa'adian story is the note on the Rabbanite attempt to assassinate Anan; it is so short and cryptic, however, and so similar to the statement about the Rabbanite plot against Jesus of Nazareth in the same chapter of al-Ḳirḳisānī's work [21] that its authenticity may well be questioned.

The conventional story of Anan's apostasy is thus left with the pseudo-Sa'adian account as its lone supporting evidence. This account was written not before the first quarter of the tenth century; indeed it is more likely, as indicated above, that it originated much later. In any case the fact remains that the story was apparently unknown to both Karaite and Rabbanite scholars for nearly 150 years following Anan's death. Moreover, the story is fairly teeming with psychological difficulties and improbabilities. The figure of Anan as a self-seeking schemer for political preferment does not square with the ascetic and rigoristic spirit permeating the whole of Anan's teaching. The account of his arrest seems inexplicable because his secession from the Rabbanite synagogue was not a crime according to Moslem law, and other Jewish sectarians of that period are known to have remained unmolested by the Mohammedan and Rabbanite authorities alike. His supposed conspiracy with a noted Moslem divine to deceive both his own followers and the caliph is highly improbable, for it presumes a gullibility on the part of the caliph and the Ananites

21. *KA,* I, ii, 9: "The Rabbanites plotted against Jesus until they put him to death by crucifixion."

and an utter lack of integrity in Anan that are exceedingly unlikely.

These apparent weaknesses of the pseudo-Sa'adian account of Anan's apostasy are not offset to any degree by what may be gleaned concerning his personality from the fragments of his theological credo, the *Book of Precepts* (Hebrew *Sefer ham-miṣwoṯ*). He appears here as a pedantic and ascetic fundamentalist, bent on fulfilling the Lord's word, as he understood it, to the letter, irrespective of any personal hardship and inconvenience involved. It is safe to say that by remaining in the Rabbanite fold Anan would have been much better off materially than he was as the leader of a small and impoverished band of ascetics.

Anan's *Book of Precepts,* far from being an attempt to produce another and supposedly better Talmud—as if a single person could have created a work of so vast a scope!—is precisely what it calls itself, a handbook of religious law according to Anan's teaching. It was written in Aramaic, which had then not yet been superseded by Arabic as the language of scholarly expression among the Jews of the East. The portions which have so far been discovered represent concise, rather dry and monotonous expositions of various points of religious law and practice, and if there were additional chapters of general dogmatics or polemics with Rabbanites or other sectarians, these have yet to be found.

Anan's methods of biblical exegesis and formulation and interpretation of law are in a large measure identical with the Talmudic ones, a circumstance that brought upon him the sharp criticism of some of his immediate successors, who accused him of excessive leanings toward Rabbanism, an inability, as it were, to divest himself completely of the errors which he had professed before he broke with the Rabbanite synagogue. The fact, however, is that while Anan freely used Rabbanite exegetical and juridical methods, he came to entirely divergent conclusions, in direct contrast to Benjamin al-Nahāwandī, who employed distinctly Karaite methods of legal exegesis but came to many conclusions identical with or closely parallel to Rabbanite legal norms. Most frequently Anan used the method of analogy (Arabic *ḳiyās,* Hebrew *heḳeš*) which he applied not only to the legal subject matter but also to the wording of the biblical text and carried to the unreasonable extreme of basing conclusions on the similarity of single words or even single letters. His rigorism led him to postulate the principle that the rules of rhetoric and literary style cannot lawfully be applied to the Bible, and that when the biblical text seemingly expresses the same idea in different words or uses several synonyms to designate the same object or action some new meaning, or shade of meaning, must be implied, indicating a modification or amplification of the particular rule or ordinance. Even grammatical variations and alternate usages were presumed to fall under the same category, and the presence or absence of a conjunction or particle, for example, was used by Anan as justification for a new regulation. In many instances this was undoubtedly not a matter of Anan's going from a new interpretation of a biblical verse to a new non-Rabbanite ordinance but rather a deliberate procedure of finding biblical support, by means of forced exegesis, for an already formulated deviation from talmudic practice in such cases where Anan deemed it imperative to reject the latter.

The same rigoristic tendency led Anan to the unswerving practice of choosing the strict and prohibitive in preference to the lenient and permissive where the wording of the biblical text was indefinite enough to permit such a choice—the principle of "in case of doubt the stricter alternative is to be regarded as obligatory." By the same token, Anan's asceticism prompted him to eliminate as far as possible all elements of joy and pleasure which are associated in Rabbanite practice with such institutions as the Sabbath or the Passover. In this, to be sure, he had some Rabbanite precedent, for there were ascetics, although comparatively few, in the Rabbanite camp who believed that mourning and sorrow for the vanished Temple and the dispersed state of Israel should be the keynote of divine worship and pious meditation, particularly on holy days, and that rejoicing in the Lord's daily bounties and celebrating past glories were out of place so long as Zion lay in ruins. Sabbaths and holy days were thus turned to a considerable extent into occasions of sadness and self-denial rather than of soul-restoring enjoyment of the fruits of God's favor and blessing. Fasting, coarse raiment, and contempt of worldly goods were elevated into virtues per se, and the more one indulged in these tokens of repentance and self-purification, the nearer one came to righteousness and the greater was one's contribution toward the redemption and restoration of Israel.

In many of his innovations and deviations Anan seems to have borrowed his ideas from other sectarians, especially the Essenes and the Yudganites, whose ascetic mode of thinking and living must have found a sympathetic echo in his own mind. Anan's debt to the Sadducee teaching is still a matter of uncertainty and controversy; in any case, the available information on the doctrines of the Sadducees is still so meager and in part so contradictory that it would be rather unfair to pass judgment on the degree of their influence upon Anan and his immediate successors. In some of his doctrines Anan seems to have gone back to old Rabbanite customs which were practiced by Jewish minority groups in talmudic times but were subsequently given up in favor of rites and customs stamped by majority approval and so recorded in the Talmud. Here, too, the evidence is rather scanty and needs further amplification.

A summary of the *Book of Precepts* is occasionally quoted under the Arabic title of *Fadlaka* (*"Summary"*). It, too, was written in Aramaic, and the title therefore is hardly authentic. Since al-Ḳirḳisānī speaks of "the book of Anan" [22]—in the singular—it may well be questioned whether the *Summary* was a separate work.

Al-Ḳirḳisānī states also that Anan was reported in the tenth century to have written a treatise on the transmigration of souls, a doctrine to which he was said to have subscribed and which was accepted by some tenth-century Ananites.[23] Since al-Ḳirḳisānī indicates clearly that he himself did not see the work, the sus-

22. See above, p. 3.
23. *KA*, I, 54, ll. 18–20.

picion arises that the claim may have been a fictitious one, invented by these Ananites to justify their belief in metempsychosis.[24]

FROM THE *BOOK OF PRECEPTS* OF ANAN BEN DAVID

I. OBSERVANCE OF THE LAW

1. The Merciful One has ordered us to perform His precepts with awe and reverence, as it is written: *Worship ye the Lord with fear* (Ps. 2:11). Even though this *Worship ye the Lord* refers ostensibly to prayer and requires of man that he should pray before the Merciful One with awe and trembling, yet since the particle *eṯ* has been added here before *the Lord* we must conclude that all other precepts likewise must be performed by us with awe. We must also treat the precepts with reverence, as it is written: *Make his praise glorious* (Ps. 66:2), meaning, "fulfill ye the Law in a spirit of reverence," i.e., "revere ye its precepts."

2. The Merciful One will sit in judgment over him who makes light of His precepts, as it is written: *Whosoever curses his God shall bear his sin* (Lev. 24:15). This "cursing" means "making light," because conversely, "making light" is likewise sometimes expressed by the word "cursing"; e.g.: *for the iniquity in that he knew that his sons have made themselves accursed, yet he did not rebuke them* (I Sam. 3:13).

3. The words *his God* denote God's precepts, for conversely the precepts likewise are sometimes called by the Name of God, as it is written: *Say unto the cities of Judah, Behold your God!* (Isa. 40:9), meaning that the Merciful One had told the herald of Zion to say unto Israel, "Behold, here are the precepts of your God!" So also *his God* here signifies his God's precepts. As for Scripture

24. Poznanski (*REJ,* XLV, 190–191), takes the existence of this treatise for certain and suggests that al-Ḳirḳisānī's detailed discussion of the doctrine of transmigration of souls (*KA,* III, xvii–xviii) includes material taken from, or based upon, that treatise. All this, in my judgment, is pure conjecture for which no factual evidence is available as yet.

saying *his God,* and not just *God,* it signifies that even if a man observes something which really is not a precept but which he thinks is a precept, inasmuch as he thinks so he is subject to judgment if he makes light of it. But if he knows that this thing is not a precept, or if someone learned in the Law tells him that it is not a precept, and yet he does not cease observing it, he is guilty of bearing false testimony about the Law and the Merciful One will destroy him, since it is written of such persons: *a false witness breathes forth lies* (Prov. 14: 5).

4. He who says that the precepts are as nothing or that the Law is as nothing, or he who says, "Who is God?" draws upon himself the punishment of death, and all Israel shall stone him until he is dead, as it is written: *And he who blasphemes the name of the Lord shall surely be put to death, the whole congregation shall surely stone him* (Lev. 24: 16). The word *blasphemes* here means "specifies," in which sense it is used also in the verse: *And Moses and Aaron took these men who had been designated by name* (Num. 1: 17). This word *blasphemes* is here preceded by the conjunction *and* and by the words *Whosoever curses his God shall bear his sin* (Lev. 24: 15); this is to teach us that it refers to him who designates the Name of the Merciful One in a light manner, and that he incurs the death penalty. The sixteenth verse then goes on to say: *For his blaspheming of the name he shall be put to death,* indicating thus that also he who speaks lightly of the Law incurs the death penalty, since the Law is sometimes called "the Lord's Name"; e.g., *to bring up from thence the ark of God, upon which was called the name, the name of the Lord of Hosts who dwells over the cherubim* (II Sam. 6: 2), meaning that the Name of the Lord was within the Ark. Now there was nothing inside the Ark but the Law, as it is written: *And he took the testimony and put it into the ark* (Exod. 40: 20); it follows therefore that the Law is called "the Name of the Lord." And since the precepts and the Law mean the same thing, as it is written: *and I will give thee the stone tablets and the Law and the precepts* (Exod. 24: 12), he who speaks lightly of the precepts also incurs the penalty of death.

II. CRIMINAL LAW

1. Since we no longer issue death sentences when someone commits a sin requiring capital punishment, we must separate ourselves from him. If it is a man, we must separate his wife from him; if it is a woman, we must separate her husband from her. We must not converse with the culprit or let him dwell with us or engage in doing business with him; neither borrow anything from him nor lend to him; neither accept charity from him nor show any pity toward him. In short, we must treat him as if he were dead.

2. Nor do we pass judgments relating to mayhem, since it is written: *Let not thine eye have pity, life for life, eye for eye, tooth for tooth, hand for hand, foot for foot* (Deut. 19: 21). The Law thus treats mayhem on an equal footing with homicide, and just as we no longer issue death sentences for homicide, we cannot likewise execute sentences of punishment for mayhem. The same applies to burns, wounds, and welts, as it is written: *Eye for eye, tooth for tooth, hand for hand, foot for foot. Burn for burn, wound for wound, welt for welt* (Exod. 21: 24–25). Just as we no longer pass judgments relating to eye, tooth, hand, and foot, so also we can no longer pass judgments for burns, wounds, and welts.

3. *Burn* signifies an injury done by fire, as it is written: *If there shall be upon its skin a burn made by fire* (Lev. 13: 24). *Wound* signifies a laceration of the head, as it is written: *And the man smote him, smiting and wounding* (I Kings 20: 37). *Welt* signifies the result of a blow to the body causing the effusion of blood and is similar to a laceration of the head, as it is written: *wound and welt and moist sore* (Isa. 1: 6); the words *moist sore* are meant to indicate that while *wound* and *welt* are also sores, they are accompanied by an effusion of blood, whereas a *moist sore* is one which is not followed by hemorrhage.

4. We also no longer pass sentences relating to fractures, as it is written: *Fracture for fracture, eye for eye, tooth for tooth . . .* (Lev. 24: 20), where *fracture* is likened to damage done to an eye or a tooth; since we no longer pass judgments relating to an eye or a tooth, we can no longer do so in cases of fracture. *Fracture*

signifies the breaking of a bone, as it is written: *I groaned till morning, and like a lion it broke all my bones* (Isa. 38: 13).

5. We also no longer judge cases covered by *If men should quarrel and hurt a pregnant woman, and her children should come out, and there should be no mischief* (Exod. 21: 22). The same applies to the case of a bailee who has been engaged to keep money or utensils and has lost them by theft. The reason for it is this: in the case of the pregnant woman it is written: *and he shall pay as the judges shall determine* (Exod. 21: 22), while in the case of the theft from the house of the bailee it is written: *The master of the house shall come near unto God* (Exod. 22: 7), and further on: *The cause of both shall come before God*. Now the word *judges* refers to the priests and judges who functioned at the time when the Temple was still standing, as it is written: *If anything relating to judgment should puzzle thee* (Deut. 17: 8), and further on: *Thou shalt come to the priests, the Levites, and to the judge . . . and thou shalt inquire, and they shall declare unto thee* (Deut. 17: 9). As for the words *unto God,* they mean that the litigants should go to the men who engage in the work of God, as it is written: *he shall be unto thee as a mouth, and thou shalt be unto him as God* (Exod. 4: 16). The words *before God* mean that they must go first to their local court, and only if the local judges are in doubt about their case are they to go to the judges at the Temple in Jerusalem.

6. Except for the cases enumerated above, all other cases in law may be judged in the Dispersion.

7. He who commits one of the aforementioned offenses which we can no longer judge, or he upon whom sentence has been passed and who refuses to submit to it, must be ostracized in the same way as the person subject to capital punishment, since inasmuch as he has committed one of these acts against his fellow man or has not submitted to his sentence he has become a malefactor, as it is written: *Wherefore does the wicked contemn God?* (Ps. 10: 13). And inasmuch as he has become *wicked,* he who does not separate himself from him thereby associates himself with him in his wickedness, as it is written: *Depart, I pray you, from the tents of*

these wicked men . . . lest ye be swept away in all their sins (Num. 16: 26).

8. If a person subject to capital punishment repents of his evil deeds, we do not accept his repentance. On the other hand, he who commits any of those other offenses against his fellow man, if he makes restitution to the injured party, we may accept his repentance. So, too, he who had refused to submit to judgment, if he repents and comes back and submits to it, we may accept his repentance. The reason for all this is that he who is subject to capital punishment comes under the biblical command: *and thou shalt exterminate the evil from thy midst* (Deut. 13:6), whereas he who has committed the other offenses is referred to in the verse: *And the priest shall make atonement for him before the Lord, and he shall be forgiven for each of his trespasses that he had committed* (Lev. 5: 26).

III. PRAYER OF THANKSGIVING

1. He who has met with mortal danger and has been delivered from it—as when one who has traveled in the desert and lost his way is saved from this deadly peril, or as when one committed to prison and chastised and put in irons is eventually released, or as when one who was gravely ill recovers, or as when one who has gone on a voyage in a ship and been overtaken by a violent storm comes through unharmed—all these must render praise to the Merciful One who has vouchsafed them His mercy and must make acknowledgment in the presence of men of the miracles which the Merciful One performed for them, since of all these it is written: *Let them give thanks unto the Lord for his kindness . . .* (Ps. 107:8).

2. How is this acknowledgment to be made? He must say before the Merciful One: *I will thank thee, O Lord my God, with all my heart . . . For great is thy kindness toward me, and thou hast saved my soul from the nethermost hell . . .* (Ps. 86: 12–13), followed by: *Blessed art thou, O Lord, teach me thy laws* (Ps. 119: 12).

3. And how before men? He must say: *O magnify ye the Lord*

with me, and let us exalt his name together (Ps. 34:4), followed by: *He has not done unto us according to our sins* (Ps. 103:10), *Many things hast thou done, O Lord my God* (Ps. 40:6), *Blessed be the Lord God, God of Israel, who alone performs miracles. And blessed be his glorious name* (Ps. 72:18–19).

4. The reason for the use of these verses is this: since with reference to the Merciful One it is written: *Let them give thanks unto the Lord for his kindness,* the prayer of thanksgiving should include the verse, *For great is thy kindness;* and because he was saved from deadly peril, he must recite the verse dealing with God's kindness and the salvation from danger. After this he must go on to pray before the Merciful One and beg that in His mercy He might teach him the Law, since the revelation of the Law is accounted as a major token of God's kindness. For it is written: *God will send forth his kindness and his truth* (Ps. 57:4)—here *his truth* signifies the Law, as it is written: *that we might turn back from our sins and become proficient in thy truth* (Dan. 9:13).

5. Before men, on the other hand, he must say, *Magnify ye the Lord with me* (Ps. 34:4), because it is written of those who had been saved: *Let them exalt him in the midst of the congregation of the people* (Ps. 107:32); since the former verse continues, *and let us exalt his name together,* it should be recited on this occasion. And since it is written of these same people: *And let them offer sacrifices of thanksgiving* (Ps. 107:22), he must make confession of his sins, for it is written: *and he shall confess that in which he had sinned* (Lev. 5:5). He must then acknowledge and praise God for His miracles, as it is written: *Let them give thanks to the Lord for his kindness and for his miracles to the children of man* (Ps. 107:8). And since the congregation is required to respond with *amen, and again amen,* they must recite along with him: *let all the earth be filled with his glory; amen, and again amen* (Ps. 72:19).

IV. DIETARY LAW

1. All birds are forbidden to us for use as food, excepting pigeons and turtledoves, since it is written concerning Noah: *And he took*

of every clean beast and of every clean bird and offered burnt offerings upon the altar (Gen. 8:20). The clause *and offered burnt offerings upon the altar* indicates that Noah used for burnt offerings only such beasts and fowl as were ritually proper for such a purpose, for if Scripture had merely said "and offered them upon the altar," it would have been sufficient; nevertheless it took pains to make the wording precise, by saying *and offered burnt offerings,* to teach us that Noah employed as burnt offerings only that which was ritually suitable.

2. Now we do not find that any birds were used for burnt offerings save turtledoves and pigeons, as it is written: *And if the burnt sacrifice for his offering be of fowls, let him bring his offering of turtledoves or of young pigeons* (Lev. 1:14). The juxtaposition of the words *of every clean bird* and *he offered burnt offerings* thus proves that the only clean birds are turtledoves and pigeons.

V. SABBATH

1. Carrying a burden, which is forbidden on the Sabbath, signifies only the act of carrying upon one's shoulder, since it is written: *they carried upon their shoulders* (Num. 7:9).

2. [It is forbidden to light fire in Jewish homes on the Sabbath or to permit fire kindled before the arrival of the Sabbath to continue burning into the Sabbath, as it is written: *Ye shall not kindle fire in all your dwellings upon the sabbath day* (Exod. 35:3).]

3. One might perhaps say that it is only the kindling of fire on the Sabbath which is forbidden, and that if the fire had been kindled on the preceding weekday it is to be considered lawful to let it remain over the Sabbath. Now the Merciful One has written here: *Ye shall not kindle fire,* and elsewhere: *thou shalt not perform any work* (Exod. 20:10), and both prohibitions begin with the letter *taw*. In the case of labor, of which it is written: *thou shalt not perform any work,* it is evident that even if the work was begun on a weekday, before the arrival of the Sabbath, it is necessary to desist from it with the arrival of the Sabbath. The same rule must therefore apply also to the kindling of fire, of which it

is written: *Ye shall not kindle,* meaning that even if the fire has been kindled on a weekday, prior to the arrival of the Sabbath, it must be extinguished.

4. In the case of work, just as one is forbidden to perform it himself, so also is he forbidden to have others perform it for him. [So, too, in the case of fire, one is forbidden to make others kindle it for him on the Sabbath, just as one is forbidden to kindle it himself.] Thus it is clear that we are forbidden to leave either a lamp or any other light burning on the Sabbath in any Jewish home.

VI. INCEST

1. It is written: *The nakedness of thy sister, the daughter of thy father or the daughter of thy mother, whether born at home or born outside, thou shalt not uncover their nakedness* (Lev. 18:9). The words *The nakedness of thy sister, the daughter of thy father or the daughter of thy mother* mean that a man may not marry his sister, whether she is the daughter of both his father and his mother or only of his father and not his mother or only of his mother and not his father.

2. The words *whether born at home or born outside* signify whether begotten in lawful marriage or by fornication or out of a male or female slave. One born legitimately is designated as *born at home* [referring to the verse: *Thy wife shall be like a fruitful vine by the sides of thy home* (Ps. 128:3)]. One born illegitimately is called *born outside,* referring to the verse: *Now she is outside, now in the streets, and she lies in ambush at every corner* (Prov. 7:12).

3. The words *thou shalt not uncover their nakedness* imply that all these are equally forbidden.

4. The words *their nakedness* are in the plural, because Scripture did not wish to say in the singular, "the nakedness of the daughter of thy father and thy mother," or "the nakedness of the daughter of a male slave," or "the nakedness of the daughter of a female slave"; [rather], it says *their nakedness,* in the plural, to tell us that all women who are our full or half sisters are equally for-

jamin appears to have written all his works in fluent and idiomatic Hebrew.[5] They are:

1) The *Book of Precepts* (*Sefer miṣwoṯ*) and the *Book of Rules* (*Sefer dinim*)—both presumably parts of a comprehensive work on religious law; the latter part, on civil and criminal law, was printed under the title *Maś'aṯ Binyamin*.[6]

2) Commentaries on some of the books of the Bible (the Pentateuch, Isaiah, Song of Songs, Ecclesiastes, Daniel).

Karaite tradition has it that Benjamin fortified the Karaite faith by purging it of Anan's excessive leaning toward Rabbanite doctrines. There is little historical evidence to support such an interpretation of his teaching. On the contrary, Benjamin exhibited little hostility toward the Rabbanites and expressly stated his view that Rabbanite ordinances may be freely adopted by Karaites, even when they have no direct support in the text of the Bible. He seems also to have been a most tolerant person toward fellow Karaites who differed from him in matters of faith and law. Indeed, he is said to be the author of an aphorism to the effect that each person may be guided by his own judgment and is not obliged to defer to the views of commonly acknowledged authorities; [7] but this is probably without historical foundation.[8]

The extracts from the *Book of Rules* given here illustrate well enough the basic difficulty which beset Karaism from its very birth. Few of the regulations contained in these extracts have any clear basis in the biblical text; at best, some may be deduced from it by means of farfetched exegesis. Others are directly taken from Rabbanite law or are formulated in imitation of it. In other words, circumstances of every day life could not, even in the nascent period of Karaism, be governed by strict and exclusive adherence to biblical legislation conceived a thousand years earlier, and Karaite

5. Mann, pp. 12–13.

6. Published (with many errors) as an appendix (6 leaves) to Aaron ben Joseph, *Miḇḥar yĕšarim*, ed. Abraham Firkovitch (Eupatoria, 1835). Fragments from the sections on holidays, diet, cleanness, circumcision, etc., were published by A. Harkavy, *Studien und Mittheilungen*, VIII, 175–184.

7. *Ibid.*, p. 176, par. 2.

8. *Ibid.*, p. 176, n. 5.

bidden to us, whether they are of high or low degree in our estimation.

5. Likewise a woman may not marry her full or half brother, even one begotten by fornication or out of a male or female slave.

VII. DIVORCE

1. It is written: *If a man should take a wife and become her husband, and if it should happen that she should find no favor in his eyes, because he has found in her something hateful* (Deut. 24:1); i.e., if he found her unworthy in his sight by discovering in her something to make him dislike her, so that he is no longer pleased with her, he may then divorce her, whether because he does not want her or because she does not want him.

2. It is written further: *and he shall write for her a writ of cutting off,* meaning that he is to write for her a deed which makes separation between him and her complete.

3. Scripture calls it *a writ of cutting off,* implying that he must not write it until he is certain that there is no offspring of his within her. If the wife is pregnant, the husband may not write the bill of divorcement for her until the offspring has been delivered. If she is not pregnant, he must withdraw from her for three months, after which he may write the bill. The reason for this is that the presence of a child within a woman becomes certain in three months from the time of conception, as it is written: *And it came to pass, after about three months, that word was brought to Judah, to say, Tamar, thy daughter-in-law, has committed adultery, and behold also, she is with child by fornication* (Gen. 38:24). This shows us that pregnancy does become recognizable in three months.

4. It is written further: *and he shall place it in her hand, and shall send her away from his house* (Deut. 24:1), meaning that he must give it to her into her own hand and dismiss her from his home. The words *from his house* indicate that even though he has withdrawn from her prior to the delivery of the writ of divorcement she remains in his house.

5. As for the bill, he writes it for her thus: "I, So-and-so, the son of So-and-so, took So-and-so, the daughter of So-and-so, to be my wife, and I became her husband. And certain things came to pass between me and her, and I have written for her this writ of divorcement, and I have placed it in her hand and have sent her away from my house. And the witnesses of her divorce are So-and-so, the son of So-and-so, and So-and-so, the son of So-and-so."

VIII. CIRCUMCISION

1. A man must be circumcised by another man and may not circumcise himself with his own hand, since Scripture says: *And ye shall be circumcised in the flesh of your foreskin* (Gen. 17:11). Were the meaning to be that a man may circumcise himself with his own hand, it would have been written, "And ye shall circumcise the flesh of your foreskin"; the wording *And ye shall be circumcised* indicates therefore that someone else must circumcise him.

2. In dealing with the "foreskin of the heart," where no severing of flesh is involved and whatever is to be done about it rests with the penitent person, Scripture says: *Ye shall circumcise the foreskin of your heart* (Deut. 10:16), without using the word "flesh" or employing the passive prefix. In speaking, on the other hand, of the actual male foreskin, where severing of the flesh is involved and where another person must perform the circumcision, Scripture uses both the word "flesh" and the passive prefix, as [in the aforementioned verse, and also] in the verse: *And the uncircumcised male who is not circumcised in the flesh of his foreskin, that soul shall be exterminated from among his people* (Gen. 17:14).

BENJAMIN AL-NAHĀWANI

BENJAMIN ben Moses al-Nahāwandī, of Na
vend) in Persia (in the ancient province o
ished in the second quarter of the ninth ce
thus one of the all but immediate successors of A
Karaite tradition he is regarded as second only to
hierarchy of the fathers of the Karaite synagogue
which is too strongly colored by the desire to present e
as a unified and cohesive movement to be credible. A
who lived a century later, states—and we have no re
believe him—that Benjamin was "learned in the lore
banites and strong in Scripture, and served for many
judge." He disagreed with many aspects of Anan's
and later Karaites did not accept all of Benjamin's view
ticular they rejected his theory [3] that God had created
angel and that it was this angel, and not God Himself,
complished all the other work of creation.

Of Benjamin's life very little is known. It seems certa
ever, that the Karaite settlement in Palestine, particularly
salem, began after Benjamin's demise; [4] hence it would
that Benjamin did not emigrate to Palestine but spent
in or near the Karaite centers in Persia and Iraq.

Unlike Anan, who wrote, so far as we know, only in Ar
and unlike his own successors, who wrote mostly in Arabic,

1. In the Karaite memorial prayer (*Karaite Liturgy* [Vienna, 1854], I,
Benjamin is listed next to Saul, Anan's son and successor in the office of the K
exilarch. To later Mohammedan writers the Karaites were the "followers of
and Benjamin" (Arabic *aṣḥāb ʿĀnān wa-Binyāmīn;* cf. Kobak's *Yĕšurun*
(1873), 35; Hastings' *Encyclopedia of Religion and Ethics,* VII, 664).

2. A summary of the characteristic points of Benjamin's teaching is give
KA, I, 55–56 (English transl., *HUCA,* VII (1930), 386–387).

3. Presumably adapted from the Hellenistic-Christian doctrine of the Crea
Word, the so-called Logos.

4. Salmon ben Jeroham says so expressly (*LḲ,* I, 22); there is other eviden
to the same effect (cf. Mann, p. 4).

leaders were compelled, no matter how reluctantly, to compose something like a Talmud of their own—a procedure which, on the Rabbanite side, they condemned as ungodly and blasphemous.

FROM THE *BOOK OF RULES* OF BENJAMIN AL-NAHĀWANDĪ

I. WITNESSES

1. Two witnesses residing in the same city and both called Benjamin son of Moses would render a deed invalid if they were to sign it with these names alone. How then should they proceed? They should write down their occupations. If their occupations are the same, they should write down the names of the streets on which they live or the names of their shops and stores. If they are partners in the same trade and in the same shop, they should write down the names of their mothers as well as those of their fathers. If these, too, are identical, they should write down some indication of the shape of their bodies and limbs, whether they are tall or short, corpulent or lean or of medium build, dark complexioned or light or yellowish or reddish, or any other mark relating to their build, their hair, their beards, arms, and legs, or their poverty or wealth, in order that their signatures should not invalidate the deeds.

II. LOANS

1. If a debtor has sent money by a messenger to his creditor, in order to pay off his debt, and this money has suffered damage in transit, he is not free from responsibility for any damage whatsoever, and he must repay the creditor in full. . . . If he has sent the money by the creditor's own messengers, at the creditor's orders, and it suffers damage in transit, he is not responsible, since the debtor has merely followed the lender's orders; i.e., he has acted, as it were, in the capacity of a servant fulfilling his master's commands, as it is written: *the borrower is a servant to the lender* (Prov. 22:7).

III. THE WIFE'S PROPERTY

1. The wife's property which forms her dowry is added to that of her husband, as it is written: *and it shall be added to the inheritance of the tribe* (Num. 36: 3); therefore the wife's property belongs to her husband, both during her lifetime and after her death. The husband has the right to repossess from the holders such part of the wife's property as she has sold or given as a gift, while her husband was living. But he cannot sell any part of her property without her permission, since they are both partners in it, whereas he may sell or give away his own property to whomsoever he wishes.

2. As for money and property belonging to the wife and not recorded in her marriage contract as her dowry to her husband, the husband has the use of the income thereof, but the principal remains hers and she may give it away to whomsoever she chooses. At the time of their parting the husband need not repay such past income received, since it does not represent an obligation on his part. On the other hand, all that which represents an obligation on the husband's part and is so recorded in her marriage contract is subject to his management only and must be repaid by him at the time of their parting. If the wife dies, the husband inherits both varieties of her property. . . .

3. A wife's property not recorded in her marriage contract as her dowry to her husband or property acquired by her elsewhere is subject to her disposal at will. On the other hand, she cannot dispose of property which is recorded in the marriage contract without her husband's permission. If she dies, her husband inherits both kinds of property. . . . If she sells such property without her husband's permission and later dies, the husband may reclaim it after her death from the possession of those who hold it, since she and her property belong to him.

4. The wife may, however, give and spend without her husband's permission as much of her property as might promote her husband's honor and be generally commendable as charity, as

it is written: *And Abigail took two hundred loaves of bread and two skins of wine* (I Sam. 25: 18)—all these she carried to King David, and he blessed her for this donation and accepted it from her, as it is written: *Blessed be thou, and blessed be thy discretion* (I Sam. 25: 33), and further: *And David received of her hand that which she had brought for him* (I Sam. 25: 35). And it is written also: *And it came to pass one day that Elisha went over to Shunem, and there was there a great woman, and she prevailed upon him to partake of bread* (II Kings 4: 8). The wife may not, however, make gifts or sales out of both kinds of such property without her husband's permission.

5. If the wife lives with her orphaned children and raises them with the income from her husband's property, whether real estate or movables, no one may dispossess her of this property, as it is written: *And Elisha spoke to the woman whose son he had restored to life* (II Kings 8: 1), and he addressed her, saying, "Thou and thy son"; he did not say, "Thou and thy husband," proving that her husband was then dead, since he was an old man, as it is written at the beginning of this story: *But she has no son, and her husband is old* (II Kings 4: 14). She then went to live in the land of the Philistines, and when she returned the king restored to her all her husband's landed property, as well as its produce, as it is written: *And the king appointed unto her a special officer, saying, Restore all that was hers, and all the produce of the field, from the day when she left the land, until now* (II Kings 8: 6).

IV. GIFTS

1. A sick person who has signed away his property as a gift and subsequently recovered from his illness may retract his action. Why so? Because he has signed it away on the assumption of his imminent death, and yet he did not die. If he has reserved anything for himself, however, to the effect that if he should recover it is to remain in his possession, he cannot retract his donation, and his gift remains a gift in perpetuity, whether he dies or re-

covers, inasmuch as the reservation proves that he had made the gift not solely because of his expected death.

2. If a sick man has signed away a gift to one person and subsequently changed his mind and signed it away to another person, the second person has the right to it while the first person has none, because so long as the gift has not passed into the actual possession of the one or the other it remains the property of the original owner, who may assign and give it to whomsoever he wishes.

V. INHERITANCE AND WILLS

1. If a man's lawful heir has migrated overseas, and if the man, not knowing whether the heir is still among the living, bequeathes his property to someone else, and if the lawful heir later returns to claim his inheritance, the man's will must be set aside, inasmuch as he has disregarded his lawful heir and has bequeathed his property to one who had no right to it; except when the man has dismissed his lawful heir with some bequest, regardless of the amount.

2. If a man commands his heirs, saying, "After my death, hand this bill of divorcement to my wife," or "Hand this bill of emancipation to my slave," his command is void, and the bills may not be served, since after his death his wife ceases to be his wife and becomes his widow, and a woman becomes divorced only by being dismissed by her husband and not by any other person, as it is written: *neither shall they marry a woman divorced by her husband* (Lev. 21:7). Likewise, the deceased can exercise no direct power over property in the form of slaves left by him, except by ordering his heirs, "After my death, do ye emancipate this slave."

3. If a man assigns his property to someone who is not his lawful heir by writing, "I assign to him all that I have acquired before and all that I shall acquire in the future," his gift is void, since he can go only by the past and cannot know what lies in the future; perchance God will inflict upon him a chastisement or give him a good reward or grant him sons or daughters.

VI. MARRIAGE

1. He who marries a woman and abides with her for ten years without her bearing him children must be compelled to marry another woman, as it is written: *And Sarah, the wife of Abram, took Hagar, the Egyptian, her maidservant . . . and gave her to her husband Abram to be his wife* (Gen. 16:3).

2. He who says, "I refuse to feed and support my wife," must be compelled to divorce her and pay her the full amount of her marriage contract, as it is written: *He shall not diminish her food, raiment, and cohabitation. And if he do not fulfill these three for her, she shall go free* (Exod. 21:10–11).

3. If he weds her and is found to be incapable of cohabiting with her, the choice is up to her; if she is willing to go on living with him, she may do so; if she is not, she may demand her divorce on the basis of the biblical verse just quoted.

4. If he weds her and cohabits with her, but does not give her full support, he must divorce her and pay her the full amount of her marriage contract.

5. If he divorces her, he must pay her the full amount of her marriage contract, and he cannot repossess any gift which he has given her. . . .

6. A man is obligated to feed and provide for his sons and daughters; the sons, until they become proficient in the Law and in a profession, as it is written: *I have nurtured and raised sons* (Isa. 1:2), *nurtured* signifying practical education, while *raised* means the teaching of morality; and the daughters, until they shall have been married to husbands, as it is written: *and she shall return to the house of her father, as during her girlhood* (Lev. 22:13), and again: *from his loaf she did eat* (II Sam. 12:3), showing that the unmarried daughter partakes of her father's loaf of bread and drinks from his cup. A father is also obligated to provide for the marriage of his sons and daughters, as it is written: *Take ye wives for your sons . . . and give ye your daughters to husbands for wives* (Jer. 29:6).

7. He who says, "I refuse to feed and support either my wife or

my sons and daughters, either during my lifetime or after my death," has no legal standing whatever.

VII. ADULTERY

1. If testimony is given against a married woman that she has lain with another man, both are subject to the penalty of death, even if no intercourse has actually occurred, as it is written: *and they shall die, even both of them, the man who has lain with the woman, and the woman* (Deut. 22:22). However, since we no longer inflict the punishment of death, she must instead remain forbidden to her husband, and both she and her paramour must be kept apart from the congregation of the Exiled, as it is written: *after that she had been made unclean* (Deut. 24:4).

2. If the only witness against her is her husband, she becomes forbidden to him on the ground of his own statement that "I saw her with another man," since his testimony, standing alone, is valid only as it affects himself and is insufficient to affect others, for which reason she becomes forbidden to him only; she may not be put to death solely on his word. The proof of this is the same verse: *after that she had been made unclean,* and the verse: *The condemned shall be put to death by two witnesses, or three witnesses* (Deut. 17:6).

3. However, she is not forbidden to either her husband or her paramour if the former has not yet cohabited with her, since it is written: *Her first husband . . . cannot take her a second time to be his wife, after that she had been made unclean* (Deut. 24:4). This cannot apply to the husband, since the words *a second time* and *had been made unclean* cannot possibly refer to him, for he never as yet had any carnal knowledge of her.

VIII. DESERTION

1. A woman whose husband has gone away and who hears a rumor that he has died and marries another man, but whose first husband subsequently returns safe and sound, becomes forbidden

to both husbands, as it is written: *after that she had become unclean, for it is an abomination in the sight of the Lord* (Deut. 24:4). In this case *had become unclean* applies to both men, and she must therefore be separated from both. Her first husband must give her a bill of divorcement, and she is free to marry other men. The second husband need do nothing, since his union with her was sheer adultery, inasmuch as betrothal, wedding, and consummation of marriage cannot apply to a woman already married. Even if she has married successively a hundred men, it is all null and void, being sheer adultery, since until she receives a bill of divorcement from her first husband she remains in his domain and is forbidden to anyone else.

IX. CONCLUSION

1. Let there be abundant peace to all the Exiled, from me, Benjamin son of Moses—may his memory be blessed together with that of all the righteous. I, who am dust and ashes beneath the soles of your feet, have written this Book of Rules for you Karaites, so that you might pass judgments according to it upon your brethren and friends. For every rule I have indicated the pertinent verse of Scripture. As for other rules, which are observed and recorded by the Rabbanites and for which I could find no pertinent biblical verse, I have written them down also, so that you might observe them likewise if you so desire.

DANIEL AL-ḲŪMISĪ

Daniel ben Moses, a native of the city of Dāmaġān in the province of Ḳūmis,[1] lived probably at the end of the ninth and the beginning of the tenth centuries. He left his native land and (possibly after a sojourn in the neighboring province of Xurāsān) [2] moved to Jerusalem, where he presumably remained until his death. He was, so far as we now know, the first notable Karaite author to settle in the Holy City.

A man of great learning and independent frame of mind, Daniel did not hesitate to differ sharply with both Anan and Benjamin al-Nahāwandī in important matters of law and belief, even to the extent of dubbing Anan a "champion fool." Yet al-Ḳirḳisānī, who is by no means generous in complimenting others, characterized Daniel in these words: [3]

I know of no one among the devotees of the use of pure reason more conscientious than Daniel al-Ḳūmisī, or more willing to give it its just due. Every conclusion arrived at by the use of reason or obtained through research or demanded by logical proof he readily accepted. What is more, he would write to his followers who had made for themselves copies of his works, informing them of any changes which had occurred in his opinions as recorded in his writings and requesting them to make corresponding corrections in their copies of his works. . . . He was strong in Scripture and in the knowledge of the Hebrew tongue.

To be sure, al-Ḳirḳisānī then proceeds to give Daniel a mild rebuke for his disrespect for Anan, but as a matter of fact al-Ḳirḳisānī himself held no especially high opinion of Anan as a philosopher and theologian.

Of Daniel's theological views the most striking is his complete denial of the existence of angels, apparently aimed at Benjamin

1. In Ṭabaristān, North Persia.
2. Cf. Mann, p. 8, n. 14.
3. *KA,* I, 4–5; a summary of Daniel's teaching is found *ibid.,* pp. 58–59; a detailed discussion of his theory of the angels is given in *KA,* II, 328–330.

al-Nahāwandī's theory of the angel-creator of the world. In Daniel's opinion the word "angel," as used in Scripture, is merely a metaphoric term for the various forces of nature, such as fire, clouds, and winds, employed by God as agents in fulfilling His decrees, while the figures of angels seen by the Prophets in their visions represent creatures made by God for each particular occasion and having no permanent existence. In matters of law he was more rigoristic and exacting than other Karaite teachers. Thus, he prohibited the consumption of the blood of fish[4] and the use of soap on the Sabbath.[5] On the other hand, he is said to have exempted men under twenty years of age from the obligation to observe all the religious ordinances, and to have accepted the testimony of Moslems regarding the appearance of the new moon and permitted its use in the fixing of the dates of holidays.

Daniel's violent opposition to Anan is presumably responsible for his neglect by the later Karaites. His name does not appear in the official Karaite memorial list, and of his writings, which must have been extensive, only fragments have so far been found, not all of them definitely assignable to him. These fragments form portions of a commentary—or rather a series of short notes interspersed with longer theological and philosophical excursuses—on the Bible and a *Book of Precepts;* the latter appears to have covered the ritual law, perhaps also the law of inheritance, but not civil law. Both works were written in Hebrew.

FROM THE WRITINGS OF DANIEL AL-ḲŪMISĪ

I. THE CLEAN SPECIES OF ANIMALS WHICH MAY BE USED FOR FOOD

1. Know ye that the cleanness of beasts, fish, and grasshoppers is known by their marks: of the beasts, by their cloven hooves and

4. Meaning that in his opinion the flesh of fish must be as thoroughly drained of blood as the flesh of cattle and sheep before it can be used for food.

5. Meaning that he regarded the use of soap as a procedure involving chemical changes and therefore prohibited on the Sabbath.

cud-chewing; of the fish, by their fins and scales; of the grasshoppers, by their legs above their feet. The cleanness of birds, on the other hand, is known by their names only, and not by any marks. The Lord did not command us, "You may eat all birds which have such-and-such a mark," but rather designated each forbidden species by its name, as it is written: *And these ye shall hold in abomination from among the birds . . . the eagle . . .* (Lev. 11: 13).

2. Now why did not the Lord also ordain the cleanness of birds by their marks, as He had done in the case of beasts and fish? Because the marks of unclean beasts differ from those of clean beasts, whereas the mark of many a clean bird is like that of an unclean one; that is why He listed the unclean birds by their names, and not by their marks. In this way you will know that he who says, "All birds having such-and-such a mark are clean," speaks falsely of the Lord in words contrived from his own heart.

3. Some say that all birds having a *mur'ah* and a *noṣah* may be used for food, but this is not so, and they speak without knowledge. They think that mur'ah and noṣah are two parts and interpret them as signifying the gizzard and the crop, which is not correct. You must know that mur'ah signifies the food collected and swallowed by the bird and contained within the noṣah, the latter being the place where this gathered food is kept, as it is written: *And he shall remove its mur'ah with its noṣah* (Lev. 1: 16)—it is not written, "its mur'ah and its noṣah"—showing that this is all one part of the bird's body, and not two. This is confirmed further by the next phrase: *and he shall throw it,* showing again that it is all one part—otherwise it would have been written, "And he shall throw them"—and indicating that these are not two parts.

4. To sum up, mur'ah signifies the bird's food while noṣah is the organ in which this food is collected. Now is there a bird in existence which does not possess an organ for the storage of food, be it a noṣah or the intestines? As for their interpretation of mur'ah as meaning the gizzard, there is no proof for it in the whole of the Lord's Law.

5. Now you must know that we are not at liberty to eat of any

birds until we shall have learned the precise meaning of these names of forbidden birds. Yet who is there today who knows the significance of these names of forbidden birds (of Lev. 11:13–19)? Rather, one person says thus-and-thus, while the other person says it is not so. Such of these names as also occur elsewhere in Scripture we are able to interpret with fair certainty; for example, the crow and the eagle. Others which occur nowhere else in Scripture we cannot identify at all; for example, the *peres,* the *'ozniyah,* the *taḥmas.* The Hebrew language has ceased being spoken among us, and we no longer know which birds these terms signify.

6. It is therefore forbidden to us to eat birds, since we are unable to distinguish unclean birds from clean ones.

7. The only exceptions are *torim* and young *yonah.* Torim signifies turtledoves, while yonah means pigeons; they do not signify cocks and chickens respectively. The proof of it is the fact that chickens are domestic fowl which dwell permanently in people's houses and have no definite time of arrival, whereas the torim have a definite time of arrival in the year, as it is written: *the tor, the swallow, and the crane observe the time of their arrival* (Jer. 8:7), showing that the tor is the turtledove. This being so, yonah clearly signifies the pigeon.

8. If you should ask, "But how could the Lord have commanded a widow to go hunting wild birds in the open field, in order to offer them as a sacrifice?"—know that this precisely is the reason why He allowed the alternative, *or two young yonah* (Lev. 12:8), for if the one species is not available, might not the other be at hand?

9. Should you say that *śeḵwi* signifies the domestic cock and that since it has been left out of the list of unclean birds it denotes the domestic fowl and is permissible for use as food, know that not all unclean birds are included in the list; rather of each species there has been mentioned one which is representative of it, as it is written: *And every raven, after its ḵind* (Lev. 11:15)—who knows how many kinds of raven there may be?—*And the falcon, after its ḵind* (Lev. 11:14), *and the cucḵoo and the hawḵ, after its ḵind* (Lev. 11:16). You will know thereby that all those birds

mentioned are merely representative of their species, which include many other kinds not designated by name. Who can tell, therefore, that śeḵwi is not such an unlisted unclean bird?

10. You must know now that he who fears God must not use any bird for food except turtledoves and young pigeons, also wild pigeons, "until such time as the teacher of righteousness shall have come," forasmuch as all those who eat forbidden fowl or fish shall perish and be reduced to nothing on the Day of Judgment, just like those who eat the flesh of swine, as it is written: *Those who eat the flesh of the swine, and of other abomination, and of mice, shall perish all together* (Isa. 66: 17); the *abomination* mentioned between the swine and the mice signifies unclean fowl and fish, implying that those who eat of them are like eaters of the flesh of swine and camel. And in general he who fears God must keep away from all things subject to doubt as to their permissibility.

II. APPEAL TO THE KARAITES OF THE DISPERSION TO COME AND SETTLE IN JERUSALEM

1. *Hear my words, ye wise men, and give ear unto me, ye who have knowledge* (Job 34: 2). Is this not the custom of the whole world? When one man waxes angry with another, does not the latter come to the former as suppliant? Likewise, the disobedient son comes to his father's door to beg for reconciliation, and the disobedient servant comes to the door of his master. If the king is angered by one of his officials and has him put into confinement, is it not for the official to mourn, to don different clothing, and to forego the customary pleasures of high officials until such time as the king may hear of it and be mollified and restore him to his former place of honor? Is it not written: *If her father had but spit in her face, should she not hide in shame for seven days?* (Num. 12: 14). Is it not for him, too, to sit in grief for seven days, like a mourner? How much less, if the Creator, God of all the world, should wax wrathful against a creature, is it fitting for the latter to enjoy food and drink before he has returned in repentance to Him and [His wrath has been mollified]!

2. How much more does this apply to us, woe unto us, for the Lord has turned His wrath upon us and has cast us out *into another land, as it is this day* (Deut. 29: 27). . . . He has abandoned us like sheep without a shepherd; *He has cast down from heaven unto the earth the splendor of Israel* (Lam. 2: 1). . . . He has burned His sanctuary; He has left His Holy Place and His Temple, the dwelling of His Holy of Holies, to be trampled under the feet of the unclean ones, the uncircumcised, men and women soiled with suppuration, menstruation, and leprosy. He has abolished His priests and their sacrifices, as well as the Levites who sang over the sacrifices to the accompaniment of lutes and harps. Our festivals have been turned into days of mourning, all our songs have become dirges, and our holidays are full of sorrow and sighs, as it is written: *My harp has turned to mourning* (Job 30: 31). Our sun has set in daylight, as if it were nighttime, and our midday is as if it were darkness, as it is written: *And it shall come to pass on that day, sayeth the Lord God, that I will cause the sun to set at noon, and I will darken the earth in daylight. And I will turn your festivals into mourning . . .* (Amos 8: 9–10); *Therefore will I wail* (Mic. 1: 8); *The roads of Zion are in mourning* (Lam. 1: 4); *For these things I weep* (Lam. 1: 16).

3. *Awake, ye drunkards* (Joel 1: 5), our brethren in Israel, who are heedless or asleep or lazy, wake up and weep over the House of the Lord . . . *Gird yourselves and lament, ye priests; wail, ye servants of the altar; come, lie all night in sackcloth, ye servants of my God!* (Joel 1: 13). And now, our brethren in Israel, in all your cities, *For this gird yourselves with sackcloth, lament and wail, for the heat of the wrath of the Lord has not turned away from us* (Jer. 4: 8).

4. Know, then, that the scoundrels who are among Israel say one to another, "It is not our duty to go to Jerusalem until He shall gather us together, just as it was He who had cast us abroad." These are the words of those who would draw the wrath of the Lord and who are bereft of sense. Even if the Lord had not made it an ordinance upon us to go to Jerusalem from the various lands of the Dispersion and to pray there with mournful and bitter tears,

would we not know with our own understanding that it is for those who are objects of the Lord's wrath to come to the door of Him who has been moved to anger, to supplicate Him, as I have said above? How much more so when the Lord himself has commanded the men of the Exile to come to Jerusalem and to stand within it at all times before Him, mourning, fasting, weeping, and wailing, wearing sackcloth and bitterness, all day and all night, as it is written: *Upon thy walls, O Jerusalem, have I appointed watchmen; all day and all night, always, they shall not be silenced; ye who mention the Lord, do ye not cease. And do ye not give him rest* (Isa. 62:6–7). And it is written also in Jeremiah (31:18a–b): *I have surely heard Ephraim*—Ephraim signifying Israel—*moving to and fro;* i.e., wandering hither and thither in exile, crying and weeping, and saying before Me, Is it not Thou, O my God, *who hast chastised me* and hast cast me into exile? And I in my exile, bereft of those who would teach me righteousness, have become *as a calf that has not been trained* to bear the yoke, inasmuch as the shepherds of the exile have not taught me to bear the yoke of the ordinances as set forth in the Law of Moses, but rather have led me astray with *an ordinance of men learned by rote* (Isa. 29:13). *Now make me turn back, and I will so turn back, for thou art the Lord my God* (Jer. 31:18c).

5. And the Lord replied to Israel in these words: My people, if thou desirest that I should turn thee back (Jer. 31:21–22): *Set up for thyself way signs*—meaning [signposts] on the road to Jerusalem to go to the House of the Lord; *make for thyself bitterness*—by weeping and wailing—*set thy heart toward the highway, the road thou hast traveled; return, O virgin of Israel, return to these thy cities!*—i.e., prior to the reassembly of the Exiled, go back to Jerusalem and there hold vigils before the Lord, day and night. *How long wilt thou wander about, O back-sliding daughter,* saying, I will not go to Jerusalem, to the seat of the Lord? If thou shouldst say, *Make me turn back, and I will so turn back,* I shall not turn thee back until thou thyself returnest to Jerusalem, *for the Lord has created a new thing in the earth.* And what is this new thing? It is that the wife should return of her own accord to her

husband, to appease his heart, without his sending a messenger to her to bring her back to him, as it is written: *A woman shall court a man,* since the relationship between the Lord and Israel is like that of a wife and her husband, as it is written: *Forsooth as a wife has betrayed her husband, even thus have you betrayed me, O house of Israel, says the Lord* (Jer. 3:20). Therefore says the Lord: *I will go and return to my place, until they realize their guilt and seek my presence; in their anxiety they will beseech me earnestly* (Hos. 5:15).

6. Therefore it is incumbent upon you who fear the Lord to come to Jerusalem and to dwell in it, in order to hold vigils before the Lord until the day when Jerusalem shall be restored, as it is written: *And do ye not give him rest* (Isa. 62:7).

7. It is written also (Ps. 84:6–7): *Blessed is the man whose strength is in thee;* blessed is the man who places his confidence in God and is strong with the strength of the Lord, who does not say, "How shall I go to Jerusalem, seeing that I am in fear of robbers and thieves on the road? And how shall I find a way to earn a living in Jerusalem?" *There are highways in their hearts*—referring to the aforementioned verse, *set thy heart toward the highway—There are highways in their hearts; those who pass through the valley of weeping*—meaning Jerusalem—*make it a well,* since the well of all godly learning is in Jerusalem.

8. Do not nations other than Israel come from the four corners of the earth to Jerusalem every month and every year in the awe of God? What, then, is the matter with you, our brethren in Israel, that you are not doing even as much as is the custom of the Gentiles in coming to Jerusalem and praying there, as it is written: *neither have ye done according to the judgments of the nations that are around you* (Ezek. 5:7)? You have refrained from following the praiseworthy laws of the Gentiles, yet have followed those that are wicked, as it is written: *ye have done according to the judgments of the nations that are around you* (Ezek. 11:12). What could be more grievous than that the Lord should designate Israel as more wicked than the Samaritans, of whom it is written: *They feared the Lord and worshiped their god* (II Kings 17:33),

while of Israel it is written: *Until this day they are acting according to their former manners: they do not fear the Lord, and do not act according to their divine laws and judgments, and according to the law and the ordinance which the Lord has ordained upon the children of Jacob* (II Kings 17:34), since Israel observes neither the holidays of the Lord nor His ordinances and judgments nor anything else but *an ordinance of men learned by rote* (Isa. 29:13), whereas of these Gentiles it is written: *And these nations did fear the Lord* (II Kings 17:41).

9. Now you, our brethren in Israel, do not act this way. Hearken to the Lord, arise and come to Jerusalem, so that we may return to the Lord. Or if you will not come because you are running about in tumult and haste after your merchandise, then send at least five men from each city in the Dispersion, together with their sustenance, so that we may form one sizable community to supplicate our God at all times upon the hills of Jerusalem, in accordance with the aforementioned verse: *Upon thy walls, O Jerusalem, have I appointed watchmen*. You will have no valid excuse before the Lord if you do not return today to the Law of the Lord and to His ordinances as prescribed in it, because since the beginning of the Exile, in the days of the kingdom of the Greeks, the Romans, and the Magians, the Rabbanites held the offices of princes and judges, and those who sought the Law could not even open their mouths in behalf of the ordinances of the Lord for fear of the Rabbanites who were [ruling over them]. Upon the arrival of the kingdom of Ishmael, however, matters improved, for the Ishmaelites always help the Karaites to observe the true faith as set forth in the Law of Moses, and we must bless them for it.

10. Now you are living in the midst of the kingdom of Ishmael, which loves those who fix the new moon by direct observation. Why, then, are you afraid of the Rabbanites? God will surely come to your assistance. Arise, therefore, draw your strength from the Law of the Lord, *strengthen ye hands that are weak* (Isa. 35:3), endeavor skillfully to teach all Israel the ordinances of the Lord, and admonish them with words of peace, not with quarreling and strife, as it is written: *And they who have understanding among*

the people shall instruct many . . . and many shall join them (Dan. 11:33–34), this being a reference to the kingdom of Ishmael, for with it the Lord broke the staff of the Rabbanites and removed it from over you.

III. COMMENTARY ON DANIEL 11:35–39

1. *And some of the men of understanding shall stumble* (v. 35). In this way the Lord informed Daniel through the angel that some of the early men of understanding in the Dispersion shall have stumbled in their interpretation of the ordinances. Now as regards Anan, if you classify him among the men of understanding, was he not one of those who stumbled, inasmuch as he was early? Or if you say that he was not a man of understanding, then you need not obey his words, and it follows that the truth was to be discovered by the later scholars, as it is written further on: *to refine among them, and to purify and whiten, even to the time of the end, for there is yet time to the appointed day of reckoning,* meaning that prior to the time appointed for the end they shall be purified and whitened.

2. *And the king shall do according to his will* (v. 36), meaning the king of Ishmael, who is greater than all kings. Therefore it is written further on: *and he shall exalt and magnify himself above every god;* i.e., over the kingdom of the Persians, the kingdom of the Romans, and the kingdom of the Turks, since the Ishmaelites also conquered many Turkish provinces, from Xurāsān through Xuwārizm, Samarkand, Šāš, Farġāna, and others, and from the province of Hinduwān to Xawlān and Kirmān. Who can enumerate all the provinces under their rule? That is why it is written: *and he shall magnify himself above every god,* since all the provinces which he had conquered were inhabited by idol worshipers, so that he was exalted, through his conquest, *above every god.*

3. *and against the God of gods*—meaning the God of Israel—*he shall speak wondrous things,* since he said, "I am the messenger of God," and spoke about His Prophets things which are not mentioned in the Scriptures. *And he shall prosper*—in his kingdom

and in his blasphemous words, when he spoke in defiance of Heaven, and his deceit shall prosper in his hand, and his kingdom shall endure for him—*until the wrath shall be fulfilled,* i.e., until the termination of the Exile, since no one else will hold imperial dominion after him until the advent of the Messiah. *For that which has been decreed shall be accomplished;* i.e., that which has been decreed to be fulfilled over Israel, all of it shall be accomplished during his kingdom, as it is written also: *And in the days of these kings the God of heaven shall set up a kingdom which shall never be destroyed* (Dan. 2: 44).

4. *And concerning the gods of his fathers* (v. 37), i.e., the idols which his fathers had worshiped, *he shall not regard them*—but only the one and only God—*and concerning the desire of women . . . he shall not regard it.* In my opinion this refers to his permission of making concubines out of all purchased maidservants, since before him the uncircumcised held that a man is permitted to have no more than one woman. Some say that this sentence refers to his prohibition of some cases of incest, such as marrying one's mother, daughter, sister, or niece, which is in accordance with the Jewish ordinance. *And concerning every god, he shall not regard him,* for he will utter and recount all his sayings in the Name of the one and only God.

5. *But the god of fortresses* (v. 38)—some say that this means al-Lāt and al-'Uzzā, since before his advent the inhabitants of the provinces around Mecca used to worship *the god of fortresses,* i.e., the local god of their provinces, *fortresses* meaning the same thing as provinces—*he shall honor in his seat,* since he left [him] there unharmed, as it is said that the people of the environs of Mecca came to him and made a covenant with him that he should not destroy the local *god of fortresses* but should leave him in his seat. *But to the God whom his fathers knew not*—which in my opinion signifies the one and only God—*he will show honor with gold and silver, and with precious stones and costly things,* the latter signifying fine vestments of expert workmanship, since they made all such things for the glory of the God of heaven.

6. *And he shall deal with the strongest fortresses* (v. 39). In

my opinion this signifies the provinces which he had captured and whose inhabitants he took into his army; they are idolaters who brought their idols with them and continue to worship them. These form the army of the kings of Ishmael: men from Xurāsān, Brahmins, and others; men from the tribes of Ya'ḳūb, 'Umar, Xuḳāran, and the latter's subtribes, who live in the mountains of Xurāsān and Ṭabaristān; also men of Daylam, likewise idolaters—all these are part of the army of the kings of Ishmael.

7. *And he shall cause them to rule over many,* since the army of war rules over the multitude of the population in every direction. *And he shall divide the land for a price,* referring to the tribute and the gifts which tax farmers give to kings to buy the tax revenue of provinces.

JACOB AL-ḲIRḲISĀNĪ

JACOB al-Ḳirḳisānī (Arabic Abū Yūsuf Ya'ḳūb ibn Isḥāḳ ibn Sam'awayh [or Sam'ūya] al-Ḳirḳisānī) [1] may be justly regarded as the greatest Karaite mind of the first half of the tenth century. His stature as a scholar and thinker has only recently been brought to light in anything approaching its full measure, and future publication of his as yet undiscovered works may well force a revision of this estimate toward an even higher level.

Of his life nothing is known beyond what may be deduced from indirect references found in his works. His surname has been variously explained as indicating that he was a native of Ḳirḳīsīyā, the ancient Circesium, in Upper Mesopotamia, or of Ḳarḳasān, a small town in the general vicinity of the capital city of Bagdad; [2] if the latter derivation is the true one, his surname should be spelled more correctly al-Ḳarḳasānī. His command of geography indicates that he knew well the lands of the Near East, and he may even have journeyed as far as northern India; [3] certainly travel was regarded by Moslem society in al-Ḳirḳisānī's time as an indispensable ingredient of every mature scholar's education.

1. This is the full name as given in one of the manuscripts (copied in 1388) of the *Book of Lights* (*KA,* V, 010; for *al-Xāzirūnī,* there and on p. 011, read *al-Kāzirūnī,* i.e., from Kāzirūn in Persia). A much earlier manuscript, copied in 1108 (*ibid.,* p. 012) omits Sam'awayh, which is presumably a Persianized form of the biblical name Shemaiah (I Kings 12: 22). The full name implies that his father was named Isaac and that his son was named Joseph. This genealogy, however, is suspect as being merely a repetition of the sequence of the biblical patriarchs and may have been supplied later by a reader who had no authentic knowledge of al-Ḳirḳisānī's family.

2. The basic information on these two places is given by the Arab geographer Yāḳūt (*Mu'ǧam al-buldān,* ed. F. Wuestenfeld, [Leipzig, 1866–73] IV, 64–66). On Ḳirḳīsīyā, see also the excellent article in the *Encyclopedia of Islam.* On the existence of Karaite communities in either of these places no information appears to have been found so far.

3. For references to India in the *Book of Lights,* see *KA,* V, 062; they deal with Hindu religion, legal procedure, marriage, and social customs. For references to China, see *ibid.,* p. 056.

He was well read in contemporary Arabic literature, theological, philosophical, and scientific, and had a more than superficial knowledge of the Mishnah, the Gemara, many midrashic and halakhic works, and Rabbanite liturgy.[4] He also read the Koran and the New Testament, or at least portions of them, although he appears to have had considerable difficulty in gaining access to copies of these sacred books; the Mohammedan authorities in particular generally frowned on having unbelievers handle the Revelation of the Prophet.

Although himself a zealous and outspoken Karaite, al-Ḳirḳisānī was nevertheless on terms of personal friendship with eminent theologians of other faiths, including Jacob ben Ephraim (Arabic Ya'ḳūb ibn Ifraym) al-Šāmī, a Rabbanite scholar,[5] and Jesus (Arabic Yasū') Sexā, a Christian "bishop" (perhaps rather a deacon).[6] About the Rabbanites he said many harsh things, but his language never reached the depths of abuse sounded by other Karaite polemicists, and toward Sa'adiah Gaon, the bête noire of all tenth-century Karaite writers, he preserved throughout a tone of respectful and calm disagreement. A firm believer in the use of reason in theology and jurisprudence, he wrote with a clarity and logic few of his contemporaries could approach, and his erudition in both theological and secular matters endowed his opinions with an impressive basis of factual support.

Fate was not kind to al-Ḳirḳisānī. He wrote in Arabic only, and his works, at least so far as is known, were never translated into Hebrew, so that they remained practically out of reach of later Byzantine and Russo-Polish Karaites who had no command of the Arab tongue. Even his Arabic-speaking contemporaries and successors seem to have been indifferent toward him, although they occasionally mentioned and quoted him with fair respect. One can only guess at the reason for this lack of popularity by reflecting that al-Ḳirḳisānī's appraisal of some Karaite sectarians

4. Cf. the list of works quoted and mentioned in the *Book of Lights* (*KA,* V, 041–043).

5. Considerable space is devoted to him in the *Book of Lights;* for list of references, see *KA,* V, 081.

6. *KA,* II, 220; al-Ḳirḳisānī speaks of him in a tone of genuine personal regard.

and their squabbles about ritual minutiae was often little short of scathing and that he minced no words, even when speaking of Anan, whenever he found himself obliged to disagree with his views.[7] This unpopularity perhaps explains also another puzzling fact: al-Ḳirḳisānī must have been of about the same age as the Gaon Sa'adiah and had published a sizable literary output during the Gaon's lifetime, including much detailed discussion of the latter's views on various subjects; yet Sa'adiah does not mention al-Ḳirḳisānī, at least not by name, in any of his works that have so far come to light. It may be that in spite of his scholarly achievements and reputation al-Ḳirḳisānī wielded too little practical influence among his fellow-Karaites to be regarded by Sa'adiah as a formidable opponent.

Al-Ḳirḳisānī's principal work is the *Book of Gardens and Parks* (Arabic *Kitāb al-riyāḍ wal-ḥadā'iḳ*), completed in 938 [8] and containing an extensive commentary on the nonlegal portions of the Pentateuch. This commentary forms the sequel to an earlier work,[9] the *Book of Lights and Watchtowers* (Arabic *Kitāb al-anwār wal-marāḳib*), which is a monumental and systematic code of law enriched with numerous excursuses on a wide variety of subjects.[10]

7. His sharpest criticism of Anan is perhaps his exasperated comment (*KA*, V, 1142), in discussing Anan's opinion on a problem in the law of incest: "I wish to goodness I knew whether Anan was asleep or out of his head when he uttered this opinion!" To be sure, al-Ḳirḳisāni branded as shameful Daniel al-Ḳūmisī's characterization of Anan as "the First of the Fools"; this was altogether too uncouth an outburst for al-Ḳirḳisānī's sense of moderation and courtesy and, on purely historical grounds, it was wholly uncalled for.

8. Cf. A. Neubauer, *Medieval Jewish Chronicles* (Oxford, 1887–95) II, 249 ff., where the concluding portion of the *Book of Gardens* is printed.

9. Composed (or completed) supposedly in 937, according to the Karaite chronicler Ibn al-Hītī (*JQR*, IX [1897], 432, 436–437, where, however, this date has been badly confused by the copyist and is therefore not wholly certain); see below pp. 231, 374.

10. For example, a philosophical disquisition on knowledge and reason (II, i–x); a treatise on dialectics (IV, lix–lxviii); on witchery and kindred crafts (VI, ix–xi); on the psychophysiology of sleep and dreams and on the interpretation of the latter (VI, xiv); on the value of the Jewish shekel (VI, xxxviii); on suicide (VI, xlvii). A mass of smaller pieces on various topics (medicine, natural sciences, astronomy, Hebrew and Arabic philology, etc.), is scattered throughout the work (cf. *KA*, V, index of subjects).

His shorter works—smaller only in point of size, not in importance—have unfortunately not yet been recovered and are known only from references to them in the *Book of Lights* and the *Book of Gardens;* they must consequently have been written prior to these two works. They comprise the following: [11]

1) A commentary on the Book of Genesis (Arabic *Tafsīr Bĕrešiṯ*) which appears to have been a very extensive work augmented with excursuses on various subjects.
2) A commentary on the Book of Job (Arabic *Tafsīr Iyoḇ*).
3) A commentary on the Book of Ecclesiastes (Arabic *Tafsīr Ḳoheleṯ*).
4) A treatise in refutation of Mohammed's claim to prophecy (Arabic *Kitāb fī 'ifsād nubuwwat Muḥammad*).
5) An essay on the art of textual interpretation and explanation (Arabic *al-Ḳaul 'alā l-tafsīr wa-šarḥ al-ma'ānī*).
6) An essay on the art of translation (Arabic *al-Ḳaul 'alā l-targama*).
7) A treatise on the oneness of God (Arabic *Kitāb al-tauḥīd*).

There is, of course, no certainty whatever that this list represents al-Ḳirḳisānī's entire literary output up to 938; he may have written other works which he had no occasion to mention elsewhere in his writings. Nor is there at present any information as to whether he had written any works subsequent to the completion of the *Book of Gardens.* The scope of his known writings and the bulk of his two major works leave little doubt that his industry was as great as the range of his learning was encyclopedic.

FROM THE WRITINGS OF JACOB AL-ḲIRḲISĀNĪ

I. HISTORY OF JEWISH SECTS

1. The first to show dissension in the Jewish religion, to sow disobedience to the Law among the people of Israel, subsequent to the establishment of the monarchy, to alter the divine ordinances and to supplant them was Jeroboam, since Scripture says of him in more than one place: *the sins of Jeroboam . . . wherewith he*

11. *KA*, V, 042–043.

has made Israel to sin (I Kings 14:16, 15:30, etc.). This refers to his making the two golden calves and to his call to the people: *Ye have gone up long enough to Jerusalem . . .* (I Kings 12:28). According to Scripture, his motive for doing this was his desire to establish himself in his kingdom and endure in it and his fear that if the people continued to travel to Jerusalem for the festivals they might long again for their legitimate king of the House of David, so that Jeroboam's kingdom would slip out of his hand, as it is written: *And Jeroboam said in his heart, Now the kingdom will return to the House of David if this people should continue to go up to offer sacrifices in the house of the Lord at Jerusalem, and the heart of this people will turn back unto their master, even unto Rehoboam, king of Judah, and they will slay me and return to Rehoboam, king of Judah. And the king took counsel, and he made two calves of gold, and he said to them, Ye have gone up long enough to Jerusalem; behold thy gods, O Israel, who brought thee up out of the land of Egypt* (I Kings 12:26–28). Some of our scholars hold that he made these two golden calves merely as a substitute for the two cherubim, and this opinion is not improbable, since in everything which Jeroboam had done in deviation from the Law his purpose was merely to imitate and duplicate that which is ordained in it. This is shown by his substitution of laymen for the Aaronite priests, as it is written: *and he appointed priests from among all the people, who were not of the sons of Levi* (I Kings 12:31). The same applies to his instituting a festival in the eighth month in imitation of the seventh month's festival observed at Jerusalem, as it is written: *And Jeroboam ordained a festival in the eighth month, on the fifteenth day of the month, like the festival which was observed in Judah* (I Kings 12:32). It is indeed possible that he made the people believe that that year was a leap year, as some of our scholars have suggested.

2. This is all the information supplied by the Scriptures as to the dissent and change introduced by Jeroboam. It is possible that he dissented in, and supplanted, many other religious ordinances, of which the biblical account, limiting itself to the few which were

the most grievous and most important, makes no mention. Actually, however, Jeroboam did not deny the Creator or disacknowledge Him or worship idols, as some people imagine. We know this in two ways: in the first place, there is the aforementioned fact that he replaced each religious ordinance which he had abolished with another of the same kind; had he abandoned the true religion as a whole, he would have abolished and abrogated the entire revealed legislation and would have had no need to introduce substitutes. Rather, the real cause of his innovations was, as we have said above, his apprehension lest the kingdom should be lost to him. The second proof that Jeroboam did not forsake the true faith and did not worship idols is that we find that Jehu destroyed the idols and slew their Israelite worshipers, as it is written of him: *And Jehu destroyed the Baal out of Israel* (II Kings 10:28)—and yet right after these words it is stated that he persevered in the sins of Jeroboam, to wit: *But as for the sins of Jeroboam, the son of Nebat, wherewith he had made Israel to sin, Jehu did not turn away from them, from the golden calves which were in Bethel and which were in Dan.* This is irrefutable proof that Jeroboam did not make the two calves in order to worship them as the heathen worship idols. And if one should ask, "But does not Scripture say that Jeroboam offered sacrifices and burned incense to them, as it is written: *to sacrifice unto the calves which he had made* (I Kings 12:32), and in another verse: *To burn incense unto the calves which he had made?*" we would answer that it is the custom of the Scriptures to use such expressions by way of metaphor. Whenever anyone undertook something which was abhorrent to God and which violated the established faith, he was designated as "worshiping" that thing; e.g.: *And there ye shall worship gods, the work of men's hands, wood and stone, which neither see, nor hear, nor eat, nor smell* (Deut. 4:28); since the children of Israel did not worship idols during their exile, this must merely mean that they practiced certain transgressions of the kind practiced by idolaters. . . .

3. As for Jeroboam's call, *behold thy gods, O Israel* (I Kings

12: 28), it is possible that he meant merely to refer to the Creator and to the new place where He might be approached by way of prayer and sacrifice. This is similar to the words of the children of Israel to Aaron: *Come, make for us a god* (Exod. 32: 1), and further on, after the golden calf was made: *This is thy god* (Exod. 32: 4). Consider now: they said to him, "Make for us a god who led us out of Egypt"; yet the exodus from Egypt had already taken place, while the god to be made was still nonexistent, so that he who was nonexistent would have done that which had already come to pass. Could anyone not bereft of reason say such a thing? Moreover, it is also possible to say that the image of the calf was the same as the image of one of the angels' faces, as it is written: *and the face of an ox on the left* (Ezek. 1: 10); and that when the children of Israel said, *This is thy god, O Israel,* they meant, "This is the image of the angel who had led us out of Egypt," as it is written: *And the angel of God who went before the camp of Israel moved off* (Exod. 14: 19). It is therefore possible that Jeroboam, too, had the same thing in mind.

4. From this time on—that is, the time when Jeroboam committed the aforementioned acts—dissent arose among the children of Israel, and similar practices were planted in their midst, one generation inheriting them from the other, since it is written about each one of their kings: *he walked in the way of Jeroboam and in his sins wherewith he made Israel to sin* (I Kings 15: 34, 16: 26, etc.). They continued in this manner until the exile of the Ten Tribes, since it is written in the story of King Shalmaneser, when he exiled Hosea, the son of Elah, at the time of King Hezekiah, together with the entire Ten Tribes: *And the children of Israel walked in all the sins of Jeroboam which he had committed, they did not turn away from them* (II Kings 17: 22). And they continued at the time of their exile in the sins of Jeroboam, meaning the practices and indulgences which he had introduced in place of, and at variance with, biblical laws; except that at that time the two golden calves were no longer in existence as a pair, since one of them had been seized by Sennacherib, as it is written: *for the calf of Samaria shall become splinters* (Hos.

8:6), and further on: *It, too, shall be carried to Assyria, for a present to the King Contentious* . . . (Hos. 10:6). We learn thus that the statement about the children of Israel at the time of the exile, *And the children of Israel walked in all the sins of Jeroboam which he had committed,* refers not to the calves but to the practices and indulgences he had introduced in place of the original biblical ordinances. Afterward the people of Judah, too, followed the Ten Tribes in this dissent, as it is written: *Judah, too, did not keep the ordinances of the Lord their God, but they walked in all the sins of Israel which they practised* (II Kings 17:19). Both kingdoms were thus carried into exile, while they held on to these practices of Jeroboam, and they were scattered all over the world still persisting in them and transmitting them from one generation to the other until the present day. . . .

5. Next after Jeroboam appeared the Samaritans, known among the Jewish people as the Cutheans, of whom it is written: *And the king of Assyria brought men from Babylon and from Cuthah* (II Kings 17:24). They are those of whom it is written that they were *the adversaries of Judah and Benjamin* (Ezra 4:1), and that they approached the chiefs of the children of Israel when they were building the second Temple, as it is written: *And they drew near to Zerubbabel and the chiefs of the families of the fathers, and they said to them, Let us build with you, for we seek your God as ye do, and to him do we sacrifice since the days of Esarhaddon, king of Assyria* (Ezra 4:2). And it is related of them that to this day they preserve the memory of Sanballat the Horanite, who was a chieftain among them.

6. After the Samaritans there appeared the Chiefs of the Community, who are the original Rabbanites; this was in the days of the second Temple. The first of them to be recorded was Simeon, whom they call Simeon the Righteous; they say that he was one of the remaining members of the Great Synagogue. These, they say, lived in the time of Ezra and Nehemiah. The Rabbanites acknowledged the authority of the Chiefs of the Community solely because they followed the practices and the indulgences inherited from Jeroboam. In particular, they sustained and confirmed these

practices, supplied them with argumentative proofs, and wrote down the interpretation of them in the Mishnah and in other works. At times one or another among them did set forth the true meaning of a biblical ordinance, but they invariably banished him and sought to do him injury, as was, for example, the case of Gamaliel who fixed the date of holidays on the basis of the appearance of the new moon, or of Eliezer, the son of Hyrcanus, who disagreed with them in the matter of uncleanness of vessels the construction of which has not been completed; they excommunicated him and kept away from him, despite miraculous proofs of the truth of his opinion. . . .

7. After the Rabbanites there appeared the Sadducees, founded by Zadok and Boethus, who were, according to the Rabbanites, disciples of Antigonus, a successor of Simeon the Righteous, and had thus received their learning from the latter. Zadok was the first to expose the errors of the Rabbanites. He openly disagreed with them and he discovered part of the truth; he also composed a book in which he strongly reproved and attacked them. However, he produced no proof for anything that he claimed but merely set it forth in the manner of an assertion, except for one thing, namely, the prohibition of marrying one's niece, which he deduced from her being analogous to the paternal and maternal aunts. As for Boethus, he was of the opinion that Pentecost can fall only on a Sunday, which is also the view of the Ananites and all the Karaites.

8. About that time there appeared also the teaching of a sect called Magarians, who were so called because their religious books were discovered in a cave (*maġār*). One of them was the Alexandrian, whose well-known book is the principal religious book of the Magarians. Next to it in rank is a small booklet called the Book of Yaddu'a, also a fine work. Of their remaining books none is significant; most of them merely resemble idle tales.

9. Next there appeared Yešu'a, who the Rabbanites say was the son of Pandera; he is known as Jesus, the son of Mary. He lived in the days of Joshua, the son of Peraḥiah, who is said to have been the maternal uncle of Jesus. This took place in the reign of Augus-

tus Caesar, the emperor of Rome, i.e., at the time of the second Temple. The Rabbanites plotted against Jesus until they put him to death by crucifixion.

10. On the shores of the Nile, in Egypt, about twenty parasangs from al-Fusṭāṭ, there is said to be a sect called Kar'ites, so named because they use utensils made exclusively of gourds (*ḳar'*). According to a certain theologian, they claim that they are the descendants of Johanan, the son of Kareah.

11. The Rabbanites subsequently split into two factions, called the School of Hillel and the School of Shammay. The Rabbanites of Iraq followed the practice of the School of Hillel, while those of Syria followed that of the School of Shammay. Hillel and Shammay received their learning from Shemaiah and Abṭalion. The conflict between the School of Hillel and the School of Shammay broke out on the third day of the month of Adar, and a number of adherents of each school was slain.

12. Next appeared Obadiah, known as Abū 'Īsā al-Iṣfahānī, who claimed that he was a prophet. This occurred in the reign of the Caliph 'Abd al-Malik ibn Marwān. It is reported that he planned to come out against the Moslem government, and a number of people became his followers until he had about him a whole army, but he was engaged in battle by the Moslems and was slain. Some of his partisans, however, say that he was not killed but rather entered a fissure in a mountain, and nothing has been heard of him ever since. The miraculous thing about him, according to his followers, was that although he was, as they say, an illiterate tailor, unable to read or write, he nevertheless produced whole books and volumes without having been taught by anyone. A group of his followers now reside in Damascus and are known as Isunians.

13. Next after Abū 'Īsā appeared Yūdġān, who was called by his followers the Shepherd, meaning that he was the pastor of his people. He is said to have been a pupil of Obadiah and to have claimed, like him, that he was a prophet. His partisans say that he was the Messiah.

14. After Yūdġān appeared Anan, who is styled the Chief of

the Dispersion; this occurred in the days of the Caliph Abū Ğa'far al-Manṣūr. He was the first to make clear a great deal of the truth about the divine ordinances. He was learned in the lore of the Rabbanites, and not one of them could gainsay his erudition. It is reported that Hay, the president of the Rabbanite Academy, together with his father, translated the book of Anan from the Aramaic into Hebrew and found nothing in it of which they could not discover the source in Rabbanite lore, excepting his view on the law concerning the first-born and the difference between a firstling conceived while its mother was owned by a Jew and one conceived while its mother was owned by a Gentile; they did not know from whom he had borrowed this view until they found it in the hymnology of Yannay. The Rabbanites tried their utmost to assassinate Anan, but God prevented them from doing so.

15. Next after Anan appeared Ismā'īl al-'Ukbarī; this was in the reign of the Caliph al-Mu'taṣim Billāh. Most of Ismā'īl's utterances lead to a suspicion of insanity, and all well-educated persons who heard him laughed at him. Yet notwithstanding his ignorance he held himself in high esteem, for in his works he made little of Anan and often called him stupid. Upon feeling the approach of death, he is said to have commanded his followers to inscribe upon his tomb the words: *the chariot of Israel and its horsemen* (II Kings 2:12).

16. In the days of Ismā'īl al-'Ukbarī lived also Benjamin al-Nahāwandī. He, too, was learned in the lore of the Rabbanites, and he was strong in Scripture; he is said to have served as a judge for many years. In much of what he said he hit upon the truth, but in some instances he did not adhere to the method of analogy; rather he widely deviated from it. His teaching shows that he was diligent in following the biblical text strictly, as well as in making deductions from it or from the results of inference based upon two premises and a conclusion, the latter being a method intermediate between that of pure analogy and that of strict adherence to the biblical text. . . .

17. A younger contemporary of these men was Mūsā al-Za'farānī, known as Abū 'Imrān al-Tiflīsī. A resident of Bagdad,

he became known as al-Tiflīsī after he had emigrated to Tiflis, a city in Armenia, where he settled. A number of people accepted his teaching, and a group professing it exists there to the present day. The followers of Ismā'īl al-'Ukbarī say that Abū 'Imrān was Ismā'īl's pupil and received his learning from him.

18. In al-Ramla lived Malik al-Ramlī, whose followers are known down to the present day as Ramlites or Malikites.

19. In 'Ukbara, after Ismā'īl, lived Mīšawayh al-'Ukbarī. In addition to being exceedingly weak in matters of speculation, he was, judging by what is reported about him, much like a man lost in perplexity. . . . There are followers of his in 'Ukbara down to the present day; they are known as Mishawites, and there is not a single man skilled in knowledge and speculation among them.

20. The last to profess an acknowledged religious system, to compose books, and to acquire followers was Daniel al-Dāmaġānī, known as al-Ḳūmisī. . . .

21. These are the well-known sects, according to the information accessible to us.

II. PRINCIPLES OF BIBLICAL EXEGESIS

1. It is our purpose to undertake a commentary upon the Book of our Lord, which He revealed to us through Moses, namely the Law, and to elucidate that part of its subject matter which is other than laws and ordinances, since we have already dealt with these in a separate work. We shall mention the problems involved in biblical passages of ambiguous and seemingly contradictory nature, which are pointed out by dissenters and deviators, such as the Mannāniyya sect and others. I intend [not to leave anything], special or general, in the way of questions raised by various persons [without mentioning and explaining it]. To be precise, I see that some of our scholars who are devotees of rational speculation and research neglect problems and subjects of general import and discuss only such as are of special interest. Yet in this they deviate from what is desirable in two ways: first, it is the general and easy which should form the point of departure in science and

theology, from which one might then progress to that which is special and difficult. Secondly, an expert scholar and theologian is often approached by an ignorant and unlearned man with a question about a general matter which the scientist had neglected to investigate, thinking that it was of small import; he attempts a reply thereto, but is covered with shame when he finds that he has no answer for it. That is why matters of this sort should not be neglected but should be dealt with before everything else.

2. Let us therefore begin with the explanation of the meaning of *In the beginning* (Gen. 1: 1), since this is the first word in the Law, embracing hidden meanings and abstruse problems which require discussion and thorough investigation, especially on the part of him who undertakes to interpret it in the light of matters rational and philosophical. Indeed, some scholars who have attempted to do this without possessing skill in both of these things, that is, the text of Scripture and rational speculation, have imagined that the biblical account of creation and of its sequence conflicts with the principles of philosophy and nature. This, however, is not so, and he who has armed himself with a true knowledge of both these disciplines knows that each one of them confirms the other; indeed, Scripture is really one of the foundations of philosophy, providing that the investigator divests himself of personal inclination and bias. We shall explain this as far as we are able, trusting in God for ultimate success.

3. Dā'ūd ibn Marwān al-Raḳḳī, known as al-Muḳammiṣ, has written a fine book containing a commentary on Genesis, which he translated from the commentaries of the Syrians. But in some places he did not say all that needed to be said about the intended meaning of the Sacred Text, while in other places he was guilty of foolish verbosity for which there was no need. Another scholar of our own time also composed a fine book on this subject in which he followed a method similar to that of Dā'ūd. We shall extract the best part of both works and we shall add thereto that which they, in our opinion, have neglected to mention or have failed to explain adequately.

4. Before beginning with this we must prove the validity of

rational speculation and philosophical postulates from Scripture by mentioning some passages in it which point and lead to them. We shall do this because some of our scholars, upon hearing an interpretation interspersed with matter pertaining to philosophical speculation, are frightened away from it, regarding it as superfluous and unnecessary; indeed, some of them consider it improper and even forbidden. But this is only because of their ignorance and the poverty of their knowledge. Were the eyes of their minds open, they would have learned that these things are tools for the understanding of Scripture and ladders and bridges toward the perception of revealed truth, inasmuch as the truth of Scripture and religion can be comprehended only by reason. Since the philosophical postulates, too, are built upon rational deductions based in their turn upon the knowledge of things perceived by the human senses and logical axioms, he who rejects rational and philosophical opinions thereby denies all data posited by cogitation or sense perception.

5. We have already mentioned a part of all this in the seventh chapter of the second discourse of our book on the biblical laws, but we shall mention a small portion of it here also, because we have need of it in the expository treatment of Scripture, particularly in the interpretation of Genesis. We have mentioned there—by way of showing the validity of investigation into matters rational and disciplines philosophical, and proving that the Sages of our nation had engaged in such investigation—the biblical account of King Solomon as the most learned of the children of Adam, in that he discoursed upon all the various kinds of plants, from the largest, which is the cedar tree, down to the smallest, which is the hyssop, and upon all the various kinds of animals, including beasts, birds, fish, and insects. Consider now, what could he have discoursed about, as regards all these things, if not in the way of describing their natural properties and causes, their beneficial and harmful qualities, and similar matters? This in fact is what the Greek and other philosophers quote in his name and is now incorporated in their books. A similar thing is related in the biblical account concerning Daniel, Hananiah, Mishael, and

Azariah; to wit, that they were skilled *in all matters of wisdom and understanding* (Dan. 1:20), indicating that the king inquired of them about various matters of wisdom and that their knowledge of it was ten times greater than that of his advisers and court philosophers. This is an incontrovertible proof that they were scholars skilled in all branches of philosophy, since they were ten times more learned than the king's magicians.

6. Even if we had no other evidence of the existence of the study of philosophy among the children of Israel than that which has just been set forth, it would have been most decisive; how much more so when Scripture mentions similar things in numerous other places, some of which we have quoted there. We shall, however, mention some of those passages also in what follows, especially such as concern biblical exegesis.

7. Thus, Scripture says, confirming the validity of the use of reason: *In order that they may see, and know, and consider . . . that the hand of the Lord has done this* (Isa. 41:20); that is, to infer by way of reasoning that a thing made presupposes the existence of a maker. Another passage, *That they may know from the rising of the sun . . . that there is none beside me* (Isa. 45:6), represents a rational proof of the oneness of God. Another verse, *Thou hast heard; see all this . . . they are created now, and not from of old* (Isa. 48:6–7), is a proof of the temporal incipiency of substance, on the ground that it is inseparable from other temporal incipients, meaning the accidences. The passage, *Remember the former things of old* (Isa. 46:9), proves the impossibility of one thing being preceded by another thing which in turn is preceded by a third thing, and so forth, without end. The verse, *Know ye that the Lord he is God, it is he who has made us* (Ps. 100:3), shows the impossibility of things being self-created. In the passage, *Behold, this have I found, said Koheleth . . .* (Eccles. 7:27)—i.e., "I have found that all things depend one upon the other"—we find the same demonstration; namely, proof for the existence of cause and effect through the dependence of all existent things one upon the other. The verses, *Does not the ear test words? . . . Is wisdom with the aged?* (Job 12:11–12),

[refer] to the validity of reasoning, as does the verse, *Now they see not the light* (Job 37: 21), meaning that he who denies the existence of God is like one who denies the existence of light, since reason perceives the existence of God by means of incontrovertible proof in the same manner as the sense of sight perceives the existence of light. The same thing is shown by the passage, *the skilled workmen, they are of mere mankind; let them all be gathered together, let them stand up* (Isa. 44: 11). The verse, *Pour down, ye heavens, from above* (Isa. 45: 8), points to the movement taking place from the direction of the ether, that is, the fiery sphere which causes the rise of vapor, as stated in the verse, *And vapor rose from the earth* (Gen. 2: 6). The next words, *and let the skies pour down righteousness* (Isa. 45: 8) allude to the precipitation upon the earth, in the shape of rain, of the part of the vapor which has been condensed into water. The next words, *let the earth open, that they may bring forth salvation,* signify the meeting of the earth with its productive powers for this purpose, the result of all of which is the sprouting of plants, as shown by the following words, *And let her cause righteousness to spring up.* Such is the theologians' proof, from the cooperation between the celestial sphere and the terrestrial nature, of the incipiency of the world and its creation by an all-wise Creator . . . as is indicated by the final words, *I, the Lord, have created it;* i.e., He Himself has placed within these things the proof of His own existence.

8. These, then, are the rational proofs built upon the knowledge based on sense perception; and it is for this reason that King David, in describing the Law and stating that it is allied with both reason and perception, says: *The Law of the Lord is perfect* (Ps. 19: 8–10); i.e., its perfection is due to its close connection with reason free from error. He says further: *The commandments of the Lord are upright, rejoicing the heart,* referring to the satisfaction felt by the human heart because of the truth of the premises and conclusions contained in His commandments; and further: *The precept of the Lord is pure, enlightening the eyes,* refers to the clarity and lucidity of the precept, caused by its freedom from

ambiguities; and further: *The fear of the Lord is immaculate, enduring forever,* meaning that the word of the Law is firmly established in the face of disputes and attacks against it, and remains irrefutable. The full truth is then made evident by the combination and union of all five of these principles in the concluding words: *The judgments of the Lord are the truth, they are righteous all together.*

9. King Solomon has said: *The words of a man's mouth are as deep waters* (Prov. 18:4), implying that God has placed it in the power of Sages to elicit the meanings of things and to bring them near to men's understanding by joining or separating or arranging and placing them in proper sequence, just as He has put into their minds the art of raising water from the bowels of the earth. Has not the person who rejects reason and its postulates, founded on inferences from proofs and analogies, reached the height of insolence, not to mention his unbounded ignorance? Do men excel one another in anything save the qualities of the mind and of the postulates of reason? Were it not for human reason and the power of reasoning, in eliciting that which is unknown and learning that which is inaccessible to the senses by means of demonstrable proofs, would man have had any advantage over beast? That is why Scripture states: *He teaches us over and above the beasts of the earth . . .* (Job 35:11); i.e., although beasts and birds do possess some wisdom—like the bees who build hives; or the ants who in the summer prepare their food for the winter, as it is written: *Go to the ant, thou sluggard . . . she prepares in the summer her food* (Prov. 6:6–8); or the spider who labors to spin a net in order to catch flies for his food; or other known instances of the wisdom of beasts and birds—this wisdom is merely a matter of natural implanted instinct. Man, on the other hand, has been favored above all animals with the wisdom of choice, i.e., of deduction and inference, as illustrated by his aforementioned contrivance to raise water from the bowels of the earth. This is also expressed by King David in the verse, *O Lord our God, how magnificent is thy name . . .* (Ps. 8:2), the following words, *Thou hast placed thy splendor over the heavens,* signifying,

"Thou hast placed in the heaven and in its construction the proof of Thy splendor and might," in agreement with the verse, *The heavens declare the glory of God* . . . (Ps. 19:2) . . . And further, *Out of the mouths of babes and sucklings* . . . (Ps. 8:3), i.e., "after Thou didst place this proof in the heavens, Thou hast brought into being the knowledge of Thy power and justice in the work of creation, so that even *babes* are able to comprehend it." For if a man were to charge a boy with performing something which is beyond his ability, the boy would reply, "I am unable to perform this task"; and if the man were to compel him nevertheless or punish him for failure in his charge, he undoubtedly would have, in the boy's opinion, acted wrongfully toward him. The knowledge of God's justice and power, on the other hand, is firmly established in the mind of everyone, even of *babes*. David continues to discuss the heavens and their evidence for the existence of their Maker, by saying: *As I look at thy heavens* . . . (Ps. 8:4); he then goes on to discuss man and what he has been favored with above all the rest of creation, and he concludes with the statement: *he passes through the paths of the seas* (v. 9); i.e., "in addition to making him master over all the animals, Thou hast given him power and knowledge to cut across seas and travel over the watery deep by means of his initiative and sagacity," as explained above. All these quotations confirm the validity of reasoning, deduction, and inference, and there are many other biblical passages of similar purport.

10. Having thus explained the validity of reasoning, of the results yielded by proofs derived from reason and analogy, and of philosophical postulates built upon the science of analogy, let us now . . . mention the necessary preliminary things pertaining to the explanation of the meaning of Scripture and the interpretation of its seeming ambiguities, so as to lay a foundation upon which to build further, when we shall demonstrate the perfection of the whole of Scripture in the way of account, address, statement, and question, relating to fact, metaphor, generalization, advancement, postponement, abridgment, profusion, separation, combination, and other of its usages. These preliminary things

are thirty-seven in number, and by setting them forth first we shall have facilitated our purpose, notwithstanding that we look to God for ultimate succor.

11. First. We must know that our prophet and master Moses was the one who wrote the Pentateuch, from its beginning in Genesis to its end. It was he who handed down to us all the accounts contained therein regarding the events from God's creation of the world down to Moses' own death, inasmuch as it is written: *And Moses wrote this Law . . .* (Deut. 31:9). That is why it is associated with his name in more than one place as his Law, for it is said concerning it: *as it is written in the book of the Law of Moses* (Josh. 8:31), and again: *Remember ye the Law of Moses, my servant* (Mal. 3:22). This is one of the fundamental principles of biblical exegesis.

12. Second. Scripture as a whole is to be interpreted literally, except where literal interpretation may involve something objectionable or imply a contradiction. Only in the latter case, or in similar cases which demand that a passage be taken out of its plain meaning—e.g., where a preceding or a following passage requires it in order to avoid a contradiction—does it become necessary to take the text out of the literal sense. If it were permissible for us to take a given biblical passage out of its literal meaning without a valid reason for doing so, we would be justified in doing likewise with the whole of Scripture, and this would lead to the nullification of all the accounts therein, including all commandments, prohibitions, and so forth, which would be the acme of wickedness. Thus we are compelled to say that the verse, *And they saw the God of Israel . . .* (Exod. 24:10), must not be understood literally and does not signify seeing with one's eye, since it is contrary to reason to assume that the Creator may be perceived with man's senses; the same applies to all similar passages. So, too, in respect to the verse, *And thou shalt sacrifice the passover offering unto the Lord thy God of sheep and cattle . . .* (Deut. 16:2), we are constrained to assume that what is meant here is not the paschal lamb sacrificed at twilight, but the paschal peace offerings, since the former must consist of sheep only. There are, however, bib-

lical passages which admit of both literal and allegorical interpretation. For example: *and the spirit of Jacob, their father, was revived* (Gen. 45: 27), which may be explained literally to the effect that when Jacob heard this news his spirit was revived, i.e., was fortified, and he was gladdened thereby, which is a figure commonly used in men's speech. It may also be interpreted allegorically to the effect that the gift of prophecy came back to him, since prophecy, too, is sometimes called "spirit," as in *and I will take of the spirit which is upon thee, and will put it upon them* . . . (Num. 11: 17). This is supported by the fact that ever since Joseph was separated from him Scripture mentions no occasion on which God addressed him, and that at the time of his setting out on the journey to Egypt he was addressed by the Lord once again. A similar case is the verse, *And for the bounty of the products of the sun* . . . (Deut. 33: 14), which may be explained literally as signifying the various fruits produced from year to year and formed under the influence of the sun traveling on its course, whereas the following *and for the bounty of the produce of the moons* signifies the fruits influenced by the moon, such as melons, cucumbers, and gherkins, which [are formed] under the influence of the moon traveling on its course, all of which is evident to our sense of observation. It may, however, be interpreted also allegorically, *the products of the sun* meaning the bounty of this world and of its cultivation which yields crops from year to year, the year being the time of a single circling by the sun around the celestial sphere; while *the produce of the moons* would signify the bounty of the time of the Messiah, when crops and fruits will ripen from month to month, the month being the time of a single circling by the moon around the celestial sphere, as it is written: *it shall bring forth new fruit according to its months* (Ezek. 47: 12).

13. Third. The Hebrew language is the primordial tongue in which God addressed Adam and other prophets. Some people say that the Aramaic language is the primeval one, and one of the proofs of the falsity of this view and of the truth of the preceding statement is the fact that you will find in Scripture psalms and

other passages built upon the order of the letters of the alphabet; e.g., the psalm beginning, *Blessed are they that are upright in the way* (Ps. 119:1), and other psalms; also the passage beginning, *A valiant woman who can find?* (Prov. 31:10), and the Book of Lamentations. When all these passages are turned into another language their alphabetical arrangement is broken. This is a powerful proof of the baselessness of their claim, and a silencer for their insolence. Another proof of our view are the derivations of names which we find in Scripture, the first of which is the passage, *And the Lord God formed Adam* (Gen. 2:7), where Adam's name is derived from the earth out of which he was created. Another instance is the verse, *she shall be called Woman* (Gen. 2:23), a name derived from man's own name, since she was taken out of him. This is not so in Aramaic, since "man" in Aramaic is *gaḇra,* whereas "woman" is *'itṯa* (*'attĕṯa*), which cannot be derived from the former; he who disagrees with our view cannot avoid this fact. Another instance is the passage, *and she gave birth to Cain* (Gen. 4:1), whose name is then derived from *I have acquired a man with the help of the Lord;* in Arabic Cain is called *Ḳābīl,* which cannot be derived from the Arabic "I have acquired." We do not say this here because someone claims that Arabic is the primeval tongue but merely in order to remove all possible doubts. Other examples are: Seth, derived from *for God has appointed me another seed* (Gen. 4:25)—the Arabic spelling is *Šīṯ,* which cannot be derived from the Arabic "God has appointed me"; Peleg, derived from *the earth was divided* (Gen. 10:25); [and many others.] . . . Nor can one claim that at that time there was, in addition to the Hebrew language, another tongue, since Scripture says: *And the whole earth was of one language* (Gen. 11:1), until there occurred on the part of men whatever did occur, and they were dispersed and divided by tongues, as it is written: *for there did the Lord confound the language of all the earth* (Gen. 11:9). Indeed, God has promised to restore this single language and that no other tongue will be spoken, namely, on the advent of the Savior, as it is written: *For then will I return to the peoples a pure language . . .* (Zeph. 3:9), and further on: *On that day,* implying that at present every nation designates the Name of God in its own tongue but on that day these will vanish and all mankind will call the Lord by His Hebrew name *Ăḏonay.*

14. Fourth. Scripture addresses mankind in a manner accessible to their understanding and about matters familiar to them from their own experience; this is what the Rabbanites mean when they say, "The Law speaks with the tongue of men" (B. Bĕrakoṯ 31b). Thus, when the Creator wished to describe Himself to the effect that nothing visible is hidden from Him, He described Himself as provided with eyes, because men are familiar with the sense of sight and know from their own experience that its seat is the member of the body which is the eye, not because He really is provided with bodily members. Likewise, when He wished to let them know that no sound is veiled from Him, He described Himself as provided with ears, because among men sounds are perceived by the sense of hearing. The same applies to all matters of this sort. This is similar to the reply of a certain scholar who was asked, "How can the Creator address mankind, seeing that His speech is of a different species from men's speech, inasmuch as it is infinitely more sublime and exalted?" To this, the scholar replied that when God created His creatures and wished to address them with commandments, prohibitions, promises, threats, and narratives, He took into consideration the fact that their constitution could not bear to hear His natural speech because of its sublimity and exaltation and its dissimilarity from their own language, and He fashioned for them a speech akin to their own, near to their comprehension, acceptable to their understanding, and bearable to their faculties. This is comparable to our own procedure with animals and similar creatures, whose constitution is different from ours, whom we must govern and manage, to whom we must communicate our wishes, who do not know our speech, and whose sounds and utterances are not akin to ours. We therefore resort to signs, hints, and noises which make known our wishes, such as whistling, bleating, and various other sounds produced by movement of the vocal organs. Thus, we call *ǧurr*

to an ass when we want him to start moving, and we call something else when we wish to make him stop. Likewise, we call *ḳišš* to some birds when we want to drive them away; to others we call *axx*. We say *axš* to a dog, while we whistle to other animals and use different sounds to signal other species of animals. This scholar's explanation is of great potency and is similar to our own view that God addresses mankind in a manner adapted to their minds and accessible to their understanding. It is for this reason, or one near it, that the children of Israel begged to be excused from listening to the Creator's address, when they said to Moses: *let not God speaḳ with us, lest we die* (Exod. 20:16).

15. Fifth. Scripture does not recount a false statement in an unqualified way, but either designates it as false or else expressly attributes it to its author, and in doing so, brands it as a lie. If Scripture were to recount an untrue statement without making its falsity known to us or making its author responsible for it, it would have been dealing in falsehood disguised as truth, and we would have been unable to distinguish the true statements from the false—but the all-wise Creator is exalted far above such reprehensible procedure. Therefore, we find, throughout Scripture, every utterance which is a prejudiced statement and a falsehood assigned to the person who made it; e.g.: *And Pharaoh said, Who is the Lord that I should hearḳen unto his voice?* (Exod. 5:2), *they say, The Lord will not see* (Ps. 94:7); the same is true in the case of the man who brought the news of King Saul's death, as it is written: *So I stood up to him and slew him* (II Sam. 1:10), which statement Scripture brands as false by making him the actual speaker. Other instances are the lying words of Gehazi: *Thy servant went neither here nor there* (II Kings 5:25), and the account of Sarah having laughed and having later denied it for fear of punishment. This refutes also the opinion of those who assert that Balaam's she-ass really did not speak and that it is all a tale propounded by a lying narrator.

16. Sixth. Where Scripture quotes the words of persons professing other faiths, who are not of the children of Israel, does it do so in the same language in which the words were spoken, or

were they spoken originally in another tongue and turned by Scripture into its own language by way of translation? Some say that whenever Scripture recounts a speech or address made by certain persons, without specifying the original language, it quotes it as it was delivered, in Hebrew; otherwise Scripture specifies that it was spoken in another language. For proof they refer to the story of the heap of stones erected by Jacob and the statement there that Jacob called it in Hebrew *gal 'eḏ,* while Laban named it in Aramaic *yĕḡar śahăḏuṯa* (Gen. 31: 47), each one naming it in his own tongue. Another example is the passage, *And the Chaldeans spoke to the king in Aramaic* (Dan. 2: 4), whereupon Scripture quotes them in their own tongue; to wit: *O king, mayest thou live forever . . .* Likewise, Jeremiah wrote to those in exile in Iraq and advised them to speak to the native Nabateans in their own tongue, saying in Aramaic: *The gods that have not created heaven and earth shall perish . . .* (Jer. 10: 11). Another instance is the passage in Ezra: *and the writing of the epistle was written in Aramaic . . .* (Ezra 4: 7), whereupon Scripture quotes it in the original language, beginning with, *Rehum the governor,* and so forth. The same is the case with the Aramaic letter beginning: *Artaxerxes, king of kings . . .* (Ezra 7: 12), where the preceding text is in Hebrew, and after the quotation of the Aramaic text of the king's edict is completed Scripture reverts to the Hebrew language once more and goes on to say: *Blessed be the Lord, God of our fathers . . .* (Ezra 7: 27).

17. Those who oppose this view say that while it is true in some instances it is not so always; rather, Scripture occasionally does narrate in its own tongue something which was told originally in another language without clearly saying so. Thus we see Scripture quoting in its own tongue copious sayings of persons of other nations, yet we perforce know that these persons spoke in their native languages. . . . Such, for example, is the biblical story of Pharaoh saying: *Who is the Lord that I should hearken unto his voice?* (Exod. 5: 2); or King Hiram's words in his letter to King Solomon: *My servants shall bring them down from the Lebanon to the sea . . .* (I Kings 5: 23); or the words of the Queen of Sheba:

It was a true word that I have heard (I Kings 10: 6), and *because of God's love for Israel* (I Kings 10: 9), and the remainder of her speech; or Balak's speech to Balaam: *I said I would do thee great honor* (Num. 24: 11), and all the rest of the conversation which took place between them; or the speech of Ben Hadad: *If they come out for peace, seize them alive* (I Kings 20: 18), and his letters to King Ahab; or the speech of Ben Hadad's servants: *Behold, we have heard that the kings of the house of Israel* (I Kings 20: 31), and the rest of the story; or the words of Naaman: *For this thing the Lord will pardon thy servant* . . . (II Kings 5: 18); or Cyrus' speech: *The Lord, God of the heavens, has given me all the kingdoms of the earth* (Ezra 1: 2); or the speech of Artaxerxes to Nehemiah: *Why is thy countenance downcast?* (Neh. 2: 2). An even stronger proof is the conversation between David and Goliath, at which there was no one else present. Is it possible that all these persons, notwithstanding the variety of their descent and tongues, should have spoken all these words in Hebrew? This is impossible; rather each one of them must have spoken in his own tongue, but his speech was recounted in the language of Scripture.

18. To this the holders of the former opinion reply, What evidence is there to make it impossible, seeing that Hebrew is the primordial language, as explained above? It is perfectly possible that in those times kings and their courtiers, and especially those of them who were men of learning, studied the Hebrew language also and mastered it, as is evidenced by the words of King Hezekiah's officers to Rabshakeh: *Speak, I pray thee, unto thy servants in Aramaic* . . . (Isa. 36: 11), and his answer, of which it is written: *and he cried in a loud voice, in the Jewish tongue* (Isa. 36: 13); from this we learn that the foreign kings and their courtiers did know Hebrew. This, the holders of this opinion continue, is further supported by the statement in the story of Ahasuerus: *and it was written . . . unto every province in its own writing, and unto every people in their own tongue, and to the Jews also in their own writing and language* (Esth. 8: 9), from which it is evident that they were skilled in Jewish writ-

ing and tongue, since they wrote to the Jews in this language.

19. Their opponents then answer that these passages are like the others and that it is indeed possible that there were some among the Gentiles who learned the Hebrew language, but this does not prove that the king and everyone in his court knew it; rather that one among them who knew Hebrew served as an interpreter between the king of the Jews and the emissaries of other kings, just as we find it nowadays that the kings of the Arabs have officials who interpret between them and the envoys of the Byzantine kings, and so do the kings of Byzantium. In fact, they say, this is shown by the very passage that you have cited from the story of Hezekiah and the words of his officers to Rabshakeh: *Speak, I pray thee, unto thy servants in Aramaic* . . . (Isa. 36: 11), where Scripture goes on to say that they knew Aramaic, whereas the common people did not.

20. To this the holders of the former opinion reply, "This argument is really in our favor and confirms what we have said; namely, that the kings and their courtiers studied and learned foreign languages, since the officers of Hezekiah were not just one [or two] persons but rather a large company, and they all said to Rabshakeh, 'Speak to us in Aramaic, for we all understand it.' This shows that the kings, together with a great part of their suite, were familiar with the languages of those peoples who were their neighbors and who exchanged envoys with them."

21. The opinion of these latter seems, up to this point, to be more convincing. There are, however, some passages in Scripture which appear to refute it; e.g., the words of Joseph's brethren: *But we are guilty concerning our brother* . . . (Gen. 42: 21), followed by: *And they did not know that Joseph understood them, for the interpreter was acting between them,* meaning that they spoke in the tongue which they understood, i.e., undoubtedly Hebrew, but they did not know that Joseph also understood it, i.e., they did not know that he understood Hebrew, since he and they had been conversing through an interpreter. We learn from this that they spoke to Joseph in Hebrew, while he addressed them in another tongue, i.e., in Egyptian, which he had learned during

his long sojourn in Egypt, and that the interpreter translated from one to the other; and yet Scripture recounts the whole conversation in the Hebrew language. Another example is the story of Esther, when it tells how Mordecai advised her not to tell which nation she belonged to, and how she obeyed this order and remained with the king all those years, she speaking to him and he speaking to her. Unquestionably she addressed him in his own tongue, and his words to her: *What wilt thou, O queen Esther?* (Esth. 5: 3), repeated twice, were spoken in the same tongue also. Likewise, Harbonah's words: *Behold also the gallows* . . . (Esth. 7: 9), and all the words addressed by the king to Haman, must have been spoken in their own tongue, yet Scripture relates all this in Hebrew. We learn from this, therefore, that not everything recounted in Scripture in the Hebrew language was originally spoken in Hebrew; rather, some things may have been spoken in other languages but were recounted in the tongue in which Scripture was composed.

SALMON BEN JEROHAM

Salmon ben Jeroham (Arabic Sulaymān, or Sulaym, ibn Ruḥaym) was born in Palestine (?) or in Iraq (?) probably some time between the years 910 and 915. As a young man, presumably about his twentieth year, he appears to have gone to Egypt to pursue his studies. For some years afterward he seems to have lived in Jerusalem; in any case, he exhibits in his writings a familiarity with the topography of Jerusalem and the geography of the Holy Land that can only have been acquired from personal experience and observation. Toward the end of his life, for some unknown reason, he is said to have moved to Aleppo, Syria, where he died. The fifteenth-century Karaite chronicler Ibn al-Hītī states [1] that Salmon's tomb was a well-known landmark in his time, and there seems to be no valid reason to doubt the authenticity of this information.

The same chronicler quotes a Karaite tradition to the effect that Salmon was the teacher of the Gaon Sa'adiah, and that Sa'adiah attended Salmon's funeral and gave public expression to his respect for Salmon's learning. The tradition is palpably unhistorical, since Salmon is known to have been still active in the sixth decade of the tenth century, a number of years after Sa'adiah's death in 942. Besides, Sa'adiah was Salmon's senior by some thirty years. Nevertheless, there may well be some truth in the legend in the way of personal contact between the two men, which would also explain to some extent Salmon's extraordinary hatred of Sa'adiah and the violent language he used in referring to him. Possibly some physical encounter or some rankling rebuff administered by Sa'adiah to the young Salmon caused the latter to become not only a zealous religious opponent but also a bitter personal enemy of his illustrious Rabbanite contemporary.

Salmon's principal work is his polemical epistle against Rabbanism in general and Sa'adiah in particular, written while the

1. See below, p. 234.

latter was still living, probably some time in the fourth decade of the tenth century. Only the Hebrew version of it, entitled *Book of the Wars of the Lord* (Hebrew *Sefer Milḥamoṯ haš-Šem*) and written in rhymed quatrains, has been preserved. Salmon himself speaks of writing an Arabic version also, probably in prose, for the general reading public who would have found his Hebrew style much too difficult, but no part of it has so far been discovered.

The epistle seems to have had considerable success among the Karaite public, although Salmon's arguments were in a large measure borrowed from older Karaite writers, notably al-Ḳirḳisānī. The poetic form and the violent and belligerent manner of Salmon's approach were, however, all his own. One may suspect, on purely psychological grounds (since no historical data are available), that Salmon had hoped that the savage force of his attack on Sa'adiah would provoke the eminent Rabbanite Gaon to issue a counterblast, thereby enhancing the young scholar's reputation among his Karaite brethren. In this, however, he was disappointed. Whether Sa'adiah was too busy with other matters or regarded it beneath his dignity to notice a young and little-known schismatic, he seems to have made no reference to Salmon in his works.[2]

In the sixth decade of the tenth century Salmon wrote, in a somewhat calmer mood, a series of commentaries in Arabic on individual books of the Bible. Of these, the commentaries on the Psalms and the Song of Songs are characterized by uncompromising denunciations of Sa'adiah's views on various matters as well as of the study of secular subjects. On the other hand, the commentaries on Lamentations and Ecclesiastes attributed to him contain nothing directed against the Gaon, or even against the Rabbanites, and consequently their authenticity is subject to some doubt. He wrote commentaries on Esther, Job, Proverbs, and Daniel as well,

2. Geiger's hypothesis, revived by Davidson, that Salmon was the same person as Ibn Sāḳawayh, against whom Sa'adiah wrote a special tract, involves such difficulties as to make it highly improbable (cf. Mann, pp. 1469–1470). Perhaps one of the reasons for Sa'adiah's silence was that a refutation of Salmon's arguments would have been essentially a repetition of the material already given in the tract against Ibn Sāḳawayh.

perhaps also on the Pentateuch and Isaiah.[3] Whether he actually composed the tract on the resurrection of the dead which he expressed his intention to write is not known.

Salmon's poetic style in the *Wars of the Lord* has been variously characterized as "wretched rhymes" by Samuel Poznanski,[4] and as "by far the best among the Karaite writings" by Israel Davidson.[5] Fairness would seem to lie somewhere between these two extremes. Certainly Salmon had no genuine poetic gift; his quatrains are the fruit of his considerable learning in biblical, Karaite, and Rabbanite lore rather than the product of inspiration. Yet his style is, on the whole, fluent and easily understood, and the epistle makes interesting and informative reading.

FROM THE *BOOK OF THE WARS OF THE LORD* OF SALMON BEN JEROHAM

REFUTATION OF SA'ADIAH'S ARGUMENTS FOR THE VALIDITY OF THE RABBANITE ORAL TRADITION

Canto I

1 To you I call, O men—
  Hearken to my explicit words,
Reinforced, clad, enveloped, and robed
  With proofs as solid as onyx and sapphire.
2 When I was at the age of vanity,
  I did search for the right road for my course,
That I might learn, as well as teach, in the midst of my
    Karaite congregation,
  And I sought to clear the stones from my path.

3. The Hebrew commentary on the Book of Ruth ascribed to Salmon and published by I. Markon, *Livre d'hommage à la mémoire du Dr. Samuel Poznanski,* (Warsaw, 1927), Hebrew part, pp. 78–96, is really a translation of Japheth ben Eli's Arabic commentary; see L. Nemoy, "Did Salmon ben Jeroham Compose a Commentary on Ruth?" *JQR,* XXXIX (1948), 215–216.

4. Poznanski, p. 13.

5. Salmon ben Jeroham, *The Book of the Wars of the Lord,* ed. I. Davidson (New York, 1934), p. xiii.

3 I was a stranger in a foreign land,
Investigating and searching the ways of the Law.
And I saw in the midst of the Jewish congregation
A man devoid of a good heart and straying away from justice.
4 He bent his bow to write complaints
And to remonstrate in all languages,
To tear up improved roads
And to pervert with nonsense and trifles the highway of understanding.
5 I understood his purpose and was overcome with apprehension,
And my wrath was kindled like a burning fire;
And I was seized with zeal for the sons of Judah,
And for the Almighty, and for the Book of the Testimony.
6 And I was afraid of the Day of Judgment and Retribution,
Lest His wrath should burn with anger.
Therefore I composed a double rejoinder against him,
In the language of Eber, and also in that of the sons of Dumah.
7 This shall be my consolation in my exile,
That there are learned men to investigate my words fairly,
Who will know that I speak out of zeal for God,
So that the men of my congregation might not be led astray.
8 He stated in his misleading discourse,
And he did utter the assertion,
That the Almighty chose to reveal Himself to Moses
At Mount Sinai, to give him two Laws for His chosen people.
9 The commandments of the one Law were set down in writing,
While the commandments of the other were kept upon the tongue.

Moreover, they were both to be, into everlasting eternity,
An heirloom for the congregation of the seed of the perfect ones.
10 My spirit advised me to reply to him in this matter,
And to place my answer among my congregation in a written epistle,
In order to remove the stumbling block, and to clear the path of stones,
So that the flock of Israel would not go astray into the waterless desert of heresy.
11 But rather that they would study it attentively,
So that my congregation might not be seduced by what is hidden from them.
And I hope that as my reward God Almighty
Will let me behold His good tidings in Zion.
12 We believe firmly that the written Law
Was in truth given to Israel by the right hand of the Almighty,
According to the testimony of the whole congregation of the Lily,
Who are scattered in every land.
13 All of them, believers as well as unbelievers,
Divided as they are by language and tongue,
All Israel, from the east to the westernmost ends of the world,
Testify to the sanctity of the written Law, all of them, the little and the great.
14 This testimony has become firmly established in their midst,
By their united and universal consent, without challenge.
Likewise, the signs and miracles which the Dweller of the heavenly abode has wrought
Are written therein and are explained for them who wish to understand.

15 Selah! They remember the splitting asunder of the Red Sea,
And they do not deny the words spoken by the Almighty on Mount Sinai;
And with their mouths they sing of the glory of the Law and of the other miracles.
Israel and all other nations speak of this as one.
16 Now if Israel and Judah are all united
Concerning the validity of the oral Law which is, as they say, perfect,
Let them offer their testimony, and let their voices be heard;
If not, then the Fayyumite's words are void and his tongue has been silenced.
17 I shall begin here with another argument,
Which I shall mention now, without delay,
And I shall ask and demand a reply to it
From everyone who holds to the oral Law and has given his preference to it.
18 You say that the Rock has given Israel two Laws,
One which is written, and one which was preserved in your mouths.
If this is as you say,
Then indeed your deeds are but falsehood and rebellion against God.
19 The Holy One has given you an oral Law,
So that you would recite it orally,
For, say you, He had deemed it, in His wisdom, a laudable command.
Why, then, did you write it down in ornate script?
20 Had the Merciful One wished to write it down,
He would have had it written down by Moses.
Now did He not give it to you to be studied orally,
And had He not ordained it not to be inscribed in a book?
21 Yet they altered God's alleged words and wrote it down,

And instead of studying it orally they transferred it into writing.
How, then, can their words be believed, seeing that they have offended grievously?
They cannot withdraw from this contradictory path.
22 They wrote down both Laws, thus contemning the commandment of the Almighty.
Where, then, is the oral Law in which they place their trust?
Their words have become void and meaningless,
And out of their own mouths have they testified that they have drawn God's wrath upon themselves.

Canto II

1 I have discovered in my heart another argument,
A handsome one, and majestic enough
To be placed as a crown for the Karaites,
To be their ornament, pride, and glory.
2 I have looked again into the six divisions of the Mishnah,
And behold, they represent the words of modern men.
There are no majestic signs and miracles in them,
And they lack the formula: "And the Lord spoke unto Moses and unto Aaron."
3 I therefore put them aside, and I said, There is no true Law in them,
For the Law is set forth in a different manner,
In a majestic display of prophets, of signs, and of miracles;
Yet all this majestic beauty we do not see in the whole Mishnah.
4 I have seen an end to every human purpose,
But there is no end to the speaking about the majesty of His ordinance and utterance.
Blessed be the Creator of what is below and of what is above,
And may His blessing rest upon His people. Selah!

5 I am young in days,
And you are older than I.
Had not the blackguard intruded among the scholars
I would never have written this epistle.
6 I have turned again to my first argument,
To fortify it with truth and uprightness, without falsehood,
And with might and power, like the power of Samson;
However, the best answer of the tongue is from the Lord.
7 I have set the six divisions of the Mishnah before me,
And I looked at them carefully with mine eyes.
And I saw that they are very contradictory in content,
This one Mishnaic scholar declares a thing to be forbidden to the people of Israel, while that one declares it to be permitted.
8 My thoughts therefore answer me,
And most of my reflections declare unto me,
That there is in it no Law of logic,
Nor the Law of Moses the Wise.
9 I said, Perhaps one of the two did not know the right way,
Wherefore he did not know how to reason it out with his companion;
Perhaps the truth lies with his companion;
Let me look into his words; perchance I will find relief from my perplexity.
10 But instead I found there other men—
Sometimes they say, "Others say,"
While anon the scholars issue a decision,
Agreeing neither with the one nor with the other, but contradicting both.
11 Had I been among them—I say, had I been among them—
I would not have accepted the words of these "others" and "scholars."
Rather would I have weighed the word of the Lord with them,

And I would have judged accordingly every word which
they had contrived.

12 Gird thyself with thy strength and hearken, and step up to
me,
And let the scholars of my congregation of Israel judge
between us,
And let them place our words upon the scales,
So that I may walk in truth upon the road of my life's
course.

13 Know that there is no difference in learning between
them and me.
When they say, "Rabbi So-and-so said thus-and-so,"
I answer and say, I, too, am the learned So-and-so.
Thine escape has been cut off by this argument, else answer me, if thou canst.

14 His heart is overlaid with stupidity as with fat, and I know
well what he says and speaks,
As he has set it forth in his written scroll;
Therefore will I turn my face toward him and do battle
with him,
And I will shake his loins and strike down his sword.

15 He has written that the six divisions of the Mishnah are
as authoritative as the Law of Moses,
And that they wrote it down so that it would not be forgotten.
I shall answer him concerning this, for I will not be silent,
Lest the blackguard think that he had uttered an unanswerable argument.

16 He who remembers forgotten things and knows what is
hidden,
Had He deemed it proper to have them skillfully
written down,
In order that they might not be forgotten upon earth,
He would have ordered His servant Moses to inscribe
them, with might and power, in a book.

17 If it is proper for men like us,

Who have none of the holy spirit in us,
To turn the oral Law into a written Law, by writing it down,
Why would it not be right for us to turn the written Law into a Law preserved only in our mouths?
18 Hearken unto me and I will speak further:
If thou shouldst say, "This took place in the days of the Prophets and in the days of Ezra";
Why is there no mention in it of these Prophets
In the same manner as the names of the Prophets are recorded throughout Scripture?
19 Be silent, and I will teach thee wisdom,
If it be thy desire to learn wisdom.
It is written: *The Law of the Lord is perfect* (Ps. 19:8).
What profit be there for us, then, in the written Mishnah?
20 Moreover, if the Talmud originated with our master Moses,
What profit is there for us in "another view,"
And what can a third and a fourth view teach us,
When they tell us first that the interpretation of this problem in law is thus-and-so, and then proceed to explain it with "another view?"
21 The truth stands upon one view only,
For this is so in the wisdom of all mankind,
And right counsel cannot be based upon two contradictory things.
Now in this one thing he has fallen down and cannot stand up:
22 If the Talmud is composed of the words of prophets,
Why are contradictory views found in it?
Now it is evident that this view of Sa'adiah's is foolishness, and the words of fools.
So testify all mankind.

Canto III

1 Where dost thou flee, O Fayyumite, to hide thyself
From utter ruin?
Let us rather come together for judgment;
Increase thine army of arguments and come out for battle.
2 I have seen also in the Talmud—
Which you Rabbanites regard as if it were your main supporting column,
And which is made by you a partner to the Law of Moses,
And is held beloved and desirable in your hearts—
3 The bellowing of the School of Shammay against the School of Hillel, to controvert their words,
As well as that of the School of Hillel against the School of Shammay, to refute their interpretations of law.
This one invokes blessings, and that one heaps curses upon their heads,
Yet both are an abomination in the sight of the Lord.
4 The words of which one of the two shall we accept,
And the views of which one of the two shall we condemn,
Seeing that each one of them has attracted a great congregation of adherents,
And each one of them turns to say, "I am the captain of the ship"?
5 Incline thine ears, if thou desirest pearls of wisdom;
The matter cannot be in both ways.
If their words require interpretation with words of men of understanding,
Then this Mishnah cannot be the Law of the Master of masters.
6 If the Mishnah be the Law of Moses, God's servant,
Why do they not mention therein the name of Moses only?

And why do they mention in each chapter of the Mishnah the names of teachers other than he?
And why do they not say, "Thus said the Lord," and "Thus said Moses," after his meeting with the Lord?

7 If thou wouldst yet double thy rascalities,
And wouldst utter more error and falsehood,
And wouldst say, "They used to engage in scholarly discussions, in awe of Him who dwells in glory,"
Remember that many fell slain among them in their stumbling.

8 God forbid that I should remain silent;
Rather will I establish the strongest proofs in the world,
And I will refute thee and despoil thee of thy claims,
With the help of Him who causes men to become rich as well as poor.

9 The text of the seven written arguments
Which are set down in thy commentary on Genesis—
If at all times thou didst mention them publicly in order to seduce
Men's hearts, yet now they will become like spears and swords over thy head and heart.

10 May thy steps be hampered in walking,
When thou sayest that my congregation has need of the Mishnah,
In order to know the precise measurements of the ordinances of the ritual fringe, the *lulab̲,* and the booth,
And that this is why they arranged it and set it down in writing.

11 Thou hast written lies, for not all ordinances have a definite measurement,
And that is why the length of the fringe is not specified in the Law.
If one should forcefully exhibit this argument, how wilt thou distinguish,

And what answer wilt thou make to him, out of the words of the Divine Testimony?

12 To heap up more lying words, thou hast written and set forth further,
And hast said, secondly, that the Mishnah is ancient,
Because in it is explained the precise amount of the heave offering,
So that Israel might know what part of what amount they are to give.

13 This argument is identical with the preceding,
And the answer to the former argument applies to the latter as well:
No precise amount or sum has been specified for it;
Rather each person is to give as much as he wishes and will meet with no complaint.

14 Thou hast said, thirdly, that we have need for the inherited tradition,
In order that we might know what day of the week is Sabbath, so that we might keep it holy.
But the Sabbath is known to all the inhabitants of the world as a day of rest,
From factual knowledge and reasoning, not merely from reckoning by three, five, and six.

15 Thou hast turned from the right road and hast labored much,
When thou hast said, fourthly, that we need the Mishnah to know which vessel is capable of becoming ritually unclean. But thou hast erred,
For thou hast not considered the verse, *whatsoever vessel it be, wherewith any work is done* (Lev. 11:32);
All such vessels are specified in the Law, if thou wouldst but turn thy heart to it.

16 Still thou holdest fast to broken arguments,
And hast said, fifthly, that there are ordinances which we must observe, and which are not explained in the Law—

Such as prayers, and other ordinances—
Yet the prayers are not mentioned in Scripture.
17 Thy mouth has not considered the verse, *and ye shall pray unto me* (Jer. 29: 12);
And prayers are mentioned also in many other places.
Thus, thou hast not remembered, when thou hast spoken, the prayer of Daniel, the man greatly beloved of God.
Therefore I reject from before me all ordinances and statutes which are not written in the Law.
18 Thy flag fell from thy bastion,
When thou hast said, sixthly, that we need the tradition, and pride ourselves upon it,
In order to know the number of years elapsed since the destruction and cessation of the Second Temple.
I will answer thee in this matter, and thy glory will wilt.
19 O thou who bindest together silly things without wisdom!
In which sacred book is it written that it is our duty
To know the reckoning of how many years
Shall elapse between the destruction of the Temple and the Dread Gathering?
20 With much labor, but uselessly, hast thou written,
Seventhly, and hast said that we need the tradition, and pride ourselves upon it,
To know the date of the period of the redemption of Israel,
And the appointed time of the resurrection of the dead.
21 In the songs of the Prophets and other seers,
All these things are already mentioned and are contained therein;
They are bound and fastened therein as firmly as with ropes,
And they do not follow from thy words and thy worthless traditions.
Here end my words concerning the Mishnah.

JAPHETH BEN ELI

Japheth ben Eli (Yefeth ben ʿAlī) Hallewi (Arabic Abū ʿAlī al-Ḥasan ibn ʿAlī al-Baṣrī) flourished in the last quarter of the tenth century, and was evidently still living in the year 1004–05.[1] He was a native of Basra, Iraq, but subsequently moved to Jerusalem where he lived for a considerable period if not until his death. Nothing more is known about his life.

Japheth ben Eli is the foremost Karaite commentator on the Bible during the golden age of Karaite literature. His commentaries, all written in Arabic, cover the entire Old Testament and are accompanied by a translation of the biblical text, done in a most literal manner, often in violation of the rules of Arabic grammar. The commentaries themselves are detailed and uniform and comprise not only a thorough explanation of the sacred text but also occasional excursuses on problems of theology (including polemics against Christianity and Islam), law, Hebrew grammar, and history. For this reason they are of considerable value as source material for the history of the early period of Karaite thought. Japheth's exegesis is not original with him, nor does he claim it to be; in fact, he leans heavily, and admittedly, on his predecessors, and occasionally borrows from Rabbanite sources, the Targumim (the colloquial Aramaic versions of the Old Testament), the Talmud, and the works of the Karaites' archenemy, the Gaon Saʿadiah. Nevertheless his commentaries enjoyed great favor and exerted a powerful influence upon later Karaite exegetes and also upon the Rabbanite, including among the latter no less an authority than Abraham ibn Ezra (twelfth century).

As might be expected, Japheth does not refrain in his biblical commentaries from polemics against the Rabbanites, and princi-

1. The British Museum MS Or. 2554, his commentary on Ruth, copied at al-Ramla, in Palestine, in that year (= A.H. 395), quotes Japheth's name with the eulogy *'ayyadahū Allāh,* "May God fortify him"—a formula usually applied to living persons only (cf. G. Margoliouth, *Catalogue of Hebrew and Samaritan Manuscripts in the British Museum* (London, 1899), I, 223–224, No. 301).

pally against Sa'adiah. To refute the latter particularly, he wrote a special work, of which, however, no part has as yet been brought to light.[2] His tone, to be sure, is usually calm and dignified and is not marred by abusive language.

In addition to writing a book of precepts, also lost, Japheth tried his hand at poetry, as the specimen here translated shows. Its merit, however, lies more in its antiquity than in any genuine poetic excellence.

FROM THE WRITINGS OF JAPHETH BEN ELI

I. COMMENTARY ON RUTH 1–2

1. Blessed be the Lord, God of Israel, the Primeval and All-powerful, who created everything to make known His might, and made the heavens the seat of the throne of His incomparable dignity and the dwelling of the angels who sanctify and glorify His Name. He made the earth the abode of His presence and of His servants whom He has honored with His choice, as it is written: *The heaven is my throne, and the earth is my footstool . . .* (Isa. 66:1).

2. Now by His exalted and incomparable nature, He has chosen the weakest and poorest of men and has honored them above all others because of their obedience to His commands, as it is written: *For all these things my hand has made, and all these have thus come to be, says the Lord. Yet will I look on him who is poor and of humble spirit, and trembles at my word* (Isa. 66:2). If to this poverty and piety there is added also nobility of descent, then the servant of God acquires a double nobility, like the nobility of the children of Israel who comprise our ancestors, our roots, our original tribes, our kings, and our sages.

3. We find further that nobility of faith ranks higher than that of descent, since we find that persons of noble descent are some-

2. The polemical epistle in doggerel verse directed against Jacob ben Samuel and ascribed to Japheth (*LK̦*, II, 19–24) was probably written by Sahl ben Maṣliaḥ; cf. Mann, pp. 26–28.

times demoted from their high positions because of their acts of disobedience to God. We find also that even he who is converted to the Jewish faith sometimes reaches a high position because of his obedience to God, as was the case with Jethro, who acquired a good and great name and an exalted station because of his belief in, and obedience to, God, as we have explained in our comment on *And Jethro heard of all that God had done for Moses and for Israel* (Exod. 18: 1).

4. All this applies not only to men, but also to women; e.g., Jael, concerning whom the prophetess Deborah in her Song speaks in a manner showing that she had acquired a high station in God's esteem, as it is written: *Blessed above all women shall be Jael, the wife of Heber the Kenite; above all women in the tents shall she be blessed* (Judg. 5: 24). This is true also of the woman whose story we are about to explain, according to what is contained in the book bearing her name—meaning Ruth—wherein there is set forth the excellence of her mind, conduct, and faith, because of which the Lord of the worlds joined her fate to that of that noble man, Boaz, who was the ancestor of our King David, so that Ruth became his wife. It will thus be shown that nobility of faith takes precedence over nobility of descent. Blessed therefore is he who dedicates himself to faith and makes it his strength and his refuge, as it is written: *Render ye sincere homage, lest he be angry and ye perish in the way, when suddenly his wrath is kindled. Blessed are those who put their trust in him* (Ps. 2: 12).

Chapter I

And it came to pass in the time when the judges ruled, that there was a famine in the land. And a certain man from Beth-lehem, which is in Judah, went to sojourn in the field of Moab, he, and his wife, and his two sons (v. 1).

And the name of the man was Elimelech, and the name of his wife was Naomi, and the names of his sons were Mahlon and Chilion, Ephrathites from Beth-lehem, which is in Judah. And they came into the field of Moab and settled there (v. 2).

5. We must first of all explain the several purposes of this scroll of Ruth. We have already set forth some of them when we spoke of the significance of Ruth herself. The scroll makes mention, furthermore, of Naomi and the excellence of her conduct, her mind, and her faith, as well as her steadfastness in the face of successive trials; also how she managed her affairs until she reached the thing which made her soul happy, as it is written: *And he shall be for thee the restorer of thy soul* (Ruth 4: 15). Next, the scroll tells us the story of Orpah, who was also a well-meaning person at first, so long as her husband was living, and who was inclined to stand by Naomi while she expected to obtain thereby something she desired, yet when her hope was frustrated she relapsed into idolatry. We learn further from this scroll the customs then prevalent among Israel regarding their behavior in matters of harvesting and gleaning and in the matter of their servants, as we shall explain when we come to the story of Boaz. We learn from it also the nature of the laws of levirate marriage and redemption, this being the most important of the lessons taught by the scroll. It tells us also the genealogy of King David, that he was a descendant of Boaz and a scion of Perez, the son of the Patriarch Judah. All these lessons which we have mentioned you must understand, for a man might learn from them the right road to follow in both this world and the next.

6. Having explained the purposes of this scroll, we shall proceed to expound the meaning of each verse in a concise yet sufficient manner, according to what we have learned from our preceptors and what we have discovered by following the principles of exegesis that they have taught us.

7. *And it came to pass in the time when the judges ruled*—this narrative is thus joined to the events which took place in the time of the Judges. Even though these events are set forth in the Book of Judges, yet the author has narrated the story of Ruth and Boaz separately, inasmuch as the Judges themselves have no part in it. The author therefore classified this scroll with the other scrolls, placing it first in accordance with its chronological position, since Boaz lived before King Solomon.

8. *When the judges ruled—judges* refers not to judges of law, of whom no account is given in Scripture, but to judges of war, such as Othniel, Ehud, Shamgar, Deborah, Gideon, and the others.

9. *When the judges ruled*—it is not written "In the days of the Judges," indicating that what is meant is the time of their being actually in office as rulers; "In the days of the Judges" would not have indicated that it occurred in the time when they exercised the supreme command over Israel.

10. Were it written, "And it came to pass in the days of So-and-so," whether Othniel or any other of the Judges whose history is set forth in the Book of Judges, it would have been a specific statement; yet Scripture does not explain which of the Judges is meant, wherefore we ask, which of the Judges was it? Now most scholars think that this happened in the time of Gideon, since it is written in his story: *and they left no sustenance for Israel* (Judg. 6: 4). I believe, however, that had this been in Gideon's time, they would have returned from the field of Moab after an interval of only seven years, as it is written: *and the Lord delivered Israel into the hand of Midian for seven years* (Judg. 6: 1); whereas after Elimelech and his family went into the field of Moab because of the famine they remained there for *ten years* (Ruth 1: 4), after which they heard *that the Lord had remembered his people in giving them bread* (Ruth 1:6), whereupon they returned to the land of Judah.

11. It is not unlikely that *in the time when the judges ruled* might refer to Judges whose history has not been recorded in detail in the Book of Judges, such as Jair, Ibzan, and Tola. And it is probable that it happened in the time of Tola, the son of Puah, and his contemporaries, before the days of Jephthah, the Gileadite, since Boaz belonged to the third generation after Nahshon, and King David belonged to the fourth generation after Boaz. Now from the time of Nahshon to the time of David there were four hundred and some years, and Boaz lived approximately in the middle of these four hundred years; moreover, Boaz was at that time an old man, as we shall explain from the words: *inasmuch*

as thou didst not follow young men, whether poor or rich (Ruth 3:10).

12. *There was a famine in the land*—this does not refer exclusively to Bethlehem, as distinct from the rest of Palestine, for it is written further on *that the Lord had remembered his people in giving them bread* (Ruth 1:6), referring to the people as a whole all over Palestine. Moreover, had there been any place in Palestine not afflicted with famine, Elimelech would have betaken himself there instead of migrating to the field of Moab.

13. Now there could have been only one cause for a famine which overtook Palestine alone, without affecting any other land, and that is the sins of Israel. For Palestine is a holy land which casts forth its inhabitants when they exceed all limits in committing acts of disobedience to God, as it is written concerning it: *Thou art a land devouring men, and hast been bereaving thy nations* (Ezek. 36:13).

14. *And a certain man went*—we are told that he departed together with his wife and children, since his wife and his children [depended upon him] for his support and their care was incumbent upon him, and this is why he took them with him.

15. We are told further that he departed from *Beth-lehem, which is in Judah*. Possibly there was in Palestine another Bethlehem, which is why it is written here: *Beth-lehem, which is in Judah.*

16. Scripture then proceeds to name the place whither they migrated, namely, *the field of Moab;* possibly this was the nearest place concerning which they had heard that there was no famine, hence they went there.

17. *To sojourn in the field of Moab*—showing that he went there not in order to reside and remain there permanently but only to sojourn until the cessation of the famine, when they would return to their native home.

18. A certain scholar has held Elimelech blameworthy for leaving Palestine, and said that he and his two sons died in the field of Moab as a punishment for it. My opinion is that this scholar's remark is unfounded, for we find the Prophet Elisha saying to

the Shunamite woman: *Arise, and go, thou and thy family, and sojourn wheresoever thou canst sojourn* (II Kings 8:1), whereupon we are informed that she went to the land of the Philistines.

19. The story then tells us that they were four persons: *he, and his wife, and his two sons.* If he had had any other children, aside from Mahlon and Chilion, he surely would have taken them with him, and the narrator would have mentioned them immediately after Mahlon and Chilion. Moreover, the continuation of this story shows that Naomi had no sons other than Mahlon and Chilion.

20. The text then gives his name, the name of his wife, and the names of his two sons. Elimelech's name is given because of his high station and descent. His wife's name is given because of her own merit, for which she was to be renowned. The names of his two sons are given so as to indicate that Ruth was the wife of Mahlon. They are mentioned here, at the beginning of the story, for the sake of their marriages which will be mentioned later on.

21. *Ephrathites*—that is, from the city of Ephrath, which is another name for Bethlehem, as it is written: *on the way to Ephrath, which is Beth-lehem* (Gen. 48:7), and again: *And David was the son of an Ephrathite man, from Beth-lehem, which is in Judah* (I Sam. 17:12). Ephrathite has also another meaning, namely, an inhabitant of the province of Ephraim, as it is written concerning Elkanah that he was *the son of Jeroham, the son of Elihu, the son of Tohu, the son of Zuph, an Ephrathite* (I Sam. 1:1). Ephrathite is used also in the sense of a man from the tribe of Ephraim, as it is written: *And Jeroboam, the son of Nebat, an Ephrathite, from the town of Zeredah* (I Kings 11:26), and again: *Art thou an Ephrathite?* (Judg. 12:5).

22. The account then repeats the statement, *from Beth-lehem, which is in Judah*—this for two reasons. First, to explain that they were Ephrathites in the sense of being residents of *Beth-lehem, which is in Judah,* which is also called Ephrath; and second, because the statement in the preceding verse, *from Beth-lehem, which is in Judah,* merely tells that they left this town to embark on their journey, which does not necessarily mean that they were

residents of it; hence the repetition of *from Beth-lehem, which is in Judah,* to show that they stemmed from there.

23. Finally we are told that having arrived in the *field of Moab,* they remained there because the place met their requirements and because it was their destination when they left Bethlehem.

And Elimelech, the husband of Naomi, died; and she was left, and her two sons (v. 3).

24. The narrator does not say how long Elimelech lived in the country of Moab.

25. The phrase, *the husband of Naomi,* coming after the statement, *and the name of his wife was Naomi,* is to show that he neither divorced her nor married any other women. It serves also to express compassion for her, inasmuch as she was left all alone, since a woman's husband is her protector and the one who looks after her.

26. From the phrase, *and she was left, and her two sons,* we are to conclude that Elimelech died before his two sons were married. We learn from it also that they both were Naomi's sons, since it was said before, *and his wife, and his two sons,* which might have led one to believe that she was Elimelech's wife without being their mother.

And they took for themselves Moabite wives; the name of the one was Orpah, and the name of the other was Ruth; and they dwelt there about ten years (v. 4).

27. The phrase *And they took for themselves*—it is not written, "And their mother took for them"—may indicate one of two things. They might have married without her consent, the wives being Moabite women—compare, for example, the statement regarding Ishmael: *and his mother took a wife for him out of the land of Egypt* (Gen. 21:21)—or else the phrase might be meant to indicate that her two sons had come of age.

28. *Moabite wives,* too, may mean one of two things: either they were native members of Moabite tribes or they were called Moabite by virtue of their residence there. In either case, we know that they

were not adherents of the faith of Israel, as we shall show further on in commenting on the phrase, *Behold, thy sister-in-law has gone back to her people and to her gods* (v. 15).

29. From the words *and the name of the other was Ruth* we learn that Chilion, who was the younger of the two brothers, was married before his elder brother, since Ruth's husband was Mahlon, the elder brother.

And Mahlon and Chilion died, both of them, also, and the woman was left bereft of her two sons and of her husband (v. 5).

30. *Both of them, also* relates to the death of their father; and the names of Mahlon and Chilion are given so that we might not think that *both of them* meant that one of the daughters-in-law died with her husband.

31. *And the woman was left . . .*—that is, left bereft of her two sons and widowed of her husband, since one cannot very well say, "A was left of B."

32. *Of her two sons and of her husband*—the reason for this statement is that her two daughters-in-law were still living, and it was still possible that one of them might have a child who would take the place of one of Naomi's dead sons.

And she arose, she and her two daughters-in-law, and she set out to return from the field of Moab, for she had heard in the field of Moab that the Lord had remembered his people in giving them bread (v. 6).

33. We are told that after the death of Mahlon and Chilion Naomi set out to return. We are further told that the cause of her return was the cessation of the famine in Palestine, which had caused them to migrate to the field of Moab. She had been inquiring all the time for news from Palestine, and as soon as she heard *that the Lord had remembered his people,* she did not delay setting out to return to Palestine.

And she went forth from the place where she was, and her two daughters-in-law with her, and they went on the way to return to the land of Judah (v. 7).

34. The preceding verse, *and she set out to return from the field of Moab,* did not indicate that her two daughters-in-law set out with her; therefore in this verse we are told that they started out with her.

35. The phrase *from the place where she was,* coming as it does after the foregoing phrase, *from the field of Moab,* may possibly signify that she resided in the place to which she had moved, up to the time of her departure, because it suited her requirements.

36. *To return to the land of Judah*—showing that her intention was to return to the land of Judah from which she had emigrated.

And Naomi said to her two daughters-in-law, Go, return each woman to the house of her mother, and may the Lord deal graciously with you, even as ye have dealt with the dead and with me (v. 8).

May the Lord grant you that ye may find rest, each one of you in the house of her husband. And she kissed them, and they lifted up their voices and wept (v. 9).

37. It is a token of the nobility of Naomi's mind that she did not speak to them until she had gone with them outside of the town and had seen that they were prepared to go on with her. Only then did she begin to probe into what was in the mind of each one of them, in order to determine whether their going with her was caused by hope of worldly gain or by devotion to her religion. If it was not a matter of longing for the true faith, she could not bear to have either one of them join her.

38. The phrase *each woman to the house of her mother* indicates that each one of the daughters-in-law had a family on her mother's side, but none on her father's, to which she would return under the scriptural law: *and she shall return to the house of her father* . . . (Lev. 22:13).

39. *As ye have dealt with the dead* was meant to show their kind behavior toward their husbands, as well as toward her. Then she went on, "May God repay you with kindness, such as you have displayed toward my sons," namely, that each one may obtain a husband to her liking and may enjoy rest with him. This state-

ment of Naomi's is indeed a graceful one. *With the dead*—meaning those who now were dead.

40. Naomi spoke of the husbands of her daughters-in-law first, and of herself secondly, for two reasons. The first is that a husband's rights take precedence over those of a mother-in-law. The second is that they continued to deal graciously with her after the death of their husbands, which again proves the nobility of their minds.

41. The phrase *May the Lord grant you* requires amplification; i.e., "May God grant you good husbands," since she goes on to say, *that ye may find rest, each one of you in the house of her husband*. This is the best blessing which one can possibly invoke upon women. We are thereupon told that she followed these words by embracing and kissing them, as if she were again requesting them to refrain from going on with her, and that they both wept out of affection and friendship for her.

And they said to her, Nay, rather we will return with thee to thy people (v. 10).

42. Their reply thus was that they would not part from her, but would go on with her to dwell in the midst of her people.

And Naomi said, Return, O my daughters! For what purpose should ye go on with me? Have I yet sons in my womb, that they may become your husbands? (v. 11).

Return, O my daughters! Go, for I am too old to have a husband. If I should say I have yet hope, I shall be tonight with a man, yea, I shall even bear sons (v. 12).

Is it for them that ye will wait, until they grow up? Is it for their sakes that ye will remain unmarried, without having husbands? Nay, O my daughters, for it grieves me exceedingly for your sakes, inasmuch as the punishing hand of the Lord has been manifested upon me (v. 13).

43. When she heard them say, *rather we will return with thee,* she wished to find out whether these words were spoken in pure sincerity or out of mere politeness; eventually she ascertained that

Orpah spoke out of politeness, whereas Ruth meant it sincerely.

44. *For what purpose should ye go on with me?*—that is, there is no profit for you in coming with me.

45. *Have I yet sons in my womb?*—that is, even if there were yet any more sons for me, in my womb, could they possibly become your husbands, so that you might wait for them and remain unmarried? This being so, she went on, *Nay, O my daughters.* This may mean [one of] two things: either, "Do not go on with me, O my daughters," or, "O my daughters, I shall never have any more sons, and even if I should ever have any, they would not be suitable for you as husbands." She thus cut off their hope in this direction, in order that she might see whether or not they would still choose to go on with her, even without such a hope. . . .

46. Some people imagine that the Rabbanites might draw proof from this story that the duty of levirate marriage applies to any two blood brothers, namely, from Naomi's words, *Have I yet sons in my womb?* This, however, is an error, since the Rabbanites do not require levirate marriage when one brother has died and left a widow while the other brother is yet in their mother's womb, but only when the other brother has already been born and is present. Accordingly, it is not fitting that Naomi's words, *Have I yet sons,* should be a legal statement to the effect that if she had sons in her womb, they would have been lawfully designated as husbands for Orpah and Ruth; it is thus clear that these words are not a legal assertion but a rhetorical question, as we have explained above.

And they lifted up their voices and wept again. Then Orpah kissed her mother-in-law; but Ruth cleaved unto her (v. 14).

47. *And wept again* relates to their having wept once before. *Then Orpah kissed her mother-in-law*—she did this because she had already determined to turn back. And the proof that she did turn back is Naomi's statement in the following verse, *Behold, thy sister-in-law is gone back;* also the above phrase, *but Ruth cleaved unto her,* i.e., she did not leave her but rather said to her, "I will not leave thee, nor will I go back."

And she said to her, Behold, thy sister-in-law is gone back to her people and to her gods; go thou back after thy sister-in-law (v. 15).

48. We are shown how skillfully Naomi found out what was in the hearts of Ruth and Orpah, through her delicate questioning. Thus she said first, *Have I yet sons in my womb,* thereby discovering what was in Orpah's heart, who thereupon went back to Moab. When Naomi saw that Ruth refrained from going back, she said to herself, "I will now find out what is in Ruth's heart in another way." And she said to her, "Behold, thy sister-in-law is gone back, for she preferred to reside in the midst of her own people and to worship her former gods; therefore go thou back likewise to thy former circumstances, prior to thy joining us, and do not estrange thyself from thy country and thy family." These words on Naomi's part are unquestionably a reproach to Orpah, and if Ruth had done as Orpah did the same reproach would have applied to her as well.

And Ruth said, Do not confront me with the like of such advice, that I should leave thee and return from following thee; rather whither thou goest I will go, and where thou lodgest I will lodge; thy people are my people, and thy God my God (v. 16).

Where thou wilt die, I will die, and there will I be buried; may the Lord do unto me thus and thus, and even more, for nought but death shall part me and thee (v. 17).

49. Ruth's answer contains everything necessary to make Naomi completely satisfied, namely, two points. First, Ruth said that she had chosen to remain with her mother-in-law, Naomi, in preference to being with her own family and relatives, since the four things that she mentioned, to wit, *whither thou goest I will go* up to *Where thou wilt die, I will die, and there will I be buried,* are proof of an exceedingly great affection, namely the affection of a child toward its parent. The second point is her answer to Naomi's words, *Behold, thy sister-in-law is gone back* . . . when she said, *thy people are my people, and thy God my God.*

50. *Do not confront me*—she meant, "Do not confront me with the like of so harsh and painful a speech."

51. *Whither thou goest*—that is, to whatever place or country Naomi might go, whether it is her own country or any other. *Where thou wilt die, I will die, and there will I be buried*—she chose to speak of that which was most probable, since fate might have had in store for them captivity or some other calamity. Similarly, in saying, *for nought but death shall part me and thee,* Ruth swore an oath concerning that which lay within her own choice and not that which was beyond it. Even though she did not make it explicit by her own words, common sense demands it, since man does not know when he will die or where.

52. Her oath, *may the Lord do unto me thus and thus, and even more,* is a curse oath; she undoubtedly mentioned the things which were to happen to her if she violated her oath, but the narrator omitted them for the sake of brevity.

And when Naomi saw that she was determined to go with her, she ceased speaking further unto her (v. 18).

53. Undoubtedly Naomi rejoiced to hear these words of Ruth; nevertheless she refrained from saying anything more to her.

And they both went on until they came to Beth-lehem. And it came to pass that as they entered Beth-lehem all the city was agitated concerning them, and they said, Is this Naomi? (v. 19).

54. We are told that Naomi set out for her native country. *All the city was agitated*—that is, the women of the place, since it is followed by *and they said.* The phrase *Is this Naomi?* shows that some of the women had known Naomi before; and yet, approximately ten years must have gone by.

And she said to them, Do not call me Naomi, rather call me Marah, for the Almighty has dealt very bitterly with me (v. 20).

55. These words of Naomi's indicate several things: first, that the women's outcry, *Is this Naomi?* was caused by their astonishment at the change in her aspect and appearance; second, that her

name signified the Pleasant One, meaning that she had been originally accustomed to comfortable circumstances; third, that when her circumstances changed for the worse her name was changed to Marah. There can be no doubt that the women, too, wept when they heard Naomi say this.

56. After saying, *for the Almighty has dealt very bitterly with me,* Naomi proceeded to specify wherein He had dealt bitterly with her.

I departed full, and the Lord has brought me back empty; why then do you call me Naomi, seeing that the Lord has answered against me, and the Almighty has tried me sorely? (v. 21).

57. It is possible that *I departed full* signifies, "I had a husband, children, and goods; and now *the Lord has brought me back* bereft of all these." *The Lord has answered against me*—that is, "He has made me a widow." *And the Almighty has tried me sorely*—"by the death of my children." I have interpreted *has answered against me* in the sense of "testified against me," on the analogy of *though our sins answer against us* (Jer. 14:7), and *he has answered falsely against his brother* (Deut. 19:18). The meaning is: "He has visited my sins upon me, and they were the cause of my widowhood, the loss of my children, and my destitute condition."

So Naomi returned, and Ruth, the Moabite, her daughter-in-law, with her, who had returned from the field of Moab. And they both entered Beth-lehem at the beginning of the harvest of barley (v. 22).

58. The statement *So Naomi returned,* coming as it does after the previous statement, *And it came to pass that as they entered Beth-lehem,* signifies that she now returned to her homestead and to her household. The repetition of the statement about their arrival at Bethlehem serves to record the time of their coming, namely, *at the beginning of the harvest of barley,* meaning that they indeed found food.

Chapter II

And Naomi had an acquaintance of her husband's, a mighty man of valor, of the family of Elimelech, and his name was Boaz (v. 1).

59. This verse serves as a prologue to what follows, and we learn from it three things: first, that Boaz was a friend of Elimelech's, since the verse says, *an acquaintance of her husband's,* and that for this reason Boaz dealt kindly with Naomi; second, that he was of Elimelech's family and that he subsequently married Ruth because of it; and third, that his name was renowned, since he was an important man of high rank, as it is written: *a mighty man of valor.*

And Ruth, the Moabite, said to Naomi, Let me go to the field and glean among the ears of barley after anyone with whom I may find favor. And she said to her, Go, my daughter (v. 2).

60. Ruth knew that Naomi was not able to go out to glean because of her advanced age, and she knew also that they both had nothing else upon which to base their hopes. It was therefore her duty to go out herself, for she was young and strong. Since, however, it was not proper for her to go out without Naomi's direct order, she had to ask her permission to do so.

And she went out and entered a field and gleaned in the field after the reapers. And it so happened to her that the portion of the field belonged to Boaz, who was of the family of Elimelech (v. 3).

61. The words *and entered* signify that she entered in the company of the other gleaners. *After the reapers* shows that she did not act deceitfully, as do gleaners who are not honest. *And it so happened to her* shows that it was a matter of pure chance and was not done deliberately by her, since she did not know Boaz as yet, and had gone there not because of her own intention concerning this matter but because the Lord of the worlds guided her to what was to be her future good fortune, for that is what He had prom-

ised to her and to all who are like her in the verse: *he loves the stranger and gives him food and raiment* (Deut. 10: 18).

And behold, Boaz had come from Beth-lehem and said to the reapers, The Lord be with you; and they said to him, May the Lord bless thee (v. 4).

62. This verse indicates two things: first, that the reapers had preceded Boaz, since they started early in the morning upon their work, while Boaz's manservant supervised them, since it is written later on: *And the manservant who was set over the reapers answered* (v. 6). Second, we are told about their manner of greeting each other; namely, the first person to give greeting would say, "The Lord be with you," and the person greeted would answer, "May the Lord bless thee." In the same manner the angel greeted Gideon: *The Lord be with thee, O mighty man of valor* (Judg. 6: 12). As for the expressions, "Peace be upon you" and "Peace be unto you," they are not used in Scripture as a greeting, but rather as a formula of reassurance from one person to another; e.g., when Joseph's steward said to Joseph's brethren when they were overcome with fright, *Peace be unto you, fear not* (Gen. 43:23); or when Amasai said to David, who was afraid of them, *peace, peace be unto thee, and peace unto thy helpers* (I Chron. 12: 19); or when the angel said to Daniel: *peace be unto thee, be strong, yea, be strong* (Dan. 10: 19).

And Boaz said to his manservant who was set over the reapers, To whom does this girl belong? (v. 5).

And the manservant who was set over the reapers answered and said, She is a Moabite girl who came back with Naomi from the field of Moab (v. 6).

63. We learn from the first of these two verses that Boaz did not know Ruth, although he undoubtedly knew the other gleaners who came out from Bethlehem. So when he saw her, a stranger in their midst, he inquired about her of the manservant who was overseeing them. And from the second verse we learn that the manservant was stationed on guard over the ripe grain and that

he did not permit her to enter the field until he was told who she was, either at the time of her arrival or before.

And she said to me, Let me now glean and gather from the sheaves after the reapers; and so she came and stood gleaning from the early morning until now; this is what she had gathered up to her sitting down, whereupon she will go home—it is but little (v. 7).

64. The manservant took pity upon her and spoke thus to his master, knowing that he was a kindly man and would likewise feel compassion for her. *And so she came and stood gleaning from the early morning until now* shows that he noticed that she was slow in gleaning, which was why he pitied her. . . . *it is but little* refers to the amount of grain which she had gathered, so that he said, "This small amount is all that she has gathered since morning until now, when she sat down, and it is all that she will carry home with her."

And Boaz said to Ruth, Hast thou not heard, O my daughter? Do not go to glean in another field, neither go away from hence, but thus do thou stay close to my maidservants (v. 8).

Let thine eyes be on the field in which they are reaping, and go thou after them; did I not command my menservants not to touch thee harmfully? And when thou art athirst, go thou to the drinking vessels and drink of that which the menservants had drawn (v. 9).

65. Now Boaz had already heard the story of Ruth upon her arrival at Bethlehem as it is written later on: *It has fully been told to me* (v. 11), but he had not seen her before and did not recognize her until his manservant told him: *She is a Moabite girl.* Having got to know her, however, he proceeded to assure her of every manner of kindness on his part.

66. The phrase *Hast thou not heard, O my daughter?* requires an amplifying interpretation, as follows: "Surely thou wilt hear and accept what I say?" It is possible, however, that he meant to say, "Hast thou not obeyed the words of thy mother-in-law and

come to my field? Now, then, observe what I am about to tell thee, namely, do not go away to glean upon someone else's property, thereby wandering far away from thy home; rather do not leave my fields, but as thou hast done today, gleaning from my grain, so also do thou continue to do. Stay close to my maidservants and do not leave."

67. *On the field in which they are reaping*—i.e., "as they complete the reaping in one field and pass on to another, go thou after them." *Did I not command my menservants?*—i.e., "in case I and my chief manservant are away, I have commanded the other menservants not to harm thee, therefore be reassured. . . ."

68. Then Boaz said, *when thou art athirst, go thou*—he did not say, "When thou art hungry, do thou eat with my menservants," because he was always present with his reapers at the time of their meals, according to his custom, as we shall see further on. He therefore said to her, "When thou art thirsty, go thou to the water flask and drink of what the menservants have drawn; there is no need for thee to bring water with thee."

69. As for his words in the preceding verse, *but thus do thou stay close to my maidservants,* there are two problems connected with them. First, what were Boaz's maidservants doing in the field? And second, when Ruth reported this conversation to Naomi, she said, *For he said to me, Do thou stay close to my menservants* (v. 21)—she did not say, "to my maidservants." The answer to the first problem is that Boaz had menservants scattered over his property, overseeing the reapers and looking after them. He likewise had maidservants overseeing the women who gleaned to make sure that none of them was stealing or appropriating the gleanings of another, a thing for which, if anyone of them did it, they would upbraid them loudly. The answer to the second problem is that Boaz had said to her also, "Do thou stay close to my menservants," but the narrator omitted this sentence here in anticipation of Ruth's repeating it in v. 21. Therefore, *in which they are reaping* refers to the male reapers, whereas *and go thou after them* refers to his maidservants.

70. *Not to touch thee* may be interpreted in two ways: first, "not

to approach thee with the intention of doing harm," as in *He who shall approach this man* (Gen. 26:11); and second, "not to strike thee," from the word *neḡa'* (wound), i.e., "I ordered them not to strike thee or hurt thee in any way. . . ."

And she fell upon her face and bowed to the ground and said to him, Why have I found favor with thee, that thou shouldst recognize me, seeing that I am a stranger? (v. 10).

71. When she heard his assurance of kind treatment, she fell upon her face and bowed to God in gratitude to Him, just as the manservant of the Patriarch Abraham had done. Then she said to Boaz, "My master, what hast thou seen on my part that I should have found favor with thee, although I am but a stranger to all of you?" She thus showed him her high appreciation of what he had promised her and her realization of her unworthiness. Whereupon Boaz proceeded to tell her that she was entitled to it, even deserving twice as much of it, because of her deeds of kindness in the past.

And Boaz answered and said to her, It has fully been told to me, all that thou hast done unto thy mother-in-law, after the death of thy husband, that thou hast left thy father and thy mother and thy native land, and hast gone to a people whom thou hast not known before (v. 11).

May the Lord repay thee for thy deed, and may thy reward be full from the Lord, the God of Israel, under whose wings thou hast come to seek shelter (v. 12).

72. He thus spoke of three acts of kindness which she had performed after the death of her husband and he invoked a blessing upon her for it. He did not mention her kind treatment of her husband as well, since Orpah had done likewise in this respect. Her first act of kindness was following Naomi, even though there was no hope of finding a new husband among Naomi's people. In spite of this lack of hope she shared Naomi's affliction, sorrow, and destitution, and went out to glean in the fields and bring the

grain to Naomi, so that the latter might have food to eat. She thus was even more devoted to her than a daughter, which rarely happens among daughters-in-law. This is what Boaz referred to when he said, *all that thou hast done unto thy mother-in-law.* Her second act was forsaking her parents, her kinsfolk, and her homestead, and going to a strange land for the sake of the true faith, just as the Patriarch Abraham did when he forsook his family because of his devotion to God. Her third deed was joining the congregation of Israel, although she was a stranger among them.

73. *May the Lord repay thee for thy deed*—Boaz meant, "May the Lord recompense thee for what thou hast done unto Naomi," i.e., "May the Lord repay thee with good fortune, to reach thee in this world, so that thy good deed with Naomi may not remain unrewarded." *And may thy reward be full*—that is, "May the Lord grant thee a full reward in the world to come for thine entering into the faith of Israel," since he said, *and hast gone to a people whom thou hast not known before.* We thus learn that the phrase *May the Lord repay thee for thy deed* signifies "the reward for thy conduct," whereas *may thy reward be full from the Lord, the God of Israel, under whose wings thou hast come to seek shelter* signifies the reward she will receive for entering into the true faith. Boaz thus gladdened her heart by speaking to her in this manner.

And she said, Let me find favor with thee, O my master, since thou hast comforted me, and hast spoken to the heart of me, thy maidservant, although I am not like one of thy maidservants (v. 13).

74. Her words, *Let me find favor with thee,* may be interpreted in two ways: either as a descriptive statement of an accomplished fact, meaning, "Behold, I have found favor with thee, since thou hast comforted me and hast gladdened my heart with thy blessing, and I do not doubt that thy blessing is acceptable to God," or as a request on her part that he might keep her in mind and take care of her, inasmuch as he was pleased with her previous deeds.

75. *Although I am not like one of thy maidservants*—she meant

to say, "My rank is not like the rank of any one of thy maidservants, for I am inferior to them, yet thou hast conferred upon me every sort of kindness."

And Boaz said to her at mealtime, Come hither and eat of our bread, and dip thy morsel in our vinegar. And she sat at the side of the reapers, and they roasted for her some parched corn, and she ate her fill, and left some of it (v. 14).

76. We are told that when mealtime arrived he called her to eat with them, for he was liberal and generous with his food, as befitted a man of his antecedents. For this reason she felt at ease to accept his invitation and she sat down a little apart from the company and ate, for she was also afraid that he might be displeased if she did not eat.

77. *At the side of the reapers*—it is not written, "with the reapers"—showing that she sat at a short distance from them, since it was improper for her to sit with them.

78. Now the season then being summer, and very warm, he served them vinegar so that they might dip their bread therein, and also gave them to drink some sour wine so as to cool their bodies. He did the same for her also, and we are told that she ate her fill and still had more to spare of both the bread and the parched corn, as it is written: *And she left some of it. . . .*

And she rose to glean some more. And Boaz commanded his menservants, saying, Let her glean even among the sheaves, and do not reproach her for it (v. 15).

And also let slip some ears for her from the bundles of corn and leave them for her to glean, and do not chide her away (v. 16).

79. After she had eaten, she rose eager for more work. Whereupon Boaz ordered his menservants to do two things: first, *Let her glean even among the sheaves, and do not reproach her;* and second, *And also let slip some ears for her*. Neither of these is the rightful due of those who do the gleaning, which is why he said, *Let her glean even among the sheaves,* and expressly outlined the regular procedure of gleaning, to wit: *and leave them for her to*

glean, and do not chide her away. But he added for her to that which she was entitled to glean, by saying, *Let her glean even among the sheaves,* i.e., "let her glean also the ears which lie among the sheaves," since it is usual with reapers, when they reap a sheaf and put it down and pass to another, to have some ears drop from their hands. He thus ordered them to let her pick up these ears. His words, *And also let slip some ears for her from the bundles,* refer to the heaped-up sheaves and the loose ears that protrude from among them. He thus ordered them to pull these ears out and give them to her. All this was done by Boaz so that she might obtain a goodly, large, and bountiful amount of food. And Ruth herself heard him issue these orders. . . .

And she continued gleaning in the field until evening, and she beat out that which she had gleaned, and it was about a wayba of barley (v. 17).

80. *About a wayba of barley*—this does not include what the menservants had given her, since it is written: *That which she had gleaned,* i.e., "she herself."

And she carried it away and entered the city. And her mother-in-law saw what she had gleaned; and she brought forth and gave to her what she had left from eating her fill (v. 18).

81. *What she had left from eating her fill* requires amplification; i.e., "What she had left after she had eaten her fill."

And her mother-in-law said to her, Where hast thou gleaned today and where hast thou worked? May he who took notice of thee be blessed! And she told her mother-in-law with whom she had worked, and said, The name of the man with whom I have worked today is Boaz (v. 19).

82. *Where hast thou gleaned today*—i.e., "in which region?" *And where hast thou worked*—i.e., "with whom hast thou worked?" *May he who took notice of thee be blessed*—she blessed him, although she did not yet know who he was. The meaning of

who took notice is, "who took cognizance of the rights of the stranger and acted properly about it."

And Naomi said to her daughter-in-law, May he be blessed by the Lord who has not left off his kindness to the living and to the dead! Then Naomi said to her, The man is a relative of ours, and one of our near kinsmen (v. 20).

83. *Who has not left off his kindness* may refer either to God or to Boaz. In the latter case it would refer to Boaz having acted with kindness and good faith toward Elimelech and his sons, i.e., *the dead;* while *to the living* would refer to Naomi herself and to Ruth. Some think that *to the living* also refers to Elimelech and his sons, i.e., "Who has not left off his kindness to them while they were living, or now when they are dead," meaning that he dealt kindly with Naomi for the sake of the dead.

84. When she said, *May he who took notice of thee be blessed,* it was before she knew who he was. But when she had learned his identity, she said, *May he be blessed by the Lord.* Then she told Ruth that he was a relative of hers and a near kinsman. By saying, *one of our near kinsmen,* after having said, *The man is a relative of ours,* she meant that he was a close relative, since he belonged to the father's family, rather than the mother's. She thus told Ruth that Boaz dealt thus kindly with her for two reasons: first, for her own sake, as he had said, *It has fully been told to me* (v. 11); and second, for the sake of her kinship with Naomi.

And Ruth, the Moabite, said, For he said to me, Do thou stay close to my menservants until they shall have completed all my harvesting (v. 21).

85. When Ruth heard Naomi bless Boaz because of his kind treatment of her on that day, she said, "He also told me, 'Stay close to me continually until the completion of my harvesting.' "

And Naomi said to Ruth, her daughter-in-law, It is good, O my daughter, that thou shouldst go out with his maidservants, so that they should not surprise thee in another field (v. 22).

86. *It is good, O my daughter*—she told her that what Boaz had said to her was right, meaning, that she should stay with his maidservants, according to his words, *but thus do thou stay close* (v. 8). *That they should not surprise thee*—i.e., "that they should not do any harm unto thee if thou shouldst glean in another place." And Ruth followed the words of Boaz and the words of Naomi.

And she stayed close to the maidservants of Boaz, gleaning until the completion of the barley harvest and of the wheat harvest. Then she dwelt with her mother-in-law (v. 23).

87. We are told that she continued to stay with them until the completion of the harvest. There is no doubt that Boaz continued to treat her kindly, even as he had done on the first day, so that she did not need to go to any other place.

88. And finally we are told that after Ruth was finished with him she did not engage in any other matter, but stayed close to the house with her mother-in-law in chaste and modest retirement.

II. HYMN

Seek, O pursuers of righteousness, the paths of the laws of God;
Treasure ye these laws which are better than pure gold and sweeter than honey.
Kiss ye the commandments which are as strong as a shield or a coat of armor;
Trust ye in the Rock of Eternity who resides in the heavens.
O noble ones among the nations, who cling to the God of their salvation,
Awake, awake, ye laggards, living without care and engaged in idle play!
Why deal ye in the vanities of this world?
Lend ye your hand to the Lord and give your longing to His worship.
Ye mourners for Zion, remember your Mother from afar;

Sit not in gladness, in the company of the playful.
Your Holy House is in the hands of strangers, yet you are far away;
The enemies of God are within it, yet you are unmindful.
Strive ye to appear before Him, be gasping and longing to do so.
Sinners will perish, and the righteous will sing and rejoice,
As it is written: *And let the righteous be glad, let them rejoice before God* (Ps. 68:4).

SAHL BEN MAṢLIAḤ

ABŪ al-Surrī [1] Sahl [2] ben Maṣliaḥ lived in the second half of the tenth century and was a (presumably younger) contemporary of the great Karaite exegete Japheth ben Eli. What little is known of his life is derived indirectly from his own writings. He was a resident, if not a native, of Jerusalem, whence he traveled abroad for missionary purposes. During one such journey, presumably to Cairo, he came into conflict with Jacob ben Samuel, an influential Rabbanite elder and a zealous follower of the Gaon Sa'adiah.[3] This Jacob ben Samuel addressed a sharp missive to Sahl, attacking Karaism in general and charging Sahl in particular with having come to stir up trouble between Karaites and Rabbanites and to procure converts from the Rabbanite ranks. Sahl seized the pretext of answering Jacob's charges to compose a long epistle written in Hebrew. Sahl himself states: "I shall perhaps make a translation of this work into Arabic, so that it might be read by those who do not know Hebrew"; [4] but whether he carried out this intention is not known.

Sahl was a fairly prolific writer. Of his *Book of Precepts* (written in Arabic, but listed under the Hebrew title of *Sefer ham-miṣwoṯ*),[5] which must have been a highly interesting work, only the Hebrew

1. On the pronunciation of this name see Poznanski, p. 4.

2. Sahl is the Arabic equivalent of the Hebrew name Yašar.

3. As Mann (pp. 25–26) rightly remarks, Sahl's designation of Sa'adiah as Jacob's "teacher" (*raḇ*) should not be taken literally, since the chronology requires that Jacob could hardly have been anything more than an infant at the time of Sa'adiah's death in 942. The same chronological considerations (as Mann, p. 26, indicates), rule out Poznanski's hypothesis that Jacob ben Samuel may have been identical with Jacob ben Ephraim (Ya'ḳūb ibn Ifraym) al-Šāmī, the friend and contemporary of al-Ḳirḳisānī. Jacob ben Samuel was associated in his opposition to Sahl with another Rabbanite elder, whom Sahl does not designate by name.

4. *LḲ*, II, 25.

5. Also *Sefer dinim;* but these two titles may really refer to the two halves of one and the same work, dealing respectively with ritual and civil law; cf. Poznanski, p. 33.

introduction has as yet been published.[6] Sahl himself mentions a tract of his devoted to the refutation of Sa'adiah's criticism of Karaism, but it and several other works by him have not yet come to light. The attribution to his pen of several extant fragments dealing with biblical exegesis is far from certain.

For a picture of Sahl's personality the epistle to Jacob ben Samuel is probably the most revealing of his literary productions. Although ostensibly a personal rejoinder to Jacob's accusations, it is clearly meant to serve as missionary propaganda urging the average Rabbanite to relinquish his faith and join the Karaite synagogue. What effect his appeal had we do not know, but the epistle is a powerful piece of writing. Sahl wrote with the consummate skill of a mature stylist and knew how to play upon the emotions of his readers. Throughout he alternates from pleading and tearful exhortation to dire threats of God's wrath; from lofty pictures of the messianic reign of justice and piety to shrewd appeals to throw off the heavy burden of exactions imposed by the Rabbanite hierarchy; from martyr-like complaints of Rabbanite persecution and defamation of inoffensive and unworldly Karaite ascetics to coarse profanities against Sa'adiah and his successors. And he is not averse to stretching the truth in order to enliven his discourse, as when he introduces a humorous, although obviously fictitious, anecdote about Sa'adiah's alleged cowardice in the face of his Karaite opponents. Nevertheless there can be little doubt of Sahl's sincerity and his profound belief in the righteousness of his cause.

As a historical document the epistle is an item of outstanding importance. It represents the earliest complete example, so far discovered, of practical Karaite propaganda, couched in simple terms and addressed not to the learned and privileged classes of Rabbanite Jewry but to the man in the street. It is reasonable to assume that many such harangues were delivered by itinerant Karaite missionaries all over the Near East, in market places and on street corners when possible, or in secret gatherings when Rab-

6. A. Harkavy, *Mĕ'assef niddaḥim,* (St. Petersburg, 1879) I, No. 13.

banite hostility made such publicity inadvisable.[7] No less valuable are the historical data contained in the epistle: the information about older Karaite leaders, the description of popular Rabbanite customs and superstitions, and the picture (no doubt exaggerated, but essentially logical) of the reprehensible behavior of some high Rabbanite officials.

FROM THE WRITINGS OF SAHL BEN MAṢLIAḤ

EPISTLE TO JACOB BEN SAMUEL

1. I have come from Jerusalem to caution the sons of my people, and who would hasten to take heed of this matter except the Karaites who meditate in the Law of the Lord? But you, why were you angered when I came to learn and to teach, to sit with the notables and the scholars of my congregation, and to lead the seduced ones among the Lord's people away from the forbidden kinds of food which their Rabbanite forerunners had allowed them to eat, such as foods prepared by Gentiles? These forerunners even caused them to think lightly of matters of ritual cleanness and uncleanness and of sexual intercourse with women who have recently been confined. They said that it was permissible to take and use oil from vessels owned by Gentiles and made out of camels' hides, or beverages and sweetmeats made by Gentile confectioners, or to use flour milled by Gentiles who do not first cleanse the grain from impurities and mice droppings. That is why I have come, in the Lord's Name, to caution them. . . .

2. And now, my brother Jacob ben Samuel, know that I have come from Jerusalem in order to caution against such things which the Rabbanite forerunners have done—and these are but few out of many—and to turn the hearts of those who fear the Lord

7. In this activity the Karaite missionaries could, and probably did, learn much from the experience of their Mohammedan contemporaries, the propagandists of Shiite and other heterodoxies. The latter, to be sure, frequently preached in mortal peril of their lives, whereas the Karaite missionary could expect, at worst, nothing more dangerous than an order to leave town.

back to His Law. Would that I were able to go into every city to warn and to reawaken the Lord's people, for is it not written: *Go through, go through the gates, clear ye the way of the people* (Isa. 62:10), and *Strengthen ye the weak hands* (Isa. 35:3), and *Cast up, cast up the highway* (Isa. 62:10), and again *Clear ye the way of the Lord* (Isa. 40:3)? Do you not know that there is no stumbling so bad as the stumbling of him who stumbles on an evil way? . . . Yet inasmuch as you have uttered out of your mouth words that are wicked, and out of your heart a thought that is not good, and have abused and denounced me, I know that you have spoken in a way that is not good, for he who holds in his heart the fear of the Lord guards his soul from the taint of wrongdoing and does not expose himself to guilt. . . .

3. It is not enough for you Rabbanites that you neither admonish others nor oblige yourselves and others to repent; you even look with hostile eyes upon the preaching of an admonisher like me, yet it is written: *He that rebukes a man shall in the end find more favor than he that flatters with the tongue* (Prov. 28:23).

4. God, for the sake of His great and awesome Name, will uphold the hand of the Karaites who, by means of their good admonition and their writings to their brethren abroad, have assembled at Jerusalem righteous and pious men and have set up alternating watches to pray and to supplicate before the Hall of the Temple and to implore their God to save the lost sheep and restore them to their cities, in order to fulfill His word: *return, O virgin of Israel, return to these thy cities* (Jer. 31:20). Behold now this loveliest of all women weeping and wailing over the sin of her youth, longing for her husband, pining after her lover, and crying for her sons who are scattered in the four corners of the earth, imploring and saying:

5. My King and my God,
How long am I to be lovesick?
How long wilt Thou have no mercy upon me?
How long wilt Thou forget me?
How long wilt Thou forsake me?
How long will zeal for Thy House consume me?

How long am I to be like a woman in mourning,
While in my heart burns a fierce fire?
How long will mine eyes shed tears,
As I observe graves
In the very gates of the capital city of Jerusalem?
How long will I cry bitterly,
As I observe all kinds of uncleanness in the Court of the Temple,
Instead of the priest burning incense?
How long will enemies stand up against me?
They exercise their hatred upon me,
They twice demolished my city,
They twice burned my Temple.
They slew my sons, did Babylon's lion,
Media, Persia the evildoer,
Greece, and Macedon the malefactor,
Ishmael, and Edom the witless.
My God, pray have pity,
Pray make haste,
Pray have mercy,
Pray have compassion
Upon Thy poor congregation,
Who wait assiduously at Thy gates,
Who knock at Thy doors,
Whose soul goes out with longing for Thy salvation,
Whose eyes are eagerly searching for Thy word.
And pray hearken to them, and be pleased with them, and have compassion upon the sheep of Thy flock!

6. This is the practice of Karaite Israelites who have sought God's pleasure and secluded themselves from the desires of this world. They have given up eating meat and drinking wine and have clung to the Lord's Law and have stood in assiduous watch before the doors of His Temple. Because of the greatness of their grief and the depth of their sighing, they have lost their strength to stand up against all stumbling blocks, and the skin of their

bodies has become wrinkled with premature senility. Yet notwithstanding all this they forsook not their goal, nor did they relinquish their hope; rather they continue to read the Law and interpret it, acting as both teachers and pupils, turning many persons away from evildoing, and saying, "O all ye who are athirst, come ye to the water!" They have abandoned their merchandise and forgotten their families; they have forsaken their native land and left palaces in order to live in reed huts. They have left the cities to go to mountains, they have suffered bitter calumny, and they have doffed handsome garments to don sack cloth, sighing and wailing and crying over Zion's disaster and rolling in the dust of ashes. May God fulfill regarding them His promise to turn the ashes covering the heads of Zion's mourners into an ornament of splendor.

7. You have thought in your heart that I have come here for the sake of monetary gain, like your companions who grind the faces of the poor, consume the flesh from their bones, and rip the skin off their bodies. . . . Were your words not like those of a mocker shooting off sparks, I would not be writing these words, for what do I possess in the way of righteousness, who am I, and what is my life worth? . . .

8. In God's mighty Name have I come to awaken the hearts of His people of Israel; to turn them back to the Law of the Lord; to arouse their conscience and their thoughts to the fear of their God; to make them dread the Day of Judgment, which is coming with terror and wrath, and the day of the Lord's vengeance upon those who forsake His Law; and to warn them not to rely upon ordinances contrived by men and learned by rote and laws promulgated by two wicked women, the observance of which cannot redeem a person from the punishment of Judgment Day. . . . How can I fail to do so, when my bowels cry out within my belly and my kidneys are consumed within my bosom with pity for my brethren and for the children of my people? Many of them have been forced to put a great distance between themselves and the Lord and to walk in a way which is not good, because of their leaders who oppress them remorselessly, who hasten to consume

their fat, to clothe themselves in their wool, to sacrifice their marrow, to eat their flesh, and to take the skin off their bodies. The weak among the people these leaders do not strengthen, the sick they do not heal, the wounded they do not bandage, the strayed they do not recover, and the lost they do not search for. Rather with force and violence do they rule them. Whosoever does not give according to their demand, they wage holy war against him; they subjugate and tyrannize him by means of bans and excommunications and by recourse to the Gentile officials. They punish the poor by forcing them to borrow at a high rate of interest and to make payment to them. Part of what they thus take from the poor they present to the Gentile officials, so that they may strengthen their hold over the people. They vaunt their holiness and purity and demand that the people bring them all kinds of sweetmeats and wine, exacted as payment of fines, so that they may eat and drink. They pasture themselves; they do not pasture the flock, nor do they teach them a useful ordinance. If one of the people opens his mouth to ask, "Whence have you taken that which you have said?" they turn their hatred upon him and make war against him.

9. God forbid, God forbid that I should keep silent and inactive! I know and I have heard of some of the shepherds and leaders of the Lord's people who have set themselves up as their pastors and who assert that they are disciples of the Palestinian academy of the Sanhedrin, yet they come into Jewish homes on the Sabbath to eat and drink in company with Gentile men who also eat and drink alongside them in the drinking chamber, and they mix with them as if they were as ritually immaculate as the children of Aaron the High Priest, without fear or awe or dread of the Lord's wrath.

10. How can I keep silent when some Jews follow the customs of idolaters? They sit among graves of saintly persons and spend nights among tombstones, while they seek favors from dead men, saying, "O Jose the Galilean, grant me a cure!" or "Vouchsafe me a child!" They light lamps at the graves of saints and burn incense upon the brick altars before them and tie bowknots to the

palm tree bearing the name of the saint as a charm for all kinds of diseases. They perform pilgrimage rites over the graves of these dead saints and make vows to them and appeal and pray to them to grant their requests.

11. How can I restrain myself when many Jews leave their houses on the Sabbath on their way to their synagogues, carrying various things, such as purses and pieces of apparel, upon their arms, while their wives wear jewelry? And as they do on weekdays, visiting from house to house, so do they also on the Sabbath.

12. How can I help worrying when some Jewish notables and many of their congregation send messengers to the Gentile market place to buy their bread and their boiled and salted provisions, notwithstanding that these are mixed and contaminated with the Gentiles' sacrifices? Yet they eat them publicly in the judgment place, as well as privately in their homes, without fear of the Lord. How can I rest when some of the holy seed of Israel . . . betake themselves, after the reading of the holy scroll in the synagogue, to the Gentile market place and buy there from the Gentiles all kinds of sweetmeats made with Gentile lard and sugar and prepared in their pots and vessels which have been contaminated by unclean food? How can I keep silent when many of them eat meat from carcasses skinned by Gentiles? The Gentiles fill their mouths with water, then sprinkle it over the flesh of the carcass which they are skinning, so that their saliva is blown between the flesh and the hide, while the carcass is suspended from pegs, according to the custom of the Gentiles with the carcasses which they butcher. Even the meat slaughtered by Jews is cut up with the same knife used to cut up the meat slaughtered by the Gentile, and the same butchering block used to cut up the flesh of the animal slaughtered by the Jew is used also for the animal slaughtered by the Gentile; one is mixed with the other, but they eat the meat nevertheless, although the basic rule is that flesh of cattle and sheep is forbidden for consumption in the Dispersion. Worse than this, they assign a watchman, a stupid boor, to guard their butchered meat so it will not be mixed with that of the Gentiles; still the Gentile butcher does as he pleases, steals Jewish meat, or

substitutes meat for meat, while the oxlike watchman notices nothing. And Jews buy this contaminated meat and eat it. How can I refrain from sighing when I know that some Jews send a sheep or a kid to the Gentile cook to have it roasted? There Jewish and Gentile meats get mixed, and the Jew receives in return and eats meat from Gentile slaughtering. And for this do I mourn and wail. . . .

13. Would that I were given strength to enable me to enter every Jewish congregation, so that I might utter a bitter cry and remind and warn the people in the Lord's name; perchance they would listen and turn back, each man from his evil way, for we know that salvation will come not through the righteousness of the few devout individuals but only upon the repentance of the majority of Israel from all their abominations and idolatries to do the will of their God. Were the performers of these evil deeds but few in number and acting in secrecy, like those who secretly commit abominable crimes in Israel, we would have merely said that these deeds are regarded by the leaders as forbidden. But inasmuch as those leaders themselves mix with these evildoers, and display good will toward them, instead of admonishing and warning them, we know that the leaders think lightly of it and regard it as lawful. And worse than this is their anger and wrath against him who stays away from them and from some of the aforementioned evil practices whereby they drive Israel away from the Lord and separate them from their God and draw His wrath upon them. . . .

14. I speak the truth when I say that I have not written all this except out of pity for my beloved brethren, so that he who can see may see and he who can read may read and fear his God and the day when the wrath shall be poured forth and may turn away from the evil road. . . .

15. Should someone say to me, "Behold, our brethren, the disciples of the Rabbanites in Jerusalem and Ramla, are far removed from doing such things," then you must know that, true enough, they walk the path of the Karaite students of the Law and do as the Karaites do; but it is from them that they learned it. There

are many of them who eat no meat of sheep or cattle in Jerusalem and who keep their mouths clean from every unclean meat. . . . And all this happened to them by virtue of the Lord's mercies and the instructions dispensed to them by those who fear God and their admonitions and warnings. . . .

16. Know, O our brethren, the children of Israel, that each one of us is responsible for his own soul. Our God will not listen to the words of him who justifies himself by saying, "This was the custom of my masters," just as He did not listen to the excuse proffered by Adam when he said: *The woman whom thou gavest to be with me, she gave me of the tree, and I did eat* (Gen. 3:12). He will not accept the words of him who says, "My wise men have beguiled me," just as He did not accept Eve's words: *The serpent beguiled me, and I did eat* (Gen. 3:13). Rather, even as He has given to each one his due and his just share, so also will the Lord deal with him who speaks thus. . . .

17. Know that he who justifies himself by saying, "I have walked in the way of my fathers," will gain nothing by it, for did not our God say: *Be ye not as your fathers* (Zech. 1:4), and again: *And might not be as their fathers, a stubborn and rebellious generation* (Ps. 78:8)? This shows that there is no duty resting upon us to follow our fathers unconditionally; rather is it our obligation to scrutinize their ways and to set up their deeds and judgments over against the words of the Law. If we find them identical, without deviation, we must accept and obey them without change and follow them. But if their words contradict the Law, we must reject them and ourselves search and investigate, using the method of analogy, because the precepts and other things written in the Law of Moses are in no need of any sign or witness to testify whether they are true or not, whereas the words of the fathers require a sign and a trustworthy witness, that you may know whether or not they are true. . . .

18. And you, O house of Israel, have mercy upon your own souls and have pity upon your children. For behold, the light is burning and the sun is shining. Choose for yourselves the good way, where the living waters are flowing, and walk thereon, and travel not in

the land that is desolate and exhausted and despoiled of water. Do not say, "How shall we do it? Do not the Karaites also differ among themselves? Whom, then, among them shall we follow?" The Karaites do not say that they are the leaders, and they have not contrived to lead the people after their own desire. Rather they search and investigate in the Law of Moses and in the books of the Prophets, and they even look into the words of the Rabbanite forerunners. For this reason they say to their brethren, the children of Jacob, "Study, and search, and seek, and investigate, and do that which occurs to you by way of solid proof and that which seems reasonable to you." . . .

19. And now you, if you have asked your questions of me for the purpose of seeking wisdom and understanding, you have done well, and God will guide you in the way of truth and will open for you the gates of understanding. But if you have merely sought a pretext to harass me, you have acted wrongly, for you have waged an evil contest, and it were more fitting for you to be satisfied with your honors, to remain in your place, and to hold your hand over your mouth.

20. You now, are you better than Sa'adiah al-Fayyūmī, the president of the Rabbanite academy? Did he dispute with the Karaites or wage war against them? Did not the Karaite scholars and disciples keep challenging him to come out to them and sit down with them in the Lord's war and to set up his judgments with them, so as to know which was the good way from among their ways? And they kept saying, "Let us choose to engage in judgment, so that we may know among ourselves which is the best" from among their words. But he would not consent and would not let himself come out to them; rather did he retire to his innermost chamber to hide, and he would not admit to his presence anyone but those whom he wished to see. Nor could the Karaites hold an assembly with him on the Sabbath, because of the lamps burning in the synagogue. Finally one of them, Ben Mašiaḥ, risked his very life to follow Sa'adiah to his innermost chamber, whereupon the latter shouted at him, saying, "What have I to do with you? Go away from me!" The works which Sa'adiah

had written against the Karaites were not released by him during his lifetime, but one of them did fall into Ben Mašiaḥ's hands, and he wrote a rejoinder to it while Sa'adiah was yet living. Salmon ben Jeroham, too, wrote a refutation in Hebrew of Sa'adiah's tract beginning with the words, "I shall begin my parable and propound my riddle." After Sa'adiah had died the death of a scoundrel, his other works fell into the hands of the Karaites everywhere, and they replied to them in words as straight as nails, set forth in many tracts; for example, Abū al-Ṭayyib, known as al-Ǧibālī; 'Alī ibn al-Ḥusayn; Ben Mašiaḥ; Ben Jeroham, who is known in Arabic as Ibn Ruḥaym; Abū 'Alī al-Ḥasan al-Baṣrī; and others. I, too, like them wrote a rejoinder to Sa'adiah's words. If you wish to examine their writings carefully until you discover the truth of the matter, search in them and you will know that the truth is with them.

21. If you imagine that you are greater than your master Sa'adiah al-Fayyūmī and that your wisdom is greater than his, and if you and those like you wish and have the ambition to hold a contest with the Karaites, multiply your armies of arguments and come out, go to their congregations with love and affection and fear of God, and ask and inquire. For this is a better way than the manner in which your forerunners have dealt with us. They went to the Gentile officials to denounce their Karaite brethren and to cause fines of silver and gold to be extorted from them, and they banned and cursed them with hatred and enmity. . . . If you wish to have them come to you and to your friends for a disputation, cease profaning the Sabbath by lighting lamps in the synagogue and wearing rings upon your fingers; then they will come and search with you in the Law. . . . Yet I know that you have not done so. On the contrary, you have used the Sabbath lamp for a fortress and a protecting wall, so as to prevent the Karaites from coming to you and revealing to everyone that which is hidden from your eyes. . . .

22. Behold, the days of reckoning for the Gentile nations and the time of salvation for Israel are near. God will bring this time nearer to us and will redeem us from the clutches of the two

women, and He will appoint as king over us the Messiah, the descendant of King David, as it is written: *Behold, thy king comes unto thee* (Zech. 9:9).

23. And now, my brethren, do not harden your hearts against us, but lend us your ears and come to examine our way and to investigate our path. Perchance the Lord will grant us a cure for our wound, will have pity upon our remnant, and will support our enfeebled hand, so that we may be among those who prosper and not among those who stumble. Amen! . . .

24. Our brethren, why do you listen to people who say that the Karaites seek to do you harm? God forbid that we should commit such a sinful deed! If this were true, how would God ever have pity and mercy upon our remnant, and how would He ever remember the covenant of love made with our forefathers? Do we not direct our prayer to God, our Savior, in appeal and supplication, saying, "Have mercy, O Lord, upon Thy people and upon the remnant of Israel?" . . .

25. Our brethren who share in our salvation, let not our words seem harsh in your eyes, for we have written all this out of the fullness of our love for you. Remove the foreskin of your hearts, for you know that if we do not cut off our internal foreskin, the cutting off of the external foreskin avails nothing. . . . There is no hope for us except in the submission of our uncircumcised hearts to God . . . as it is written: *If my people, upon whom my name is called, shall humble themselves, and pray, and seek my face, and turn from their evil ways, then will I hear from heaven, and will forgive their sin, and will heal their land* (II Chron. 7:14).

26. God, for the sake of His great and awesome Name, will cleanse the hearts of the children of Israel, His people, and will give them a new heart and a new spirit and will fulfill upon us, and upon you, and upon all His people, the house of Israel, His good words and His upright and soothing consolations.

27. My brethren, the time has come to wake up from the slumbers of our exile, as it is written: *The burden of Dumah. One calls unto me out of Seir, Watchman, what of the night? Watch-*

man, what of the night? The watchman says, The morning comes . . . (Isa. 21: 11–12). God will console Zion in our days and in your days . . . and He will console those who mourn for Zion in our lifetime. . . . He will yet rebuild His sanctuary and His Temple and He will set us down in His sacred courtyards. He will fulfill upon us and upon you and upon the entirety of His people, the house of Israel, the written promise: *Yet again shall they use this speech in the land of Judah and in the cities thereof, when I shall turn their captivity, The Lord bless thee, O habitation of righteousness, O mountain of holiness!* (Jer. 31: 22).

28. May we all together be deserving to behold the graciousness of the Lord and to visit His Temple, so that there may be fulfilled upon us the consolation: *Behold, how good and how pleasant it is for brethren to dwell together* (Ps. 133: 1). Amen!

29. The Lord be blessed forever. Amen, and again amen!

JESHUAH BEN JUDAH

JESHUAH ben Judah (Arabic Abū al-Farağ Furḳān ibn 'Asad) flourished in the second half of the eleventh century [1] and lived in Jerusalem. He was a pupil of Joseph ha-Ro'e ("The Seeing," euphemistically for "The Blind"; Arabic Yūsuf al-Baṣīr), an eminent Karaite exegete, jurist, and philosopher.

Jeshuah was one of the foremost figures among the Karaite scholars of his century. His learning in biblical exegesis, law, and Arabic philosophy lent him a well-earned prestige, although his philosophical and exegetical works were in later centuries rather neglected, probably because of their abstruse style and difficult method of exposition.

Among the Karaites themselves Jeshuah has enjoyed the highest esteem, particularly for his opposition to the so-called catenary theory of incest which, if developed consistently to its logical conclusions, would have meant for the Karaites something approaching group suicide. His fame in this respect, to be sure, is not entirely justified, since serious opposition to the catenary theory was offered already by Joseph ha-Ro'e.[2] Nevertheless, Jeshuah's tract against the theory dealt with it systematically and in great detail, and having been translated from the original Arabic into Hebrew while the author was yet living, it remained readily usable by later Karaites who knew no Arabic.

In addition to this treatise (entitled, in the Hebrew version, *Sefer hay-yašar,* and possibly forming an installment of a projected large and comprehensive work on all branches of law), Jeshuah made an Arabic translation of the Pentateuch, with a longer and a shorter commentary written in a philosophical strain. Another homiletic commentary on Genesis, entitled in Hebrew

1. His shorter commentary on the Pentateuch is dated 1054 (Mann, p. 34).

2. Even Joseph ha-Ro'e, however, was reputedly not the originator of the anticatenary movement; the real founder of it is said to have been David ben Boaz (second half of the 10th century), a direct descendant of Anan. Cf. Mann, pp. 140–141, n. 20.

Běrešiṯ rabbah, may possibly be a part of the aforementioned large commentary on the Pentateuch; while a commentary on the Decalogue, likewise known only in a Hebrew translation, may be a portion of the shorter pentateuchal commentary. Of all these only fragments have so far been discovered. A short Hebrew tract on the law of incest, entitled *'Iggereṯ hat-těšuḇah* or *Těšuḇaṯ ha-'ikkar,* was printed at Eupatoria (in the Crimea) in 1834 under Jeshuah's name, but his authorship of it would seem to require further proof.

In his works Jeshuah occasionally engages in polemics against Rabbanites in general and Sa'adiah in particular. His argumentation is of considerable power and insight, while his tone is calm and moderate with an undercurrent of respect for Sa'adiah's learning and sincerity.

Jeshuah's role in Karaite history is enhanced also by the fact that among his pupils were Tobiah ben Moses and Jacob ben Simeon,[3] natives of Byzantine Greece, who by their Hebrew translations of important Arabic Karaite works contributed greatly to the preservation of learning among Byzantine and later Russian and Polish Karaites who could not read Arabic. Another eminent pupil of Jeshuah's was the Spanish Karaite Ibn al-Tarās, who distinguished himself, as did his widow after him, by conducting an energetic missionary campaign in his native Castile with such success that his Rabbanite opponents felt constrained to put an end to it by force.

The following two short extracts from the *Sefer hay-yašar* give a fair idea of Jeshuah's method and of his complicated style of exposition, made even more difficult by the atrocious Hebrew diction of the translator. Often, in fact, the Hebrew version seems nearly unintelligible until one translates the text back into Arabic and reconstructs, in a fashion, Jeshuah's own wording. The subject matter itself is rather difficult and involved; moreover, the often highly complicated degrees of relationship assumed and discussed here, involving repeated marriages and divorces, sometimes between persons of wide disparity in age, appear very im-

---

3. Jacob ben Simeon was the translator of the *Sefer hay-yašar.*

probable to modern western eyes. They were, however, quite conceivable at that time, when Karaites lived in small communities, each more or less self-sufficient and comparatively limited in contact with the others. The result was that eventually most individuals in each settlement were more or less related to each other, and since marriage was regarded as the normal state of every adult person and was often dictated by considerations of family and property, the age of the contracting parties, however dissimilar, was of but minor import.

In a social situation of this kind the continued observance of the catenary theory made it increasingly difficult for Karaite men and women to find mates whom they could lawfully marry. According to the catenary theory,[4] the biblical dictum that *man . . . shall cleave unto his wife, and they shall be one flesh*[5] (Gen. 2:24), was to be taken literally, in the sense that the wife's relatives automatically became as closely related to the husband as they were to the wife. By the same token, if the wife was divorced and then remarried, her new relatives by marriage would in turn become closely related to the first husband, and every subsequent marriage in the family would extend even further the rapidly growing circle of persons and families who could not intermarry without being accused of incest and the consequent branding of their issue as illegitimate.

In other words, if the man A married the woman X, all of X's relatives became, according to the catenary theory, ipso facto relatives of A in the same respective degree; i.e., X's sister became A's sister, X's aunt A's aunt, and so forth. If some time later X divorced A and married a second husband B, A and B having thus become *one flesh* by virtue of their marriage (though at different times) to the same woman, all of B's relatives became relatives of A as well. This was continued up to, and including, the fourth degree, the holders of the catenary theory themselves thus admitting that to carry it further would have meant catastrophe;

4. In Hebrew *rikkub,* i.e., the theory of repeated "compounding" or pyramiding one forbidden degree of relationship upon another.
5. I.e., "shall be regarded as one."

yet they could offer no valid reason why the stopping point should be fixed at the fourth degree or why there should be any stopping point at all. Nor was this all. From the considerable number of prohibited degrees of relationship thus elicited directly from the biblical ordinances, new forbidden degrees were derived by using the method of analogy, and by piling analogy upon analogy the multiplication of forbidden relatives was pursued ad infinitum. A source of additional prohibitions was found also in conclusions drawn from the biblical use of certain words; for example, from the biblical use of the term *sister* in speaking of one's stepsister (the daughter of one's stepmother by a previous marriage) it was argued that she should be regarded as one's blood sister, and her relatives by blood and marriage as one's own blood relatives.

Since this theory dated back to Anan himself and was supported in a greater or lesser measure by all the subsequent eminent Karaite scholars (Benjamin al-Nahāwandī, Daniel al-Ḳūmisī, Jacob al-Ḳirḳisānī, Sahl ben Maṣliaḥ, Japheth ben Eli, and others),[6] it required considerable courage on the part of Joseph ha-Ro'e and Jeshuah ben Judah to break with it as openly and outspokenly as they did, nor is it surprising that it took some time before the new reform struck firm root.

Jeshuah's argumentation against this ever tightening noose upon the physical survival of the Karaite group as a whole ran in this manner:

1) The biblical dictum about man and wife becoming *one flesh* has nothing to do with the law of incest, but signifies rather their mutual love and affection or their sexual intimacy.

2) The biblical custom of referring to the *nakedness* of a wife as being at the same time the *nakedness* of her husband also has no bearing on the law of incest but is merely meant to convey the idea that it is the husband's duty to protect and guard the chastity of his wife, and that any violation of it is as much an injury to him as it is to her.

3) The biblical use of the term *sister* in speaking of the daughter of one's stepmother by a previous marriage does not mean that she

6. Cf. Mann, pp. 140–141, n. 20.

really becomes one's blood relative; rather that one must treat her with the same chaste modesty as one would use toward one's blood sister, because her mother's marriage has made her forbidden to her stepbrother. The same thing applies to the biblical usage of similar familiar terms (e.g., *aunt*), when speaking of adopted or distant relatives.

4) The forbidden relatives subject to the law of incest are those expressly mentioned in the Bible,[7] their blood relatives,[8] and those who may be derived from them by the method of analogy used only once. To pile up analogy upon analogy is both unlawful and absurd, since it has no definable limit.

Jeshuah's definition of incest became the standard rule in Karaite law, and the pertinent chapters in most of the later legal codes are based more or less upon Jeshuah's treatise. Although the Karaite law of incest remained more stringent than the Rabbanite system of forbidden degrees of relationship, Jeshuah's reform marked a definite relaxation in one of the cardinal points of the Karaite faith.

FROM THE *SEFER HAY-YAŠAR* OF JESHUAH BEN JUDAH

I. THE THIRD ALLEGED PROOF OF THE CATENARY THEORY

1. They say that it is written: *The nakedness of thy father's wife's daughter, begotten of thy father—she is thy sister, thou shalt not uncover her nakedness* (Lev. 18:11). This daughter of the father's wife, they say, is not really begotten of his father, because if she were Scripture would have related her to him instead of to his wife. It thus necessarily follows that she was begotten of someone else, and yet Scripture made her his father's daughter. Now it is evident that except for her mother's marriage to his father there would have been no way to make the daughter a child of his father, and if her mother's marriage to his father had not made the mother

7. I.e., expressly characterized by the Bible as *šĕ'er*, "one's *flesh*."
8. So-called *šĕ'er haš-šĕ'er*, "*flesh of the flesh*."

and the father one individual, the mother's child would not have become the father's child as well.

2. Know, then, that what they have said about this is not correct, since the falsity of what was just said about this verse has been demonstrated in more ways than one, for different scholars have interpreted it in various ways, and if it were our purpose to explain this verse, it would have been proper to recount all of them and to discuss them. Our design, however, is not to do this, but rather to explain—granting for the sake of argument the correctness of their interpretation of the verse—that their aforementioned conclusion that the father and the mother, of the son and of the daughter respectively, had become one individual is not cogent.

3. Now from their reasoning it follows that if the wife and her second husband have become one individual, then she and her first husband had likewise become one individual. This being so, it is impossible that the wife and the daughter should be the family of each of the two husbands without the two husbands also becoming thereby one individual; rather is it to be assumed that the one husband and the other also become one individual, since the child of the one becomes the child of the other as well.

4. This being proven, it follows that if the first husband had a wife other than the one who later married the second husband, this other wife and the second husband also become one individual, because she and her husband are one, and her husband and this man who is the second husband are also one, wherefore the second husband and the other wife of the first husband are likewise one. The same would be true if this other wife of the first husband subsequently had another husband, and if this latter had another wife, and so on, since the same cause governs the relationship of all of them. In this event, the relatives of these various husbands and wives would be forbidden in the same way as the relatives of the original wife who is the mother of the daughter referred to in Scripture.

5. According, then, to this principle a person has no less than five fathers, to wit:

1) The real father.

2) The mother's new husband who, by marrying the mother, becomes the father, just as the husband of the mother of the daughter is the daughter's father, for it is impossible that Scripture should call her his daughter without his becoming her father. The term "husband of the mother" applies equally whether the mother's child is male or female; the term "mother" applies equally whether the mother is the real father's widow or his divorced wife; and by analogy to the daughter of the wife of the father becoming a sister, the son of the new husband of the mother becomes a brother and the daughter of the new husband of the mother becomes a sister. These two fathers alone are fathers.

3) The third father is the husband of the wife of the father in accordance with what we have said above that if two men successively married to the same woman become one individual because each one of them has become one individual with that woman, it necessarily follows that if one of them is the father of A, the other man also is A's father; otherwise their principle that a woman acting as intermediary between two successive husbands makes them one individual is demolished.

4) The fourth father is the man who marries the other wife of the husband of the mother, which is proved thus: the husband of the mother is A's father, on the basis of what has been demonstrated above that if the woman's daughter becomes the child of the husband of her mother, he conversely becomes her father. Now if the husband of the mother is the father, and if he and the husband of his other wife have become one individual, as shown above, then the husband of the other wife also is the father, since he and the stepfather, i.e., the husband of the mother, are one individual.

5) The fifth father is any man who marries any other woman who at any time was married to one of the aforementioned four fathers, since by being married to the latter she and he had become one individual; consequently she likewise makes her second husband one individual with whichever of the four fathers she had formerly been married to. And since those four are fathers, he too becomes a father.

6. At this point they limit the fatherhood to these five fathers

without any compelling reason for such a limitation, since the fifth father likewise may at one time have been married to a woman other than those referred to before, who had previously been married to another man. In this case this man and the fifth father would, through the mediation of this woman, have to become one individual; and since this fifth person is a father, why should not the previous husband of the other wife likewise be one? And so forth, in this same manner. If they should admit the cogency of all this, they will at least have followed their principle. If, on the other hand, they do not follow in this case that which they themselves have made a basic principle, they themselves will have violated it. If they should retort that in their view it is highly improbable that this sixth man should be forbidden, the answer would be that there is no possible way for it to be improbable if the principle which leads to it is assumed to be sound.

7. Some of them proceed in the same manner with regard to the husbands of the daughter's real mother and consider four of them as her fathers, to wit:

1) The first, the husband of her mother, who is the daughter's father by virtue of the biblical phrase *begotten of thy father*.

2) The second, the husband of the other wife of the husband of her mother, because the woman who came between the husband of her mother and the other husband has caused them to become one individual; since her mother's husband is her father by adoption, it necessarily follows that the other husband is likewise her father.

3) The third is the husband of the wife of the husband of the other wife of her father, since the husband of the other wife of her father is her father by adoption, by virtue of her father's wife having caused her father and the first husband to become one individual; furthermore, the first husband and the other man have become one individual by virtue of the woman who came between them. Now since the husband of the wife of her father [is her father], the other man who is one individual with the other wife must also be the daughter's father.

4) The fourth, any man who marries any other wife of the aforementioned three fathers.

8. The same observation which we have made before, that there is no compelling reason for the limitation to these aforementioned four persons, applies here also.

9. They prohibit also the relatives of these several fathers in the same manner as they do the relatives of the true father; so much so that some of them prohibit even their metaphorical brothers and sisters, i.e., those whom they treat like sisters, as, for example, the daughter of the wife of the father would treat the son of her mother's husband.

10. They say also that as there are five fathers, so are there five sons, to wit:

1) One's real son.
2) The son of one's wife.
3) The son of the husband of one's wife.
4) The son of the wife of the husband of one's wife.
5) The son of the wife of the husband of the wife of the husband of one's wife. . . .

11. This aforementioned verse is one of the major principles of the catenary theory, and most of the rules thereof are derived from it.

II. A PROBLEM

1. Question: If one should ask, What would you say in the case of two men who were married to the same woman at different times—is it permissible for one of them to marry the other's mother, and for the other to marry the former's sister, or is it forbidden? In other words, let us suppose that A, the son of X, was married to a woman who at another time was married to B, the brother of Y; is it permissible for B to marry X, and for A to marry Y, or is it forbidden?

2. Answer: If B marries X, who is A's mother, after he had been married to A's former wife, it is not wicked, except according to

the teaching of those who incline toward the catenary theory; for according to the latter, when B marries A's former wife, A becomes his brother, whereby A's mother, X, becomes B's mother as well. If, however, this catenary principle is null and void, there remains no objection to B marrying the mother of A, who was his wife's first husband.

3. As for A's subsequent marriage to B's sister, Y, it is necessarily illegal, since the blood relative of the mother's husband is forbidden by virtue of the biblical prohibition of marrying the daughter of his father's wife; if she is forbidden to him, then conversely he is forbidden to her, according to the general principle . . . that all degrees of incest are applicable both ways. Thus, a man's son, who is unquestionably his blood relative, is thereby forbidden to marry the daughter of his father's wife; we have also said elsewhere that all other blood relatives of the father's wife, as well as of the mother's husband, are likewise forbidden. This being so, it necessarily follows that after B had married A's mother, X, A may not marry any of the blood relatives of his mother's husband, meaning in this case B's sister, Y.

4. Likewise, if A's marriage to B's sister, Y, takes place first, it becomes unlawful for B to marry A's mother, X, on this same principle.

MOSES BEN ABRAHAM DAR'Ī

Moses ben Abraham Dar'ī was a member of a Spanish family which settled in the small Moroccan town of Dar'a.[1] He himself was born in Alexandria, Egypt, but he seems to have spent some time traveling in Syria and Palestine. By profession he was a physician. Of his personal history only bits may be culled from his poetic works. His married life must have been far from happy, and his wife appears to have been an unkind and domineering person, judging from his bitter tirades against the alleged greed and perfidy of women and their tyranny over their menfolk. His two sons, to whom he was deeply attached, died during his lifetime.

The period of Moses Dar'ī's life remains a puzzle, and none of the contemporaries mentioned in his poems have so far been definitely identified. The only certain thing is that he lived later than the great Rabbanite poets of the Spanish period (Ibn Gebirol, Judah Hallewi, Abraham and Moses ibn Ezra), i.e., not before the middle of the twelfth century, since his poetry shows unmistakable traces of their influence in both subject matter and style.

Moses Dar'ī is justly regarded as the greatest poet of medieval Karaism. He was undoubtedly possessed of a genuine poetic talent and was a skillful master of the rather ornate and involved style used in medieval Hebrew poesy. It is no reflection upon his literary merit to state the simple fact that with all his accomplishments he did not attain the lyric heights and the stylistic brilliance of the best poets among his Rabbanite predecessors in Spain.

Moses' poems were gathered into a collection (Arabic *dīwān*), of which, however, only extracts have so far been published by Pinsker and others. A work of his youth, entitled *Alexandrian*

1. Near the city of Siğilmāsa; the town was the seat of a sizable Jewish community, engaged mainly in commerce (cf. Yāḳūt, *Mu'ğam al-buldān,* ed. Wuestenfeld, II, 567).

Notebooḵ (Hebrew *Maḥbereṯ No-Amon*), in prose and verse, has recently been discovered and published.[2]

SELECTED POEMS

I. ON THE CITY OF DAMASCUS

A

I came to the city of Damascus, and in my soul I thought that in
The men thereof there would be for me a rock of help.
But I found evil instead of the good which I had hoped for
From them, since because of them my pain waxed great.
My friends said, "They resemble in the stiffness
Of their necks the wolf of the forest and the lion."
But I would rather compare them with dogs,
For like dogs they also hate the stranger.

B

The pain of my sorrow, and my moaning, came upon me on the day I entered the city of Damascus.
I forgot all good things on the day when I settled down in it; that day turned my robe of splendor into sack-cloth upon my skin.
The sadness of my sorrow waxed great, and my heart was burdened with the grief caused by it.
My body was in sore straits because of the gravity of my illness, and I could not lift my leg to depart.
O God! For the sake of Thy Name and Thy might, pour the flame of Thy wrath upon it, that it may burn down!

2. By I. Davidson, *Maddaʿe hay-yahăḏuṯ,* II (1927), 295–308.

II. AGAINST THE RABBANITES

God forbid that I should join a wicked people to walk along their path;
Or that I should give heed to their lying jeers or to their scoffing;
Or that I should turn to the false claims of their books or to their vanity;
Or that I should study the ordinances of their Mishnah, invented by themselves.
Rather do I deny that it is a tradition and a secret commanded by the Rock to His congregation on Mount Sinai to cherish these false things,
And I believe only in the written Law given by God to His own people;
One Law, to which I add nothing; one rule, to which I assign no second.

III. TO HIS OWN MUSE

My song, fear not if scoffers as numerous
As grains of sand rise to attack thee.
Know that thou art the great king,
And that they will yet be servants unto thee;
And against their will, forever and ever,
They will bow down before the feet of the horse which thou art riding.
And this is the sign for thee that thou shalt yet live:
Behold, thine enemies are even now vanishing.

IV. ON THE PERFIDY OF WOMEN

Even if a man has treated his wife with generosity and uprightness, and has spent his wealth upon her,

Yet when he becomes poor, all his generous deeds which he had done will not be remembered by her in his favor.

V. ON ENVY

As for him who envies thee thy wealth and wisdom,
Never make any rejoinder to his words,
Lest the flame of his hatred should be assuaged, when thou repliest to him,
By his knowledge that his words have provoked thee.
Rather leave him to burn in the fire of envy which is within him,
Until his inwards shall be consumed inside him,
And his heart shall die a villain's death within him,
And his innermost soul shall be rent by his envy.

VI. ON FALSE FRIENDS

A

On the day when my silver and gold were gone,
My friends drew far away from my company.
I reproved them for their departure, but they said
They desired only the gold of each other, and
Their souls longed only for the company of
Their friend's wealth, not for that of the man himself.
In their slavery to gold, its chains are not to be loosened from their necks.
I commended them for speaking justly,
Even if their actions are contrary to justice.
For gold is like the soul—if
It leaves the carcasses of men, they disintegrate.
And I said, while both mine eyes
Dripped tears of blood, because my hands were helpless,
"If your attachment is solely to a man's gold,
Then ye who have gold, divest yourselves of it!"

B

Say ye to him who deserted me when I was in sore straits,
And who fled from me when poverty overtook me:
"Thou hast thought that God will not anoint
The sore of my poverty with the balm of riches.
Thou hast been mistaken and stupid, for
Thine understanding is vain and thy mind weak.
A tree that withers and whose leaves
Wilt will yet blossom and send forth flowers again."

VII. GUARD THY TONGUE

Guard thy mouth and thy hand with friends,
And do not laugh much with companions.
Know that fire may be kindled by the smallest of sparks,
And a fierce quarrel by a few words.
How many loving friends has mine eye seen
Turned by a playful phrase into bitter enemies!
Therefore place a bit and a halter upon thy mouth,
And bind fast thy hands in thy play.

VIII. ON GREY HAIR

Why should I worry when white enters the forest
Of my hair to chop down all the black,
Seeing that it is written in God's Law: *And God*
Saw the light that it was good (Gen. 1:4)?

IX. ONCE BURNED

They said, "Hast wed a wife?" And
I replied, "A woman more bitter than wormwood!"
They said, "Take another!" I exclaimed,
"Woe shall not strike me twice!"

X. RESIGNATION

When I am in sore straits I quarrel with my own soul,
And I pour out my wrath upon my own spirit.
I concede justice to my Maker for bringing upon me
The misfortune which is the cause of my wounds.
For if I were doing what He wishes me to do,
He would have done for me more than I could wish for.

XI. THE SPOKEN WORD

A wise man, when silent, cannot be known,
Whether he is wise or foolish.
It is as with cinnamon, which is thought to be ordinary wood
By all who see it, until it is burned with fire;
Then it is recognized. So also a man's word reveals him and shows
Whether he is a person of understanding, or one bereft of it.

XII. THE BURDENS OF MANKIND

The Rock has decreed that the hearts of the rich
Shall be burdened with the accounts of their wealth until they die,
While He afflicts the bodies of the poor with
Hard labor, from which they have no rest, day or night.

XIII. THE TYRANNY OF WOMEN

Perverted age, in which the females rule
Over every male and watch his footsteps!
Man's desire has delivered him into the hands of his wife,

And he is like a prisoner in the hands of his oppressor and captor.
Each wife beguiles her husband until the fruit of
His labor is exhausted and his gold spent.
In her own good time she forgets his kind deeds
Which he has done for her, and comes forth to quarrel with him.
Because of her vehement denial of his many kindnesses to her
He feels much distressed and his heart within him is hot with indignation.
It seems, then, as if every man were like one who hires
With his own money someone to make his heart weary,
Or like one who purchases with all his wealth and riches
Someone to make him wrathful and sorrowful.
How unfortunate is man, that he brings his enemy
Into his own house to enjoy his goods!
Why is it that every mother's daughter rules over every mother's son,
And that every tail is raised above every head?
The women rule over their menfolk like creditors over their debtors
And plow a deep furrow upon man's neck and back.
It seems as if the time has truly come of which God had
Spoken to His people, saying: *and women rule over them* (Isa. 3:12).

XIV. TO ONE WHO ASKED FOR THE LOAN OF A BOOK

Cease thine asking, thou borrower of books, since
A request for the loan of books is an abomination to me.
My book is ever like my beloved.
Does a man lend his beloved to others?

XV. DEVOTIONAL

Sufficient unto me is the honor that I find in being
Thy servant, O Rock, and in Thy keeping Thine eye upon me.
Sufficient unto me is the grace that I find in Thy being my
Lord, all my days, in Thy majesty.
I implore Thee, just as Thou art my Lord to my
Satisfaction, so make Thou me Thy servant to Thy satisfaction.

XVI. MEN'S FATE

Hearken, all ye sons of understanding and men of learning,
To the similes of the sons of man in this world.
They are like sleepers, all of whose slumber is a dream,
While the tongue of death interprets the dream.
Or like fowls gathered in a cage, whose feet are
Being drawn to the hands of the slaughterers.
Or like sowers, this one with his seed barren, while that one
Will harvest his seed tomorrow with a song on his lips.
Or like merchants, men of equal perfection and rectitude,
This one turned into a pauper, while that one is waxing greater in wealth and merchandise.
Or like sheep pursued by the lion,
Who does not desist until he devours them in his might and power.
Or like travelers who sail upon the sea of thought in the ship of
Hope, but whose vessel is crushed by the hand of death.
Or like those who eat honey and afterward subsist on wormwood,

Or who are forced to forsake sweetness and to dwell in bitterness.
Or like those who conceive a passion for a wicked maiden that destroys all
Who love her, while she is left to prosper.
Or like runners hastening to travel,
Or like those who go down to sea in a skiff.
Or like guests who spend the night at an inn of desire,
And in the morning depart for the pit.

XVII. THE FOOL

The fool, when he overlooks the virtues
Of his friend, in order to uncover his vice,
Is like a fly that disregards all
The healthy parts of the body, and alights upon a pustule.

XVIII. THE WORLD IS A SCALE

If thou seest a rogue raised high,
While an honorable man is brought low—
Behold, the world is like a scale, which raises
The lightweight, and lowers the heavyweight to the ground.

XIX. LITURGICAL HYMNS

A

My King, observe the heart of Thy people, how it melts
Before its enemies, as it labors for them in payment of tribute,
And is trodden under their feet in their land—
And the earth was filled with violence (Gen. 6:11).
Almighty One, who art the first of all that are first,
Relieve the cities of Thy Holy Land from Jetur and Dishon,

Lest in the city of Jerusalem there should establish himself a man of evil tongue,
And lest in the Land of Palestine there should be established a man of violence.
Have Thy sons no children that Thou hast exiled them
From their Land, and hast conducted thither strangers in their stead?
Have compassion with them and bring them forth from the hostile country,
O Lord, for *the earth was filled with violence.*
Have mercy, O Rock, upon them and demand revenge for my blood;
Take my vengeance upon mine adversaries.
Bear with the transgression of Thy people until it shall have turned back from
Its evil way and from the path of violence.
Arise and fortify the breach of the city of Zion,
And turn into fine dust those who now rule over it.
Then Zion shall again be filled with justice and righteousness,
On the day when no more violence shall be heard within her.
As for the sick of exile, remove their affliction.
Bring nigh the splendor of the grace of the throne of the Prince of Peace,
Their shepherd, who, seated upon it, will pass judgment upon the poor of his people,
And will redeem their souls from oppression and violence.

B

Refrain: They acknowledge Thee, O God,
and seek Thee, Thy holy sons.

Heaven and earth are filled with Thy
Glory, Thy majesty, and Thy splendor.
They are witnesses for Thee that Thou alone
Art primeval, whereas they are recent

And powerless. (*Refrain.*)
Remove Thy wrath and Thine anger,
As well as Thine irritation, from over Thy whole congregation,
Who always guards Thy covenant,
Since the time when Thou hast abandoned them in exile
In the midst of vipers. (*Refrain.*)
Accept their supplication, as well as their fasting,
And write their names for a long life.
Forgive their transgression for so long as they shall live.
Their fasting, of men, O Rock, and of women,
Accept as fire offerings. (*Refrain.*)
Holy One, and Creator of every soul,
Bear with their wickedness and transgression, and render
Them forgiven of sin and guilt.
O Lord, cause the sins of the heavily afflicted ones to be taken from them and broken
Into bits. (*Refrain.*)
O Lord, wipe out my sin with my repentance,
So that I may soon go up purified to the House of the Beloved City,
And may the High Priest be therein,
As of this day, clad in linen garments,
To consecrate the holy sacrifices. (*Refrain.*)
I shall rejoice, and my sorrows shall depart
From me, because of my knowledge that my sin
Has been borne away by the scapegoat,
Who before mine eyes was sent and driven away
To the dismal land. (*Refrain.*)
O people of God, thou shalt soon receive the glad tidings of forgiveness,
And that thy sin has been removed and wiped out.
Rejoicing ye shall soon take hold and possession
Of the Land of Beauty,
Taking it and cherishing it. (*Refrain.*)

C

My God, there is none like Thee among the gods; Thou art great, and Thy deeds are great.
Thy Name is as pleasant as honey to hungry men; it is a joy to the anxious and a balm to the sick.
Thy right hand has spanned the heavens, and has extended them over Thy throne like a canopy.
The earth is filled with Thy majesty and splendor, and Thou art awesome and great of deed.
Thy Name is I-Am-That-I-Am, it will endure into eternity, and will outlive the heathen idols.
Bring back the multitude of Thy people, redeemed, to Thy Sacred Hall—Thou Thyself, according to Thy promise.
Heal its wound and brighten its light, and in its outcry make high its succor above the head of the fools.
Let it raise the sound of its supplication above the sound of flutes in its Sacred House, wherein lies its soul's joy.
Accept, O Rock, from Thy lofty abode, the fruit of its prayer and the fragrance of its pious sacrifice.
I shall glorify Thee in Thy world, and Thy Name in Thy might I shall praise with rejoicing.
As for the poor people of Israel, whose eyes shed tears in streams, scatter its sins and gather balm for it.
For the healing of its wound send to it the Prince of its tent, and render its misdeeds and transgressions forgiven.
Then shall I rejoice at the coming of the Offspring of David, whose entire thought shall be that there are yet those who mourn Israel's wounds,
And who will ever be saying and testifying before Thee: My God, there is none like Thee among the gods.

D

Refrain: Here have I done nothing, that they should put me into the dungeon (Gen. 40:15).

Almighty One, observe the poor abused people
That has found no liberty in its slavery.
Every nation is at ease in the world,
Yet it is wandering about, without rest or respite.
It is driven by its rulers, yet must it keep mute.
Its bread is coarse, and its water muddy.
All its enemies surround it,
In order to destroy its life,
For they have taken counsel together,
And have cast it into the dungeon. (*Refrain.*)
Remove from me Thy wrath,
O Rock, and do not reprove me angrily,
But in Thy mercy and Thy grace
Wash me clean of my sin.
Lend me Thy good will,
And cleanse me of my transgression.
Hearken to my voice before Thee,
O Rock, do not turn a deaf ear toward me,
Lest Thou shouldst keep silent concerning me,
And I should be like those who go down into the dungeon. (*Refrain.*)
Have mercy upon me, O Lord, in Thy grace,
And illuminate Thy countenance toward me,
And by Thine own self, and with Thine own hand,
From all trials and woes
Redeem me, for I am Thy servant,
And in Thee do I place my trust, and I have no fear.
Put my tear into Thy
Water skin, O dreadful and terrible God,
And hearken to my voice,
For I have called Thy Name, O Lord, from the dungeon. (*Refrain.*)

The Holy One, God of Israel,
Will appear over me in His brilliance.
He will exalt my head above Esau
And Ishmael, and will humble their heads.
Then shall I be glad in the company of the Redeemer,
And my heart, at all times and at all hours,
Will rejoice, for God will have been pleased with me,
And will have turned toward me His salvation
From captivity, and will have heard my outcry,
And will have brought me up from the dungeon. (*Refrain.*)
Strengthen, O Lord, my hand,
To rebuild the House of my Sanctuary as of old.
Bring near the time when I shall rule over my rulers,
And shall reign over those who have reigned over me and have conquered me,
When my secret righteousness shall be revealed
To the eyes of all those who revile me and confound me.
And it shall become known to my brethren and to my servants
That Thou art the Rock who hast exalted my head,
Hast lifted my soul from Sheol,
Hast revived me from among those who have gone down to the dungeon. (*Refrain.*)

MOSES BEN SAMUEL OF DAMASCUS

Moses ben Samuel, a native of Safed in Palestine, moved some time before 1354 to Damascus, the principal city of Syria, evidently in search of wider opportunities to earn a living in a manner suited to his extensive knowledge of both Jewish and Arab lore. There he married the daughter of a Karaite who held a post in the service of the emir of Damascus, and it was perhaps through his father-in-law that Moses also joined the emir's staff as secretary [1] in charge of the management of the emir's private estates, the supervision of their local overseers, and the collection of their revenues.

The employment of Christian and Jewish officials by the Moslem government dates back to the very beginning of the empire, following the conquests made by the Arabs who burst out of the Arabian peninsula in the seventh century. In the early period the retention of Christian officials of the overthrown Byzantine administration, who had governed Syria, Palestine, and Egypt prior to the Mohammedan conquest, was a matter of necessity, since the Arabs, in taking over a complex governmental machine, had neither the knowledge nor the experience required to run it. The highest supervisory posts were, of course, filled by Moslems, but many of the subordinate functions, particularly such as required considerable technical knowledge, continued to be performed by Christians and, as time went on, also by Jews, some of whom rose to positions of great trust, influence, and emolument.[2] The reasons were many and varied in individual cases; usually, however, the Moslem ruler or high official could be fairly certain that a Chris-

1. Arabic *kātib,* Hebrew *sofer;* literally: "scribe," or "clerk," but embracing much wider duties and responsibilities than just taking dictation and writing official letters and documents.

2. Jews particularly distinguished themselves in the profession of medicine, and many served as physicians-in-ordinary to Moslem sovereigns and dignitaries. An outstanding example is Maimonides (12th century). The same thing was true in Christian Europe during the Middle Ages.

tian or Jewish subordinate would be more competent, reliable, and hard working, and far less willing to risk disaster (for his coreligionists no less than for himself) by engaging in subversive plots, embezzlement, or graft, than his Moslem colleague.

The presence of these non-Moslem officials and their occasional high favor with their royal masters naturally evoked the envy and resentment of some Mohammedans as well as the stern disapproval of the Moslem clergy at the unseemly spectacle of unbelievers placed in positions of authority over the Mohammedan population. An occasional unwise display of arrogance or ostentatious wealth on the part of such a non-Moslem official [3] would produce an explosion in the shape of a pogrom—looting, vandalism, and murder—and an official persecution resulting in the conversion to Islam, under penalty of death, of the offenders and their families, the closing or destruction of churches and synagogues, and the imposition of degrading disabilities on the Christian and Jewish minorities in general.

One such outburst of intolerance affected the destiny of Moses ben Samuel. In 1354 an Egyptian delegation led by the confidential secretary of Sultan al-Ṣāliḥ waited upon the sovereign with the claim that the presence of non-Moslem clerks in the government was inimical to the safety of the state. At a state council summoned for the consideration of the matter the vezier and the judges (*ḳāḍis*) concurred with the delegation's views and prevailed upon the sultan to issue a decree excluding unbelievers from government service and requiring them to wear inconspicuous garments, carry identifying tokens when visiting the public baths, prevent the display of jewelry by their womenfolk, and conduct their religious services in low voices so as not to offend the sensibilities of their Mohammedan neighbors. Although the decree did not

3. The majority of such instances recorded by Arab historians involved Christian officials, which is quite understandable, considering the occasional successes of the Crusaders and other Christian forces against Moslem arms, the continuously rising prestige of the European powers, and the progressive decline of the Mohammedan states. Jewish officials, on the other hand, who could look to no foreign power for moral and physical support, had little temptation to deviate from a policy of painstaking correctness.

expressly say so, it was understood that those non-Moslem clerks who could not possibly be spared because of their efficiency and skill in certain work were to be retained, but were to be forced to embrace Islam.

The emir of Damascus, who owed allegiance to the Egyptian sultan and was only too willing to comply with this particular decree, regarded Moses ben Samuel as just such an indispensable servant. Moses himself learned of the promulgation of the decree at Shechem (the modern Nāblus) in Palestine, where he was on a tour of inspection of the emir's estates. At first he and his father-in-law thought of leaving the country, but finally they decided to return to Damascus and remain in hiding in the hope that the zeal of the authorities would subside and that the decree would be tacitly nullified. Within a few days, however, Moses was discovered by the emir's police and dragged before his master, who ingeniously accused Moses of having made disrespectful remarks about the Mohammedan faith—a crime punishable by death. Two witnesses were produced to support this obviously manufactured indictment, and Moses' denials resulted only in his being interrogated under torture. To escape execution he finally consented to become a Moslem,[4] although in his heart he remained true to his ancestral faith.

When soon afterward the emir set out on a pilgrimage to the holy cities of Medina and Mecca, Moses ben Samuel was compelled to go along. What he saw of the pilgrimage rites, especially the worship of the black stone at Mecca, must have struck him as downright idolatry, for he resolved to give up his secretarial post upon his return to Damascus. In this he was helped by the fact that his master fell into disgrace with the sultan. But some time later, upon the emir's reinstatement as ruler of Damascus, Moses was ordered to resume his official duties. When he begged to be

4. The act of conversion to Islam consists, strictly speaking, of the mere recital of the confession of faith (Arabic *šahāda,* "testimony"), "There is no god but Allah, and Mohammed is the messenger of Allah." Once this is made, the convert becomes subject to all the other duties incumbent upon a true believer, such as prayer, almsgiving, pilgrimage to the holy places.

excused the emir threatened to punish him, but even as he spoke he was stricken with an attack of illness from which he never recovered, and thus Moses was once more rid of a heartless master.

The subsequent events in Moses' life are obscure. He appears to have moved to Egypt where he became—willingly or not we do not know—a clerk on the staff of the vezier,[5] going about in constant anxiety lest he be obliged to profane the Sabbath by doing any writing on that day. Fortunately for him the vezier, too, soon died, and his successor appears to have permitted Moses to spend his Sabbaths at home.[6] Possibly he ended his days in the new vezier's service.

Moses ben Samuel's literary exercises, all in verse, were gathered by one of his sons into a compact collection containing an account of his tribulations, as well as occasional pieces, epistolary missives, hymns, etc. His style is fluent and clear and shows a thorough knowledge and command of the Bible, while his liturgical pieces display a deep feeling and occasionally a genuine lyrical inspiration.

The story of his forced conversion and his pilgrimage to Medina and Mecca is extant in two versions, of which the second, written in a more factual manner, is unfortunately fragmentary. The first version, given here in translation, consists of five cantos, each made up of several quatrains; the last line of each quatrain is a biblical quotation adapted, sometimes rather awkwardly, to the context of the narrative. This scheme, however, is not always consistently observed, and biblical quotations are sometimes introduced, in unchanged or modified form, into the other lines of a quatrain. Nor is the choice of quotations for the concluding lines of individual quatrains always appropriate, and in the present

5. Presumably he there returned openly to the Jewish faith, hoping that his former conversion to Islam would remain unknown. The risk involved, however, was great, since in Moslem law such a relapse carries an automatic sentence of death.

6. It should be noted in this connection that the institution of the Sabbath as a day of rest has no counterpart in Islam. The Moslem Friday is distinguished solely by public prayer and sermon at the cathedral mosque and is accompanied by no prohibition of work or any other exertion.

translation some violence had to be done occasionally to the original meaning of these quotations in order to accommodate them to the context.

FROM THE WRITINGS OF MOSES BEN SAMUEL OF DAMASCUS

ACCOUNT OF HIS CONVERSION AND PILGRIMAGE TO MEDINA AND MECCA

Canto I

1 I shall begin by praising God the All-High,
Who searches the human heart and kidneys,
Who has granted me redemption,
And a refuge on the day when I was in sore straits (Ps. 59:17).
2 He who places his trust in Him will not return empty-handed,
And a lie will not, nor ever did, stand up before Him.
He will not reduce to nought the just due of His poor ones,
For He showed me his wondrous kindness (Ps. 31:22).
3 He is great of counsel and great of deed,
Dispenser of wise judgment,
Ruler of all living creatures and all animals,
The God who executes vengeance for me (Ps. 18:48).
4 I speak of His deeds
And of His deep thoughts and inscrutable actions;
Who among those who praise Him can recount them in full?
Blessed is the man who hearkens to me (Prov. 8:34).
5 Incline your ears toward me, friends,
And praise the Name of the Lord, for it is sweet,
And hear what evildoers have done to me—
They have set snares for me (Ps. 140:6).

6 And it came to pass in the year seven hundred and fifty
And five of the reign of the Ishmaelites,
The wrath of the Lord fell upon Israel in full force—
In such manner did he do unto me (Gen. 39:19).
7 The ire of the Lord went forth in anger,
And He delivered His people into the hands of the sons of the maidservant.
And they also raised a hand against Israel—
The prideful ones have hidden a snare for me (Ps. 140:6).
8 The men of the Dispersion did indeed sin,
And their guilt grew unbearable,
And each one of them said, without thought of mercy for his brethren,
I shall be safe (Deut. 29:18).
9 Even before this the Egyptians gathered together
In the houses of the great and the nobles,
And they contrived words against the people of the tribute—
The more they were increased, the more they sinned against me (Hos. 4:7).
10 They advised an evil counsel,
These men of guilt, transgression, and wickedness,
That our congregation should be uprooted from their midst—
And I said, I waste away, I waste away (Isa. 24:16).
11 For in the hearts of these great ones there burned a fire against us,
Because our nobles and chiefs stood nigh unto the Moslem princes;
And they sought to banish us from their midst—
Mine enemy sharpens his eyes upon me (Job 16:9).
12 Their leader said to the elders: "Where is our discretion?
The people of the tribute are many in our midst;
Some of them are secretaries to our king—
Did I say, give me your advice? (Job 6:22).
13 Hasten ye to take vengeance upon them,

And see what ye can do in a prudent manner;
Do not let them retain the upper hand—
Even so that they might not show contempt toward me (Song 8:1).

14 Let us write documents against them,
And let us proclaim them in this city and in other towns;
Let us send letters to the cities,
With the menservants who belong to me (Ruth 2:21).

15 That none of them shall evermore serve as a secretary,
And that their voices in prayer shall not be loud,
And many other such grievous laws"—
For the Almighty has dealt bitterly with me (Ruth 1:20).

16 This counsel of theirs was written down in an epistle,
And they took it into their hands for safekeeping,
And went to see the king, at the time of the first night watch, like
A bear lying in ambush against me (Lam. 3:10).

17 They found the king sitting with his men of understanding,
And they read the epistle before him.
The king listened to it, and it seemed good in his eyes—
All their plans against me (Lam. 3:60).

18 The king approved their requests,
And gave them authority over the people of the tribute;
Let them be appalled by reason of their shame,
They who say to me, Aha, aha! (Ps. 40:16).

19 He called the judges and the men of understanding,
Who made ready to answer him,
And he said: "Hearken, O true believers,
And ye who have knowledge, give ear unto me (Job 34:2).

20 Look ye at this epistle, and answer me,
What did the Prophet Mohammed have to say concerning them?"
And everyone of them replied fiercely as a lion,
For they thought to do me mischief (Neh. 6:2):

21 "Hear, O king, my lord,
For thou art a man of great wisdom."
And the viceroy, named So-and-so, spoke thus—
And he instructed me and spoke to me (Prov. 4:4):
22 "The soul of the king will be enclosed
In the receptacle of life, if he will uphold
With his might the words of the viceroy;
Attend, therefore, *I will tell thee, do but hear me out* (Job 15:17)."

Canto II

1 He said further: "For the people of the tribute are rogues;
Therefore let none of them be great in our midst,
Nor be possessed of authority like Ishmaelites—
Yea, the strength of their hands, whereto should it profit me? (Job 30:2).
2 Let us multiply the laws against them,
That they may not be free from the yoke,
And let us thus fortify our false religion—
I would bind it unto me as a crown (Job 31:36).
3 Let them make for themselves tokens for use in the public bathhouses,
And let their clothes be devoid of well-cut shape;
And let everyone of them cut the length of his turban—
Whosoever of them has sinned against me (Exod. 32:33).
4 Let them all be excluded from secretarial office,
And let them strip their married women of their jewels,
And let them not raise their voices in their prayers—
If I have erred in anything, do ye explain it to me (Job 6:24)."
5 The king heard this speech,
And became like a man who had drunk to intoxication.
And he came to a decision,
And answered the people, saying:
"The Lord has given me all the kingdoms of the earth (II Chron. 36:23).

6 This people—we shall subdue them,
For their religions are different from that of all Moslem peoples,
And their offspring is known among the nations,
So that it may be well with me (Gen. 12:13).

7 Hasten, therefore, and write letters,
And announce in provinces and cities,
And let nothing be omitted of all the aforementioned things,
And ye shall be agents for me (Exod. 19:6)."

8 There was summoned before him the confidential secretary,
Who acted as instigator of this counsel,
And the king said to him: "Write most emphatically
As thou didst speak unto me (Lam. 1:22)."

9 They issued forth hurriedly with fiercely joyful faces,
Because their advice to degrade and bring contempt upon the people of the tribute had been accepted.
May the sins of the Jewish people be expiated by this calamity!
Behold, O Lord, for I am in sore straits (Lam. 1:20).

10 In the fifth month there arose the sigh of anguish,
For this is the month of weeping and moaning;
There is no relief for the soul in this month,
For I am the unloved one, and he gave me sore trials (Gen. 29:33).

11 The aforementioned confidential secretary sat down
And summoned all the secretaries,
And he said: "Write quickly according to the king's word;
Did he not say to me these very words? (Gen. 20:5)."

12 They all heard these words,
And they quickly wrote the letters,
For God is the Judge who makes men low or high—
Because of this did the Lord do so unto me (Exod. 13:8).

13 He hastened the preparation of the letters and went to and fro,
Sealing them with the king's signet ring, as he had been instructed;
For he was a man laden with honor and high esteem—
So has it fully been told unto me (Ruth 2:11).
14 And he sent them off by couriers,
And the Egyptians urged them on to greater haste,
Because what they had wished for has been fulfilled—
They were mine enemies and my foes (Ps. 27:2).
15 They reached Damascus, my city, in the sixth month—
The letters containing the trap set for me—
And the fire of anxiety was kindled in my heart,
Because of this net which they had hidden against me (Ps. 31:5).
16 They set the date for the gathering of the people of the tribute,
That they might come and hear the decree and observe it.
And they came and submitted to the decree—
For many are those who wage war against me (Ps. 56:3).

Canto III

1 I served at first
As a secretary, in a wholehearted and well-intentioned manner,
With a prince who was a wicked and foul-tongued man—
That has been my lot in life (Job 7:3).
2 Before the letters had reached him he directed me
To apportion the administration of his towns, and he commanded me thus:
"Go and collect my revenues—*For God*
Has dealt graciously with me, and I have everything (Gen. 33:11).
3 *Curse not the king even in thy thought* (Eccles. 10:20),
When thou wilt receive his command to profane
Thy faith, and tell not thy secret to others—

My son, give me thy heart's attention (Prov. 23:26)."
4 I heard his words and went forth
With his menservants to his villages, and I apportioned them;
But my ways became crooked, for I acted foolishly,
And wearisome nights were my lot (Job 7:3).
5 At first I was like them when I was in their company,
But when they heard the king's counsel they widened their mouths in glee.
May the Lord refuse to forgive them,
Mine enemies said I was in an evil state (Ps. 41:6).
6 The seventh month came around,
And my goblet was filled from the cup of wrath.
My beloved and my friend grew distant from me,
And my mouth spoke up in my distress (Ps. 66:14).
7 I was seized with terror of the evildoers,
For they told me that a calamity had overwhelmed my dear friend
In Egypt, David Hakkohen, my favorite one,
And it became a reproach unto me (Ps. 69:11).
8 My heart was filled with wounds,
And my intestines groaned within me;
Plowers plowed deep furrows upon my back,
And the fear of Isaac was with me (Gen. 31:42).
9 I hid my pain, yet was I unable to repress it,
Because of mine enemies with whom I was consorting.
But my spirit was exhausted, and I submitted,
For mine enemies said I was in an evil state (Ps. 71:10).
10 I knew that they had opened their eyes at me with evil intent,
Because of the rumor which had reached them,
And I sought to flee from the wrath of their wicked deeds—
I would hasten to a shelter for me (Ps. 55:9).
11 I suppressed my anger until my arrival in the city of Damascus,

And while my Moslem companions went in one direction,
I went in another,
And I hid myself and went nowhere,
But it profited me not (Job 33:27).

12 I entered the synagogue to supplicate my God,
And I directed my heart toward prayer;
And I begged my God for mercy, and I said:
"Be gracious unto me, O Lord, for I am in sore straits (Ps. 31:10).

13 Of Thee I ask refuge from thunder,
For a little moment, until the terror shall have passed,
When I shall again worship the Lord in comfort,
For thou art a hiding place for me (Ps. 32:7).

14 My heart is submissive before Thee;
Look down upon me from Thy lofty abode,
And open Thine eyes to my prayer;
Incline thine ear unto me (Ps. 17:6)."

15 My flesh was rigid, and I was seized with trembling,
Because of the rumor which had reached me,
And the misfortune which had overtaken me—
O Lord, be a helper unto me! (Ps. 30:11).

16 I prayed until the night of *Šĕmini 'Ăṣereṯ,*
And having completed my prayer I fell into slumber.
The morning came, and I was apprehended,
For I had not the understanding of a wise man (Prov. 30:2).

17 Mine eyes shed tears in streams,
For the Lord did not hear my prayer;
Also my male and female relatives and the members of my household,
When they heard of my arrest, let me hear their weeping (Ps. 18:45).

18 Anxiety and oppression found me out,
And they brought me to my master and his brother, the evildoers—
The fear which I feared has overtaken me,

And that which I dreaded has come to me (Job 3:25).
19 I was summoned by the evil malefactor,
The brother of my master, who has committed many crimes.
And he spoke alternately roaring and scoffing at me,
And he said, Bring him near unto me (Gen. 27:25).
20 He multiplied his wickedness against me, and he spoke fiercely, saying:
"Has such a monstrous thing ever happened before?
Dost thou dare to scorn the faith of Ishmael,
By saying, I have no desire for it (Eccles. 12:1)?"
21 Two witnesses, worthless fellows,
Did he produce to accuse me of rebellion and malefaction,
And they testified against me before I could rise to defend myself;
They became mine enemies (Ps. 139:22).
22 My sin was complete, and the end had come,
And I became among the Gentiles like a target for the arrow;
The time of evil oppressed me,
Even as it has done unto me (Prov. 24:29).

Canto IV

1 He oppressed me and caused me great pain.
Observe and see, O my brethren, the sons of my mother and my father,
If there be any pain like unto my pain,
Which was done unto me (Lam. 1:12)?
2 I was trapped on the holiday,
On the twenty-second of the month of Tishri,
And he removed the crown which was upon my head—
If I have acted wickedly, woe unto me (Job 10:15).
3 May the Lord look down from his lofty abode
And judge that man with all his multitude of officials,
Who has multiplied his wickedness and malice—
Lord, I have called thee; hasten to me (Ps. 141:1).

4 Because of the chastisement which was inflicted upon me,
They carried me to my house in a state of grave illness;
My heart was rent beneath my clothes,
Even as they had done unto me (Judg. 15:11).
5 My illness lasted three months;
Because of my pain, my wound was aggravated,
And I asked my Rock to receive my repentance—
May the Lord do thus unto me (Ruth 1:17).
6 While the illness was yet within me,
I heard a rumor which was painful to my heart,
That the same affliction which overtook me had overtaken my brother also,
For it grieved me bitterly (Ruth 1:13).
7 When I heard these bad tidings I uttered a bitter cry,
For it was disaster heaped upon disaster and bad rumor upon bad rumor.
Mine eyes were exhausted from weeping and my spirit was unsteady—
May the Lord consider it in my favor (Ps. 40:18).
8 My heart was submissive and my flesh was rigid,
Because my God has held my sin against me.
And I prayed to the Lord and said:
"O Lord, create a pure heart for me (Ps. 51:12).
9 Observe, my God, that my spirit is submissive,
And see the affliction which has overtaken me and my brother.
How can this be, seeing that Thou hast delivered me from my mother's womb?
What is this that thou hast done unto me (Gen. 3:13)?
10 I have sought Thee, my God, with all my heart;
Do not lead me astray, O my Rock, from Thine ordinances,
For I have stored Thy sayings in my heart;
Until thy wrath be past, appoint me a set time and remember me (Job 14:13).

11 May Thy kindness be pleased to console me
With a repentance that will bring me back to Thee,
So that Thou wouldst appoint me a set time and wouldst remember me—
Then shall I be at rest (Job 3:13).

12 Come back to me in Thy mercy,
Let me come back, and I shall return to Thee;
Then will I teach the wicked Thy ways,
Which I shall behold for myself (Job 19:27).

13 Rescue me from the sin of the Gentiles,
And pull me out of the abyss of their spiritual darkness.
Mayest Thou, in Thy great kindness, console me;
Let not mine enemies triumph over me (Ps. 25:2).

14 And until I reach old age and hoariness,
Remember this, my God, in my favor.
Let my salvation be near—
This, too, remember in my favor (Neh. 13:22)."

15 After these things God remembered me
And redeemed me from my illness,
And gave me strength and endurance,
For he inclined his ear toward me (Ps. 116:2).

16 But the affliction of my heart did not pass away,
And my pain was locked within me,
And I said: "How did I reject wisdom?—
Yet all this avails me nothing (Esth. 5:13)."

17 The prince reinstated me in my secretarial position,
Against my will and not for my own good,
And he promoted me because of my desertion of my ancestral faith,
And surpassing greatness was added unto me (Dan. 4:33).

18 He spoke to me of peace, yet he was my undoing,
And he seduced me with his words,
And he said: "Now thou belongest to me,
As a friend and a brother of mine (Ps. 35:14)."

19 It occurred to his heart that he would go to Mecca
To celebrate the festival there and to pray.
And he spoke to me soft words—
Would that thou wert like a brother unto me (Song 8:1).

20 He told his whole entourage to be ready,
Women, fathers, and children,
To celebrate the festival at Mecca, amidst the multitudes—
And thus also did he do unto me (Judg. 18:4).

21 He said this to all his favorites, and he thought in his heart
That I would obey without question his order about going to Mecca;
He felt certain of it,
Saying, Thus will he do for me (II Sam. 3:35).

22 He arranged his baggage and supplies,
So that there might be no obstruction on his way;
And he sent me word by his messengers, saying:
"*For he is but seeking a pretext with me* (II Kings 5:7)—

23 Hearken to me and go with me,
Thou, together with my men who attend in my chamber,
For thou art as one of my people—
If thou wilt not, hearken unto me (Job 33:33)."

24 His servants came to me
And related his words to me,
And I cried: "O my great and mighty masters,
Hear me, and entreat for me (Gen. 23:8)

25 Before the prince, my master, and implore him,
And say to him that this man is sick
And is unable to go, so let him remain in his house—
Thus shall ye give me a token of your kindness (Judg. 14:13)."

26 They relayed to him my words, and his wrath waxed hot,
And he multiplied his anger and irritation,
And he said: "Bring him hither,
So I might understand clearly what he would say unto me (Job 23:5)."

27 He sent to me one of his senior servants,
A man deceitful in his deeds,
And he said to me: "Hasten and say to him,
Here I am, for thou hast called me (I Sam. 3:6).
28 Go back and speak to him,
Then his wrath will recede from thee;
Thou art in his opinion an elder and an important official;
Listen to my voice and go, take my advice for me (Gen. 27:13)."
29 I hastened to go, but my heart was not in it,
And I reached him, and he maltreated me,
And he said: "Behold, thou hast mocked me,
And hast not told me the truth (Judg. 16:15).
30 This very day I shall renew thy tribulations,
And I will not permit thee to reach thy desires,
Nor to go back to thy house,
Lest they make thee sin against me (Exod. 23:33)."
31 From among his servants he appointed over me
Two men to watch my actions;
And he did not permit my relatives to have contact with me;
And he said, God forbid that I should countenance thy disobedience! (Gen. 44:17).
32 Early in the morning he gathered his servants
And the men of his suite, and his friends,
And they set out, all together;
But as for myself, God forbid that I should (I Sam. 12:23)
33 Go along, except against mine own heart,
For my pain was locked within me,
And because of the gravity of my trespass before my Rock and my Refuge
All who saw me, jeered at me (Ps. 22:8).
34 We went from province to province and from town to town,
While the flame of remorse was burning in my heart,
Until we reached Mount Seir—

Whosoever heard this tale would laugh scornfully at me (Gen. 21:6).

35 I came to the city of their prophet;
Upon leaving it or entering it they pronounce a blessing upon him,
And they imagine that he hears and sees them from his seat in heaven—
It made me laugh (Gen. 21:6).

36 The pilgrims gathered at his tomb,
And they saw at night a light shining upon its minaret.
And one of his congregation said to me:
Art thou envious of me? (Num. 11:29).

37 I hastened to summon one of the native men of the city,
And I asked him: "Where does the light come from?
Swear to me by God, right here,
That thou wilt not lie to me (Gen. 21:23)."

38 He hastened to speak truthfully, without falsehood,
Saying: "The true light of our Prophet does indeed shine at night as if it were morning,
But in these days it is no longer seen, as it has become rare,
But behold, they will not believe me (Exod. 4:1).

39 In the street encircling this place there are eunuchs marching around me,
Each one holding a lighted torch and waving it to and fro,
So as to make the light shine over the Prophet's tomb,
Which they make holy for me (Lev. 22:2)."

40 His fellow townsmen heard his words,
And they rose to slay him and to curse him,
But he stood fast against them and demonstrated the truth of his words—
Strangers yield feigned obedience to me (II Sam. 22:45).

41 My mouth utters the praise of the Lord,
Because He brought to me this man to cleanse my hand;
And I bowed to God upon my face,
Because the Lord, my God, has given me rest (I Kings 5:18).

42 From his words my heart drew pleasure, after it had been heavy,
And I said: "*And there has not arisen a prophet since in Israel like unto Moses* (Deut. 34:10),
And his memory shall not be forgotten in the mouths of all nations,
For he has made with me an eternal covenant (II Sam. 23:5)."

43 They remained there three days,
And then went to Mecca, barefoot and naked.
I went with them for twelve days, full of desolation, and would have perished,
Were it not that the Lord was of help to me (Ps. 94:17).

44 We reached the house of their worship,
To which they turn their faces in their prayer,
And I observed the black stone which leads them astray in their faith—
It looked to me as if it were a plague spot (Lev. 14:35).

45 And they walked around it and reeled like drunkards,
For they said: "We are observing the custom of our Prophet and commemorating it."
O God, mayest Thou sell these people into slavery for their sin,
And may the divine king not account it a sin on my part (II Sam. 19:20).

46 I departed from there, while they were yet engaged in great celebration,
And I said: "O Lord, avenge Thy profaned name and Thy neglected Law;
And remove anxiety from our hearts,
And these troubles which thou hast given me (I Kings 9:13).

47 Turn Thine eyes to Thy devastated Temple,
And restore Thy glory to it and raise its foundations;
Exalt Thy humbled people—
So that ye shall be holy men unto me (Exod. 22:30).

48 Behold this Moslem house and those who come to it,
While Thine own House is in ruins and we are far away from it;
Bring us back to dwell in its shadow,
For thou hast been a refuge for me (Ps. 61:4).
49 Let me sojourn in Thy tent forever,
Myself together with Thy desolate people,
For Thou hast chosen us from among all the nations—
Wonderful was thy love to me (II Sam. 1:26).
50 I desire, O my God, to do what Thou wishest,
Yet now I am caught in my sin.
But from of old have I observed Thy word,
For it is ever with me (Ps. 119:98)."

Canto V

1 After this we traveled to Mount Paran,
We, and the men from Egypt,
And the men from the lands of Ishmael and Haran,
Their guilt offering, which they rendered unto me (Num. 18:9).
2 We stood there from midday until sunset,
Our flesh and our heads bare,
For they said: "This is our holy mountain—
This shall be holy unto me (Exod. 30:31)."
3 My God has dealt kindly with me and did not reveal my secret,
For He knew that I had gone along against my heart and my desire,
And He brought me back safely and did not abandon me in the land whither I had wandered;
Behold, God is my helper (Ps. 54:6).
4 They went back to their land by the same road which they had traveled,
They who said that they made me earn merit, and have earned merit themselves,
And I came back to my relatives who have sustained me.

After I had been worn out, I had relief (Gen. 18:12).
5 I gave thanks and praise to God,
And implored Him to let me offer full repentance,
When I shall pay what I have vowed,
And he shall be unto me my openly acknowledged God (II Sam. 7:14),
6 And when I shall do no more secretarial work,
For the dread of it is engraved within my heart;
When I shall pass from slavery to freedom,
He will recompense me according to the cleanness of my hands (Ps. 18:21).
7 This I asked from the Rock of Ages,
That I and my seed might walk the perfect road before Him,
And that He might save me from among the nations,
That the Lord might cure me (II Kings 20:8).
8 His kindness inclined His ears toward me, and He waxed angry with my master,
And the king banished him to Aleppo, in fulfillment of my desire,
And I and my family dwelt secure in our homestead,
And the Lord recompensed me for my suffering (Ps. 18:25).
9 The Lord is good to those who trust Him, to the soul that seeks Him;
He is always available to him who searches for Him.
Every day I beseech Him in my behalf and I seek Him,
And in the night, I am not silent (Ps. 22:3).
10 After this the king went out of his own land,
And he came to our land to do what he wished to do;
His end had come to the hostile prince,
And my sleep was sweet unto me (Jer. 31:25).
11 When my master, the prince, and his brother heard of this, they came back from Aleppo,
And presented themselves before him, and he lavished favors upon them,

And he said to them: "Go from before me with my affection,
And keep my covenant, and ye shall be in favor with me (Exod. 19:5)."

12 At this news my heart was stricken with illness and consternation,
And I went to the Synagogue of Elijah the Prophet, fasting, clad in sackcloth, and weeping;
And I spread my supplication before Him in the inner chamber:
"My God, what wilt Thou grant me in relief of my affliction? (Gen. 15:2).

13 My King, see how my master is restored to his position,
And I am full of anxiety lest he might request me to be with him again.
My God, save my soul from his snare;
I would hasten my escape (Ps. 55:9)."

14 I placed the letter in the Holy Ark,
And I prayed before the Lord as fervently as I could,
And I said: "I know that Thou art able to do all things;
Thou hast set me free when I was in sore straits (Ps. 4:2)."

15 To sum up, the king elevated the head of my master,
And he placed him in the ranks of his officers.
And my master asked me to apportion the administration of his cities among his servants,
But I said, God forbid that I should do this (Gen. 44:17).

16 I answered him, and my heart was submissive:
"My master knows of my sworn promise made at the tomb of the prophet
That I would not bring my soul back to this secretarial work;
If thou wouldst do thus unto me, then I pray thee, slay me (Num. 11:15)."

17 He turned his face to his servants, and they surrounded me,
And he said to them: "Bring him near to me,

To multiply upon him the harshness of my deeds."
But the Lord was a support unto me (Ps. 18:19).

18 My Rock laid him low at the very time that the word issued from his mouth,
And his flesh was shaken and he became ill,
And He cast him into the abyss and into the depths of death;
And the Lord recompensed me for my suffering (Ps. 18:25).

19 The awesome and fearful God accepted my prayer,
And He put him to death at the end of seventeen days,
And my God granted me redemption from him—
He heard my voice and gave me relief (Gen. 30:6).

20 God, the Merciful One, Searcher of hearts and kidneys,
Rescued the lamb from the mouth of the lions,
And He in His graciousness will save the remainder of the lambs.
I rejoiced at those who said to me, Let us go to the house of the Lord (Ps. 122:1).

21 I shall give song and praise to Thee all my days,
For Thou hast rescued me from mine enemies and mine adversaries.
I ask from Thee my bread and my water—
I am thine, and all that I have (I Kings 20:4).

22 My lips utter praise,
For Thou hast saved me with Thy compassion and pity,
And hast endowed me with Thy sublime Law;
Thou hast turned for me my mourning into dancing (Ps. 30:12).

AARON BEN ELIJAH

Aaron ben Elijah, known as Aaron the Younger,[1] was a native of Nicomedia, the present Izmīd, in Asia Minor. He died a comparatively young man [2] in 1369, presumably at Constantinople where he is said to have settled.

Aaron the Younger undertook to cover the entire range of Karaite theology by composing three extensive works dealing with philosophy of religion, (*'Eṣ ḥayyim,* composed in 1346), law (*Gan 'eḏen,* composed in 1354), and the interpretation of the Pentateuch (*Keṯer Torah,* composed in 1362), each covering its subject in full detail. He was well acquainted with Rabbanite literature and frequently quotes the Talmud, as well as Sa'adiah, Rashi, Abraham ibn Ezra, David Ḳimḥi, Maimonides, Naḥmanides, and the Rabbanite grammarians Judah ibn Ḳurayš, Judah Ḥayyūǧ, and Jonah ibn Ǧanāḥ. His Hebrew style is strongly colored with Arabic constructions, as he was proficient in that language, but it is much easier to read than the corrupt Hebrew of the early Byzantine Karaites.

As a jurist Aaron depended to a considerable extent upon his predecessors; he generally inclined, however, toward a more rigorous interpretation of biblical ordinances and opposed most relaxation of the letter of the law, except in the face of definite and certain calamity. On the other hand, he followed Jeshuah ben Judah in the more liberal theory of forbidden marriages and rejected the general prohibition, favored by the extreme Karaite ascetics, of the eating of meat in the Dispersion.

As an exegete Aaron sided with those who preferred the simple explanation of the biblical text according to its literal meaning;

1. Hebrew *ha-'aḥăron,* literally: "the latter," in distinction from his predecessor and namesake Aaron ben Joseph or Aaron the Elder (*ha-rišon,* literally: "the former").

2. A Karaite tradition has it that he was 18 years old when he wrote the *'Eṣ ḥayyim* (Mann, p. 1417), which would mean that he was born in 1328; this seems somewhat too late. He is said to have been a victim of an epidemic,

but this did not prevent him from using allegorical interpretations where they seemed advisable.

Aaron's fame among his correligionists rests mainly on his activity as a philosopher, and the Karaites generally regarded him as their counterpart of Maimonides—an appraisal which is more complimentary than justified. He did, to be sure, thoroughly acquaint himself with the available writings of Mohammedan and Jewish philosophers, and in undertaking his *'Eṣ ḥayyim* he clearly meant to create a Karaite equivalent of Maimonides' philosophical magnum opus, the *Guide of the Perplexed* (Hebrew *More nĕḇuḵim*). However, since he could not break with scholasticism, which through the mediation of Arab thinkers had strongly influenced both Rabbanite and Karaite philosophers before the twelfth century, he was compelled to take a long step backward. In Rabbanite philosophy scholasticism, nearly two centuries before Aaron, had given up its dominant place to Aristotelianism as finally formulated by Maimonides. There was no corresponding shift in Karaite thinking, however, and Aaron's Karaite forerunners, among them Joseph ha-Ro'e and Jeshuah ben Judah, were all staunch scholastics. Aaron's work, therefore, while more logical and orderly than the works of his predecessors, is in a sense a restatement of a system long outworn and discarded. This fact explains also Aaron's occasional vacillation in taking a clear stand on some scholastic doctrines and his considerable borrowing of Aristotelian terminology and argumentation. It is as if Aaron himself did not really believe wholeheartedly in all that he was setting forth in his philosophical treatise yet could not bring himself to break loose from his Karaite forerunners.

FROM THE WRITINGS OF AARON BEN ELIJAH

I. THE KARAITE HOLIDAYS (First Half Year)

The Day of Trumpeting

1. Since the first day of the seventh month, Tishri, is called *the day of trumpeting* (Num. 29:1), we must know the significance of the word *trumpeting*.

2. We say that we find *trumpeting* used in the sense of uttering a loud sound. We find it used of a loud sound expressing joy, as in *for the people were uttering a loud trumpeting* (Ezra 3:13), i.e., in praise of God, as an expression of joy; also to the contrary, to express grief, as in *Now, why dost thou utter a trumpeting?* (Mic. 4:9). Again, it is written: *And when Joshua heard the noise of the people in their trumpeting . . . And he said, It is not the voice shouting of power, nor the voice shouting of weakness, for I hear only the voice of shouting* (Exod. 32:17–18), meaning that it was an indefinite sound which might signify either alternative.

3. As for the Rabbanite doubts as to the kind of sighing or wailing which this trumpeting expresses, does not Scripture, on the contrary, define this Day of Trumpeting as one of joy, as it is written of it: *mourn not, nor weep . . . for this day is holy* (Neh. 8:9)? Furthermore, it is well known that Scripture does not indicate that this trumpeting signifies the sound of a horn. We know rather that in all places where Scripture mentions trumpeting along with trumpets and the sound of the horn—like *With trumpets and the sound of the horn trumpet ye before the King, the Lord* (Ps. 98:6), *God is gone up amidst trumpeting, the Lord amidst the sound of the horn* (Ps. 47:6), and probably in all similar passages—this trumpeting is not identical with the sound of the horn, but signifies trumpeting produced by the voice issuing from the mouths of the people, joined with the sound of a trumpet or a horn.

4. The proof of this is the fact that in many places we find

trumpeting clearly used solely of the raising of the voice in song and chanting; e.g.: *Come, let us sing unto the Lord, let us trumpet to the rock of our salvation, let us come before his presence with thanksgiving, with psalms let us trumpet unto him* (Ps. 95:1); *Trumpet ye unto the Lord, all the earth, break forth and sing for joy* (Ps. 98:4); *Sing, O ye heavens, for the Lord has done it; trumpet, ye lowest parts of the earth* (Isa. 44:23); *Sing aloud unto God, our strength; trumpet ye unto the God of Jacob* (Ps. 81:2). Where we find trumpeting joined with horns or trumpets, it does not signify that the sound of trumpets or horns is identical with trumpeting—the proper term for the former is "blowing"—rather that trumpeting is the raising of the human voice, joined with the blowing of horns or trumpets. . . .

5. The Rabbanites draw an analogy between the Day of Trumpeting and the Day of Atonement which precedes the Year of the Jubilee, of which it is written: *Then shalt thou sound the horn of trumpeting in the seventh month, on the tenth day of the month, on the Day of Atonement* (Lev. 25:9). They say that just as this trumpeting was done with a horn, so also must the trumpeting on the Day of Trumpeting have been done with a horn. We have already explained that it really means the raising of the voice, joined with the sound of the horn, as it is written: *for thou hast heard, O my soul, the sound of the horn, the trumpeting of war* (Jer. 4:19). *The day of trumpeting,* therefore, signifies nothing but the raising of the voice in song and praise, inasmuch as there is no mention of a horn in connection with it. Moreover, why should we draw an analogy between a thing which is obligatory every year, and one which is obligatory only once in fifty years, the year of the Jubilee? . . .

6. It is the custom in all Israel, in the ten days between New Year's Day and the Day of Atonement, to rise in the night and to recite prayers of confession and supplication, in order to obtain forgiveness of sins. Although man should practice repentance at all times, during these ten days especially he should scrutinize his deeds, since he cannot offer true repentance on the Day of Atonement while his sin is yet in his hand. There are even some sin-

fearing persons who also fast these ten days. All these are commendable customs and may be practiced in order that when the Day of Atonement, which is devoted especially to the atonement of sins, arrives, men may be ready with complete repentance, so that they may obtain forgiveness and atonement for all that they have sinned, as is written: *For on this day shall atonement be made for you, to cleanse you; from all your sins shall ye be clean before the Lord* (Lev. 16:30).

7. This day, i.e., the Day of Trumpeting, is called a Sabbath and a holy convocation; but it is not called a festival. Work of labor is prohibited on that day . . . excepting work entailed in the preparation of food. . . .

8. Some scholars call this day "New Year's Day," for which there is no evidence in Scripture. The Rabbanites likewise do so, and add that the world was created in the month of Tishri, although . . . there is a controversy among them as to whether it was created in Tishri or in Nisan. We have already shown elsewhere, with convincing proof, that the world was created in the first month, Nisan. . . .

9. The Rabbanites say that the Day of Trumpeting is the day when the world was conceived and when the deeds of all men are brought up for review, both their merits and their sins. He whose merits outnumber his sins is written down as destined for eternal life in Paradise, while he whose sins outnumber his merits and who does not repent is written down as destined for Hell. He whose merits balance his sins, if he repents before the Day of Atonement, is written down as destined for eternal life in Paradise; if he does not repent, he is written down as destined for Hell. The great perplexity engendered by this view of theirs is that if this day be the Day of Judgment, how could the Giver of the Law have ordained that it be a day of rejoicing and a holy convocation? Yet it is written of this day: *mourn not, nor weep . . . for this day is holy unto our Lord* (Neh. 8:9). On the contrary, if this were the Day of Judgment, it should have been devoted to submission and humility before God. . . .

The Day of Atonement

10. The tenth day of the seventh month, Tishri, is designated by Scripture as a holy convocation and a Sabbath of rest; it is not called a festival, and it is written of it: *Ye shall do no manner of work on that same day* (Lev. 23:28), exactly as it is written of the Sabbath. Therefore what is forbidden on the Sabbath is likewise forbidden on the tenth day of Tishri; there is no difference between them, except that he who deliberately profanes the Sabbath is liable to death by stoning and to being cut off, as it is written: *one that profanes it shall surely be put to death, for whosoever does any work therein, that soul shall be cut off from among its people* (Exod. 31:14); whereas he who violates this Day of Atonement is liable only to being cut off, as it is written: *And whatsoever soul it be that does any manner of work in that same day, that soul I will destroy* (Lev. 23:30). . . .

11. In addition to this, the Day of Atonement carries also the commandment of self-mortification, which follows after the commandment of rest, as it is written: *A sabbath of rest shall it be for you, and ye shall afflict your souls* (Lev. 23:32). This means that everything that is connected with eating is also forbidden on that day; e.g., the fetching of vessels necessary for the cooking and serving of food.

12. The mortification required on that day consists of abstention from food and drink, since all mortification mentioned in connection with the soul signifies fasting, as it is written: *I have afflicted my soul with fasting* (Ps. 35:13), and *satisfy the afflicted soul* (Isa. 58:10).

13. There are some people who are in doubt as to whether mortification mentioned in connection with the soul signifies fasting. They say that if this were so there would have been no need to say: *I have afflicted my soul with fasting;* it would have been sufficient to say, "I have mortified my soul," which would have implied fasting, assuming that all mortification connected with the soul signifies fasting. This, however, is not a valid argument, since *with fasting* serves to express the idea with greater

detail and breadth. Although the literal meaning of these words, "to mortify the soul," does not refer exclusively to fasting but to anything whereby the soul is mortified, as in *Every vow and every binding oath to afflict the soul* (Num. 30:14), where fasting is not expressly mentioned, nevertheless in actual usage of the Hebrew language we do not find this expression employed except with particular reference to fasting, as in *Wherefore have we fasted, and thou seest not? Wherefore have we afflicted our souls, and thou takest no knowledge?* (Isa. 58:3). Here clearly *have we fasted* and *have we afflicted our souls* are a duplication of the same meaning, as is proven by the following phrase: *Behold, in the day of your fast ye pursue your business, and exact all your labors,* which corresponds exactly to the two foregoing sentences.

14. Nor could it be argued that *I have afflicted my soul with fasting* means really "on a certain day of fasting," which they knew of, since the definite article makes such an interpretation impossible.

15. To sum up, we do not find mortification of the soul used of anything other than abstention from food and drink, as exhibited in the usage of Scripture. However, since the literal meaning of these words points to other things as well, these things cannot be ruled out, except that they have not been indicated to us by the Bible.

16. As for the way the Rabbanites have widened the meaning of the phrase *ye shall afflict your souls* (Lev. 16:29), in order to include in it the prohibition of other things, by applying it to other biblical instances of the use of the word "affliction" alone, without the addition of the word "soul," they have no justification for it. These additional prohibitions include the prohibition of anointing the body with oil, lying with women, wearing sandals, and washing the body with water. Do they not themselves admit that the penalty of being cut off applies solely to eating and drinking? Nevertheless one should observe carefully all other things which also mortify the soul, providing that such observance does not involve any violation of this Day of Atonement, since all these things are conducive to repentance, which alone brings about

atonement for sins. The basic meaning of these words, "afflicting the soul," however, according to the intention of Scripture itself, is abstention from food and drink; therefore he who violates this ordinance is liable to be cut off, as it is written: *For whatsoever soul it be that shall not be afflicted on that same day, he shall be cut off from his people* (Lev. 23:29).

17. While mortifying one's soul, one should concentrate one's heart upon repentance, for fasting without the concentration of the heart is useless. That is why Scripture has connected mortification with the soul, meaning that one should isolate one's soul from all physical pleasure.

18. From the wording of this ordinance it is evident that it is, strictly speaking, obligatory upon adults only, since it carries the penalty of being cut off, and also since it is meant as an atonement of sins. However, we of the community of Israel subject our children also to mortification, even prior to their coming of age. We do this by the analogy of the Sabbath, of which it is written: *Thou shalt not do any work, thou, nor thy son, nor thy daughter* (Exod. 20:10), by which analogy we restrain our minor children from doing work on the Day of Atonement also. In the same manner, even though the prohibition of work on the Day of Atonement is caused by its being a day of atonement of sins, and this cause does not embrace those who are not of adult age, yet we apply the same rule to the mortification of the soul and extend it to include minors as well. The children, however, should be subjected to it at an age when their lives are not endangered, and only to a degree which they are able to bear, in order to instruct them in the observance of these ordinances.

19. The scholar was right who said that this moderate mortification of our children is conducive to the improvement and inspiration of ourselves as well because, as we observe the mortification of our children, our own souls are broken with pity. Moreover, in times of suffering it was the custom of Israel to have their children and infants share the suffering with them, as it is written: *And all Judah stood before the Lord, with their little ones, their wives, and their children* (II Chron. 20:13), and again: *sanctify a fast,*

call a solemn assembly . . . Gather the elders, assemble the infants and the suckling babes (Joel 2:15–16).

20. For this mortification Scripture requires us to take also portions from the weekday at both ends of the Day of Atonement, as it is written: *and ye shall afflict your souls on the ninth day of the month, at even, from even unto even shall ye keep your sabbath* (Lev. 23:32). . . .

21. It is a good custom to pray on the Day of Atonement, all through the day, from morning until the appearance of the stars in the evening, to confess and to implore forgiveness for all sins, inasmuch as when the Temple in Jerusalem was yet standing they were wont to devote the entire day to the performance of the service of the Day of Atonement.

The Feast of Tabernacles

22. We must know first on what scriptural grounds we are obliged to construct the festal booth. The learned Rabbi Joseph explained that the obligatory construction of the booth is derived from what is implied in Scripture, and not from an expressed statement therein, namely from the verse, *In booths shall ye dwell seven days* (Lev. 23:42)—if dwelling in the booth indicates the obligation to build it, then we are indeed in duty bound to do so. For the verse, *And ye shall take for yourselves on the first day the fruit of goodly trees* (Lev. 23:40) does not, on the face of it, indicate the construction of the booth, since it does not say, "And ye shall take these fruits and build a booth," but only, *ye shall take for yourselves on the first day* such-and-such things, which is then followed by *and ye shall rejoice before the Lord, your God, seven days.* That is why the views of the commentators are in disagreement as to whether the verse *And ye shall take for yourselves* was meant to imply that these things were to be used for the building of the booth, in accordance with the ordinance *In booths shall ye dwell seven days,* or whether *And ye shall take for yourselves on the first day* was meant to signify some other purpose, while the construction of the booth was to follow log-

ically from the obligation to sit in it, in accordance with the verse, *In booths shall ye dwell seven days.* However, he who prefers to see the implication of the building of the booth in the verse *And ye shall take for yourselves* says that while Scripture does not expressly direct its building, it is impossible that the ordinance of its building should not be manifestly indicated in Scripture; we must therefore say that this verse does direct its building, by implication.

23. This implication may be strengthened by reference to the verse in the Book of Ezra: *Go ye out to the mountain and bring leaves of the olive tree, and leaves of the oil tree . . . to make booths, as it is written* (Neh. 8:15), showing that the Law somewhere does expressly indicate the making of the booth. Moreover, some of the same kinds of trees as are mentioned in the verse *And ye shall take* are mentioned also in the Book of Ezra, in the verse, *Go ye out . . . and bring.* Therefore, even though the construction of the booth is not expressly indicated in the verse *And ye shall take,* the purpose of this taking must clearly be the preparation for the building, as in the verse *they shall take to them every man a lamb, according to their fathers' houses, a lamb for a household* (Exod. 12:3).

24. Now if we grant that *And ye shall take* signifies the preparation for the building of the booth, we must ask those who think so, "What is the meaning of *the fruit of goodly trees?*" In reply to this they are compelled to interpret this word *fruit* in the sense of *so it brought forth branches and shot forth sprigs* (Ezek. 17:6), which, they say, is parallel to *tree bearing fruit* (Gen. 1:12), embracing both fruit-bearing trees and firewood trees.

25. Others interpret *fruit of goodly trees* as a transposition of "majestic fruit trees."

26. According to the former interpretation, this is the reason why Scripture goes on to say *branches of palm trees* (Lev. 23:40), without the conjunction "and"; if *branches of palm trees* were something other than *fruit of goodly trees,* Scripture would have said "and branches of palm trees."

27. According to the latter interpretation, Scripture says: *the*

fruit of goodly trees, meaning "majestic fruit trees," because it wishes to mention next firewood trees; that is why it says: *fruit of goodly trees,* in order to define the following *branches of palm trees.*

28. Furthermore, if *And ye shall take* signifies taking in order to construct the booth, then all the species of trees mentioned in the book of Ezra, in the verse, *Go ye out to the mountain,* should have been mentioned in the verse, *And ye shall take;* yet this is not the case. To be sure, scholars have proposed various explanations in order to reconcile these two verses, to the effect that all species of trees mentioned in one are really mentioned in the other also. Now the difference between them is that the *willows of the brook* (Lev. 23:40), mentioned in the Law, are not mentioned in Ezra, while *leaves of the olive tree, and leaves of the oil tree, and leaves of the myrtle* (Neh. 8:15), mentioned in the Book of Ezra, are not mentioned in the Law. If the two verses are as one, they must be made to signify the same thing. That is why scholars have been constrained to say that *the fruit of goodly trees* includes olive and oil trees, because they found it written: *and his beauty shall be as the olive tree* (Hos. 14:7)—beauty and goodliness, say they, are the same thing. As for the difference between *leaves of the olive tree* and *leaves of the oil tree,* Rabbi Anan said that although both are olive trees, yet they are of two kinds: an olive tree which produces oil, and one which does not. However, were this so, Scripture should have said "and branches of palm trees."

29. Rabbi Daniel al-Ḳūmisī said that *fruit of goodly trees* is more suitably applied as a synonym of *branches of palm trees,* for it is written: *thy stature is like to a palm tree* (Song 7:8).

30. With regard to the myrtle tree mentioned in the Book of Ezra, they say that it is a synonym of the *willows of the brook* (Lev. 23:40), as it is written: *the myrtle trees which were in the bottom-land* (Zech. 1:8), which may fittingly signify willows. Rabbi Benjamin said that the reason *willows of the brook* are not mentioned in the Book of Ezra is because it is written there: *Go ye out to the mountain,* i.e., "Go ye up to the mountain and fetch branches

of such trees as are found upon the mountain, while we shall fetch the *willows of the brook.*"

31. In this way were they constrained to force these two verses into agreement. Those, however, who dispute with them and maintain that these two verses cannot possibly be synonymous, say that the verse *And ye shall take* does not direct the construction of the booth, because the expression *fruit of goodly trees* does not fit the construction of the booth. The fact that in the verse in Ezra there have been added three species of leaves, namely, *leaves of the olive tree, and leaves of the oil tree, and leaves of the myrtle,* while the *willows of the brook* have been omitted, also shows, according to them, that the two verses are not as one. As for the aforementioned argument from the words *to make booths, as it is written* (Neh. 8: 15), *to make,* they say, has the sense of "to observe"—as in *to make the sabbath day* (Deut. 5: 15)—while *as it is written* refers solely to the word *booths,* not to the words *to make.*

32. Now it is evident that the matter must be one of two things: either the phrase *And ye shall take* is synonymous with *Go ye out to the mountain* or it is not synonymous. If it is synonymous, there should have been no addition or subtraction of kinds of trees; yet such there are, therefore the two phrases are not synonymous. Here again the matter must be one of two things: either the phrase *And ye shall take* signifies that the booth may be made from any kind of leaves, and not exclusively from these particular kinds—these latter being mentioned only by way of example, as the Israelites knew at the time that these were what the Prophet Moses had intended, after which Ezra came and added to, and subtracted from, them on his own authority—or else we must say that *And ye shall take* refers not to the making of the booth but to other matters.

33. Since it is difficult to say that this verse was not meant to restrict the choice to these particular kinds of leaves and to make them obligatory, it would seem that this verse does not refer to the making of the booth, and the fact that the Book of Ezra commands the making of the booth from some of these kinds of leaves

does not indicate that these two phrases are synonymous. Rather, inasmuch as the passage in Ezra deals with the booth, it had to say, "Take the leaves of such-and-such species of trees"; on the other hand, the passage in the Law, having nothing to do with the making of the booth, did not need to say, "leaves of such-and-such species of trees," but said, *branches of palm trees, and boughs of thick trees, and willows of the brook* (Lev. 23:40).

34. In interpreting the phrase *And ye shall take for yourselves,* some of our Karaite scholars say that it means taking the *fruit of goodly trees,* like citrons, apples, and others, in receptacles made of *branches of palm trees*—which would require the addition of the preposition "in" to the scriptural text—and taking *boughs of thick trees, and willows of the brook* in order to fashion them into baskets for festal use in eating the fruit and carrying it, as it is written: *And ye shall take . . . and ye shall rejoice* (Lev. 23:40).

35. The Rabbanites say that this "taking" signifies actual taking with the hand of the four species named. Of these, they say, *fruit of goodly trees* means the citron—for *goodly* (*hadar*) *trees* they read, "which remains (*had-dar*) upon the trees from year to year." The phrase *branches of palm trees* requires, they say, the addition of the conjunction "and," and these branches signify the *lulab*. *Boughs of thick trees,* they say, signifies the myrtle tree, since its branches come in thick clusters of three; but this is wrong, since it is written in the book of Ezra: *leaves of the myrtle . . . and branches of thick trees* (Neh. 8:15), showing that these are two different species. Moreover, it is impossible that the Hebrew word *'abot,* "thick," should signify "coming in threes," since it is spelled with the full vowel "a," whereas *'ăbot,* signifying a triple braid, is spelled with the reduced vowel "ă." . . .

36. The Rabbanites say also another thing in this connection, without any ground in Scripture, to wit, Scripture says: *And ye shall take for yourselves on the first day,* thus limiting the taking to the first day only; yet they extend the ordinance of the lulab over all the seven days of the festival. The Exalted Name alone knows the truth in this matter.

37. Second, it is clear that in any case the booth should be con-

structed of something similar to the species mentioned in the account of the making of the booth in the Book of Ezra, namely in the verse, *Go ye out to the mountain* (Neh. 8:15). It is evident also that the meaning is not that the booth must be made only out of all these species alone but rather that it may be built out of anything else, so long as it does not have an unpleasant odor; the species mentioned in the Book of Ezra were simply those available at that time and place. As for the order in the Book of Ezra implying that *leaves of the oil tree* are different from *leaves of the olive tree,* some interpret *leaves of the oil tree* as leaves of nut trees, while others say that it means a tree which burns brightly because of its abundant oil content. Regarding *thick trees,* some think that it is a species of cedar, as it is written: *and its top was among the thick boughs* (Ezek. 31:3). Others say that it is the pistachio tree, as hinted in the verse *and under every thick tree* (Ezek. 6:13). . . .

38. Third, as to the time of its building, those who believe that the obligation to make the booth is implied in the phrase *And ye shall take you on the first day* (Lev. 23:40) must assume that this phrase indicates that the booth should be constructed on the same day—yet would not doing that violate the holiday? Therefore it could not be constructed after the arrival of the holiday. Moreover, Scripture says: *In booths shall ye dwell seven days* (Lev. 23:42), which means days complete both at their beginning and at their end. The booth must therefore be ready prior to the arrival of the holiday.

39. However, if we agree that the phrase *And ye shall take* directs the construction of the booth, and seeing that we find the preposition "on" used also in other senses, e.g., *when Joshua was at Jericho* (Josh. 5:13), meaning "in the vicinity of Jericho," we may assume also that *on the first day* means at some time near the first day.

40. Fourth, as to who is to build the booth, scholars differentiate between ordinances rooted in reason and those not so rooted, and they say that the former may be executed also by non-Jews, e.g., the duty of making a balustrade on the roof, as a precaution against

accidents. On the other hand, ordinances not rooted in reason may not be executed except by Jews, e.g., the making of the booth, the wearing of the ritual fringe, and the rinsing of vessels—these may be done only by a believer. This seems to be a well-justified view.

41. Fifth, as to where the booth is to be made, some people limit the making of the booth to the Chosen Place, because the booth has been made obligatory jointly with the celebration of the festival at Jerusalem, and the latter is bound up with the Holy Land. Now . . . we find other things bound up with the celebration of the festival at Jerusalem—these particular matters connected with the booth are bound up only with the particulars of this celebration—yet we regard them as obligatory even in the absence of the celebration of the festival at Jerusalem. . . . This matter of the booth is like them. Such matters, therefore, remain as obligatory in the Dispersion as they were in the days of the Temple at Jerusalem, and the absence of the particulars bound up with the Holy Land does not affect them. Moreover, Scripture says: *that your generations may know that in booths have I made the children of Israel to dwell* (Lev. 23:43), lumping together all the future generations, both those who were to live at the time of the Temple and those who were to live in the Dispersion.

42. Sixth, as to whether it is obligatory upon every one of the children of Israel, it is self-evident that if every one of the children of Israel is obligated to dwell in a booth, then every one of them is likewise obligated to make one. However, if one of them has anticipated the rest of them and has built it all by himself, all the rest are free from the duty of building it, since it is one of the ordinances involving mere fulfillment, whereas the dwelling in the booth is a duty extending to every one.

43. Scripture makes it a duty for homeborn citizens, but not for strangers, as it is written: *all that are homeborn in Israel shall dwell in booths* (Lev. 23:42). While the Passover has been made obligatory for strangers as well, this is not so with the booth. The reason for this, say the scholars, is that the Holy Name gave His protection during the Passover in Egypt to all true

believers, both homeborn Israelites and strangers, whereas the cloud in the wilderness served as a cover for the camp of Israel alone, even though strangers were permitted to enter it; that is why the entrance of strangers into the booth is permissible to them but is not obligatory for them, in the opinion of those who say that the making of the booth is caused only by the cloud which served as a cover for Israel in the wilderness. However, in the opinion of those who do not concede that the making of the booth is caused by the cloud, but rather ascribe it to the fact that the children of Israel dwelt in booths upon their exodus from Egypt, the reason citizens alone were singled out is that strangers dwell in booths at all times. This being so, what sense would there have been in the Scripture obligating them to dwell in a booth? One might supply another reason, namely, that all ordinances have been handed down on the basis of the people's ability to perform them. Consequently, dwelling in booths has been made a duty only for those who have landed property of their own, as it is written in the Book of Ezra: *each one a booth upon his roof, and in their courtyards* (Neh. 8:16). The stranger, on the other hand, has no landed property; how then could Scripture make it a duty for him?

44. Seventh, as to the manner of "dwelling" in the booth, this is not to be taken literally but should be interpreted in relation to its cause, i.e., to the statement: *in booths have I made the children of Israel to dwell, when I brought them out of the land of Egypt* (Lev. 23:43). The meaning of this "dwelling" is clearly general, i.e., sitting, lying, eating, drinking, reading the Scriptures, praying—in short, doing all the things that one does in one's house. However, one should not do ordinary kinds of work in it, since one ought to perform the ordinance of sitting in the booth in a reverent and respectful manner.

45. The booth should be built in the open, and it should have the shape of a house, with a door and doorposts; walls of branches are not necessary, and bare walls of stone or wood may be used instead. Its size should be at least sufficient for a person to sit and lie comfortably, but one may make it as large as one is able to.

46. If a man lets pass the time proper for the making of the booth and fails to build it at the beginning of the seven days, or if he builds it and it collapses of itself, he may build it in the middle of the seven days; even if it happens on the last day of the seven, it is his duty to make a booth and dwell in it. Those who draw their rules for the manner of constructing the booth from the phrase *And ye shall take for yourselves on the first day* say that the building must take place at the beginning of the festival only. The truth, however, is that Scripture makes it our duty to dwell in the booth all through the seven days. Since the duty of building it is caused by the duty of dwelling in it, it follows that it is our duty to build it at any time within the seven days, in order that we may fulfill the duty of dwelling in it. It seems that this is why Scripture did not expressly direct the making of the booth. Had Scripture done so, it would have had to specify also the time of its building, and it would have appeared as if the making of the booth were to take place only at that particular time and at no other. That is why the duty of building it has been made to depend upon the duty of dwelling in it, with the result that as long as these seven days last it is our duty to have it built.

47. The Law explains the reason for the making of the booth by saying: *that your generations may know that in booths have I made the children of Israel to dwell* (Lev. 23:43). Scholars, however, are in disagreement. Some say that *that in booths have I made the children of Israel to dwell* alludes to the cloud which served as a screen for them in the wilderness, as it is alluded to also in *He spread a cloud for a screen* (Ps. 105:39). Others say that the cloud was not really used for a screen, and that *He spread a cloud for a screen* alludes to the cloud serving as a beacon to indicate the way for them in the daytime, just as it is written of the nighttime: *And a fire to give light in the night* (Ps. 105:39). There was only one cloud, not seven, as the commentators think, or three clouds. Moreover, in the verse, *He spread a cloud for a screen, screen* does not indicate that the cloud was situated directly over them. Rather, it is possible that it went ahead of them, just as the curtain is called *the veil of the*

screen (Exod. 35:12), although it was placed in front of the Ark of the covenant, and not over it; nor could it have been called *the veil of the screen* with reference solely to the time when the children of Israel were traveling, at which time it might conceivably have been placed over the Ark. Therefore, say they, the true reason for *in booths have I made the children of Israel to dwell* is that when they came out of Egypt and camped at Sukkoth, each one of them made a booth for himself, to dwell in it and to provide shade from the heat of the sun; that is why the making of the booth has been made a duty, so that it might serve as a memorial.

48. However, the question suggests itself that if this happened so soon after their exodus from Egypt, why was the matter adjourned until the seventh month? Scholars answer this question in various ways: some say that because the Feast of Passover takes place in the early part of the first month of Nisan, it was necessary to delay the Festival of Booths until the seventh month, so that the hearts of the people might exhaust the joy of the Feast of Passover and be ready to receive the Festival of Booths with overwhelming affection. Also because Passover falls in the month of Nisan, which is the first of the months of the civil year, it was proper to assign the Festival of Booths to Tishri, which is the first month in the reckoning of sabbatical and Jubilee years. Others say that it has been put off until this late time because then the leaves of trees are fresh and full of natural moisture. It is possible to say also that the reason was that the children of Israel did not make any booths in the wilderness until the time of Tishri, because they had no need for booths until the arrival of winter, when such would serve as a shelter from the rains; and the beginning of the arrival of winter and cold is the time of Tishri.

49. An additional possible reason is that the Sabians believed in the divinity of the heavenly host of stars and ascribed all the actions and happenings in the lower world of the earth to the power of the heavenly lights and to their influence, as demonstrated in the growth of plants, and as formulated in the verse, *And for the precious things of the fruit of the sun, and for the precious things of the yield of the moons* (Deut. 33:14). Now when

they observed the weakening of the powers of the heavenly bodies over the earthly plants at the time of the sun's entrance into the sign of Libra, which is the season of the year that we are speaking of, they were plunged into sadness and mourning, in contrast with their joy in the spring month of Nisan. That is why the Law purposely appointed the making of the booth at this time, to be a time of gladness, pleasure, and enjoyment of the plants of the earth. That is also why God in His Law commanded us to take the branches not of trees subject to wilting but of those whose leaves are ever fresh and do not wilt with the waning of the power of the heavenly lights as these decline in their course. All this was done in order to controvert their mistaken belief and to demonstrate that all things stand under His providence and that if some actions seem to be performed by intermediaries, the latter are but like a chisel in the hands of the stonecutter.

50. The Eighth Day of Solemn Assembly is not properly an integral part of the Festival of Booths, and is not called a day of festival, but only a day of assembly. Scholars interpret the word "assembly" in the sense of "congregation," from *An assembly of treacherous men* (Jer. 9:1). The truth, however, is that it is derived from "detention," i.e., we are to detain ourselves in the House of the Lord longer than during other holidays. The scholars go on to explain that the children of Israel used to detain themselves in the House of the Lord during all holidays, but that this day alone was so designated because there was no other matter pertaining to it by which it might be designated, and that is why it was named simply the Day of Assembly. The rejoinder to this explanation is that the seventh day of the Feast of Unleavened Bread is likewise designated as a day of assembly. It would seem, therefore, that the children of Israel used to make a particularly lengthy assembly on those days because they marked the end of these holidays.

51. As for the reason why this assembly has been appointed on that day, which is the twenty-second day of the month, it might be because the average lunar month consists of twenty-eight days, from the starting point to the ending point, or a little less. Now

the days of the month comprise four periods; during the last period, because of the paucity of the light of the moon, they used to make no rejoicings or holidays; that is why the Law commanded us to make the first day of this last period a holiday, which is the Eighth Day of Solemn Assembly, in order to refute their false belief.

II. REWARD AND PUNISHMENT

1. I observe that scholars hold varying views as to what happens to a man who has both merits and sins on his record; namely, three views. Some say that the man receives reward for his merits and punishment for his sins, and they refer for proof to the verse *For the work of a man will he requite unto him, and cause every man to find according to his ways* (Job 34:11). Others say that a man can belong only to one of the two permanent categories: he can be among the men of everlasting reward or among the men of everlasting punishment; and they refer for proof to the verse *some to everlasting life, and some to reproaches and everlasting abhorrence* (Dan. 12:2), no other category being mentioned therein.

2. The adherents of the third view say that if the merits are more numerous than the sins, both are weighed one against the other, and the man is judged favorably on the basis of the remaining merits; or he is judged unfavorably, if the sins are more numerous. If the merits and the sins are equal, his reward is canceled by his loss, and he comes out devoid of both reward and punishment. This is the theory called "the weighing on the scales." This weighing on the scales is done not according to the mere number of sins and merits but by their size, since obviously if a man, on the one hand, has killed another, and, on the other hand, has returned a lost article to its rightful owner, these two deeds cannot cancel one another. For proof of this view they refer to the verse *None of his righteous deeds that he has done shall be remembered* (Ezek. 18:24), which could not possibly mean that because he had committed a minor sin he has forfeited all his merits. This would not be fair, as he would be like a person

who had done us many favors worth a thousand ducats and then had caused us a minor bit of damage worth one ducat; we could not in justice condemn him utterly for this one bit of damage. The same would be true of this righteous man spoken of by Ezekiel, were it not that the enormity of his sin outweighed all his merits, and he was judged by the remaining balance of his sin. The same is true of a sinner who has performed a deed of outstanding righteousness. This, then, is the just judgment, according to this view, and in fact the Law states expressly that merit steps into the place of sin and cancels it, namely, in the verse, *But unto the damsel thou shalt do nothing* (Deut. 22:26), her merit being set forth in the following verse, *For he found her in the field; the betrothed damsel cried, and there was none to save her.*

3. To be sure, the Law says in another place, regarding the rule for sacrifices offered as a vow or as a donation: *And when ye offer a sacrifice of peace offerings . . . It shall be eaten the same day ye offer it, and on the morrow; and if aught remains until the third day it shall be burned with fire. And if it be eaten at all on the third day, it is a vile thing, it shall not be accepted* (Lev. 19:5–7), i.e., it shall not be counted as a sacrifice for the man who offered it, meaning that the sacrifice eaten in a proper fashion during the two previous days shall be annulled by the fact that it had been eaten unlawfully on the single third day. This seemingly contradicts the weighing on the scales. Two explanations of this are possible. The phrase *it shall not be accepted* may be construed as referring to the last part of the sacrifice only, and not to that eaten previously. Or else the last part of the deed may be the major one, and the demerit caused by the eating on the third day may not be equal to the merit earned by what was eaten on the preceding two days, but may exceed it, which is similar to the verse in Ezekiel, *None of his righteous deeds that he has done shall be remembered.*

4. As for the first view, that man receives reward for his merits and punishment for his sins, it is impossible, inasmuch as merit involves commendation and sin involves reprimand, and it is im-

possible that a man should be the recipient of reprimand and commendation at the same time. The second view, which holds that a man must belong to one of two categories, is likewise impossible, because if his merits are less than his sins he would belong with those who suffer eternal punishment. Where, then, would be the reward for his merits? This is clearly contrary to justice, and even more so if a man has an equal share of both merits and sins.

5. [The Rabbanites say that] man's [deeds] are calculated on New Year's Day. If it is found that his sins are more numerous than his merits, he becomes one of the people of Hell, even if he has some merits; however, if he repents he may cancel the punishment for his evil deeds, so that only his merits will remain. If his merits are more numerous than his sins, he becomes one of the people of Paradise, and his few sins are regarded as of no account. In case his sins and his merits balance each other, if he repents his sins within the ten days of mercy from New Year's Day to the Day of Atonement, he is regarded as meritorious and is counted with the righteous. If he does not earn the merit of repentance, he is counted with the wicked, and all his merits are as nothing. They thus divide them into three groups: those perfectly righteous, those absolutely wicked, and those who are intermediate; and it is the latter group that is referred to in their aforementioned opinion. This theory, however, clearly constitutes a perversion of justice, since it implies that God does not repay everyone exactly according to his deeds.

6. According to the third and preferable view, i.e., the belief in the weighing on the scales, a man's merits are weighed against his sins according to the relative weight and importance of the merits and the sins, and the man is judged by the remaining balance, whether merit or sin, as it is written: *Let me be weighed in a just balance, that God may know my integrity* (Job 31:6). We are therefore to believe that even the righteous fall into several categories according to the relative quantity of the balance of their merits; were this not so, *He who sits in judgment upon all the earth would not be doing justice* (Gen. 18:25).

7. As for him whose merits and sins are equal, his reward is

canceled by his punishment, and he comes out bereft of both, just like a person who has done neither good nor evil and has neither reward nor punishment due him. However, if he earns the merit of repentance, for the purpose of canceling the punishment due him for his sins, he is granted the merit of receiving the reward for his merits. This is what a thorough examination of the problem forces us to believe, both from the viewpoint of pure reason and from that of the scriptural text. And now let us commence explaining the matter of repentance.

8. Know that the matter of repentance is a great kindness and bounty which the Holy Name has vouchsafed to mankind, so that if a man commit a sin, he might repent, and the Holy Name would forgive his sin and cancel the punishment due him for it, and he might become again one of the community of the meritorious, since the punishment for evil deeds is, in one way, subject to cancellation by the Almighty.

9. We do not say that repentance is an absolute kindness on God's part. Rather, we say that man is composed of opposites, and accordingly, his actions are also of opposite nature, flowing from his deficient or superficient qualities. Therefore it is just that man should be vouchsafed the privilege of acquiring merit by repentance, for the Holy Name does not pervert justice, as it is written: *As I live, says the Lord, I have no pleasure in the death of the wicked* (Ezek. 33:11); that is why *there is a wicked man that prolongs his life in his evil-doing* (Eccles. 7:15).

10. The root of the concept of repentance is our belief that man is possessed of complete ability and perfectly free will to do whatever he wishes, whether good or other than good . . . provided that it be nothing so evil as to involve punishment. . . . That is why repentance, as explained by scholars, has two aspects, one of obligation and one of necessity. The aspect of necessity flows from our knowledge that it is the only way to cancel the punishment for evil deeds. The aspect of obligation flows from the Law, since repentance is one of the duties contained therein, as it is written: *thou wilt return to the Lord, thy God* (Deut. 4:30); i.e., in order to receive the reward for it. For inasmuch as man has been

vouchsafed the privilege of earning merit by repentance, and is under the necessity of performing it in order to cancel the punishment for his evil deeds, the Law has made it obligatory for him to receive a reward for it, just as he does receive a reward for performing other positive ordinances. That is why it is fitting for us to give praise to Him for it.

11. Man needs to do repentance only in order to cancel a sin or an evil deed, as it is written: *Return, O Israel, unto the Lord, thy God, for thou hast stumbled in thine iniquity* (Hos. 14:2), showing that Israel did not become liable to repentance except by reason of their stumbling in their sin. The incitement to repentance, however, is a matter of absolute kindness on the part of the Holy Name, and not a matter of necessity for Him.

12. Man may be moved to repentance in four ways. First, when he observes another man being rebuked for something similar to what he himself is guilty of, he, too, ought to do repentance for his deed. Second, when he sees his neighbor being chastised by suffering for his sins, he ought to search his own actions to see whether they might be similar to the actions of the chastised man; if they are similar to the chastised man's actions, he ought to do repentance for them. This, however, is true only if the actions of the chastised person appear to be contrary to rectitude; if they are seen to be in accordance with rectitude, the sufferings imposed on the chastised person may be a manifestation of God's love for him. Third, when he himself is exhorted by word of the divine mouth to do repentance, he ought to repent. Fourth, by way of chastisement and sufferings inflicted on himself for his evil deeds, whereat he ought to repent and turn back from the evil deeds he has done and thereby save himself from further punishment. There is a hint of this in the verse, *For God speaks in one way, even in two, though man perceives it not* (Job 33:14).

13. The Holy Name is not under any obligation to spare the evildoer until he repents, since this might serve as an incitement to the wicked to do evil, like the person who says, "I will sin now and repent later." If, therefore, the Holy Name does occasionally lengthen the days of the evildoer, it is, according to the scholar,

not a frequent occurrence. The same principle applies in the case of the true believer in the one and only God, whom the Holy Name is not obliged to remove from life before he strays into the belief in many gods, if He knows that he will so stray eventually.

14. There are twelve aspects to proper repentance. First, the true essence of repentance is regret of one's evil deeds. Second is the abandonment of the evil deed. Third is the hatred of it. Fourth is the submission to repentance with all its conditions. Fifth is confession. Sixth is the condition imposed by the Law as an accompaniment of repentance; while the Temple at Jerusalem was yet standing, this was the duty to offer a sacrifice, but now there remains only the utterance of our lips, as it is written: *so will we render for bullocks the offering of our lips* (Hos. 14:3). Seventh, man must not postpone repentance for long after the feeling of regret—like the one who says, "I will sin now and repent later"—unless he is compelled by circumstances beyond his control to do so. Eighth, he must renounce the evil deed for the sake of its very vileness. Ninth, he must also not do anything like it in the future. Tenth, he must take it upon himself not to do it again at another time. Eleventh, he must do repentance with the intention of canceling the punishment for his evil deed. Twelfth, he must do repentance because it is a duty, like all other positive ordinances in the Law.

15. Repentance does not cancel the punishment due from a human tribunal but only the punishment to come from the hands of God since He alone knows the contents of the human heart.

16. The gates of repentance are open to receive full repentance from all who are penitent for their sins, so that the Holy Name might forgive them their punishment and grant them the good reward for their fulfillment of a positive ordinance. The gate of repentance is open equally to all men—not, as others say, that men are divided into categories in this respect—providing repentance is offered according to its proper order. To be sure, men are divided there into categories according to the great or small number of their merits, but they all are granted entry through the gate of repentance, as it is written: *and let him return unto the Lord, and*

he will have compassion upon him, and to our God, for he will abundantly pardon (Isa. 55:7).

17. Inasmuch as man knows not beforehand the time of his death, he should be [prompt] to repent, so that the time of his death might not overtake him and send him on without penitence; rather should he repent before this, as well as acquire the merit of good deeds.

18. The Law makes our repentance in our Dispersion a condition of our redemption, as it is written: *And thou shalt return unto the Lord, thy God, and hearken unto his voice . . . then the Lord, thy God, will turn thy captivity and have compassion upon thee* (Deut. 30:2–3).

19. Man should do penitence constantly and should conquer his desires in order to be saved from the punishment for evil deeds, since he cannot be certain but that his deeds may contain something which requires repentance. He should be among the humble and the subdued, so that the glory of the Holy Name might dwell in him, for this is the goal of all human endeavor, as the Prophet has expressed it: *For thus said the high and lofty One, who inhabits eternity, whose name is holy: I dwell in the high and holy place, and also with him who is of a contrite and humble spirit, to revive the spirit of the humble, and to revive the heart of the contrite ones* (Isa. 57:15), i.e., to make them deserving of the life of the world to come.

SAMUEL BEN MOSES AL-MAĠRIBĪ

SAMUEL ben Moses al-Maġribī was, as his surname indicates, a member of a family of North African origin. He himself, however, lived in Cairo,[1] in Egypt, where he earned his living as a physician.

In 1434 Samuel completed his code of Karaite law, which he wrote in Arabic and entitled *The Guide* (Arabic *al-Muršid*). It is divided into twelve sections and is written in a concise, orderly, and easily understandable style. Although he occasionally attacks Rabbanite views and customs, his tone is generally moderate and he readily adopts Rabbanite customs when they seemed to him commendable and in keeping with Karaite law.

Samuel's code is the last major Karaite work of its kind written in Arabic; all later ones, so far as we know, were written in Hebrew. It was soon completely overshadowed by the legal code of Elijah Bašyatchi, but as late as 1722 a full Hebrew translation of it was made, and in 1757 a new Hebrew rendering of the portion dealing with the calendar was prepared, showing that it was still held in considerable esteem. Only a few portions of it have so far been published.

FROM *THE GUIDE* OF SAMUEL BEN MOSES AL-MAĠRIBĪ

THE KARAITE HOLIDAYS (Second Half Year)

I. Passover

1. . . . You must know that the Creator imposed the ordinance of Passover upon the children of Israel at the time of their exodus from Egypt. In it are mentioned several obligations, some of which applied only to them who were in Egypt and not to future

1. Simḥah Isaac Lutzki's (18th century) statement that Samuel was "one of the scholars of Damascus" (Mann, p. 1418) is evidently an error.

generations; e.g., *On the tenth day of this month, they shall take to them every man a lamb, according to their fathers' houses, a lamb for a household; and if the household be too little for a lamb, then shall he and his neighbor . . . take one . . . and ye shall keep it until the fourteenth day of this month . . . and they shall take of the blood . . . and thus shall ye eat it* (Exod. 12:3–11). So also concerning the Prophet's command to them: *And ye shall take a bunch of hyssop . . .* (Exod. 12:22).

2. Other obligations applied both to them and to future generations; e.g., *but on the first day ye shall put away leaven out of your houses* (Exod. 12:15), which implies the removal of all leaven before the arrival of the time of the slaughtering of the paschal lamb, meaning before the first part of the first day of the seven days of unleavened bread. This is similar, in its application to future generations, to the ordinance *Ye shall kindle no fire throughout your habitations upon the sabbath day* (Exod. 35:3). . . . This is confirmed by the verses *Thou shalt not offer the blood of my sacrifice with leavened bread* (Exod. 23:18), and *Thou shalt not offer the blood of my sacrifice with leavened bread* (Exod. 34:25). It follows from this that we must remove all leaven in its entirety before the arrival of the aforementioned time, and we must leave no trace whatsoever of it with us, either visible or hidden, in so far as this lies within our power.

3. We must also purify our vessels from all trace of leaven. Those vessels that are made of copper or iron are to be cleansed with boiling water and then scoured with a polishing agent, while tools like knives, roasting spits, pothooks, and the like must be cast into the fire and kept there until their surfaces are at white heat. As for vessels made of wood, water should be brought to a boil in a large copper tub and the vessels should be immersed in it until whatever grease and juices are contained within them are extracted. Vessels made of clay, such as bowls, plates, jugs, and others, cannot be perfectly cleansed of what they have absorbed and must therefore be thoroughly washed with water and put aside, not to be used until after the holiday.

4. Just as we are obliged to remove all solid leaven, so also is it

our duty to remove all things derived from it by fermentation, such as acid things, like vinegar sauce, sour milk, acid sauces, sour groats, fruit beer, and beer made of wheat or barley; likewise preserves containing starch or flour, and similar things.

5. As for antimony powders and eye powders which have a slight admixture of starch, or compresses and poultices, in the compounding and preparation of which a pinch of flour is added, or bread and biscuit which have spoiled and have changed their nature entirely by being turned into something resembling caked dust—all these we need not remove. Nor are we forbidden to wear clothes having a glossy surface composed partly of starch, since such starch has undergone a chemical change and has been converted from leaven into something else.

6. Just as we are obligated to remove the aforementioned leaven and its fermented derivatives from our immediate vicinity, so also is it forbidden to us to have them present and at hand anywhere in our dwellings and on our property during the seven days of the festival, as it is written: *seven days shall there be no leaven found in your houses* (Exod. 12:19), and again: *and there shall no leavened bread be seen with thee, neither shall there be leaven seen with thee in all thy borders* (Exod. 13:7), and again, in the Book of Deuteronomy: *And there shall be no leaven seen with thee in all thy borders seven days* (Deut. 16:4).

7. Just as we are forbidden to have leaven in our possession, so also are we forbidden to eat it during that period, as it is written: *Thou shalt eat no leavened bread with it* (Deut. 16:3), and again, *Ye shall eat nothing leavened* (Exod. 12:20). He who eats anything leavened incurs the penalty of death, as it is written: *for whosoever shall eat leaven, from the first day to the seventh, that soul shall be cut off from Israel* (Exod. 12:15), and again, *for whosoever shall eat leaven, that soul shall be cut off* (Exod. 12:19).

8. Even as we are forbidden to eat leaven, so are we obligated to eat unleavened bread during the aforementioned seven days, from the first day to the last. We shall mention this again after we have mentioned the Passover sacrifice.

9. The prohibition of possessing leavened bread and leaven

products after the Passover sacrifice during the remainder of the seven days, the prohibition of the eating of it, and the obligation of eating unleavened bread during those seven days did not apply to the Jews who came out of Egypt, since they were not charged with these duties; they were charged solely with the Passover sacrifice and with the eating of unleavened bread in conjunction with it. They were also charged with the removal of leavened bread and leaven products solely before the offering of the sacrifice, and they were forbidden to possess leaven at the time of the offering only. After they had made the sacrifice, none of the aforementioned things were obligatory upon them; this was explained by our Sages in their writings.

II. The Passover Sacrifice

1. The time of the Passover sacrifice is the first part of the first evening of these aforementioned seven days, i.e., the eve of the fifteenth of Nisan. This time, which is regarded as belonging to the fourteenth of Nisan of the regular calendar, is called "twilight," as it is written: *In the first month, on the fourteenth day of the month, at twilight, is the Lord's Passover* (Lev. 23:5). Its beginning is the setting of the sun, and its end the disappearance of the last brightness of daylight, and this is the period of dusk which lingers for some time after the sinking of the last portion of the disk of the sun.

2. This time is designated by three names: first, "twilight," as mentioned above; second, "evening," as in the phrase *And it came to pass in the evening, that the quails came up* (Exod. 16:13), following the statement in the preceding verse, *At twilight ye shall eat flesh;* third, "sunset," as in the phrase, *at sunset, at the time when thou didst come forth out of Egypt* (Deut. 16:6).

3. This time is regarded as part of two days: of the common day, which is the fourteenth of Nisan, as mentioned above; and of the legal day, which is the fifteenth. The common day begins after the sinking of twilight and continues until its next sinking; this is the day as reckoned for the purpose of offering the sac-

rifice. The legal day begins with sunset and lasts until the next sunset.

4. The Passover should consist of both lambs and kids, as it is written: *ye shall take it from the sheep and from the goats* (Exod. 12:5). A person may take either a lamb or a kid, as he may choose, but the people collectively may not take lambs exclusively, or kids exclusively, inasmuch as they are obligated to take of both; the choice of only one kind of animal is thus open to individuals but not to the community as a whole. The animal chosen must be a male, perfect and free of blemish, and aged exactly one year, no more and no less, as it is written: *A perfectly formed lamb, a male, one year old, this shall it be for you* (Exod. 12:5).

5. Should someone say, "Scripture says: *And thou shalt sacrifice the Passover unto the Lord, thy God, sheep and cattle* (Deut. 16:2); why, then, have you limited it to those two kinds, lambs and kids, only?" the answer would be as follows: the two species mentioned, sheep and cattle, are not both meant to be offered as Passover; rather are the sheep alone to be used for the Passover, while the cattle are to be offered as holy offerings, i.e., peace offerings, for the sake of the women and children of the household. For only the adult males, who have been obligated to make the pilgrimage to Jerusalem, are permitted to eat of the Passover, as it is written: *all thy males shall appear before the Lord* (Deut. 16:16), which is analogous to *thou shalt smite every male thereof* (Deut. 20:13), meaning the grown-up male persons, since it is written in the following verse: *But the women, the children, and the cattle . . . thou shalt take for a prey*. The members of the household thus require another sacrifice to supply their needs, wherefore the cattle should be sacrificed as peace offerings, so that they may eat of them to their satisfaction. All this, however, applies only to the Passover observed by succeeding generations, since the Passover offered in Egypt consisted exclusively of lambs and was eaten by both adult males and others, as it is written: *according to the number of the souls* (Exod. 12:4).

6. What we have said about the cattle being meant for peace

offerings is confirmed by the statement in the story of King Josiah: *And Josiah gave to the people, from the flock, lambs and kids, all of them for the Passover offerings, to all the people that were present, to the number of thirty thousand; and from the cattle, three thousand; these from the king's substance . . .* (II Chron. 35:7). This is followed by the statement that they prepared the Passover sacrifices for themselves and cooked the peace offerings for the members of the household, as it is written: *And they roasted the Passover in the fire, according to the ordinance; as for the holy offerings, they boiled them in pots, and in caldrons, and in pans, and carried them quickly to all the people* (II Chron. 35:13). This shows that they used the sheep for Passover and the cattle for peace offerings.

III. Place, Manner of Preparation, and Time of the Passover

1. The place of the slaughtering of the Passover is the House of God, as it is written: *Thou mayest not sacrifice the Passover within any of thy gates . . . but only at the place which the Lord, thy God, shall choose* (Deut. 16:5). This necessarily refers specifically to the Passover of the post-Exodus generations.

2. It must be prepared by way of roasting only, as it is written: *And they shall eat the meat in that night, roasted with fire* (Exod. 12:8). In this respect the Passover in Egypt and the Passover of the succeeding generations are alike.

3. The place of the eating of the Passover is likewise the House of the Lord, as it is written: *And thou shalt roast it and eat it in the place which the Lord, thy God, shall choose* (Deut. 16:7). This cannot refer to Jerusalem, since it is written next: *and in the morning thou shalt turn and go to thy tents.* If we assume that it does refer to Jerusalem, it would follow from the sentence *and in the morning thou shalt turn and go to thy tents* that we are permitted to travel in the morning to our homes. Now it is well known that traveling during the holiday is forbidden, wherefore it necessarily follows that the aforementioned tents were set up in the squares of Jerusalem around the sanctuary, and that after the

pilgrims had spent the night observing the Passover, they went in the morning to their tents close by. This is further confirmed by the fact that the pilgrimage is required to continue for seven days, which is why we are obligated to remain in the place of the sanctuary until the expiration of this period. How then could it be possible for us to leave Jerusalem every morning to go to our homes? The interpretation given above is, therefore, the only one possible. This rule, too, refers only to the Passover of the succeeding generations and not to the Passover of Egypt.

4. The Passover may not be eaten raw or boiled in water, as it is written: *eat not of it raw, nor sodden with water* (Exod. 12:9).

5. The time of its eating is all through the night, but no part of it may be left until the morning, as it is written: *And ye shall let nothing of it remain until the morning* (Exod. 12:10), and again: *neither shall the fat of my feast remain all night until the morning* (Exod. 23:18). Nevertheless, if anything is left until the morning, it must be burned, as it is written: *but what remains of it until the morning ye shall burn with fire* (Exod. 12:10). Nor may any bone of it be broken, as it is written: *neither shall ye break a bone thereof* (Exod. 12:46).

6. In all these things the Passover of Egypt is equal to the Passover of the succeeding generations; but it differs in others, over and above those mentioned before. First, the blood of the Passover of Egypt was applied to the lintels and to the side doorposts, whereas the blood of the Passover of the succeeding generations was poured upon the altar. Second, the disposition of the fat of the Passover of Egypt is unknown to us—some say that the people ate it, since the prohibition of eating fat had not yet then been handed down—whereas the fat of the Passover of the succeeding generations was burned upon the altar, as it is written: *in offering the burnt offering and the fat, until night* (II Chron. 35:14).

7. As the Passover is offered and eaten, song and prayer of glorification of the Lord are to be recited over it, as it is written: *Ye shall have a song, as on the night when a feast is hallowed* (Isa. 30:29). This, too, applies only to the Passover of the succeeding generations.

8. The Passover is to be eaten with unleavened bread and with bitter herbs, as it is written: *roasted with fire, and unleavened bread; with bitter herbs shall they eat it* (Exod. 12:8). In this respect the Passover of Egypt is the same as the Passover of the succeeding generations. We shall mention the unleavened bread and the regulations concerning it later on, God willing.

IV. Passover Falling on a Sabbath

1. When that night, i.e., the night of the fifteenth of Nisan, falls on the Sabbath, the Passover should not be postponed until after the Sabbath but should be performed at its exact time; this is by analogy of the supplementary sacrifices which are offered on the Sabbath. And in another place it is written: *the matter of each day upon its day* (Lev. 23:37), following the preceding sentence: *to offer a fire offering to the Lord*. There can be no doubt that the Passover comes under this rule of *the matter of each day upon its day,* since it is mentioned in the first of the series of sections of which this rule is the concluding one; to wit, in the verse *In the first month, on the fourteenth day of the month, at twilight, is the Lord's Passover* (Lev. 23:5); furthermore, the Passover comes also under the rule of *to offer a fire offering to the Lord,* inasmuch as it is an offering to God.

2. This is confirmed by the fact that the Law imposes the death penalty upon him who does not offer the Passover sacrifice at its appointed time, while able to do so, as it is written: *But the man who is clean, and is not on a journey, and forbears to perform the Passover, that soul shall be cut off from his people* (Num. 9:13).

3. This is thus similar to circumcision, which must not be postponed until after the eighth day, except for a legal cause of delay, as we have explained in our discussion of the law governing circumcision. Also, the ordinance of the Passover was handed down prior to the ordinance of the Sabbath, and the latter was established subject to the observance of the Passover, just as it was established subject to the observance of circumcision. . . . Moreover, the Passover is not a sacrifice involving any revenue to the

priest, nor is it a species of individual sacrifice, by reason of which it could be deferred until after the Sabbath.

V. Postponement of the Passover

1. The hindrances which prevent the observance of the Passover at its exact time are ritual uncleanness caused by contact with a dead body, or a journey which makes it impossible for a person to reach the sanctuary in time. The performance of the Passover is then postponed until the second month, Iyyar, as it is written: *If any man be unclean by reason of a dead body, or be on a journey afar off . . . he shall perform the Passover unto the Lord. In the second month, on the fourteenth day, at twilight* (Num. 9:10–11). . . . By analogy, the same applies to persons afflicted with flux and leprosy, and to those gravely ill. It follows also that one should not undertake a journey knowing in advance that he might be prevented thereby from performing the Passover; nor should one deliberately expose one's self to ritual uncleanness which would have the same result. All those who are not prevented by any of the aforementioned hindrances, and yet fail to perform the Passover, incur the penalty of death. . . .

2. He who has been prevented by any of these hindrances must come on the fourteenth of the second month to the House of the Lord; he must cleanse one of the chambers of his house from all leaven; he must eat therein the Passover with unleavened bread and bitter herbs; and he must burn the remainder of the Passover by daybreak. On the next day he may eat leaven and go about his daily business, since he is obligated to perform the Passover sacrifice only, this being the only thing from which the legally valid hindrance had exempted him in the first month. As for making the fifteenth of Nisan a day of festival and a holy convocation and eating unleavened bread for seven days, all these had remained obligatory upon him in the First Passover, just as they were obligatory upon persons not subject to the aforementioned legal hindrances. . . .

3. As for a proselyte, the rule is that he is subject to all the duties

incumbent upon an Israelite, which we have mentioned, as regards the First Passover and the Second Passover, since it is written of the First Passover: *One law shall there be for the homeborn and for the stranger sojourning among you* (Exod. 12:49), and of the Second Passover: *And if a stranger shall sojourn among you, he shall perform the Passover unto the Lord, according to the statute of the Passover and according to the ordinance thereof* (Num. 9:14).

VI. Rules of the Passover

1. The ordinance of the Passover comprises the six things mentioned in the section beginning: *And the Lord said unto Moses and Aaron, This is the ordinance of the Passover* (Exod. 12:43). First, *No alien shall eat thereof*. Second, *But every man's servant, bought for money, when thou hast circumcised him, then shall he eat thereof*. Third, *A sojourner and a hired servant shall not eat of it*. Fourth, *In one house shall it be eaten*. Fifth, *thou shalt not carry aught of the meat abroad out of the house*. Sixth, *neither shall ye break a bone thereof. . . .*

2. The statute of the Passover comprises the other things mentioned concerning it, in addition to these six.

3. Some parts of this ordinance and statute apply only to the Passover of Egypt, others apply only to the Passover of the succeeding generations, while still others apply to both; all this has been explained above.

VII. Was the Passover Performed in the Wilderness of Sinai?

1. If one should ask about the generation of the wilderness, whether or not they performed the Passover during the forty years of their sojourn in the wilderness, the answer is this: in the second year after the Exodus they performed it according to its rules and ate unleavened bread, as it is written: *And they kept the Passover in the first month, on the fourteenth day of the month, at twilight, in the wilderness of Sinai* (Num. 9:5); this is

in conformity with God's command to them: *according to all its ordinances and all its statutes shall ye keep it* (Num. 9:3).

2. As for the remaining years of their sojourn in the wilderness, all those who were themselves circumcised and had no uncircumcised person in their possession did not fail to perform the Passover. This is demonstrated by the praise bestowed by the Prophet Moses upon those who were about to enter the Land of Palestine, as it is written concerning them: *And ye who did cleave unto the Lord, your God* (Deut. 4:4); he could not possibly have praised them had they neglected to observe this important ordinance in the absence of any legal hindrance. Had they been so neglectful, Scripture would have branded them with reproof, yet this we do not find to be the case.

3. If one should ask, "Whereof, then, did they make the unleavened bread which they were required to eat with the Passover?" I would answer thus: The Israelites received whatever they required for baking unleavened bread by importation from the settled localities in their vicinity. This is proved by the fact that they were charged with other things for which they did not have the material necessary to make them, e.g., the showbread, the candles to be lighted in the sanctuary, the meal offerings, the wine for the drink offerings; the wherewithal for these was evidently brought to them for sale from settled places nearby. The same must have been true also with regard to flour for unleavened bread.

4. Today, however, by reason of our many sins, we are scattered over the four corners of the earth, we are dispersed in the lands of the Gentiles, we are soiled with their ritual uncleanness and unable to reach the House of the Lord, and our status is equivalent to that of persons ritually unclean or traveling far away. That is why this ordinance of the Passover sacrifice no longer applies to us, and the reason for this is our fathers' exceeding disobedience to God and our own following in their sinful footsteps. We therefore ask God, in His manifold mercies and great kindnesses, that He might fulfill upon us that which He had promised us through our Prophet Ezekiel, as it is written: *And I will sprinkle clean water upon you, and ye shall be clean* (Ezek. 36:25), and again:

And I will take you from among the nations, and I will gather you out of all the lands (Ezek. 36:24), *And ye shall dwell in the land that I gave to your fathers . . .* (Ezek. 36:28).

VIII. Other Rules Concerning the Passover

1. It is our duty on this first night of Passover to recite in our prayer the scriptural passages relating to the Passover. After this we are to gather in our houses and recite the biblical verses containing the account of the distressing servitude in which our fathers were living; of the two messengers, Moses and Aaron, who were sent to them to rescue them and who performed miracles in the presence of the pharaoh and his people; of the slaughter of the first-born of the Egyptians and the salvation of the first-born of the children of Israel; and of the exodus of the people of Israel from Egypt. We are to make this recitation in the most wondrous manner and add our own praise to God for all these mercies.

2. After this we are to pronounce the blessing over the unleavened bread and eat as much as we please of it, with bitter herbs, such as lettuce, endive, and celery.

3. During most of the night we are to recount to our children, wives, and guests what God had wrought in Egypt, as it is written: *And in order that thou mayest tell in the ears of thy son and of thy grandson what I have wrought upon Egypt* (Exod. 10:2). To be sure, it is our duty to discourse upon it always, throughout the year, as it is written: *that thou mayest remember the day when thou camest forth out of the land of Egypt all the days of thy life* (Deut. 16:3). But on this night we are to dwell on it to the greatest possible extent, and we are to do the same during the remainder of the seven days of the festival.

4. We are to regard this day, i.e., the first of the seven days of the festival, as a day of holy convocation, a holiday, and the Festival of Unleavened Bread, and we must refrain on that day from the kinds of work forbidden to be performed on holidays, which we shall mention in detail later on. The same thing applies to the seventh day. The proof of it is the verse *And on the first day there*

shall be for you a holy convocation, and on the seventh day also a holy convocation (Exod. 12:16), and again, *These are the holidays of the Lord, holy convocations . . . In the first month . . . And on the fifteenth day of the month . . . On the first day ye shall have a holy convocation . . . And ye shall bring a fire offering unto the Lord, seven days; on the seventh day there shall be a holy convocation* (Lev. 23:4–8); and in the section of Phinehas it is written: *And on the seventh day ye shall have a holy convocation* (Num. 28:25).

5. The first day has this additional mark over the seventh day in that its night is specifically designated as "the night of watching," as it is written: *It was a night of watching unto the Lord,* (Exod. 12:42); and its entire day is specifically designated as "the day of remembrance," as it is written: *And this day shall be unto you a day of remembrance* (Exod. 12:14).

6. The additional mark of the seventh day is that it is "the Day of Assembly," as it is written: *and on the seventh day shall be a solemn assembly unto the Lord, thy God* (Deut. 16:8). . . .

7. You must know that Scripture uses the word "festival" in reference to both of these days. Concerning the first day it is written: *and ye shall keep it a festival unto the Lord, throughout your generations* (Exod. 12:14); and concerning the seventh: *and on the seventh day shall be a festival unto the Lord* (Exod. 13:6).

8. All the seven days together are designated as "holidays," as it is written at the beginning of the list of festivals: *These are the holidays of the Lord* (Lev. 23:4). They are called also "the Feast of Unleavened Bread," as it is written in the Book of Chronicles: *And the children of Israel that were present at Jerusalem kept the festival of unleavened bread, seven days* (II Chron. 30:21), and in the Book of Ezra: *And they kept with joy the festival of unleavened bread, seven days* (Ezra 6:22); and in the Book of Ezekiel, speaking of the days to come when Jerusalem shall be rebuilt, it is written: *a feast of seven days, unleavened bread shall be eaten* (Ezek. 45:21).

9. The meaning of *holy convocation* is public recitation of that

which is holy, i.e., the recitation of the sections of the Law in which this festival is mentioned. Or it could mean a public announcement that it is a sacred or important day set aside for abstention from kinds of work forbidden on such days.

10. The meaning of *festival* (*ḥag̱*) is pilgrimage to Jerusalem from the villages and the cities and the tent camps surrounding Jerusalem, in fulfillment of the biblical ordinances, just as we say in Arabic, "we are making a pilgrimage" (*naḥuǧǧu*) and "So-and-so has made a pilgrimage" and similar expressions. This is in conformity with the biblical command: *all thy males shall appear before the Lord, thy God* (Deut. 16:16).

11. The word *festival,* that is, "pilgrimage," embraces also the circumambulation of the sanctuary; this is derived from the expressions: *They reeled to and fro* (yaḥoggu) *and staggered like a drunken man* (Ps. 107:27), *he walks in the circuit of heaven* (Job 22:14), *He sits above the circuit of the earth* (Isa. 40:22). This meaning of *festival* agrees with the expression *I will walk around thine altar, O Lord* (Ps. 26:6). Pilgrimage includes also the offering of sacrifices, i.e., the sacrifice of the Passover and others, as it is written: *the sacrifice of the festival of Passover* (Exod. 34:25), and again: *Bind ye the festival with cords* (Ps. 118:27), meaning the animal itself which is being sacrificed for the festival.

12. All these things are obligatory upon the people of the time of Israel's kingdom only, and not upon others.

IX. Kinds of Work Prohibited on Holidays

1. The kinds of work which are forbidden to us on a holiday and from which we must abstain during the two days of Passover are these:

2. We must not sell or buy or do any kind of work other than that which God has expressly permitted us to do in the way of the preparation of food, as it is written: *no manner of work shall be done in them, save that which every man must eat* (Exod. 12:16).

3. It follows from this that we are to prepare for ourselves all

that we need before the festival in the way of food, drink, etc., and have it ready in our possession and keeping. We are to slaughter before the festival whatever meat we wish to cook, since slaughtering is a kind of work independent of eating and there are several intermediate kinds of work between slaughtering and eating, such as skinning and cutting up the meat. Slaughtering thus signifies a means of transferring the animal from the state of life to the state of death and is thus similar, in its relation to eating, to cutting vegetables, grapes, and fruits from their stalks, all of which is forbidden on a holiday.

4. Likewise, it is forbidden to pick up what has dropped down from trees upon a holiday, be it fruit or anything else.

5. It is further forbidden to milk milch animals or grind and sift flour. And it is forbidden to catch fish or birds or pick up any that have dropped on our property or take eggs that have been laid by chickens and other birds on a holiday.

6. It is forbidden to split firewood with an ax or grind rock salt, seeds, or grains of perfume in a mortar.

7. We must not kindle fire or extinguish it. We are not, however, forbidden to have in our dwellings a fire previously kindled, since we have to leave it burning for the preparation of food. This being so, it follows that we may use it for lighting as well.

8. We must not sharpen knives or fan the fire with a blacksmith's or goldsmith's bellows.

9. We must not carry things in the streets and lanes and other public places, for this is designated as work, since it is written in the account of the Tabernacle: *Let neither man nor woman do any more work for the offering of the sanctuary* (Exod. 36:6), and their fulfillment of this command is expressed by the following phrase: *So the people were restrained from bringing;* this shows that the carrying of things in a public domain is called work; in fact, the Rabbanites count carrying as one of the principal varieties of work. Moreover, no exception was made in this respect, since Scripture says only: *save that which every man must eat* (Exod. 12:16). As for what they claim concerning the verse *and send portions to him for whom nothing is prepared* (Neh.

8:10), it is not a strong piece of evidence, that one might be guided by it, but is rather susceptible to varying interpretations; that is why we should adopt the safest explanation and prohibit carrying altogether.

10. We must not go out upon the public highways, into the outskirts of the city, or outside it; this is on the analogy of the laws governing the Sabbath. Likewise, it is forbidden to swim or to do any handclapping and dancing or to indulge in any other kind of sport and play, since all of this is the opposite of the sanctity required to be observed.

11. It is forbidden to hold judgment between litigants or undertake any labor from which we would benefit after the holiday.

12. In general, all work that is forbidden on the Sabbath is forbidden also upon the feast day, save what Scripture has excepted pertaining to the preparation of food.

13. All that we have said here concerning these two days of Passover applies also to the other holidays, which are days on which all kinds of work are forbidden, since it is written concerning these two days: *no manner of work shall be done in them, save that which every man must eat* (Exod. 12:16); and it is written concerning each one of these two days: *Ye shall do no work of labor* (Num. 28:18, 25). It follows that these two injunctions mean the same thing. Now the same injunction, *ye shall do no work of labor,* is repeated with reference to all the other holidays; it follows, therefore, that work essential to the preparation of food is permitted also on these other holidays.

14. These are the rules resulting from a rational examination into the requirements set forth in Scripture and from the opinions of the majority of scholars.

15. The expression *save that which every man must eat* (Exod. 12:16) means that which shall be consumed by thyself, myself, and others who are like us according to our daily requirements. As for anything in excess of it, which might be left over until after the holiday, the preparation of it is not permitted.

16. It is incumbent upon us to eat unleavened bread all through these seven days as a matter of duty and not as a voluntary matter,

as it is written: *Seven days shall ye eat unleavened bread* (Exod. 12:15), *Seven days shalt thou eat unleavened bread* (Exod. 13:6), and *Unleavened bread shall be eaten these seven days* (Exod. 13:7). These seven days, therefore, are to be complete, both at their beginning and at their end, as it is written: *In the first month, on the fourteenth day of the month, at even, ye shall eat unleavened bread, until the twenty-first day of the month, at even* (Exod. 12:18). . . .

17. A confirmation of what we have said concerning the duty of eating unleavened bread is contained in the fact that the biblical prohibition of eating leaven is immediately followed in the same verse by the command to eat unleavened bread, as it is written: *Thou shalt not eat with it any leaven, but for seven days thou shalt eat with it unleavened bread, the bread of poverty* (Deut. 16:3). Scripture thus forbids one thing in the beginning of the verse and requires another thing in the end of the same verse; just as the former is forbidden, so is the latter obligatory.

X. *Unleavened Bread*

1. We shall now deal with the subject of unleavened bread: its ingredients, the place of its making, the manner of its making, who is to make it, what conditions are to be observed in its making, how much dough is to be kneaded in each batch, and the meaning of its designation as *bread of poverty* (Deut. 16:3).

2. We say that unleavened bread denotes dough baked in an unleavened state, without any leaven whatever added to it.

3. As for what it should be made of, it may be made of wheat or barley or spelt or oats or rye. It may not be made of anything other than these five species of grain, since only these five are subject to leavening, whereas other grains are not.

4. The kneading should be done with cold water kept overnight in a vessel, after it has been drawn from the spring and has been well guarded from contamination by any leaven. The dough must not be kneaded with hot or tepid water.

5. The place of the making of the unleavened bread should be

away from the sun and its heat, so that the dough may not become heated and develop any leaven within it.

6. As for the manner of making it, it should be made into thin cakes. They should not be made thick, lest a part of some of them remain heated and develop leaven within it, which would make them forbidden to be eaten.

7. As for those who are to undertake the making of it, there should be not less than three persons. One person is to carry the dough from the kneading trough to the place where the baker takes it up and must see to it that no leaven gets mixed with it; the second person is to flatten the cakes of bread; and the third is to act as baker. If there are more than three persons, so much the better. All this applies to the work done after the dough has been kneaded. These men must be pious Israelites. A Gentile must not be charged with this work, unless indeed there be an emergency making it unavoidable [and even then] an Israelite should be associated with him to watch over him. Nor can it be entrusted to a person of disordered mind or a deaf-mute, i.e., one who can neither hear nor speak.

8. As for the conditions to be observed in its making, the baker should have at hand a container of cold water to moisten the bread cakes one at a time, and as soon as the water becomes warm he should replace it with another container of cold water and pour it out in a place where it will quickly scatter, without any particle of dough becoming mixed with it and remaining in it and thus forming a nucleus for fermentation.

9. As for the amount to be kneaded in one batch, each batch of dough should amount to no more than seven hundred and twenty drams. Those who prefer to be on the safe side, knead a little less than this amount.

10. As for the meaning of *bread of poverty,* scholars have uttered many different opinions concerning it, and we shall confine ourselves to the opinions of those who seem nearest to the truth.

11. Some say that this means literally the bread of the poor because poor people, in the severity of their destitution, will take some flour, knead it, and bake it into unleavened cakes which they

eat immediately, and because this is the sort of bread they have most often. Others say that it means bread that is injurious to the digestive apparatus of the body and causes harm to it. Still others say that it signifies bread suitable for the hardships of travel, since Scripture speaks of hardship in connection with travel, e.g., *He subjected my strength to hardship on the road* (Ps. 102:24); i.e., the traveler is hardly able to afford the delay of letting his dough ferment, since he is usually in a hurry to go on. This is confirmed by the words following the command to eat unleavened bread: *for in haste didst thou come forth out of the land of Egypt* (Deut. 16:3). Thus it is explained why we, too, must act in haste by making the necessary amount of unleavened bread close to the time of the eating of it, so that we may eat it in the prescribed legal manner and without anything harmful happening to it.

12. Having discussed the unleavened bread and its regulations, we shall now proceed to deal with the remaining matter, namely, the rest of the seven days, called "the workdays of the holiday."

XI. The Workdays of the Holiday

1. We say that these workdays, too, are designated as holidays and holy convocations, since they come under the statement *These are the holidays of the Lord, holy convocations* (Lev. 23:4), which forms the preamble to all the holidays. They are also comprised in the statement *These are the holidays of the Lord which ye shall proclaim to be holy convocations* (Lev. 23:37), which concludes the account of the holidays.

2. These workdays are called holidays because they differ from regular workdays in that we are forbidden on these days to engage in gainful occupations, commerce, and trades, except to the extent that we are compelled to, in order to provide for the expenditure we may be in need of and to prevent any danger to life. This applies, for example, to the irrigation of gardens and fields and the clearing of springs and streams which have become clogged. Likewise, we may prepare the necessary medicaments and do blood-

letting and other things required in the treatment of diseases and for the preservation of health. We may also dig graves and bury the dead and do all things necessary for human safety, such as repairing balustrades of stairs, locks, keys, doors, and walls. Likewise, we may press fruits which would otherwise dry out, such as olives, or gather fruits which might spoil, such as grapes, and we may sell and receive payment for them.

3. We may store crops in storehouses and remove flax from the vats in which it is soaking when there is danger of its rotting; we may likewise remove wool from the dyeing vats before it becomes damaged. In general, we may do everything that is urgent and cannot be neglected when failure to do it might cause harm.

4. As for other worldly things and things which are not urgent, we are not permitted to exert ourselves about them during these sacred days, so that the latter are distinguished thereby from other workdays. We also may not, during these days, contract or consummate a marriage, unless indeed it be a case of remarrying a divorced wife.

5. On each of these seven days we are obligated to offer an additional sacrifice over and above the permanent daily sacrifice; it is mentioned in the section of Phinehas and it is the same throughout the seven days—it is not larger on one day than on another. This, however, does not apply to the people of the Dispersion, wherefore there is no need for us to go into its particulars. . . .

XII. The Waving of the Sheaf

1. Scripture says, concerning the waving of the sheaf: *on the morrow after the sabbath the priest shall wave it* (Lev. 23: 11). The word *sabbath,* with the definite article, is meant to define the indeterminate noun *a sabbath,* mentioned previously at the beginning of the section dealing with the holidays, as it is written: *a sabbath unto the Lord in all your dwellings* (Lev. 23: 3). No one denies that this signifies the Sabbath in the sense in which the word is used in the story of Creation, since biblical usage has transferred this word from the general meaning of a day of abstention from work to the

particular rest on the seventh day of Creation and all the subsequent seventh days of every week.

2. It therefore remains for us to find out precisely which Sabbath this is, out of the several Sabbaths of the entire year. This can be done through the definition of the word *morrow* in the above verse, because when the *morrow* shall have been defined by proofs which we shall presently mention, it will thereby become clear which Sabbath is meant.

3. We say now that this *morrow* signifies one of the seven days of the Feast of Unleavened Bread. This is demonstrated by the fact that on that day there is mention of an extra sacrifice, in addition to the supplementary holiday sacrifice, as it is written: *And on the day when ye wave the sheaf, ye shall offer an unblemished lamb, one year old* (Lev. 23:12), and so on, to the end of the account of this extra sacrifice. Since this extra sacrifice comes under the general command *to bring a fire offering to the Lord* (Lev. 23:37), which covers the whole range of *These are the holidays of the Lord, holy convocations* (Lev. 23:4), and *These are the holidays of the Lord which ye shall proclaim to be holy convocations* (Lev. 23:37), it follows that this day called *morrow* must be one of the days of these several holidays. Now there is no other holiday mentioned in this chapter of Leviticus prior to the seven days of unleavened bread, to which we might possibly refer this extra sacrifice; nor does the order of subject matter in this chapter admit of it, since this extra sacrifice is mentioned immediately after the mention of the seven days of unleavened bread. Nor is there any holiday between Passover and Pentecost to which we might possibly refer it. Moreover, the general consensus of opinion is that there are no holidays other than the eighteen days expressly mentioned in Scripture. There remains, therefore, nothing else but that this day is one of the seven days of unleavened bread.

4. This being established, we say further that one of these seven days must be a Sabbath, and that it is to this Sabbath that the biblical ordinance refers, providing its morrow is part of the seven days. If this is not so, and its morrow is not part of the seven

days—a thing that would happen if the first of the seven days of unleavened bread fell on a Sunday—then this Sunday must be the day of the waving of the sheaf, and it is the preceding Sabbath which would be meant by *the sabbath* (Lev. 23:11), for the above-mentioned reason that its morrow must be part of the seven days of unleavened bread.

5. This is confirmed by the account of what was done by Joshua and the people who entered the Land of Canaan with him, of whom it is written: *And they ate of the produce of the land, on the morrow after the Passover, unleavened bread and parched grain, on the selfsame day* (Josh. 5:11). Now *the morrow after the Passover* was the fifteenth of Nisan, as it is written: *And they journeyed from Rameses in the first month, on the fifteenth day of the first month, on the morrow after the Passover* (Num. 33:3); i.e., the Passover being on the night of the fifteenth, its *morrow* was the day of the fifteenth. Now it is well known that the eating of unleavened bread and parched grain from the new crop is not permitted until after the waving of the sheaf, as it is written: *And ye shall eat neither bread, nor parched corn, nor fresh ears, until this selfsame day* (Lev. 23:14). This being so, it follows that in that year the Feast of Passover fell on a Sunday and that on that day they also made the offering of the sheaf and ate the unleavened bread and the parched grain. All this confirms what we have said about this day, namely, *the morrow after the Sabbath*.

6. We are then obligated to count fifty consecutive days, the last of which is the Feast of Pentecost. These fifty days comprise also seven Sabbaths and seven full weeks, as it is written: *And ye shall count for yourselves from the morrow after the sabbath . . . seven complete sabbaths. Until from the morrow after the seventh sabbath, ye shall count fifty days* (Lev. 23:15–16), and again in the Book of Deuteronomy: *Seven weeks shalt thou count for thyself* (Deut. 16:9).

7. The expression *seven complete sabbaths* means that each Sabbath is to serve as the concluding day of the week, by way of distinction from a Sabbath which falls in the middle of a different period of seven days, such a week not being regarded as complete

since it is not uniform with the sequence of the seven days of Creation. The meaning of *complete* is thus that the week is to conclude with a Sabbath, which conforms with the ordinance, *Seven weeks shalt thou count for thyself* (Deut. 16:9), each week ending with a Sabbath. This is the decisive proof in the hands of the Karaites, seekers of the truth, against the dissidents, who hold different opinions on this subject.

8. The reason Scripture (Lev. 23:15) mentions *sabbaths* before *days* is because the *sabbaths* are meant to be directly connected with *the sabbath* quoted before, namely, the one mentioned in *on the morrow after the sabbath the priest shall wave it* (Lev. 23:11).

9. In the following sentence, *Until from the morrow after the seventh sabbath* (Lev. 23:16), the preposition *from* is redundant, the meaning being "until the morrow," as in *to from within the veil* (Lev. 16:15), which means "to within the veil."

10. The phrase *ye shall count fifty days* (Lev. 23:16) requires that the *morrow* of both the first and the last Sabbaths should be included in it. . . .

XIII. The Count of Seven Weeks

1. Scripture says: *Seven weeks shalt thou count for thyself from the time the sickle is first put to the standing corn* (Deut. 16:9). This does not mean from the very first day on which the grain harvest is begun; rather the people may have been harvesting for a day or two days or even five days—all this time may properly be called the beginning of the harvest, inasmuch as only a small amount of harvesting has as yet been done. This is similar to the phrase, *And he said, Since the people began to bring the offerings into the house of the Lord, we have eaten and had enough, and have left plenty* (II Chron. 31:10). It is impossible that the abundance and the left-over should have resulted from the offering of just one man or two men or even three men, nor is it likely that all the people had brought their offerings at one and the same time; nevertheless it was called the beginning. There-

fore, *Since the people began* does not denote a narrow period of time but an ample one. The same is true of *the sickle is first put to the standing corn,* which may signify that a few days of harvesting had already elapsed, notwithstanding which it may properly be called a beginning.

2. This applies especially to leap years, when the harvest is bound to begin several days before the Feast of Passover.

3. The first sheaf harvested must be deposited at the House of the Lord with the priest until the day when it shall be waved, from which day on the aforementioned count is to begin.

4. The counting is to be done at the beginning of the daytime, as it is written: *on the morrow after the sabbath the priest shall wave it* (Lev. 23:11); the word *morrow* is never used with reference to the night, but only to the daytime, e.g., *And David smote them from the twilight of that day until the evening of the morrow* (I Sam. 30:17). This being established, it follows that the counting should be done early in the morning of the day, immediately after the sacrifice, for two reasons: first, in order to hasten the performance of a religious obligation as much as possible when it falls due; second, in order that the fulfillment of the one ordinance—the sacrifice—might be followed immediately by the fulfillment of the other ordinance—the counting. And since in the Dispersion prayer takes the place of sacrifice, it follows that the counting should take place right after the morning prayer.

5. The counting should be done aloud by each member of the community, since it is written: *And ye shall count* (Lev. 23:15), and again in the next verse: *ye shall count,* both in the plural. Possibly this was intended by God to serve as an emphasis of the great importance of this ordinance, and also as an assurance of general knowledge of the correct count.

6. The manner of the counting is this: we are to begin counting from *the morrow after the Sabbath,* day by day, stating the number of each day in the week, until we shall have reached the Sabbath concluding that week. The Sabbath we are to count, mentioning it first, and the total number of the days second, out of respect for the Sabbath's sanctity, then the number of the week third. The

same procedure is to be observed for the remaining Sabbaths and days of the count.

7. It is the custom in most Jewish communities to forbid marriages during these fifty days; this, however, is not a legal prohibition. These days are characterized by frequent changes in the weather, with the resulting danger of damage to crops and injury to health, as Jeremiah has said, in reproving those who did not acknowledge the bounties of the Lord and did not dread His punishment: *Neither say they in their heart, Let us now fear the Lord, our God, who gives rain, the early rain and the late rain, in due season, and keeps for us the appointed weeks of the harvest* (Jer. 5:24). That is why the Jews have made these days a period of performing divine worship and praying to God for security from harmful mutations and changes which might occur at that time. This is what the true Karaite scholars have said in explanation of this custom. As for the dissenters' claim that the custom is meant to commemorate the ten martyrs, it has, in our opinion, no bearing whatever on the matter.

XIV. Pentecost

1. The last day of the count, i.e., the fiftieth day, Scripture commands us to regard as *a holiday,* as *a holy convocation,* as *the feast of weeks,* as *the day of the first fruits,* and as *the feast of the harvest.*

2. It is called *a holiday* and *a holy convocation* because it is part of the eighteen days mentioned in the section beginning: *These are the holidays of the Lord, holy convocations* (Lev. 23:4), and ending: *These are the holidays of the Lord which ye shall proclaim to be holy convocations* (Lev. 23:37). Moreover, the term *holy convocation* is applied specifically to this fiftieth day in two places, first in the verse *And ye shall make proclamation on the selfsame day, there shall be a holy convocation unto you* (Lev. 23:21), and second in the verse *And on the day of the first fruits . . . ye shall have a holy convocation* (Num. 28:26).

3. It is called *the feast of weeks* because it marks the conclusion

of the count of seven weeks, as it is written: *with your seven weeks* (Num. 28:26), meaning "after your seven weeks," the preposition "with" having the force of "after," as in *With the coming of all Israel* (Deut. 31:11), and *With the completion of the days of her purification* (Lev. 12:6).

4. It is called *the day of the first fruits* because on this day there takes place the offering of the two loaves of showbread made of the first ears of new wheat, as it is written: *And ye shall present a new meal offering unto the Lord* (Lev. 23:16). It consists of two cakes of leavened bread made of white-flour dough and weighing two tenths of an ephah, which is baked and then brought to the sanctuary, as it is written: *From your dwellings shall ye bring the bread of the waving of the sheaf* (Lev. 23:17). With it there are to be offered seven lambs, a bullock, and two rams, forming the burnt offering; the meal offering and the drink offering belonging to it are to be ordered according to the rules set forth in the section: *When ye are come into the land of your habitations . . . and will make an offering by fire unto the Lord, a burnt offering, or a sacrifice* (Num. 15:2–3), and what follows thereafter. The same is true of all the other references to meal offerings and drink offerings which are not specified in detail—they are meant to conform to the rules explained in that section. This burnt offering is followed by a kid of goats as a sin offering, augmented by two lambs for a peace offering, to be eaten by the priest and his sons and daughters. . . .

5. It is also called the *feast of the harvest,* because at that time wheat reaches the state of being ready for harvest and the people begin to do the harvesting. That is why the offering brought consists of two loaves of bread made of the first ears of this new wheat, as it is written: *And the feast of the harvest, the first fruits of thy labors which thou hast sown in the field* (Exod. 23:16).

6. You must know that private peace offerings are not permitted on the days when work is forbidden; consequently the peace offerings mentioned on that day must necessarily be public offerings, which belong to the priest, as stated above. Nor are even public peace offerings permitted on the Sabbath—a matter agreed upon by

the consensus of all Jewry. This is thus another proof that this Day of Pentecost could not possibly fall on a Sabbath. Were the count of fifty days—of which this Day of Pentecost is the last—permitted to begin on the second day of the Feast of Unleavened Bread, whatever day of the week it might happen to be, as the dissenters assert, the Day of Pentecost would accordingly fall on varying days of the week, sometimes on the Sabbath, sometimes on other days, depending on the day on which the Feast of Unleavened Bread happens to begin. It follows, therefore, that it must fall always on the same weekday, namely, on Sunday and never otherwise.

7. If they should fall back upon the faulty principle which they have set up for themselves, namely, that Passover must not fall on a Monday, a Wednesday, or a Friday, it is merely based upon a gross misinterpretation of the statement in the Book of Ezra: *For on the first day of the first month began he to go up from Babylon* (Ezra 7:9), to *And on the fourth day the silver and the gold and the vessels were weighed* (Ezra 8:33). The true Karaite scholars have already explained this matter in their writings and have shown the falsity of all such deferments on the basis of these same biblical passages and the utterances of the dissidents' own scholars. Whosoever wishes to inform himself about it, let him peruse the well-known works on the subject.

8. The Karaites have another argument in this matter which we shall mention here, namely, that all the other holidays are set on definite days of definite months, whereas this Feast of Pentecost is not; it necessarily follows that, as we have said above, it must forever fall on the same weekday, without variation, namely, on Sunday.

9. We are also obliged to proclaim on this day in our gatherings and meetings, "Today is a holy convocation," as it is written: *And ye shall make proclamation on the selfsame day, there shall be a holy convocation unto you* (Lev. 23:21). This is followed in the same verse and in others by *ye shall do no work of labor*. We have already explained the meaning of this prohibition in the discussion of the Feast of Unleavened Bread, and there is no need to repeat it here.

10. We are obliged to celebrate this festival in all places and at all times, as it is written: *a statute forever, in all your dwellings, throughout your generations* (Lev. 23:21). This is similar to the phrase regarding the prohibition of eating the fat and the blood of animals: *a statute forever, throughout your generations, in all your dwellings* (Lev. 3:17). Therefore, he who believes that this festival is not obligatory in the Dispersion is a sinner and a transgressor making false claims, inasmuch as he says that this festival depends upon the beginning of the count after the waving of the sheaf, which latter depends on the beginning of the harvest, while this in turn depends on the deliverance of Palestine into the possession of Jewry and consequently does not apply to the Jews in the Dispersion. He who says this would be bound thereby to invalidate the Feast of Tabernacles as well, since concerning it Scripture says: *and the feast of ingathering, at the end of the year* (Exod. 23:16), making it depend upon our gathering of the crops which are the produce of Palestine. If he invalidates the former festival, he should invalidate the latter likewise, since there is no difference between the two of them in this respect.

11. Proof of our obligation to observe all the festivals at all times and in all places is that a person prevented by a valid cause from performing the Passover in the first month is not thereby relieved of the duty to observe the first and seventh day as holidays and holy convocations, nor is he relieved of the duty to eat unleavened bread throughout these seven days; rather is he obliged to perform all these things. This shows that each of these things is an independent ordinance not affected by the voidance of another ordinance. The same thing applies to the rest of the ordinances; i.e., any one of them is not made void solely by reason of its close connection with another ordinance, from the observance of which a person might be excused at a certain time. Rather we are obligated to observe all the ordinances that we can; as for such as we are unable to observe for a valid reason, they are temporarily not binding upon us by reason of our lacking the means to perform them. Likewise, in our present situation in the Dispersion only such ordinances have ceased to be obligatory upon us as have be-

come impossible for us to observe, e.g., sacrifices, the performance of which is out of our reach until such time as the Holy Spirit shall be poured forth upon us from above; until the Lord shall look out upon us from heaven and shall rebuild His Temple, shall gather us from the four corners of the world, shall enthrone over us a descendant of King David, and shall teach us the good and straight way, so that we shall observe His ordinances and statutes and testimonies, as it is written in the Law of His servant, Moses, and as He has promised us.

XV. The New Wheat Crop

1. It remains for us now to deal with the question of the new wheat crop, and whether or not we may eat of it before the offering of the two loaves of bread. The most probable answer is that we may not, on the analogy of the new barley crop. Just as we are not permitted to eat bread, parched grain, or green ears from the new barley crop before the offering of the sheaf, so also is it forbidden to us to eat anything of the new wheat crop before the offering of the two loaves of bread. However, this analogy does not apply to beans, lentils, or peas, since the prohibition is applicable only to crops similar to that from which the offering is made up, otherwise the offering would have included these other crops also. This prohibition applies with equal force to us in the Dispersion, as well as to those who lived at the time of the Jewish kingdom, and there is no difference between us and them in this respect.

2. It is the custom on that day to mention the array of Israel before Mount Sinai, both in the prayer proper and in the following liturgy. The reason for it is that this great and important array took place in the third month of the year, Siwan, but we do not know for certain the precise day when it happened, so that we might mention it on that same day. Now this day, i.e., the Feast of Weeks, falls always in that same third month, and it is a holy and honored day suitable for matters of worship; that is why the people of Israel placed the mention of this great array on that day.

3. As for the Rabbanites' claim that the Day of Pentecost is the

very day of the array at Mount Sinai, it is a claim devoid of proof, and the Sacred Book rather testifies to the exact opposite thereof. We pray God, therefore, that He may open their hearts and eyes, so that the truth may be revealed to them and they may follow it and turn back from the acts of disobedience in which they are now indulging and perform the true requirements of that which He has ordained and prescribed for them, as it is written: *And thou shalt return unto the Lord, thy God, and shalt hearken to his voice, according to all that I command thee this day* (Deut. 30:2).

XVI. The Fasts of Tammuz and Ab

1. In the fourth month of the year, called Tammuz, on the ninth day, it is incumbent upon us to fast and mourn. This is called *the fast of the fourth month* because on that day the Holy City was captured and the king of Judah was seized and his children were slain before him, as were the leaders and chiefs of the people, whereupon the king was blinded and exiled to Babylon, as it is written: *In the eleventh year of Zedekiah, in the fourth month, on the ninth day of the month, a breach was made in the city, and all the princes of the king of Babylon came in . . .* (Jer. 39:2–3), and in a second account of the same event: *In the fourth month, on the ninth day of the month, the famine was sore in the city . . . Then a breach was made in the city, and all the men of war fled . . .* (Jer. 52:6–7).

2. In the month of Ab, on the seventh day, we are to observe again a fast and a great mourning and sorrow because on that day Nebuzaradan, the captain of the guard, entered the House of the Lord and set fire to it, as well as to the king's palace and other palaces and houses in Jerusalem; he broke some of the Temple's vessels and seized the rest of them, and he carried off the chiefs of the people and later slew them at Antioch, as it is set forth in the Book of Kings, in the section beginning: *And in the fifth month, on the seventh day of the month, which was the nineteenth year of king Nebuchadnezzar, king of Babylon . . . And*

he burned the house of the Lord . . . (II Kings 25: 8–9). The same account is found also at the end of the Book of Jeremiah, except that there it is dated on the tenth day of the same month of Ab, and the wording has been partially altered, as it is written: *And in the fifth month, on the tenth day of the month, which was the nineteenth year* . . . *And he burned the house of the Lord* . . . (Jer. 52: 12–13).

3. Scholars have assigned definite reasons for all these variants in the wording, but since this is not the place to discuss them all, we shall consider only the change in date. Some scholars explain it by assuming that Nebuzaradan did not actually do what the Book of Kings attributes to him, on the day mentioned there, but merely decided to do it, and had not yet done it, so that the doing had been ascribed to him as of the seventh of Ab, although he actually did it on the tenth.

4. Others say that he did begin the burning and several other acts, of those mentioned in the Book of Kings, on the seventh, but when Nebuchadnezzar himself arrived in Jerusalem on the tenth, Nebuzaradan resumed the burning and completed the acts ascribed to him.

5. Still others say that Nebuzaradan entered the House of the Lord on the seventh and then did the things attributed to him in the Book of Kings, but that on that day he did not dare to set fire to anything except the Temple Court. However, when Nebuchadnezzar arrived in Jerusalem and entered the House of the Lord on the tenth and set up his throne there, he ordered Nebuzaradan to set fire also to the proper portion of the Temple, i.e., to the Holy of Holies and the adjoining parts of the Temple Hall, the vestibule, and the courtyard of the priests, as well as to those palaces and houses which Nebuzaradan had not dared to burn. This latter view seems more probable than the foregoing two.

6. For this reason we must fast and exhibit mourning and sorrow on that tenth day also. . . .

XVII. Rules of Fasting

1. We shall now explain the meaning of the word "fast." We say that fast signifies total abstention from food and drink during a certain period of time, as is proven by the verse *and fast ye for me, and neither eat nor drink three days, night or day* (Esth. 4:16), and again in the story of Nineveh, *Let neither man nor beast, herd nor flock, taste anything* (Jonah 3:7). It follows that on a fast day nothing must enter our mouths that has any taste or flavor. Consequently, rinsing one's mouth must also be forbidden, inasmuch as it affects the sense of taste; moreover, since the region of the stomach is contiguous to that of the mouth, it is unavoidable that some of the mouth rinse should spill into the former. This prohibition is thus similar to the prohibition by which no particle whatever of forbidden food or drink may enter one's mouth, as it is written: *neither came there abhorred flesh into my mouth* (Ezek. 4:14). Further support is lent by the fact that when Daniel was overcome with grief and withdrew from all pleasures he said of himself: *neither came flesh nor wine in my mouth* (Dan. 10:3). This confirms what we have said: that no particle of food or drink may enter our mouths on a fast day.

2. Scholars disagree as to the exact beginning of these and similar fasts. Some say that a man may eat and drink on the night of the fast, so long as he is wakeful; but if he falls alseep, even if only for the shortest while, he may not thereafter, in their opinion, partake of anything whatsoever. Others say that a fast begins with the end of the first quarter of the night, and this is the preferable view, since it is the general custom of people to eat and drink until this time of the night prior to the fast.

3. If after having partaken of food and drink a man falls asleep and then wakes up in the night and desires to eat, he may not do so, since he would be in the position of eating a daybreak meal, like the one consumed by Moslem fasters in order to forestall the feeling of hunger during the ensuing fast day; this is forbidden on Karaite fasts. However, if he wakes up before the third watch of the night and feels exceedingly thirsty, he may drink as much

as will quench his thirst. But if he is not thirsty and wishes merely to drink in order to forestall thirst during the ensuing fast day, he may not do so, since this likewise would come under the heading of a daybreak meal.

4. From the expression *Should I weep in the fifth month and keep apart, as I have done these many years?* (Zech. 7: 3), there follow several things, e.g., abstention from eating meat, drinking wine, frequenting bathhouses, using incense and perfume, and wearing fine raiment. On these days we must wear coarse clothing, indulge in great sorrow, put on sackcloth, seek solitude, and speak but little. All this is to commemorate the afflictions which overtook our fathers, particularly the great catastrophe, the like of which never happened elsewhere in the entire world, namely, the one which occurred in Jerusalem, as it is written: *so that under the whole heaven there has not been done the like of what has been done upon Jerusalem* (Dan. 9: 12), meaning that starving fathers ate the flesh of their children, and children ate the flesh of their fathers, as it is written: *Therefore fathers shall eat their sons in thy midst, and sons shall eat their fathers* (Ezek. 5: 10) and the additional afflictions which cannot be properly recounted or sufficiently soothed, as it is written: *What shall I take to witness for thee, what shall I liken to thee?* (Lam. 2: 13).

5. We pray God, the Dispenser of mercy to His creatures and the Fulfiller of His covenant, that He may look down upon Jerusalem with the eye of His mercy and fulfill for us the covenants which He has made with our fathers and that He may bring to pass for us the intent of the prophecy of Zechariah: *Sing and rejoice, O Daughter of Zion, for lo, I come . . . And many nations shall join themselves to the Lord on that day . . . And the Lord shall inherit Judah as his portion . . .* (Zech. 2: 14–16).

6. Only these four fasts are obligatory upon us—and not the additional ones mentioned by the Rabbanites—because these four were observed in the days of the Prophets and recorded in Scripture, and the promise was applied to them alone. As for what the Rabbanites say about the destruction of the second Temple, there is no certainty but that the opposite is true. Namely, they claim that

it was destroyed on the ninth of Ab and assign the same date to the destruction of the first Temple. But since the biblical text proves that this is not true with regard to the first Temple, we need not rely upon their assertion, inasmuch as it contradicts Scripture; rather are we to disregard it. Had there been a prophet present at the destruction of the second Temple and had he recorded the date of it for us, we would have been obliged to observe it also as a day of mourning and fasting; but since this did not happen, we are not obliged to observe it.

IBN AL-HĪTĪ

DAVID ben Sĕʿaḏel[1] ibn al-Hītī, a native, as his surname indicates, of the town of Hīt on the Euphrates, appears to have settled in Egypt, where he engaged in scholarly studies. He was a younger contemporary of Samuel ben Moses al-Maġribī and hence must have lived in the second quarter of the fifteenth century.

Ibn al-Hītī's only known work is a concise Arabic chronicle of Karaite scholars. Although a mere jumble of badly phrased short notes on eminent Karaites of various ages, without any critical or even strictly chronological arrangement, the work is of considerable value, inasmuch as the author appears to have had at his disposal some old autograph manuscripts and perhaps also other sources, such as oral traditions, which are no longer in existence. He mentions, furthermore, several names which are not recorded anywhere else.

THE CHRONICLE OF IBN AL-HĪTĪ

1. I shall proceed to mention the names of Karaite scholars of whom I have found a record.

2. The first of them was our master Anan. He was the first to exert himself in discovering the truth in religion, after it had been long obscured, and to establish it firmly, although in doing so he exposed his life to the danger of death. It is said that he lived at the time of Abū Ǧaʿfar al-Manṣūr, who assumed the office of caliph in the year 136 of the Hegira. Anan served as exilarch of all Israel at Bagdad and induced a number of Rabbanites to come back to the truth, i.e., the teaching of the Karaites.

3. After him lived Daniel al-Ḳūmisī and David al-Muḳammiṣ, the latter being the author of a work on the principles of faith. These two lived before al-Ḳirḳisānī, since the latter mentions them

1. A variant of the name Saʿadiah.

in his *Book of Lights,* together with several other scholars, namely, Ismā'īl [al-'Ukbarī, and others], as well as [the scholars of] 'Ukbara, Tustar, Bagdad, Basra, Fārs, Xurāsān, Ǧibāl, and Syria, whose names he did not give, but merely recorded their differing opinions in matters of law.

4. The learned Jacob ben Isaac al-Ḳirḳisānī composed his work, the *Book of Lights,* in the year 1278 of the Seleucid era, corresponding to the year 315 of the Hegira.

5. Our master David ben Boaz composed his commentary on the Book of Ecclesiastes in the year 383 of the Hegira. He wrote also a commentary on the Pentateuch and a work on the principles of faith.

6. The learned doctor Abū al-Surrī lived after Sa'adiah al-Fayyūmī, since he refuted the views of al-Ḳirḳisānī in his commentary on the Pentateuch and in his *Book of Precepts.* Now Sa'adiah al-Fayyūmī lived before al-Ḳirḳisānī, since he was refuted by Israel ben Daniel. Sa'adiah is also mentioned by the prince Solomon, in his *Book of Incest,* before al-Ḳirḳisānī and the learned doctor Abū al-Surrī. It is probable that when Solomon listed the Karaite scholars he arranged them in chronological order, since he mentions first Anan, then Benjamin, Daniel al-Ḳūmisī, al-Ḳirḳisānī, Abū al-Surrī, Abū 'Alī al-Baṣrī and his son, David ben Boaz, the prince, and finally, the learned doctor Abū 'Alī.

7. It is probable that Abū al-Surrī was a contemporary of the learned Abū Ya'ḳūb Yūsuf ibn Nūḥ, since he wrote an extensive refutation of the latter's views on the search for fresh ears; also, the learned Abū Ya'ḳūb al-Baṣīr and the learned Abū al-Faraǧ Hārūn were among those who came down to attend the lectures of the learned Abū Ya'ḳūb Yūsuf ibn Nūḥ, and these two are mentioned in a copy of a work of his dated in the year 393 of the Hegira.

8. The learned doctor Abū 'Alī, in his refutation of Ibn Nūḥ, mentions the names of several scholars whom he calls warriors and mighty and God-fearing men. They are Abū Sa'dān ben Abraham, Abū 'Isḥāḳ Abraham ibn . . . al-Iṣfahānī, the learned doctor Salmon ben Jeroham, Abū Ibrāhīm ibn 'Ilān, Abū Ezra

ibn 'Abūna, and the learned Abū Ya'ḳūb ben Abraham ibn Ğils; the latter may be identical with Joseph al-Baṣīr. All these lived before Abu 'Alī, since he says of them, "May God have mercy upon them and remember them when He shall turn His grace toward His people."

9. Salmon ben Jeroham was a contemporary of Sa'adiah al-Fayyūmī.

10. The learned doctor Abū Sa'īd, son of the learned doctor Abū 'Alī, was the teacher of Abū al-Farağ Furḳān ibn 'Asad, since the latter quotes some views of his with the formula, "our teacher So-and-so." He lived in the time of Abū al-Surrī Sahl ben Maṣliaḥ, since he made an abridgment of his commentary and refuted his views in his *Book of Precepts*. Al-'Arīšī also mentions the learned doctor Abū Sa'īd in his *Book of Precepts,* in the discourse on fresh ears.

11. The aforementioned Abū Ya'ḳūb ibn Nūḥ presided over a college in Jerusalem in which there are said to have been seventy students, among them the learned Abū Ya'ḳūb al-Baṣīr and the learned Abū al-Farağ Hārūn. The college continued in the same flourishing condition after his death, and among those who went on with their studies in it were Abū al-Farağ Hārūn and others. In the Karaite synagogue at Damascus I have seen a fragment of a commentary on the Book of Leviticus, written on parchment, and in Abū al-Surrī's refutation of Ibn Nūḥ, contained in this commentary, he says that he had been living in Jerusalem for thirty years; "yet," said he, "I have not succeeded in discovering in all these years the true nature of fresh ears, so how can I describe their exact appearance?" This indicates that he continued to teach for this long while.

12. The two scholars, Abū Ya'ḳūb al-Baṣīr and Abū al-Farağ Hārūn al-Muḳaddasī, were, as was stated above, among those who received instruction from Ibn Nūḥ, since they mention him in their works with the formula, "our teacher So-and-so said." The learned Abū Ya'ḳūb al-Baṣīr passed away before the learned Abū al-Farağ Hārūn, since the latter mentions him with the formula, "May God be gracious unto him." I have also found a fragment

of the *Book of Investigation* of Abū Ya'ḳūb al-Baṣīr, dated in the year 428, in which the author refers to him with the formula, "May God prolong his dignity." I have, moreover, found a tract of his in refutation of both opinions, which was dictated by him in the year 458. It is probable that both these scholars, together with the learned Abū Sa'īd, lived at the same time and studied together at the college of Ibn Nūḥ. The learned Abū al-Farağ Furḳān ibn 'Asad mentions all three of them, saying of each of them, "our teacher So-and-so." It is said that he used to attend the lectures of the learned Abū al-Farağ Hārūn and that about this time he began his commentary on the Pentateuch, the shorter version, which he wrote down with his own hand in the month of Rabī' the First of the year 446. Part of it is a commentary on the Book of Exodus, in two divisions, in his own handwriting, the composition and copying of which took seven months.

13. In al-Ramla, in Palestine, lived the learned 'Alī ben Abraham al-Ṭawīl. He lived after the learned Abū al-Farağ Furḳān ibn Asad, since he mentions him in his book, with the formula, "May God be gracious unto him," and wrote a commentary on the entire Bible.

14. The prince Solomon, known as Prince Abū al-Faḍl, was also one of the great Karaite scholars. He was the leader of the Karaites in Egypt, and his orders and legal decisions went forth to the east, to the west, and into Syria. No legal work by him is known to exist, except for the *Book of Incest.* He was an outstanding person in general learning, as well as in jurisprudence, and he wrote also a *Book on Such Matters Pertaining to the Principles of Faith as Ordinary Persons Have Difficulty in Comprehending*. He departed this life in the year 600.

15. The scholars of Bagdad and Iraq were the following: the two learned men, Abū al-Ḥasan ben Mašiaḥ and Salmon ben Jeroham, who lived in the time of Sa'adiah al-Fayyūmī. Ben Mašiaḥ wrote many refutations of the latter at Bagdad, while Ben Jeroham did the same thing at Aleppo. Ben Jeroham passed away at Aleppo while al-Fayyūmī was yet living, and the latter attended his funeral clad in torn garments, girded with a coarse

rope, and barefoot. When he was reproved for it, he said, "Both I and he derived great profit from our controversy, and there can be no doubt of his great learning; that is why I have done what I have done, in attending his funeral." The tomb of Salmōn ben Jeroham is known in Aleppo to this day, even among the Gentiles and others, as the "tomb of the Righteous Man," and they make vows to it down to the present time.

16. Abū [ʻAlī] ʻĪsā ibn Zarʻa, in his *Epistle to Ibn Šuʻayb,* engaged in polemics against the Jews. Then he ran into the aforementioned Ben Mašiaḥ and they disputed with each other. The epistle just referred to was composed in the year 387.

17. Abraham al-Harzalānī wrote a refutation of the Rabbanites and their views, and among the scholars whom he mentioned in his work is Joseph ben Ṣabtiyya.

18. I have found two works on scholastic philosophy, one by ʻAlī ben Joseph Samiyya dated in the year 459, in which the scribe refers to the author with the formula, "May God be gracious unto him"; and the other by Ṣadaḳa ben Šomĕron.

19. The learned Hananiah ben Jacob was one of the most outstanding and profound scholars of his time; he was exceedingly learned in jurisprudence and scholastic philosophy and wrote a dissertation [in] theological research [entitled] *Book of Secrets,* in five volumes—an exceedingly fine work. Only the first two volumes of it are now extant. He mentions some of his father's opinions which indicate that the latter likewise was an [outstanding] scholar. It is said that he was personal trimmer of reed pens to the caliph, who held him in great esteem. His erudition places him in the same class with Joseph al-Baṣīr and Abū al-Farağ Furḳān ibn Asad.

20. Ibn Sāḳawayh wrote a refutation of the Rabbanites and Saʻadiah al-Fayyūmī in the matter of the observation of the new moon, the searching for fresh ears, the date of Pentecost, and the permissibility of eating the fat tail and other fat, as well as the authority of the Rabbanite tradition; he refuted their claim that they have received their teaching from the Prophets by direct tradition.

21. The learned Abū Anan Isaac ben ʻAlī ben Isaac was also

a great scholar. He refuted Sa'adiah al-Fayyūmī in his *Book of the Lamp,* and he wrote also a work on the equinox. It is probable that he was one of the most learned men of his age.

22. The learned Samuel ben Asher ben Manṣūr, known as Abū al-Ṭayyib al-Ǧabalī, lived in the time of Abū al-Faraǧ Hārūn, and they disputed with one another concerning the searching for fresh ears and the order of the legal year. Samuel held to the view of the learned Abū 'Alī in matters of the calendar and wrote a discourse in refutation of the Rabbanite cycle and calculation of the time of the New Moon. He also wrote a refutation of Menahem, head of the Rabbanite academy, after he had read a tract addressed to Abū Ṯābit by Menahem's son.

23. The learned Abū Sa'īd refuted the same Menahem on the subject of scholastic philosophy and wrote an excellent book about it.

24. The learned Yašar ben Ḥesed ben Yašar al-Tustarī was one of the great scholars of his time. He composed the *Book of Clarification,* containing an exposition of the science of scholastic philosophy, its terminology and evidences. He also wrote a refutation of Sa'adiah al-Fayyūmī, a work on the equinox, many works on law, and the *Book of Introduction.*

25. After him came the learned Solomon ben Mubārak ben Ṣaġīr, author of the *Book of Facilitation;* then the learned 'Alī ben Solomon, author of the *Abridged Lexicon;* then the learned Aaron ben Elijah al-Ḳisṭanṭīnī; then Judah ben Elijah Hadasi, the Mourner; then the learned Israel, the Judge; then Japheth ben Ṣaġīr, known as the Sterling Physician; then Isaiah ben Uzziah hak-Kohen, known as the learned doctor Fāḍil; then the learned doctor Samuel ben Moses, known as al-Sinnī; then Samuel ben Moses al-Maġribī, the physician, author of the *Book of Question and Answer,* the *Book of Precepts,* and *Prefaces to the Pentateuch.*

26. The latter was the last of the scholars and wise men who are true guides to the truth, and of whom Scripture says: *And they that are wise shall shine* (Dan. 12:3). There have been, however, other scholars among the Karaites about whom we do not know much and whose writings we have not studied.

27. May there be peace upon all Israel.

ELIJAH BAŠYATCHI

Elijah ben Moses Bašyatchi [1] was a member of a scholarly family residing at Adrianople [2] in European Turkey, where he presumably was born about 1420. He subsequently moved to Constantinople, where he continued his studies, profiting from both Karaite and Rabbanite teachers, with the result that he acquired not only a thorough knowledge of Karaite theology and literature but also a substantial grounding in Rabbanite lore, as well as astronomy and its mathematical auxiliaries. His learning and his lucid and systematic method of treatment of theological and legal problems soon earned him the reputation of an outstanding authority, and his opinions were eagerly sought not only in Constantinople but also in the Karaite settlements of Poland. He was thus led to engage in a copious learned correspondence, some of which has been preserved.[3]

For over thirty years Elijah labored to produce his code of Karaite law entitled *The Mantle of Elijah* (Hebrew *'Addereṯ 'Eliyahu*), but he died (in 1490) without completing it. His brother-in-law, Caleb Afendopolo,[4] undertook to continue the work on the basis of Elijah's own notes and remembered conversations, but he too died in the middle of his task. All this careful and long labor produced a work characterized by abundant content, logical reasoning, systematic exposition, and a style that makes it easily understandable to laymen as well as scholars. It is not surprising, therefore, that it quickly superseded in authority all the older

1. Sometimes misspelled Bashyazi or Bashyatzi; the surname is of Turkish derivation, but its meaning is obscure.

2. His father, Moses, and his grandfather, Menahem, occupied the position of pastor (Hebrew *ḥaḵam*) of the Karaite community in that city. Elijah's descendants were also prominent.

3. Mann, pp. 1143 ff.

4. Or perhaps more correctly Efendopolo. He was Elijah's pupil, as well as his relative, and a fine scholar in his own right in both the theological and the secular fields. He was a prolific author in theology, philosophy, poetry, astronomy, and mathematics.

Karaite codes of religious law and became the standard manual of belief and practice, esteemed and deferred to by the Karaites about as much as Joseph Caro's[5] *Šulḥan ʿaruḵ* was revered by the Rabbanites.[6]

While Elijah foreswore any violent enmity toward the Rabbanites and freely used the works of their great authors, especially Maimonides, in writing his code of law, he nevertheless did not mince words in expressing his conviction of the righteousness of the Karaite faith and his condemnation of Rabbanism as a whole. Occasionally he shows a preference for the Sephardic Jews, who naturally were better known to him, since they included his Rabbanite neighbors in Turkey, rather than the Ashkenazic Jews from Germany, Poland, and the adjacent lands, who repelled him by their allegedly outlandish garb, ostentatious piety, and coarse diet. One is rather less inclined to forgive him his assertion that such Rabbanite notables as Abraham ibn Ezra and Maimonides realized the error of Rabbanism and the truth of Karaism, but deliberately misled their correligionists to believe the opposite. Elijah could hardly have failed to perceive from his reading of Maimonides' works that the latter, at any rate, was the last person on earth to succumb to the vice of hypocrisy.

The great prestige of the *'Addereṯ* gave rise to a number of commentaries, mostly to portions of the code. The numerous quotations from early Karaite authors contained in it make the work also an important source of literary history.

In addition to his code of law, Elijah composed three epistles on individual legal problems; namely, on fasting on the Sabbath (*'Iggereṯ haṣ-ṣom*), on the prohibition of eating the sciatic nerve (*'Iggereṯ giḏ han-naše*), and on the law of inheritance (*'Iggereṯ hayrušah*).[7] He was also a prolific poet, although without any

5. Caro, born in 1488, was an infant at the time of Elijah's death.

6. In contrast to the numerous editions of Caro's code, Elijah's *'Addereṯ* was issued in print only three times: first, by Elijah's grandson and namesake, at Constantinople in 1530–31 (the printing was done by the great Rabbanite printer, Gershom, *italicè* Girolamo, Soncino); second, by Abraham Firkovitch, at Eupatoria in the Crimea, in 1834–35; and third, by Isaac Beim, at Odessa, in 1870.

7. Included in the 1834–35 edition of the *'Addereṯ*.

real poetic talent, and the Karaite prayerbook contains a versified exposition of the Mosaic ordinances [8] and some hymns from his pen.

An astronomical work, entitled *Kĕli han-nĕḥošet* and ascribed to Elijah, has not been recovered as yet.

FROM THE *'ADDERET 'ELIYAHU* OF ELIJAH BAŠYATCHI

I. FUNDAMENTALS OF LAW

1. *The Law of the Lord is perfect, restoring the soul* (Ps. 19:8) to the sublime place from which it had been hewn, so that it might enter the palace of divine wisdom and so that knowledge of God might be upon the earth and God's glory fill the world. This takes place in three ways: through ethical qualities, practical ordinances, and rational ordinances.

2. Ethical qualities may be learned from the stories of the Patriarchs who are mentioned in the Law, as well as from the tales of the Prophets, the kings, and the wars recounted in the books of prophecy, since all these accounts induce a man to arrange his personal affairs according to the politic order; this is what scholars call perfection of ethical qualities and politic wisdom. And together with this ethical perfection man must acquire also the other two perfections, i.e., perfection in the practical and rational ordinances.

3. This is the reason why the Giver of the Law placed at its beginning the tales of the Patriarchs, and it is to this perfection that King David referred when he said: *the testimony of the Lord is sure, making wise the simple* (Ps. 19:8); for by means of these tales any simple person may learn, so far as it is possible for his natural ability, to acquire the perfection of ethical qualities, in order that he may do the proper thing at the proper time for the proper reason and in the proper place.

4. These tales are called *the testimony of the Lord* because the

8. Limited, however, to the ordinances still in force in the Dispersion.

prophetic tales mentioned by the Prophets, and especially the patriarchal tales mentioned by Moses, were all, or most, of them given by the Lord to the Prophets with His testimony as to their truth, and they recorded them in the books of prophecy. The Prophets themselves did not witness the events mentioned in them, since they lived long after the time of their occurrence; they merely knew of them by way of prophecy, the Lord having given the Prophets His testimony concerning them. Thus, the events of the stories of the three Patriarchs written down by Moses in the Law did not occur in his time but were communicated to him by the Lord exactly as they had occurred. That is why they are called *the testimony of the Lord,* i.e., stories attested by the Lord Himself.

5. The reason that the Law does not prescribe for us the observance of ethical qualities in the same admonitory manner as it does the practical and rational ordinances is that had the Law prescribed these for us in the same fashion as the other ordinances, we would have found ourselves everlastingly in sin, since ethical qualities are characteristics of the soul which do not remain in the same state. For example, let us suppose that the Law had commanded us not to let ourselves succumb to anger, except at the proper time for the proper cause and in the proper place, and had done the same for gladness. Now anger and gladness are states of the soul which are always found only in conjunction with the soul, and the soul, too, does not remain in the same state since it, in turn, is joined to matter—i.e., to the human body—which is constantly subject to change. For this reason we would have been everlastingly in a state of sin, and there would have been no man on earth righteous enough to do only good and never to sin. Therefore, matters of this kind are not suitable for being prescribed in the manner of an ordinance and an admonition.

6. Moreover, this would also have caused men to make light of other fundamental ordinances, because as a man would observe that he is unable to fulfill perfectly most of the ethical ordinances imposed upon him, he would inevitably grow careless about all ordinances, including the fundamental commandments. This

would be as if a master were to give many orders to his servant and tell him that if he did not fulfill all of them perfectly he would be flogged unmercifully; now this servant, observing that he could not possibly perform them all and knowing that his master would therefore assuredly flog him, of necessity would lose all hope and would not carry out even one of his master's orders.

7. That is why the Prophet has said: *Even thus shall the children of Israel eat their bread unclean among the nations* (Ezek. 4:13), and that is why scholars have said that the ordinances of the Law were imposed upon men according to their ability to understand and perform them and that when we do not know an ordinance perfectly we must fulfill it approximately. It was therefore a wise procedure on the part of our divine Law to set forth the politic wisdom in the form of tales, and not in the form of commands.

8. Moreover, the opinions of men are more likely to be fortified in fulfilling this politic ordinance by the method of tales, for they observe that So-and-so among the Patriarchs had acted thus-and-so with such-and-such results and are guided by this in their own actions. In fact, for this very reason even some practical ordinances have been set forth by way of tales and stories mentioned in Scripture.

9. The practical ordinances are ordinances like: *And the children of Israel shall keep the sabbath* (Exod. 31:16); *And thou shalt sacrifice the Passover to the Lord, thy God* (Deut. 16:2); *Ye shall surely destroy all the places* (Deut. 12:2); *In booths shall ye dwell seven days* (Lev. 23:42)—in general, all ordinances making some action obligatory. These practical ordinances are the road and the entrance to the reception of the rational ordinances, and scholars have said that the practical ordinances are the preparation for, and the introduction to, the rational ordinances. They said also that the excellence of the ordinances imposed by the human intellect requires their being obligatory, while the obligatory nature of the ordinances imposed by the Law requires their being excellent. They said further that each practical ordinance has a reason and a cause appropriate to its own character, and the fact that we are unable to learn the reasons for some

ordinances is solely because of the insufficiency of our knowledge. In the case of some ordinances, however, the Law itself explains the reasons for them, e.g., the ordinance of the Sabbath is explained by *For in six days did the Lord make the heavens and the earth* (Exod. 20:11); this tells us also of the incipience of the world and the eternal existence of the Lord. Likewise, the ordinance commanding the eating of unleavened bread, bitter herbs, and the flesh of the Passover lamb is explained by their being a memorial of the exodus from Egypt, which also tells us of the existence of the Lord and His care of what exists underneath the heavens. So also the command *Whoso sheds the blood of man, by man shall his blood be shed* (Gen. 9:6), is explained by the following: *for in the image of God did he make man,* referring to *Let us make man in our image, after our likeness* (Gen. 1:26). Similarly, the ordinance concerning the ritual fringe worn on the borders of men's garments is explained by *that ye may look upon it, and remember all the commandments of the Lord, and do them* (Num. 15:39), and the reason for the sabbatical year is *that the poor of thy people may eat* (Exod. 23:11). There are many instances like this; and this is what is meant by the verse *the commandment of the Lord is pure, enlightening the eyes* (Ps. 19:9), meaning that by means of the practical ordinances man enlightens the eyes of his heart and purifies his soul of all shortcomings, so that it becomes as spotless as a polished mirror in which to behold the Lord in the land of life.

10. The rational ordinances are the fundamental ordinances established and planted in man's heart, as King David expresses it: *The precepts of the Lord are right, rejoicing the heart* (Ps. 19:9); i.e., they are planted and rooted in the heart, which is the fountainhead of wisdom, as it is written: *In the heart of him who has discernment rests wisdom* (Prov. 14:33), and again: *The spirit of man is the lamp of the Lord, searching all the inward parts* (Prov. 20:27).

11. These ordinances are known to man as a result of mental consideration, which is the reason why they were known prior to the revelation of the Law, from the time of the Patriarch Abraham

onward, as it is written of him: *and he kept my charge, my commandments, my statutes, and my laws* (Gen. 26:5). This is true also of the Ten Commandments, excepting the one ordaining the Sabbath. However, the truth is that the mystery of the Sabbath also is a matter of reason, as we shall explain in another place. It is also true of the summons: *Hear, O Israel, the Lord, our God, the Lord is one* (Deut. 6:4); *Know this day, and lay it to thy heart, that the Lord, he is God* (Deut. 4:39); *To love the Lord, thy God, to hearken to his voice, and to cleave unto him* (Deut. 30:20). Most of them, however, are negative ordinances.

12. You must know also that if the believer in the divine Law takes these rational ordinances to heart by way of example from the deeds of the biblical personages, they are bound to be established and planted in his heart more firmly than if he had received them only by way of tradition. However, the proper thing for every believer in the Law is to receive these ordinances first by tradition, and only afterward, with the help of his divine Rock, to seek the knowledge of the cause for every ordinance, according to its interpretations, particulars, and biblical examples. This is the way of him who desires and longs for the achievement of moral perfection, and that is what the psalmist referred to when he said: *Then should I not be shamed as I look at all thy commandments* (Ps. 119:6). If he were to endeavor first to learn the reasons and the biblical examples for every commandment, and accept it by tradition only afterward, he would be like a man who refuses to eat bread until he learns how it was sown, how it was harvested, how it was ground, and how it was baked, and who would consequently go hungry a long time until he shall have learned its causes and beginnings.

13. The root and basis of these rational commandments is the existence and oneness of the Lord, and the denial of His corporeality, which is the reason why the Ten Commandments begin with *I am the Lord, thy God* (Exod. 20:2); for the relation of this commandment, . . . which affirms the existence of God, to the others is like that of the substance to the accidences which it carries. The second commandment, *Thou shalt have no other*

gods (Exod. 20:3), alludes to the oneness of God, as does the summons, *Hear, O Israel, the Lord, our God, the Lord is one* (Deut. 6:4). The verses *for ye saw no manner of form on the day when the Lord spoke unto you* (Deut. 4:15), and *To whom, then, will ye liken God, and what likeness will ye compare unto him?* (Isa. 40:18), constitute the denial of His corporeality.

14. The ordinances are also divided into two other groups, the positive and the negative. Examples of positive ordinances are: *And thou shalt sacrifice the Passover unto the Lord, thy God* (Deut. 16:2); *And thou shalt keep the feast of weeks* (Deut. 16:10); *And thou shalt love the Lord, thy God, with all thy heart* (Deut. 6:5); *that they shall make for themselves fringes* (Num. 15:38); *and thou shalt make a parapet for thy roof* (Deut. 22:8). And it is to these positive ordinances that King David alluded in saying: *the ordinances of the Lord are true, they are righteous altogether* (Ps. 19:10). The Rabbanites have made a reckoning of these positive ordinances and they say that there are two hundred and forty-eight in all.

15. Examples of negative ordinances are: *Thou shalt have no other gods before me* (Exod. 20:3); *Thou shalt not take the name of the Lord, thy God, in vain* (Exod. 20:7); *Thou shalt eat no leaven with it* (Deut. 16:3); *Thou shalt not carry tales among thy people* (Lev. 19:16). The Rabbanites have made a reckoning of these also and have found them to be three hundred and sixty-five, and it is to them that King David alluded when he said: *The fear of God is clean, enduring forever* (Ps. 19:10), for the word *fear* cannot refer to anything except negative ordinances.

16. The positive ordinances are the path and the point of contact for the negative ones, which are the fundamental ones, for we find positive ordinances the essence of which is negative. For example, *And the children of Israel shall keep the sabbath* (Exod. 31:16), implies the obligation to rest, and resting is not action but lack of action. So also: *ye shall afflict your souls* (Lev. 16:29) implies "ye shall not give yourselves the pleasure of eating and drinking"; and *sanctify yourselves* (Lev. 11:44) implies "ye shall not defile yourselves."

17. Some scholars say that there are ordinances which are outwardly commands, while inwardly they are admonitions, and others which are the reverse. For example, *thou shalt not leave a soul alive* (Deut. 20:16) implies "thou shalt slay." We also find one ordinance which embraces all the ordinances together, namely, *The Lord, thy God, shalt thou fear, and him shalt thou serve* (Deut. 6:13); the words *shalt thou fear* embrace all the negative ordinances, while the words *and him shalt thou serve* comprise all the positive ones. King Solomon likewise said: *The end of the matter, all having been heard: fear God and keep his commandments, for this is the whole man* (Eccles. 12:13).

18. However, the negative ordinances are more stringent, as commands of the Lord, than the positive ones, because he who does what he had been commanded not to do, yet does it notwithstanding, causes greater wrath on the part of the Lord than he who is too lazy to do what he had been ordered to do. The latter, in not performing what he had been commanded to do, may have been prevented by some restraining cause, whether a matter of time or place. On the other hand, he who does that which he had been ordered not to do, yet does it nevertheless, is deliberately rebelling against the intent of Him who had issued that ordinance. That is why the extreme punishment of being cut off is, under the Law, imposed mostly for violation of negative ordinances and only in a few instances for violation of positive ordinances, like those of circumcision and Passover, the violator of which draws the punishment of being cut off only because these two ordinances are among the original fundamental ordinances of the Jewish faith.

19. However, we find one ordinance which embraces all the positive ordinances together and involves the punishment of being cut off, namely, *Cursed be he that confirms not the words of this law* (Deut. 27:26). *Cursed be he* implies the divine punishment of being cut off by way of death, since the crimes referred to are committed in secret, and in fact the several occurrences of *Cursed be he* in this section of Deuteronomy refer to secret crimes, inasmuch as transgressors who lie with an animal or a mother-in-

law or a sister, or accept a bribe, act in secret. In the case of crimes openly committed, human law exacts its due from the perpetrators, but where they act in secret their punishment consists in their being cut off by the hand of God, and therefore *Cursed be he that confirms not the words of this law* must signify that his punishment shall be his being cut off.

20. You must know also that all ordinances fall into three other categories: first, those fulfilled by way of the belief of one's heart, i.e., the commands of the Lord which are planted in the human heart; second, those fulfilled by word of mouth; and third, those fulfilled by action, as it is written: *For this word is very nigh unto thee, in thy mouth, and in thy heart, to do it* (Deut. 30:14). All, however, are also meant for the heart, since the heart is the principal thing, as it is written: *for the Lord searches all hearts, and understands all the imaginations of the thoughts* (I Chron. 28:9); *thou didst well that it was in thy heart* (I Kings 8:18); *but the Lord looks into the heart* (I Sam. 16:7). The heart is the principal thing because it is the foremost member of the human body. It is the abode of the sublime soul, as it is written: *The spirit of man is the lamp of the Lord, searching all the inward parts* (Prov. 20:27), and again: *In the heart of him who has discernment rests wisdom* (Prov. 14:33).

21. Ordinances fulfilled in the heart are such as *I am the Lord, thy God* (Exod. 20:2); *And thou shalt love the Lord, thy God* (Deut. 6:5); *Thou shalt have no other gods* (Exod. 20:3); *thou shalt love thy neighbor as thyself* (Lev. 19:18)—in general, all the rational ordinances.

22. Ordinances fulfilled by word of mouth are such as *Thou shalt keep the utterance of thy lips* (Deut. 23:24); *And thou shalt speak and say before the Lord, thy God, A wandering Aramean was my father* (Deut. 26:5); *And thou shalt teach them to thy children* (Deut. 6:7); *Thou shalt not take the name of the Lord, thy God, in vain* (Exod. 20:7); *Thou shalt not bear false witness against thy neighbor* (Exod. 20:16).

23. Ordinances fulfilled by action are the practical ordinances mentioned above.

24. You must also know that there are ordinances applying to one man only, such as a king or a priest; others apply to a certain group, such as the priests or the Levites; still others apply to single individuals, such as the nazirite or the leprous person. There are ordinances applying exclusively to men or to women, to all the individuals of the particular sex. In the case of particular things the pertinent ordinance may apply only at a certain time, as with the redemption of first-born sons and the tithe; others apply only at a certain place, e.g., in Palestine or in a far-away place; some apply only on certain days, some in the daytime, others at night; some once a week, some once a month, some once a year, some once in seven years, some once in fifty years.

25. You must know also that there are many ordinances which are not expressly mentioned in the Law but which issue from the validity of other ordinances or from the accounts of prophetic utterances, and their excellence requires their being obligatory. These ordinances are derived by means of analogy, in several ways, as is evident from the words of scholars.

26. The first variety: when an ordinance is found in the Law in one place and its precise meaning is explained in another place, either in the Law or in the prophetic books, we assume that the explanation of the ordinance as first formulated is the same as that found in the other place. For example, with regard to the verse *If brethren should dwell together, and one of them should die* (Deut. 25:5), one might be in doubt as to whether *brethren* signifies brothers by blood or brothers by common family. Now from the story of Ruth, the Moabite, we learn that redemption of the deceased brother's wife and property belonged in Ruth's case to a brother by family. Since the Law forbids the application of this ordinance to brothers by blood, we therefore interpret *If brethren should dwell together* to refer only to brothers by family. Likewise, we assume that the verse *Thou shalt not take a wife in addition to her sister, to make enmity* (Lev. 18:18), refers to sisters by religion, and not by blood, in accordance with what scholars have explained in this matter.

27. The second variety: from the rule governing the particular

we learn the rule governing the general. For example, the verse *Thou shalt not plow with an ox and an ass together* (Deut. 22:10), forbids the combination of two specific kinds of animals, one of which is clean and the other unclean; it also mentions plowing, which is a particular kind of work used here in lieu of all kinds of work. We conclude therefore that it is forbidden to use all sorts of unclean and clean animals together in all kinds of work, because one is strong while the other is weak, since unclean beasts are always stronger than the clean, for which reason the flesh of the unclean is forbidden, as is well known to practitioners of medicine. We thus learn that unclean and clean animals of any species whatever may not be used jointly in the same work, of whatever type it may be.

28. The third variety is called comparative analogy or, as the scholars term it, "equal nature." For example, it is written: *Thou shalt not uncover the nakedness of thy father's brother* (Lev. 18:14), from which we learn by way of comparative analogy that the same prohibition applies also to the mother's brother.

29. The fourth variety is analogy leading from the minor to the major, for the Law sometimes forbids a minor thing without prohibiting the corresponding major, the illegality of which is therefore derived by way of this variety of analogy. For example, it is written: *Thou shalt not uncover the nakedness of thy son's daughter, or thy daughter's daughter* (Lev. 18:10), but Scripture does not expressly forbid marrying the daughter herself. That the latter, too, is forbidden we learn by arguing from the minor to the major, i.e., if the daughter's daughter is forbidden, how much more so the daughter herself.

30. The fifth variety is analogy based on the wording of the ordinance, i.e., on the words used in it. For example, the prohibition of marrying one's grandmother and his grandmothers in ascending line is deduced from the words *The nakedness of thy father, and the nakedness of thy mother, shalt thou not uncover —she is thine own mother* (Lev. 18:7). Likewise, in interpreting the verse *This month shall be for you the beginning of the months* (Exod. 12:2), we learn its meaning from the literal significance

of the word *month,* i.e., "the renewal of a thing," meaning the renewal of the visibility of the moon to the inhabitants of the earth. So also from the expression *A moon of days* (Deut. 21:13), meaning a month, we learn that this renewal takes place in the moon as viewed by those living upon the earth.

31. The sixth variety is logical preference, as for example, the prohibition of marrying the step-brothers of the father, which Rabbi Jeshuah ben Judah forbade by way of logical preference, i.e., preference demanded by both reason and common knowledge. This applies to cases for which we find no pertinent ordinance written in the Law, nor one that might be derived by analogy from another written ordinance; in such cases reason supplies the pertinent ordinance, whether permissive or prohibitive. Most of the laws governing inheritance are derived by way of logical preference, as will be explained in the proper place.

32. The seventh variety is analogy based upon similarity, i.e., what is prohibited to one of two of a kind, is forbidden to the other also, as required by both reason and common knowledge. For example, if marrying the daughter of the father's wife is forbidden because two closely related persons may not be married to two other closely related persons, then likewise wherever the marriage of two close relatives to two other close relatives is involved, the same prohibition should apply.

33. These are the varieties of analogy used by scholars in investigating the laws of the ordinances. There are, however, other ordinances in the observance of which we have been raised since the days of our fathers, and their fathers before them, and which are a matter of custom with us. They are not recorded in the Law and have become as second nature with us; nevertheless, they flow in a sense from the intent of prophetic utterances. Such ordinances are called by scholars "the burden of inheritance" or "tradition"; for example, the slaughtering of animals which must be performed by means of a slaughtering knife and by proper cutting of the prescribed parts of the body; the sanctification of the new month which must be determined by the appearance of

the New Moon, even though this latter may be derived also by analogy, as shall be explained in another place.

34. The learned Rabbi Tobiah states that he who says that there are traditions which have no support in Scripture does so merely because of his insufficient comprehension of the particular ordinance. That is why scholars have said that all ordinances are valid, whether written in Scripture or derived by way of analogy or transmitted by tradition; and they have said also, "the observance of Scripture rests on three things: the written text, analogy, and the 'burden of inheritance.'"

35. Karaite tradition, however, is not like the tradition believed in by the Rabbanites, since the latter add to and subtract from Scripture and say that tradition overcomes the written biblical text, notwithstanding that Scripture says expressly: *Ye shall not add unto the word which I command you* (Deut. 4:2). If their intention be merely to interpret the prophetic utterances, it is not seemly for them to say that tradition overcomes the written biblical text. For example, with regard to the ordinance *Forty stripes may he give him* (Deut. 25:3), they say that the meaning is forty less one. They say likewise that the husband should inherit his wife's property, referring to the verse *And he shall inherit her* (Num. 27:11); a few among them say that this is a matter of mere assumption. Yet it is evident from Scripture that this verse deals only with hereditary landed property, since it is written: *If a man should die, having left no son, ye shall transfer his landed property to his daughter. And if he have no daughter, ye shall give his landed property to his brothers. And if he have no brothers, ye shall give his landed property to the brothers of his father. And if his father have no brothers, ye shall give his landed property to his nearest kinsman, from among his family, and he shall inherit her* (Num. 27:8–11); they thus clearly added to Scripture an ordinance of their own when they said that the husband should inherit his wife's estate. Karaite tradition, on the other hand, is such as is acknowledged by all Israel, and it does not stand up against that which is recorded in the Writ of divine truth; and our

scholars have said that every tradition which does not stand up against Scripture, does not add to what is stated in Scripture, is acknowledged by all Israel, and has indirect support in Scripture, is to be called genuine tradition, and we must accept it. They said further that most of the Mishnah and the Talmud comprises genuine utterances of our forefathers, and Rabbi Nissi ben Noah has said that our people are obligated to study the Mishnah and the Talmud.

II. THE TEN PRINCIPLES OF FAITH

1. All physical creation, i.e., the planets and all that is upon them, has been created.
2. It has been created by a Creator who did not create Himself, but is eternal.
3. The Creator has no likeness and is unique in all respects.
4. He sent the Prophet Moses.
5. He sent, along with Moses, His Law, which is perfect.
6. It is the duty of the believer to know the language of the Law and its interpretation.
7. God inspired also the other true prophets after Moses.
8. God will resurrect all mankind on the Day of Judgment.
9. God requites each person according to his ways and the fruits of his deeds.
10. God has not forsaken the people of the Dispersion; rather are they suffering the Lord's just punishment, and they must hope every day for His salvation at the hands of the Messiah, the descendant of King David.

III. COMMENTARY ON THE SIXTH PRINCIPLE OF FAITH

1. I say that the language of our divine Law is the tongue spoken since ancient times by Eber and his children and children's children, and that Moses used this language in writing the Law from the Lord's own mouth. In olden times it was called the tongue of

Eber, but since the time of Moses and down to our own time it has been designated as the holy tongue, since it is connected with holiness, being the tongue of a holy people, as it is written: *Ye shall be holy* (Lev. 19:2), and again: *and be ye holy* (Lev. 20:7).

2. Some say that it is called holy because it does not include words for the sexual organs, either of the male or of the female, for the act of union which results in the birth of offspring, and for human sperm, urine, or excrement. This, however, is not true, since we find in the Law the word *yišgalennah* (Deut. 28:30), signifying the very act of sexual intercourse. Moreover, were this so, it would have been more fitting to call it the pure tongue. Nor was it called the tongue of the people of Israel or the tongue of the Land of Israel, because the holy tongue included both these aspects as well.

3. There is no doubt that in the time of the Temple in Jerusalem this language was spoken in its utmost perfection, but after the people of Israel were exiled to a foreign land the holy tongue was submerged under the local secular languages, so that we have nothing left of it at present but the twenty-four sacred books and the few additional words used by the scholars of the Mishnah, even though some of these latter were borrowed from other languages.

4. Inasmuch, then, as our divine Law was written in this tongue, every believer must study the Law in this very tongue, and not in any other, for even though the meaning of the Law may be well understood in other languages, He Who revealed it cannot be understood as thoroughly as in its own tongue. Moreover, the proper names in the Law cannot be translated, and there are various metaphors in every tongue which cannot be exactly rendered into other languages. Do you not observe the books of the philosophers, originally composed in Greek, which were translated by Arab scholars into their own language, with the result that many obscurities have crept into these translations? Afterward Jewish scholars have turned these Arabic versions into Hebrew, doubling the number of these obscurities. Moreover, the nations which have made translations of the sacred books of Scripture into their own languages could not render all the words contained therein, but

had to leave some of them in the original Hebrew because of the difficulty of translating them. And the fact that our older scholars composed their own writings in Arabic is no proof to the contrary, for their contemporaries were not sufficiently conversant with the holy tongue, so that our scholars followed the proverb "If you cannot do that which would satisfy you, you must be satisfied with what you can do."

5. This being so, every person of the holy seed of Israel must himself study the holy tongue and must teach his children to know the language of our Law and of the words of the Prophets in a proper and fitting manner, with special conditions which would facilitate its study, to wit:

6. First, the pupil must be not less than six years old. If he is of exceptionally strong bodily build, he may be only five years old, but not less, unless he should go to school merely for his training, without being subjected to the travail of study, since a little boy's brain is tender, and if he overtaxes his intellect with study the sinews of his brain become enfeebled, he acquires a permanent weakness of the brain, and his study is retarded.

7. Second, the teacher must be fit to do his teaching. He must be a person of good disposition, neither too lenient nor too irascible, else his pupils will grow weary of him, and his occasional outbursts of anger must be dictated by his zeal for the pupil's perfection and not for anything else. He should not flog his pupils with whips or canes but only with a small strap, so that the pain may last only for that moment and not longer.

8. Third, the student should be trained to assign descriptive marks to each lesson, because verbal definition is the necessary introduction to the acquisition of knowledge, since that which is not clearly defined cannot be encompassed by knowledge. This is why Ezra the Scribe established sections in the text of the Bible, some closed and others open.

9. Fourth, the recitation should be confined to one biblical book until that book shall have been completed; one should not change from book to book, for such change in reciting, and more so in writing, weakens the memory, since movement from one subject

to another fatigues the person who is exerting his memory. Do you not observe that boys, because of their constant mobility, have a less retentive memory than young men, even though the greater moisture of their humors contributes to the sharpness of their memory?

10. Fifth, recitation should be done from a book that is handsome as to both its handwriting and the parchment upon which it is written. The schoolhouse itself should be well built, for two reasons: first, out of respect for the dignity of the books and the teaching, as it is written: *to beautify the place of my sanctuary* (Isa. 60:13). He who takes care of this earns a great reward from the Lord, since by doing so he does honor to His Law. Therefore, wealthy persons who themselves have no learning should endeavor to take care of this in lieu of their lack of education, for even though they were not so fortunate as to excel in the knowledge of the Law, they will have contributed to its extension and propagation. Second, the beauty of the book and of the school building encourages the students' desire to take part in the recitation. For this reason all teachers whose schoolhouses are not free from ugly things and are not pleasingly decorated to the best of their ability should not be permitted to teach, for they would only cause their pupils to lose all desire to study and would thereby decrease the knowledge of the Law, unless indeed the teacher is so poor that he cannot afford it, in which case the members of the congregation should contribute money, according to their ability, to build schoolhouses in order to propagate and glorify the Law. Books contributed to the library of the synagogue and kept in it should be given to indigent students, so that they may study therein in their school. If there are no such books in the synagogue library, the congregation should contribute them for the poor students' benefit and should also provide the students with their daily needs, as far as possible, out of respect for the Law.

11. Sixth, recitation should be done in a voice loud enough to be audible to the student's ear, so as to draw the attention of the cells of his mind to what is read, as it is written: *With my whole heart have I sought thee, let me not err from thy commandments* (Ps.

119: 10), i.e., "after I have sought Thee with all the strength of my heart, let me not err from Thy precepts, for I have already traveled the road which prevents error, which is the road of seeking Thee with all the strength of my heart." This can be achieved only by a voice that is audible; an inaudible voice weakens the strength of the student's heart and multiplies his errors. An additional support for this condition is the fact that scholars call the words of sacred prophecy "Recitation," meaning that they are learned by recitation in an audible voice. Do you not observe the musical accents which are attached to the prophetic text, each one of which has a tone other than that of its fellow, but which form jointly a regular combination of tones so as to produce an audible well-arranged melody? Had this been of no consequence for the divine Author of the Holy Writ, what need would there have been for these accents? Moreover, it is written: *The loud voice of rejoicing and salvation is in the tents of the righteous* (Ps. 118: 15). To sum up, recitation of the books of prophecy should be done in a voice that is loud and pleasing, with observance of the accents, according to the usage of each locality. If it can be done with the melody of the accents as used by the Jerusalemite exiles of Spain, so much the better, since they have this melody by ancient tradition handed down from one generation to the other. Moreover, this pleasant melody encourages the student's desire to engage in recitation and contributes to the balance of the nature of the reciter, for the spirit of the Lord does not come to rest upon a person unless his nature is balanced, as it is written: *And it came to pass, when the minstrel played, that the hand of the Lord came upon him* (II Kings 3: 15). This may also be the reason for the word *mĕnaṣṣeaḥ,* meaning that pleasing music produced by well-coordinated voices gains mastery over a nature which is uneven and returns it to a balanced state. Moreover, philosophers say that this science, i.e., the practical part of the science of music, or practical singing, is active in stimulating the powers of the human organism and in balancing the nature of man's humors, until he is restored to good health. It is for this reason that when the men of the Exile were asked by their captors to sing some songs of Zion they replied: *How shall we sing the Lord's song in a foreign land?* (Ps. 137:4), i.e., how could they deliberately balance the nature of their enemies?

12. Seventh, one student should teach another to recite, since this strengthens his own memory, for it causes him to repeat what he knows, and repetition translates his potentialities into action. Perhaps that is what King David alluded to when he said: *I have gained more understanding than all my teachers* (Ps. 119:99); and the Rabbanites say: "I have learned much from my teachers; more from my fellow-students; but most of all from my pupils" (B. Ta'ănit 7a).

13. Eighth, the teacher and the pupil should recite together with attention and deliberation, and without haste, so that the recited matter may make an impression upon the student's memory; especially since hasty speech often brings about stumbling in the flow of talk and causes a person to utter improper words, the opposite of what he means to say, thereby leading others to heresy.

14. Ninth, the reader should set a limit to the time employed for his recitation, but should not limit the amount of material which he is to recite within that period, i.e., he should not say, "Within such-and-such a period of time I shall recite this biblical section," or "this biblical book." Knowledge and learning cannot be circumscribed by a certain period of time, since they are a gift from God and are above time, for time encompasses and circumscribes only physical things, not spiritual ones. A definite time for recitation, however, should be set, in order that a person may not spend it doing something other than studying. Although, strictly speaking, one is obligated to meditate in the Law at all times, day and night, as it is written: *and in his law does he meditate day and night* (Ps. 1:2), yet, it being a matter of natural law that man cannot do this, especially in the Dispersion where he is compelled to attend to the needs of his body, to earn money, and to manage his household, it is sufficient for him to designate three periods of time, in the evening, in the morning, and at noon, for study, as it is written: *Evening, morning, and noon will I complain and moan; and he has heard my voice* (Ps. 55:18), i.e., three times in a complete day of twenty-four hours. In the winter, on the other

hand, it is proper to meditate longer during the long nights, as it is written: *Arise, cry out in the night* (Lam. 2:19). Night work is generally work which is most productive of results for the worker. A certain scholar was asked how he managed to gain more learning than his fellows, and he replied that he had added more to his expenses for lamp oil than they had spent for wine. That is why people call winter nights "nights of wisdom."

15. Tenth, the reader should repeat his recitation as often as he can until it shall have impressed itself upon his memory, for repetition of what one has learned impresses it on one's memory, as it is written: *And thou shalt teach them diligently to thy children* (Deut. 6:7).

IV. ON ONE'S CONDUCT TOWARD HIS FELLOW MEN

1. It is written: *thou shalt love thy neighbor as thyself* (Lev. 19:18); this is the general rule in man's relations with his brethren, namely, that which is unacceptable to him he should not inflict upon another. It is written further: *Thou shalt not hate thy brother in thy heart* (Lev. 19:17); this is a particular of the aforementioned general dictum. It is also written: *Thou shalt not carry tales among thy people* (Lev. 19:16); this, too, is a particular, as is also the command: *Thou shalt not harbor revenge, nor bear a grudge, against the children of thy people* (Lev. 19:18), for all these things a man finds unacceptable to himself and should therefore not do them unto his brethren.

2. While all these injunctions serve as particulars to the general dictum *thou shalt love thy neighbor as thyself,* they are at the same time the source of other ethical matters, and from them one may deduce by analogy many things.

And these are the things that one should avoid, which may be deduced from the general dictum *thou shalt love thy neighbor as thyself:*

3. It is forbidden to admonish one's fellow in public, either in private matters or in matters concerning religious ordinances, e.g.,

accusing him of violating the commands of the Law. Only if others among his people imitate him in his violation is it proper to reprove him gently in public, in order to make him cease. For the Rabbanites say, "He who publicly causes his fellow's face to go pale with shame has no share in the world to come" (Mish. A̱ḇoṯ 3:11), and the biblical command, *thou shalt surely rebuke thy neighbor* (Lev. 19:17), does not mean doing it in public.

4. This latter command thus imposes a biblical obligation upon a person to admonish his fellow, in order that no hatred might arise between them. If the man who is admonished proves to be innocent and the admonisher asks for forgiveness, the admonished should grant it willingly, because God himself is forgiving and it is also written: *Thou shalt not harbor revenge, nor bear a grudge.*

5. The admonition should be given in an even tone and with soft language, in a manner that would convince the admonished that it is meant for his own good, and it should be repeated time after time, so long as he knows that he is meant to benefit by it. However, if the admonished does not turn back from his evil way, he is to be publicly shamed and rebuked until he does turn back. If he does not, the religious court alone should impose a ban upon him; if he persists further, both the court and the entire Karaite congregation should issue a general ban against him—all this providing one is certain that he will not "change his clothes."

6. It is likewise forbidden to speak any words that would cause shame or damage to another person, and in general one should treat one's fellow as one would wish to be treated one's self.

7. "Bearing tales" signifies reporting one person's words to another person, by saying, "I heard him speak thus-and-thus." Even if the talebearer does not add anything of his own, he disrupts the good order of society, inasmuch as he causes people to quarrel.

8. The same thing applies to a person who gives a bad name to another person, even if what he says is perfectly true, for he is even worse than the aforementioned talebearer, and he is branded as a man of evil tongue. This sort of person is, for example, he who says, "So-and-so's forefathers used to do such-and-such dis-

honorable work," or "They cheated So-and-so of his property," and of him it is written: *May the Lord cut off all flattering lips, the tongue which speaks exaggerated things* (Ps. 12:4).

9. There is a somewhat less reprehensible kind of evil tongue, for example, one who says, "So-and-so is a pious man," or "So-and-so is a righteous man," in a sarcastic tone. Likewise to be condemned is he who lauds his favorite in the presence of the favorite's enemy, for he thereby causes the latter to speak maliciously of the former, as it is written: *He who blesses his friend in a loud voice early in the morning, it shall be regarded by others as if he had uttered a curse* (Prov. 27:14). And just as one is forbidden to have an evil tongue, so also is he forbidden to sit among other men of evil tongue, as it is written: *Blessed is the man . . . who sat not in the seat of scorners* (Ps. 1:1).

10. A person is said to harbor revenge when he inflicts upon his fellow the same injury as the one the latter had caused him, even after he had accepted the latter's apology; for example, when he says to his fellow, "Lend me a thousand silver coins," and the latter refuses, but later the former accepts the latter's apology. When subsequently his fellow asks him for a loan, he should not say in reply to the request, "I will not lend thee, because thou didst refuse to lend me before."

11. A person is said to hold a grudge when he nurses his revenge for a long time, even after he had accepted his fellow's apology, whereas a vengeful person executes his revenge within a short period of time. However, in the case of men who have done evil and have not repented and offered apologies, harboring revenge and holding a grudge are not forbidden. In fact, Rabbi Japheth said that there are evil men upon whom one may take revenge, just as the Creator takes revenge upon such of His creatures as are incorrigibly evil, as it is written: *He does not quarrel into eternity, nor bear a grudge forever* (Ps. 103:9), i.e., He does not quarrel with the righteous man who repents an evil deed or hold a grudge against him who comes back to Him in repentance, as it is written also: *Will he bear a grudge forever?* (Jer. 3:5); but where there is no repentance, the Lord relents not from His vengeance. There-

fore one may take revenge upon one's evil fellow and hold a grudge against him if he persists in his wickedness, just as King David held his grudge against Shimei all his life and finally ordered his son, King Solomon, to slay him.

12. From the dictum *thou shalt love thy neighbor as thyself,* follows one's duty to ransom captives at their fair valuation and up to one sixth as much more, this one sixth being the fixed market increase. One is not obligated to pay more than this, in order that Gentiles may not deliberately hunt for Jewish captives in order to extort money from Israel. The ransomed person should work off his purchase price for six years and should go free in the seventh. However, slaves who are perpetual property, i.e., Gentile slaves, even if they are converted to Judaism at our hands, remain slaves forever, since liberation in the seventh year applies only to our Jewish brethren, as it is written: *If thy Hebrew brother should be sold to thee . . . he shall serve thee six years; and in the seventh year thou shalt let him go free* (Deut. 15: 12). Likewise, if a free proselyte has been taken captive, we are obligated to ransom him and to set him free in the seventh year.

13. From the same dictum *thou shalt love thy neighbor as thyself,* follows an Israelite's duty to donate to his destitute brother that which is sufficient to fill his need, although there are other biblical verses indicating the duty of giving alms, e.g., *Thou shalt surely open thy hand* (Deut. 15: 8), and *If thy brother be waxen poor . . . thou shalt uphold him, even a proselyte and a settler, and he shall live with thee* (Lev. 25: 35). This has been made obligatory also by way of admonition, as it is written: *Thou shalt not harden thy heart, nor shut thy hand, from thy needy brother* (Deut. 15: 7).

14. For the purpose of fulfilling the ordinance of almsgiving, it is the custom of congregations to appoint an alms collector, who is entrusted with the collection of alms and their distribution among the poor. He should not be required to submit a regular accounting, as it is written: *But there was no reckoning made with them of the money that was delivered into their hand, because they dealt faithfully* (II Kings 22: 7). The alms collector should give

preference to the poor of his own congregation over those of another, and to the poor of his own city over those of another city, as it is written: *unto thy poor and needy brother, who is in thine own land* (Deut. 15:11).

15. Just as he who gives alms earns a reward—as it is written: *Zion shall be redeemed with justice, and they that return to her with righteousness* (Isa. 1:27)—so also he who moves another person to charity earns a reward, and our Sages have said that his reward is even greater than the reward of him who gives alms himself; of those who move others to charity it is written: *and they who turn the many to righteousness shall shine like the stars* (Dan. 12:3).

16. One should give alms according to one's ability. If he gives more than that, let him do so; but he who gives less, his punishment shall be great indeed.

V. ON HONORING ONE'S FATHER AND MOTHER, AND ON THE MANAGEMENT OF CHILDREN

1. It is written: *Honor thy father and thy mother* (Exod. 20:12). Since Scripture does not give the particulars of the honoring, it must be taken in its general sense, i.e., they are to be honored in every manner, in both words and actions. As for words, by saying good things in a respectful and deferential manner when speaking of them, or even when merely mentioning their names.

2. As for actions, there are two kinds of them: the first, by spending money to support them and to clothe them fittingly, according to one's means. The other kind are acts of honoring, pure and simple, e.g., by rising in their presence and advancing to meet them—as King Solomon did for his mother, as it is written: *And the king rose up to meet her and bowed down to her* (I Kings 2:19)—and by accompanying them wherever they may go; by not disobeying their command; and by not contradicting them in whatever they may say, excepting in grave matters of the Law which concern the faith. However, as regards simple textual interpretation of Scripture and matters pertaining to secular sciences,

which are not of the essence of the faith, one should not contradict them, since to do so would be a violation of the ordinance of honoring one's father and mother. One should also not speak insolently to their faces, and one should hold them in awe, as it is written: *Ye shall fear every man his mother, and his father* (Lev. 19:3).

3. Just as one is obligated to honor one's parents during their lifetime, so is it one's duty to honor them after their death, by burying them according to their dignity in life, by mourning for them, and by building up their burial place so that it may be recognizable. One must also fulfill their testament, just as King Solomon fulfilled the testament of his father, and take care of the needs of one's father's orphans.

4. One is also obligated to honor one's older brother in the same manner as described above, but to a somewhat lesser degree. Likewise one should observe the same distinction in honoring one's mother, as compared with the honor paid to one's father, since the father is more to be honored than the mother, even though Scripture sometimes mentions the mother before the father. One should also honor in the same lesser degree the brothers of the father and the brothers of the mother, but the grandparents, meaning the father's father and the mother's father, should be honored in the same degree as the father, since honoring one's father has no other basis than the fact that he has taught and raised his son, as it is written: *but make them known unto thy children and thy children's children* (Deut. 4:9).

5. If the parents reach old age and deviate from the proper line of conduct, one should not show contempt for them on that account, as it is written: *and despise not thy mother when she is old* (Prov. 23:22).

6. You must know that he who did not observe the ordinance of honoring one's father and mother and other relatives used to be conducted by his father and his mother to the court, as it is written: *Then shall his father and his mother lay hold on him and bring him out to the elders of his city* (Deut. 21:19). And there he was charged with being a rebellious son as well as a glutton and a

drunkard. These rebellious propensities in most cases originate with him, and not with his parents, nor could in most cases the habit of gluttony and drunkenness come from them; it would seem that these evil attributes cause one another.

7. He who openly curses his father and his mother used to be judged in the court; he who does so secretly is subject to being eventually cut off by the hand of God, as it is written: *Cursed be he who dishonors his father or his mother* (Deut. 27:16). On the other hand, he who observes the duty of honoring his father and mother, his reward is longevity, as it is written: *so that thy days may be long* (Exod. 20:12)—a hint that he, too, shall reach their station as a father of children and that just as they are now a burden upon him, so shall he some day become a burden upon his own children, wherefore he should not show weariness of their old age.

8. Just as the son is obligated to honor and obey his father, so is the father obligated to teach his son the Law and good morals, to arrange for his marriage, and to instruct him in the ways of business, so that he may earn his own livelihood. The father should also give him a portion of his capital, while he is yet living. If the father does not do all this for his son, the latter may very well become a glutton and a drunkard and be put to death for it, so that the father would be the cause of his execution. The father has brought the son into this world, therefore it is his duty to guide him, just as the Creator who has created the world guides it in an orderly and well-knit manner in its perpetual existence, even though He Himself does not derive any personal benefit from it, whereas the father is bound to benefit from his children at the end of his days; it is thus to his own advantage to raise them properly. It is written: *he who mistreats his flesh and blood is a monster* (Prov. 11:17), and again: *As a father has compassion upon his children* (Ps. 103:13).

9. Rabbi Japheth holds that if the father takes care only of his son's physical needs, yet does not teach him the Law, but lets him remain an ignoramus, the son is under no obligation to honor him, since it is the father's duty to teach his children the laws of

the faith, as it is written: *And ye shall teach them diligently to your children* (Deut. 11:19). The father may do the teaching himself or hire a teacher; in the former case, the father has a greater claim to his son's respect than if he had taught him solely by spending money for the hire of a teacher.

VI. ON HONORING THE AGED AND THE SAGES

1. It is written: *Thou shalt rise before the hoary head, and honor the face of the old man* (Lev. 19:32). Scholars differ as to whether hoariness signifies old age or something else. Rabbi Joseph al-Ḳirḳisānī holds that old age indicates greater age than hoariness, because a man is not called old until he has advanced considerably in age; this is why Scripture requires honoring for old age and mere rising for hoariness. Honoring is greater than rising, since there is no honoring that does not involve rising; hoariness, on the other hand, signifies merely whiteness of the beard.

2. Others say that old age and hoariness are the same thing and that Scripture mentioned both of them in order to say both *Thou shalt rise* and *honor;* both commands apply equally to old age as well as to hoariness, i.e., it is one's duty to rise before, and honor, both old and hoary-headed men.

3. Still others say that hoariness refers only to the gray color of the hair, this being the literal meaning of the word, whereas *old man* is used here in the sense of wise old man, as in *I have more understanding than mine elders* (Ps. 119:100), and *And unto the elders he said, Tarry ye here for us* (Exod. 24:14). And they rightly conclude from the fact that Scripture added honor to the respect due a wise old man that one is obligated to rise before him as well as honor him. The verse is therefore to be explained thus: *Thou shalt rise before the hoary head,* i.e., before a man with a hoary head; but even if his hair is not hoary, on account of his beard being sparse, it is one's duty to rise before him for the sake of his advanced years; and before the *old man* one should both rise and do honor, since the conjunction *and* preceding the word *honor* indicates the addition of *honor* to *rise.*

4. Doing honor consists in advancing to meet the old man and accompanying him to wherever he is going. Rabbi Japheth holds that when an old man passes by on the road while you are standing still upon your feet, it is your duty to go to meet him, turn to face him, do him honor, and invoke a blessing upon him. If you are seated when he passes by, you must rise to your feet before him, with a courteous expression upon your face, bow to him, and walk with him for a short distance upon his way. This is the additional honor which is due a wise old man, as compared with the honor due a man with a hoary head, providing the old man is a wise as well as a God-fearing person.

5. From the verse *Thou shalt not curse the deaf, nor put a stumbling block before the blind, but thou shalt fear thy God* (Lev. 19:14), scholars conclude that even if the gray-headed or old man has weak sight, one must not withhold the honor due him. Scholars say further that it is a positive biblical ordinance to rise before a hoary-headed man, and one must do honor and show respect to scholars in general, especially if they are famous for their wisdom, even if they have no gray hair. The honor should consist of rising in their presence, advancing to meet them, and going along on their left side to accompany them. If two men meet a scholar, the older should walk at his right, and the younger at his left, so that the scholar may always be in the middle. One should not contradict them, and one should obey them, except where profanation of the Lord's Name may be involved.

6. Rabbi Levi holds that it is the duty of the congregation to honor and obey any person who is superior to them in age or wisdom. Scholars say also that an older man must rise in the presence of a younger one if the latter excels him in wisdom or good works. Rabbi Jeshuah holds that if an old man lacks both wisdom and fear of God he has no claim to honor, since it is written: *The hoary head is a crown of glory, if it is found in the way of righteousness* (Prov. 16:31). He holds also that a young man who is possessed of both wisdom and piety outranks an old man possessed of piety alone, and that when two men are of equal rank in piety or wisdom, or in both, they should do honor to each other. The same

scholar said that failure to show honor to old and high-ranking men is a sure indication that the place where this happens will be devastated and that its inhabitants will perish, as it is written: *the child shall behave insolently against the old man, and the base against the honorable* (Isa. 3:5).

7. All that has been said before about the duty of honoring old men does not apply at all times, since at the time of prayer one is relieved of this duty, because the obligation to pray is the greater one, inasmuch as it is a mark of honor toward one's Creator. Likewise, if a company of people are staying at the shop or the house of a scholar or an aged man, and he passes to and fro many times in their midst, they are not obligated to rise and do honor to him every time he passes, but rather twice only each day. However, if there should be among them other men who were not present when they had first done honor to him, they all should rise once more in his presence, in order that they might not be reproached with lack of respect for scholars.

8. Rabbi Jeshuah holds that if a father and his son operate a shop and the son is seated in it at his work, while his father is going in and out repeatedly, the former is not obligated to rise every time, but only once, the first time, excepting when other men have entered the shop, who have not been there before.

9. Scholars are of varying opinions regarding him who neglects his own dignity and prevents others from doing him honor. Some say that he who disregards his own dignity may do so. Others say that he is not permitted to do so, since Scripture has made honoring him an obligation; moreover, the person who honors him earns thereby a heavenly reward, and he should not deny to that person the opportunity to earn this reward. They say furthermore that if it were permissible for him to disregard his own dignity, it would have been permissible for a father to forgive his rebellious and disobedient son, and save him from the punishment of death. Moreover, Aaron the High Priest, although older than Moses, subordinated himself to him and addressed him respectfully, saying: *Let not the anger of my lord wax hot* (Exod. 32:22), and *I pray thee, my lord* (Num. 12:11); and so also all the people

stood up respectfully before Moses, each at the door of his tent; yet, although no one was ever more modest than Moses, nevertheless he did not prevent them from showing him all these marks of respect. For this reason, they say, a scholar should not disregard his own dignity, out of consideration for the dignity of scholarship itself.

10. Rabbi Levi, however, holds that it is more likely that one is permitted to disregard one's own dignity, because we do not observe anyone among venerable and learned men saying to a person who did not rise before him, "Why did you not do honor unto me?" This is the correct view.

11. Just as ordinary people are obligated to do honor to scholars, so is it proper for scholars not to walk to and fro in their midst to an excessive extent or engage in idle talk with them, in order not to inconvenience them or lose their respect, thereby injuring also the veneration due to the Law.

VII. CONCERNING THE DICTUM,
Thou shalt not boil a kid in its mother's milk (Exod. 23: 19)

1. Some commentators have explained this verse in strange ways, but its literal meaning is clearly that one must not boil a kid together with its mother's milk. This rule is a general one, applying to all domestic and wild animals, to the effect that one must not boil the offspring in the milk of its mother. Just as in the case of the dictum *And whether it be a cow or a ewe, ye shall not slaughter it and its young in one day* (Lev. 22:28), which speaks only of domestic animals, we have extended it by means of analogy to wild animals as well, so do we proceed here, since all ordinances are intended to apply to the general, not to the particular, since the general is better known than the special.

2. It follows from this that joining also must be forbidden, i.e., joining the mother's milk with the young's flesh; this applies also to the reverse case, i.e., to joining the young's milk with the mother's flesh, as well as to joining the young's flesh with the

flesh of the father or of the mother, and vice versa. The reason for all these is that the root and the meaning of this ordinance flow from the meaning of the ordinance *ye shall not slaughter it and its young in one day*.

3. Some scholars are in doubt as to whether only the boiling of these is forbidden or the eating of milk and flesh thus boiled together as well, on the ground that they found some other things the doing of which is forbidden, but not the usufruct of them. For example, the mixed breeding of trees or animals is forbidden, while the eating of the fruit of such mixed trees and the riding of the offspring of mixed animals are permitted; thus, we find that King David and King Solomon rode mules.

4. Others say that *Thou shalt not boil* amounts to the same thing as "Thou shalt not eat," just as *ye shall not slaughter* amounts to the same thing as "Ye shall not eat"; they therefore forbid both the boiling and the eating and say that one also must not eat the flesh of a calf in its mother's milk or vice versa. This is the correct view, and not that of the Rabbanites, who say that one must not eat milk and meat together at the same table, no matter what meat it may be.

5. To sum up, it is forbidden to eat an animal's meat with milk obtained from its mother, i.e., mixed with the milk; but it is permitted to eat meat mixed with milk definitely known not to belong to the mother. This applies to both domestic and wild animals.

VIII. ON WHETHER DANGER TO LIFE DOES OR DOES NOT NULLIFY THE LAWS GOVERNING THE SABBATH

1. Scholars say that in all matters in which a man's judgment convinces him that his life is in peril, he may violate the Sabbath on that account, so as to eliminate the danger to his life. By analogy they apply this rule also to the actions performed by a midwife attending a woman in childbirth, such as cutting the navel cord and tying it up, and all the other services required by the mother and the newborn child. All these are, strictly speaking, forbidden

on the Sabbath, in so far as they come under the heading of work, but they are permitted for the sake of the deadly peril which would otherwise be very likely to arise. Moreover, it is written: *that he may live by them* (Lev. 18:5). Another example is the case of a man who has fallen into the sea on the Sabbath and who would drown and die, unless he is pulled out of it. Likewise, if a house has burst into flames and this has placed several lives in danger, one may extinguish the fire, or demolish the houses around it, in order to prevent the burning of the entire town, with the consequent peril to many lives. Similarly, it is permitted to cook medicines and food for a sick person whose life would be imperiled without them. So also is it permissible to make war on the Sabbath by the use of weapons and by transporting supplies on public thoroughfares, for the same reason of deadly peril, for if the Gentiles should know that the Jews would not offer battle to them on the Sabbath, they would always attack on that day and kill them all. This is proved by the fact that Goliath the Philistine stood for forty days against the array of Israel; had the Israelites not fought with their weapons on the Sabbaths included in these forty days, they would all have been slain, which is a supposition intolerable to the reason of any understanding person.

2. Rabbi Joseph ha-Ro'e says that when such danger is subject to doubt, one should not violate the Sabbath; it may be violated only when the probability of peril is decidedly greater than that of safety.

3. The Rabbanites say, "A man should let himself be slain rather than commit any one of three sins, namely, idolatry, adultery, and shedding of blood." To this Karaite scholars reply that in the case of idolatry a man should indeed let himself be slain, rather than commit it, the proof of which is the story of Daniel and his companions, who delivered themselves to be put to death. In the matters of adultery and shedding of blood, however, the fact is not the same. As for adultery, we find that in the case of the affianced virgin who had intercourse with a man in the open field Scripture does not require her to be put to death. According to the dictum of the Rabbanites she should have been slain, yet it is

written: *But to the damsel thou shalt do nothing, there is no deadly sin upon the damsel* (Deut. 22:26). As for the shedding of blood, it is written: *If a thief be found breaking in, and be smitten, so that he dies, no blood shall be spilled for him* (Exod. 22:1), from which we learn, on direct biblical authority, that when a man comes forth to slay you, you may strike first and slay him, which amounts to the exact opposite of what the Rabbanites say.

4. To sum up, the scholars have ruled that danger to life takes precedence over the sanctity of the Sabbath, providing sound reason tells us that peril is more probable than safety.

5. A problem which arises in this connection is the case of a patient who is attended by two physicians. One says that the patient is in danger, whereas the other says that he is not. The proper solution is to follow the verdict of the more expert physician, and if he so advises, to violate the Sabbath for the sake of the patient's needs by performing any kind of otherwise prohibited work, such as kindling fire, cooking various kinds of food, and preparing concoctions and all sorts of medicines. Nor should one in such a case delay the profanation of the Sabbath in order to ascertain the true state of the patient by saying, "Perhaps we shall have no need for them." The ordinances of the Law are not meant to exact vengeance from men, but were rather given to them as a mark of God's grace and mercy, so that they may earn the life of this world and the life of the world to come. And those who say that this is nevertheless a profanation of the Sabbath and that it should not be done even in the face of deadly peril come under the biblical verse *Wherefore I gave them also statutes that were not good, and judgments whereby they should not live* (Ezek. 20:25).

6. Therefore anyone who violates the Sabbath on account of danger to life is free from punishment, whether it is the physician who has violated it or the apothecary or the midwife attending the mother and the newborn child or any Jew who profanes the Sabbath to save a life or two Jews, or three or more, whatever their number may be—all are free from punishment. However, if one of the attendants completes all the work required to meet the danger and no more of it is needed, no one else may do anything

more to violate the Sabbath. And the Rabbanites say that when such things in violation of the Sabbath have to be done, they should not be entrusted to Gentiles or to minors or to servants or to women, in order not to lower the dignity of the Sabbath in their eyes; rather should these things be done by the great and the learned in Israel.

KARAITE LITURGY

When Anan set out to construct a complete new form of religious life for his adherents, he turned his attention also to the ritual of divine service. He was, of course, well versed in the Rabbanite order of service, but like Rabbanite law, it did not meet with his approval. The Rabbanites, he decided, traveled the same false road in liturgy as they did in matters of divine law—they forsook the only true form of divine service, the one used at the Temple in Jerusalem, and substituted for it a form of worship of their own making. And so Anan's motto here, too, became "Back to the Bible!"

To be sure, a complete return to the Temple service was physically impossible, because one of the cornerstones of that service was the animal sacrifice, offered twice daily, at dawn and at sunset, with additional sacrifices (Hebrew *musaf*) on the Sabbath and holidays. Anan, like the Rabbanites, admitted that as long as the Temple was nonexistent no ritually proper sacrifices could be offered, and that a scriptural lesson and a solemn prayer had to be substituted in their stead. But as the fragments, so far discovered, of the liturgical portion of his *Book of Precepts* seem to indicate, he endeavored to model his liturgy as closely as possible upon the original service of the Temple.

To parallel the two daily sacrifices at the Temple, Anan prescribed only two daily prayers, at dawn and at sunset, thus rejecting the afternoon prayer (Hebrew *minḥah*) of the Rabbanite ritual. The daily lessons from the Pentateuch, which were substituted for the discontinued sacrifices, were to be read only by men of priestly descent, inasmuch as only priests could perform offerings of animal sacrifices at the Temple. And by the same token, the daily psalm (Hebrew *šir hay-yom,* "song, or hymn, of the day") was to be recited only by a man of Levitic lineage, thus continuing the duty performed by his ancestors in the Temple at Jerusalem. Again, the Holy Ark containing the scrolls of the

Law was to be venerated by kneeling before it and bowing to the ground, as was its prototype, the Holy of Holies. Nor could prayer be offered anywhere, except at a special place (meaning the synagogue, the substitute for the Temple) uncontaminated by any extraneous touch (Anan's term for it was "court," Hebrew *ḥaṣer*).

It was a logical arrangement, but it met, like some other ordinances promulgated by Anan, with immediate opposition. His guiding principle that prayer equaled sacrifice met with the objection that while prayer does indeed take the place of sacrifice it is not its equivalent, since a sacrifice, to be valid, must be offered by a consecrated priest at the Temple in Jerusalem, whereas prayer may be offered by any person, who need be only ritually clean, and not consecrated, and at any place, which need be only ritually undefiled, and not holy. The same distinction applied to the Ark of the Law in the synagogue, which was, according to Anan's opponents, a substitute for the Holy of Holies, but not its equivalent, and therefore to kneel and bow before it, in each of the several synagogues, was an act dangerously akin to polytheistic idolatry.

Anan's number of daily prayers, too, was found unsatisfactory by later Karaites who must have felt uncomfortable when they observed the three daily prayers of the Rabbanite ritual and the five daily orisons of the Moslem worship. The majority of the later Karaite leaders seem to have acknowledged the validity of the afternoon-prayer prescribed by Rabbanite law, but they salved their consciences by pointing out that the Rabbanites unlawfully recited it late in the day, whereas it was really meant to be a noon prayer and should properly be recited at midday.

On one principal point, however, the early Karaites were unanimous, and that was their conviction that formal prayer should consist exclusively of biblical quotations, mainly the Psalms of David, and that the Rabbanite practice of composing and introducing into the official liturgy new material in the form of prose prayers and versified hymns was unauthorized and unlawful. It was a logical enough line of thought, from the Karaite point of view, and it led them not only to the rejection of such ancient and basic portions of the Rabbanite liturgy as the so-called Eighteen Benedictions (Hebrew *šĕmone ʿeśre bĕrakot*), but also to the adoption of different prophetic lessons (Hebrew *hafṭarot*), which are read as appendices to the lessons from the Law. But here again this attempt to go back to biblical usage could not stand up in the face of the changing times and ideas, particularly in view of the extensive growth of the Rabbanite liturgy and its enrichment by the magnificent hymns and prayers composed by the foremost Rabbanite poets and scholars of the Middle Ages.

The absence of a generally accepted order of divine service and the divergence among various Karaite communities in matters of liturgy, as well as the gradual infiltration of nonbiblical matter —in spite of ancient prohibitions—finally made a reform of the prayer book imperative. As in law, so also in prayer, the Karaite could not, try as he would, live by a formula kept unchanged for over a thousand years. His religious fervor, his need for expression of his veneration and love for God, and his trust in His justice and mercy were just as great as his Rabbanite cousin's, and magnificent as the biblical psalmody is, it could satisfy only a portion of his longing for intimate communion with God.

Two early attempts to codify the Karaite liturgy, one by an ancient author whose name was lost and the other ascribed to a certain Joseph [1] who lived in the first half of the thirteenth century, proved unsuccessful, although they apparently were not entirely discarded, since copies of these two prayer books were available as late as in the second half of the fifteenth century.[2] A third prayer book, compiled by Joseph's son, Aaron ben Joseph (known as Aaron the Elder), who lived in the second half of the thirteenth century,[3] met with general approval, induced not only by the skillful and logical arrangement of the material but also by the authority of the compiler, who was revered as an out-

1. Mann, pp. 705, 1158.
2. Mann, *loc. cit.*
3. Cf. Poznanski, pp. 76–78.

standing scholar, philosopher, and physician. Aaron was also a gifted poet, and he introduced into his manual of liturgy a number of his own hymns, thus giving final sanction to the abolition of the ancient insistence upon biblical prayer only. Once the dam was thus breached, a great many hymns by other liturgical poets found their way into the Karaite prayer book; nor was entry denied to non-Karaites, for a number of pieces by Rabbanite authors were incorporated as well.

The present Karaite prayer book, the final result of this long evolution, is a voluminous work comprising the order of prayer and ceremony for daily and festival service, for various special occasions from childbirth to death and burial, and for semi-liturgical recital of hymns outside the official divine worship. As in the Rabbanite prayer book, many of the prayers are constructed from biblical quotations, either a complete passage or an amalgam of phrases taken from various portions of the Bible and joined together. The poetic quality of the hymns composed by Karaite poets is on the whole inferior to the hymnology of the Rabbanite prayer book, and even their choice of borrowed Rabbanite pieces is not always the best possible. But to Karaite worshipers it has been a good and purposeful handbook for man's communion with his Maker, instilled with a deep and sincere feeling of piety and devotion, of faith in God's justice and loving-kindness, and of confidence in the ultimate triumph of good over evil.

FROM THE KARAITE PRAYER BOOK

I. THE MARRIAGE RITUAL

1. As the Bridegroom Proceeds to the Synagogue or to the House Where the Wedding Is to Take Place, His Friends Are to Chant the Following Hymn in a Pleasant Melody:

From His abode in heaven a light is shining
Upon thee, O my bridegroom, and rejoicing is growing
for thee.
Refrain: Mayest thou always have only gladness!

Restitution for Zion, and the year of recompense,
The day of final judgment—may they be revealed
To thee in thy lifetime, together with the Son of Peace,
The Messiah, to restore the spirit of Israel. (*Refrain.*)

He who dwells amidst the cherubim, may He turn his face
To thee in His heaven.
May He direct toward thee, as abundantly as the stream of His gardens,
Peace that shall endure until the moon shall shine no more. (*Refrain.*)

May the Rock, from heaven,
Make thee as fruitful as Manasseh and Ephraim.
He has planted thee by the side of streams of water;
Thy flourishing flower bed is spreading its fragrance. (*Refrain.*)

On the day of the gladness of heart caused by his wedding,
God, too, surely rejoices at his gladness,
Granting prosperity and joy
To the bridegroom with his bride. (*Refrain.*)

2. If They Do not Reach the Synagogue or the House Where the Wedding Is to Take Place by the Time This Hymn Is Concluded, It Is to Be Followed by the Following Psalm (Ps. 67):

God be gracious unto us and bless us;
May He cause His face to shine toward us. Selah!
That Thy way may be known upon earth,
Thy salvation among all nations.
Let the peoples give thanks unto Thee, O God,
Let the peoples give thanks unto Thee, all of them.
Let the nations be glad and sing for joy
That Thou wilt judge the peoples with equity,
And lead the nations upon earth. Selah!

Let the peoples give thanks unto Thee, O God,
Let the peoples give thanks unto Thee, all of them.
The earth has yielded her increase;
May God, our God, bless us.
May God bless us,
And let all the ends of the earth fear Him.
Blessed be the Lord in eternity. Amen, and again amen!

3. As the Bridegroom Enters the Synagogue, the Following Psalm Is to Be Recited (Ps. 122):

I rejoiced when they said unto me, Let us go to the House of the Lord.
Our feet are standing within thy gates, O Jerusalem.
Jerusalem, thou art built like a city that is compact together,
Whither the tribes went up, even the tribes of the Lord, as a testimony unto Israel, to give thanks unto the Name of the Lord.
For there were set thrones for judgment, the thrones of the house of David.
Pray for the peace of Jerusalem, may they who love thee prosper.
May there be peace within thy walls, prosperity within thy palaces.
For the sake of my brethren and companions I will now say, Peace be within thee;
For the sake of the House of the Lord, our God, I will seek thy good.

4. After This the Bridegroom Is to Take the Following Oath at the Hands of an Esteemed Man, Either in the Synagogue or in the House Where the Wedding Takes Place:

According to the covenant of Mount Sinai, and according to the statutes of Mount Horeb, and by the testimony of the Lord of Hosts, and by the testimony of our elders and notables, I, So-and-so, son of So-and-so, do betroth and sanctify unto myself

So-and-so, daughter of So-and-so, to be my wife, in purity and holiness, by way of bridal gift, writ of marriage, and marital intercourse, according to the law of Moses and Israel.

5. After This the Groomsmen Conduct the Bridegroom to the Bride, Chanting the Following Psalm (Ps. 91):

O Thou who dwellest in the covert of the Most High,
who abidest in the shadow of the Almighty!
I will say unto the Lord, who is my refuge and my fortress,
My God, in whom I trust,
That He will deliver thee from the snare of the fowler,
From the noisome pestilence.
With His pinions He will cover thee,
And under His wings shalt thou take refuge;
His truth is a shield and a buckler.
Thou shalt not fear the terror by night,
Nor the arrow that flies by day,
Nor the pestilence that walks in darkness,
Nor the destruction that wastes at midday.
A thousand may fall at thy side,
And ten thousand at thy right hand,
It shall not come near unto thee.
Only with thine eyes shalt thou behold,
And the recompense of the wicked shalt thou see.
For thou hast made the Lord, who is my refuge,
Even the Most High, thy habitation.
No evil shall befall thee,
Neither shall plague come near thy tent,
For He will give His angels charge over thee,
To keep thee in all thy ways.
They shall bear thee upon their hands,
Lest thou dash thy foot against a stone.
Thou shalt tread upon the lion and the asp,
Thou shalt trample upon the young lion and the serpent.
Because he has set his love upon Me, therefore will I rescue him,

I will exalt him, because he has known My name.
He shall call Me, and I will answer him;
I will be with him in trouble;
I will deliver him and make him honored.
With long life will I satisfy him,
And make him to behold My salvation.

6. If the Way Be Long, the Following Psalm Is to Be Added (Ps. 121):

A song of ascents.
I will lift up mine eyes unto the mountains,
From whence shall come my help?
My help comes from the Lord,
Who made heaven and earth.
He will not let thy foot stumble,
He who guards thee, will not slumber—
Behold, He that keeps Israel
Does neither slumber nor sleep.
The Lord is thy keeper,
The Lord is thy shade, upon thy right hand.
By day the sun shall not smite thee,
Nor the moon by night.
The Lord shall keep thee from all evil,
He shall keep thy soul.
The Lord shall keep thy going out and thy coming in,
From this time forth and for ever.
Blessed be the Lord in eternity. Amen, and again amen!

7. As the Bridegroom Arrives At the Bride's House, One of the Notables Is to Draw Nigh and Perform the Betrothal with a Ring or Another Object of Value, Beginning to Recite in a Whisper (Hos. 2:21):

And I will betroth thee unto me for ever;
And I will betroth thee unto me in righteousness, and in justice, and in lovingkindness, and in compassion;

And I will betroth thee unto me in faithfulness;
And thou shalt know the Lord.

8. The People Who Are Present Are to Repeat This Aloud. Thereupon They Are to Conduct the Bridegroom to the Synagogue or to His Own House to the Strains of the Following Hymn, One of the Groomsmen Starting off in a Loud Voice and with a Pleasant Melody:

Refrain: The ornament of my bridegrooms,
And the people of my trust,
Come, let us walk
In the light of the Lord.

Perfect of ways
And of paths,
For thee is waiting
The congregation of the Lord. (*Refrain.*)

Rest yourselves, O friends
And dear ones;
Answer thus to those who stand
In the House of the Lord. (*Refrain.*)

With might and humility
Step thou along the way,
And I will bless thee
In the Name of the Lord. (*Refrain.*)

Trust and hope
In God, and thou shalt have thy fill
Of His goodness and
Of the truth of the Lord. (*Refrain.*)

Hold fast to the faith,
And walk rejoicing,
And lead once more
The people of the Lord. (*Refrain.*)

Among notables
Do thou dwell, and among friends,
And among the remnants of Israel
Who belong to the Lord. (*Refrain.*)

Multiply, so that thou mayest live
Forever, and become
The fruit which
The Lord loves. (*Refrain.*)

Abundant in blessing
Be thou, in thy very name,
And a veil of royalty
In the hand of the Lord. (*Refrain.*)

Rejoice in thy helpmeet,
When entering thy chamber.
Thus shall be blessed
He who fears the Lord. (*Refrain.*)

Take possession of thine acquired bride,
And cling to her,
And hold her fast,
According to the Law of the Lord. (*Refrain.*)

Hearken to the words of
Truth, and thou shalt multiply,
And then shalt thou be blessed
By the Lord. (*Refrain.*)

9. If They Do not Reach the Aforementioned Place, They Are to Add the Following Psalm (Ps. 46):

God is our refuge and strength,
Help in trouble, surely present.
Therefore we will not be afraid, though the earth be moved,
And though the mountains be moved into the heart of the seas,
Though the waters thereof roar and foam,

Though the mountains shake at the swelling thereof.
Selah!
There is a river, the streams of which gladden the city of
God,
The holiest dwelling place of the Most High.
God is in her midst, she shall not be moved;
God will help her, at the approach of morning.
Nations were in tumult, kingdoms were moved;
When He uttered His voice, the earth melted.
The Lord of Hosts is with us,
The God of Jacob is our high tower. Selah!
Come, behold the works of the Lord,
Who has made desolations in the earth.
He makes wars to cease unto the ends of the earth,
He breaks the bow and cuts the spear in sunder,
He burns chariots with fire.
Let be, and know that I am God,
I will be exalted among the nations, I will be exalted upon
the earth.
The Lord of Hosts is with us,
The God of Jacob is our high tower. Selah!
Blessed be the Lord into eternity. Amen, and again amen!

10. The Bridegroom Is then Seated in His Chair, While the Groomsmen Go Back to Fetch the Bride and Bring Her to the Synagogue or to the House Where the Wedding Is to Take Place. One of the Groomsmen then Begins to Recite in a Pleasant Melody (Prov. 18:22; 31:10–31):

Refrain (*repeated after each verse*):
Whoso finds a wife, finds a great good,
And obtains favor from the Lord.

A valiant woman, who can find?
For her price is far above rubies.
The heart of her husband does safely trust in her,
And he has no lack of gain.
She does him good, and not evil,

All the days of her life.
She seeks wool and flax,
And works willingly with her hands.
She is like the merchant ships,
She brings her food from afar.
She rises while it is yet night,
And gives food to her household,
And a portion to her maidens.
She considers a field, and buys it,
With the fruit of her hands she plants a vineyard.
She girds her loins with strength,
And makes strong her arms.
She perceives that her merchandise is good;
Her lamp goes not out by night.
She lays her hands to the distaff,
And her hands hold the spindle.
She stretches out her hand to the poor
And reaches forth her hands to the needy.
She fears not the snow for her household,
For all her household are clothed in scarlet.
She makes for herself coverlets;
Her clothing is fine linen and purple.
Her husband is known in the gates,
Where he sits among the elders of the land.
She makes linen garments and sells them,
And delivers girdles to the merchant.
Strength and dignity are her clothing,
And she laughs at the time to come.
She opens her mouth with wisdom,
And the law of kindness is upon her tongue.
She looks well to the ways of her household,
And eats not the bread of idleness.
Her children rise up and call her blessed;
Her husband also, and he praises her:
Many daughters have acted valiantly,
But thou hast excelled them all.

Grace is deceitful, and vain is beauty;
But a woman that feareth the Lord, she shall be praised
Give ye her of the fruit of her hands,
And let her works praise her in the gates.
So shalt thou find grace and good favor in the sight of
God and man (Prov. 3:4).

11. After This the Groom and Bride Are to Stand Before the Holy Ark of the Synagogue, the Bride on the Left Side of the Groom. One of the Groomsmen Is then to Read the Following Marriage Contract:

A. On such-and-such a day of the week, being such-and-such day of such-and-such month, in the year so-and-so since the creation of the world, according to the reckoning which we employ here in the congregation of Karaites; in the district of so-and-so, in the domain of the lord So-and-so, may he live forever. On that day there came So-and-so, son of So-and-so, before the elders of the congregation of Karaites, and he said to them:

B. "Be ye witnesses for me, and accept from me in legal terms, and write down and sign that which I am about to say before you. I am not laboring under compulsion or error or misunderstanding or force; rather with perfect heart, full knowledge, will, and intention, I admit before you and make you witnesses for me, to the effect that I have betrothed and sanctified unto myself the lady So-and-so, daughter of So-and-so, the virgin maiden, to be my wife, in purity and holiness, by way of bridal gift, marriage writ, and marital intercourse, according to the Law of Moses, the man of God, and according to the statutes of Israel, the pure and holy ones.

C. "I will clothe and cover and hold dear and support and feed her, and I will work for her to supply all her proper needs and desires, according to my strength and to the extent that I can afford. I will not oppress or despise her, nor will I betray her, and I will not diminish her food, clothing, and marital intercourse, as prescribed in the Law. And I will conduct myself toward her with truth, pity, and mercy, and I will treat her in the manner of the sons of Israel, who feed, honor, hold dear, and clothe their virtuous wives, and do all that is proper for them in faithfulness and uprightness.

D. "And the bridal gift which I stipulated, set, and imposed upon myself, the bridal gift for her virginity, as prescribed in the Law and proper for her, I shall give her."

E. And this lady So-and-so, the bride, heard the words of So-and-so, the groom, and she agreed, with perfect heart, to be his wife, companion, and woman of his covenant; to obey his voice and to hold him dear and to honor him and to do in his house all that the daughters of Israel do in the houses of their husbands, and to be under his rule, her desire being directed only toward him.

F. Both of them also willingly took upon themselves, by the free choice of their hearts, and by the covenant of Mount Sinai and the laws of Mount Horeb, to keep the holidays of the Lord, as sanctified by the observation of the moon and the finding of the fresh ears in the Holy Land of Israel, if they can find them.

G. And a covenant was made between So-and-so, the groom, and this lady So-and-so, the bride, embodying all that is written and explained above.

H. And the legal force of this deed of agreement is to be like that of all deeds in Israel, which are clear, fortified, customary, and proven, from this day into eternity.

I. And that which took place before us and which we have heard and seen, we have here written and signed, and we have given this deed into the hands of this bride, to serve in her hand as proof and title in any court in Israel, so that it may emerge true, upright, established, strong, clear, and lasting. And may they build a household and prosper. Amen!

12. The Proper Qualified Witnesses Are then to Sign It, and the Groom Is to Hand It to the Bride, Together with a Ring or Some Other Object of Value. The Person Who Recites the Blessing Is then to Recite to Them Softly, if the Bride Be a Virgin (Hos. 2:21):

And I will betroth thee unto me for ever;

And I will betroth thee unto me in righteousness, and in justice, and in lovingkindness, and in compassion;
And I will betroth thee unto me in faithfulness;
And thou shalt know the Lord.

Or if She Be a Widow, He Is to Recite (Isa. 54:4):
Fear not, for thou shalt not be ashamed;
Neither be thou confounded, for thou shalt not be put to shame.
For thou shalt forget the shame of thy youth,
And the reproach of thy widowhood shalt thou remember no more.

Or if She Be a Divorcée, He Is to Recite to Her (Isa. 62:4):
For thou shalt no more be termed Forsaken,
Neither shall thy land any more be termed Desolate;
But thou shalt be called, My delight is in her,
And thy land, Espoused;
For the Lord delights in thee, and thy land shall be espoused.

13. After All These Ceremonies the Person Who Pronounces the Blessing Is to Place the Curtain Over the Heads of the Groom and the Bride, and Is to Begin, in a Pleasant Manner, the Following:
The blessing of the Lord be upon you;
We bless you in the Name of the Lord (Ps. 129:8).
Blessed be he who comes in the Name of the Lord (Ps. 118:26).
So God give thee of the dew of heaven and of the fat of the earth, and plenty of corn and wine (Gen. 27:28).
And all the people who were in the gate, and the elders, said, We are witnesses; the Lord make the woman who is coming into thy house like Rachel and like Leah, which two did build the House of

Israel. And do thou worthily in Ephrath, and be famous in Beth-lehem.

And may thy house be like the house of Perez, whom Tamar bore unto Judah, from the seed which the Lord shall give thee out of this young woman (Ruth 4:11).

The Last Sentence Is to Be Pronounced Again, in Song, and Is to Be Repeated a Second Time by Those Present:

And may thy house be like the house of Perez, whom Tamar bore unto Judah, from the seed which the Lord shall give thee out of this young woman.

14. This to Be Followed by This Hymn:

The Lord, abiding in the mighty heavens,
Maker of heaven and earth,
Whose eyes roam over the whole earth,
May He bless the groom and cause him to become like the house of Perez.

Refrain: And may thy house be like the house of Perez.

The God who is sanctified in Israel and in Judah,
And is praised with singing and thanksgiving,
May He make fruitful and multiply this girl,
Like Perez whom Tamar bore unto Judah. (*Refrain.*)

And may the Almighty God bless thee,
And give thee the benediction bestowed upon Abraham;
And may He grant thee young sprigs around thy table,
From the seed which the Lord shall give thee. (*Refrain.*)

May they study this Law;
And those who fulfill the precepts in the midst of the congregation of Who is this,
Mayest thou be privileged to behold them
From this girl. (*Refrain.*)

Thou who dwellest in the highest heaven under the Name
of the Lord,
Do Thou strengthen and fortify the poor agitated people
of Israel,
To gather them in the rebuilt city of Jerusalem—
And then every soul will praise the Lord. (*Refrain.*)

15. The Person Reciting the Blessing Is then to Take Up a Cup of Wine in His Hand and Recite These Seven Benedictions.

The First Benediction:

Give ye thanks unto the Lord, for He is good,
For His mercy endureth for ever.
Give ye thanks unto the God of gods,
For His mercy endureth for ever.
Give ye thanks unto the Lord of lords,
For His mercy endureth for ever (Ps. 136:1–3).
I will lift up the cup of salvation,
And call upon the Name of the Lord (Ps. 116:13).
I will proclaim the Name of the Lord—
Ascribe ye greatness to our God (Deut. 32:3).
Blessed be the Lord, the God of Israel, from everlasting and to everlasting. Amen, and again amen! (Ps. 41:14).
Thou hast put gladness into my heart,
More than when their corn and their wine increase (Ps. 4:8).
Blessed art Thou, O Lord, our God, King of the universe, who growest the vine from the earth, and with its wine makest glad the heart of the children of man;
As it is written: And wine which gladdens the heart of man, causing his face to shine more than with oil, and bread which sustains man's heart (Ps. 104:15).

Blessed art Thou, O Lord, our God, King of the universe, who givest us joy and gladness, and dost create the fruit of the vine. Amen!

16. The Second Benediction:

Blessed be the Lord God, God of Israel, who alone does wondrous things;

And blessed be His glorious name forever; and let the whole earth be filled with his glory. Amen, and again amen! (Ps. 72:18–19).

I, even I, have made the earth, and have created man upon it;

I, Mine own hands, have stretched out the heavens, and all their host I have commanded (Isa. 45:12).

Yea, My hand has laid the foundation of the earth,

And My right hand has spread out the heavens.

When I call unto them, they stand up together (Isa. 48:13).

Thus said the Lord, thy Redeemer, and He who formed thee from the womb,

I am the Lord who makes all things, who alone stretches forth the heavens, who spreads out the earth, by Myself (Isa. 44:24).

Blessed art Thou, O Lord, our God, King of the universe, who hast created all things for the sake of Thy majesty. Amen!

17. The Third Benediction:

Blessed be the Lord, God of Israel, from everlasting even to everlasting; and let all the people say, Amen, praise ye the Lord! (Ps. 106:48).

For thus said the Lord, Creator of the heavens, He is God who formed the earth and made it; He established it, He created it not a waste, He formed it to be inhabited—I am the Lord, and there is none else (Isa. 45:18).

Thus said God, the Lord, who created the heavens and

stretched them forth, who spread forth the earth and its produce, who gives breath unto the people upon it, and spirit to those who walk therein (Isa. 42:5).

And the Lord God formed man of the dust of the ground, and He breathed into his nostrils the breath of life, and man became a living soul (Gen. 2:7).

Blessed art Thou, O Lord, our God, King of the universe, who hast formed man. Amen!

18. The Fourth Benediction:

Blessed be God who has not turned away my prayer, nor His mercy from me (Ps. 66:20).

And now thus says the Lord who has created thee, O Jacob, and who has formed thee, O Israel, Fear not, for I have redeemed thee, I have called thee by thy name, thou art Mine (Isa. 43:1).

And God said, Let Us make man in Our Image, after Our Likeness, and let them have dominion over the fish of the sea, and over the fowl of the air, and over the cattle, and over all the earth, and over every creeping thing that creeps upon the earth.

And God created man in His image, in the image of God did He create him, male and female created He them.

And God blessed them, and God said to them, Be fruitful and multiply, and replenish the earth and subdue it, and have dominion over the fish of the sea, and over the fowl of the air, and over every living thing that creeps upon the earth (Gen. 1:26–28).

Male and female created He them, and He blessed them, and called their name Man, on the day when they were created (Gen. 5:2).

Two are better than one, because they have a good reward for their labor (Eccles. 4:9).

And the Lord God said, It is not good that the man should

be alone; I will make him a help meet for him (Gen. 2:18).

And the Lord God caused a deep sleep to fall upon the man, and he slept; and He took one of his ribs, and closed up flesh in its place.

And the rib, which the Lord God had taken from the man, made He a woman, and He brought her to the man.

And the man said, This now is a bone of my bones, and flesh of my flesh; she shall be called Woman, because she was taken out of man.

Therefore shall a man leave his father and his mother, and shall cleave unto his wife, and they shall be one flesh (Gen. 2:21–24).

Blessed art Thou, O Lord, our God, King of the universe, who hast formed man. Amen!

19. The Fifth Benediction:

Blessed be the Lord out of Zion, who dwells in Jerusalem. Praise ye the Lord! (Ps. 135:21).

Sing, O barren one, thou who didst not bear,

Break forth into song and shout, thou who didst not travail,

For more are the children of the desolate than the children of the married wife, says the Lord (Isa. 54:1).

Sing, O daughter of Zion; shout, O Israel,

Rejoice and be glad wholeheartedly, O daughter of Jerusalem! (Zeph. 3:14).

Sing and rejoice, O daughter of Zion, for behold, I am coming, and I will dwell in the midst of thee, said the Lord (Zech. 2:14).

Thus says the Lord, I am returning to Zion, and I will dwell within Jerusalem,

And Jerusalem shall be called the city of truth, and the

mountain of the Lord of Hosts shall be called the holy mountain (Zech. 8:3).
They shall yet say in thine ears, the children of thy bereavement,
The place is too strait for me; give place to me that I may dwell.
And thou shalt say in thy heart, Who has begotten me these, seeing that I am bereaved and lonely, exiled and wandering; and who has brought these up? Behold, I was left alone; these, where had they been? (Isa. 49:20–21).
Let Israel rejoice in their Maker,
Let the children of Zion be joyful in their King (Ps. 149:2).
Blessed art Thou, O Lord, our God, King of the universe, who causest Zion to rejoice in her children. Amen!

20. The Sixth Benediction:
Blessed be the Lord;
Day by day He bears our burden, the God who is our salvation. Selah! (Ps. 68:20).
Rejoice in the Lord, O ye righteous ones,
And give thanks to his holy Name (Ps. 97:12).
Rejoice in the Lord and be joyful, O ye righteous ones,
And shout for joy, all ye upright of heart (Ps. 32:11).
Rejoice with Jerusalem, and be joyful with her, all ye who love her;
Rejoice with her in joy, all ye who mourn for her;
In order that ye may suck and be satisfied with the breast of her consolations,
That ye may drink deeply with delight of the abundance of her glory (Isa. 66:10–11).
Then shall the virgin rejoice in dancing,
And young men and old men together;

For I will turn their mourning into joy,
And I will console them and make them rejoice from their sorrow.
And I will satiate the soul of the priests with fat,
And My people shall be satisfied with My goodness, says the Lord (Jer. 31:12–13).
And let the righteous rejoice, let them be joyful before God,
And let them be glad with joy (Ps. 68:4).
Blessed art Thou, O Lord, our God, King of the universe, who causest bridegroom and bride to rejoice. Amen!

21. The Seventh Benediction:
Blessed art Thou, O Lord, teach me Thy statutes (Ps. 119:12).
I will greatly rejoice in the Lord,
My soul will be joyful in my God,
For He has clothed me with the garments of salvation,
He has covered me with the robe of righteousness,
As a bridegroom puts on a priestly diadem,
And as a bride adorns herself with her jewels (Isa. 61:10).
But be ye glad and rejoice for ever in that which I create,
For behold, I create Jerusalem a rejoicing, and her people a joy;
And I will rejoice in Jerusalem,
And joy in My people,
And no more shall there be heard within her the sound of weeping and the voice of crying (Isa. 65:18–19).
Lift up thine eyes round about and behold,
All these gather themselves together and come to thee;
As I live, says the Lord, thou shalt surely clothe thyself with them all, as with an ornament,
And gird thyself with them, like a bride (Isa. 49:18).
For as a young man espouses a virgin, so shall thy sons espouse thee,

And as the bridegroom rejoices over the bride,
So shall thy God rejoice over thee (Isa. 62:5).
Blessed art Thou, O Lord, our God, King of the universe, who givest joy to the bridegroom with the bride, who givest happiness and joy to the bridegroom with the bride. Amen!
Give thanks to the Lord, for He is good, for His mercy endureth for ever (Ps. 136:1).
May joys be many in Israel!
May consolations be many in Israel!
May salvations be many in Israel!
May good tidings be many in Israel!
May love multiply in Israel!
May blessing multiply in Israel!
May rejoicing multiply in Israel!
May joy multiply in Israel!
May splendor multiply in Israel!
May counsel multiply in Israel!
May merit multiply in Israel!
May bridegrooms be many in Israel!
May brides be many in Israel!

As of this day, and in Jerusalem, may they rejoice and be glad in the rebuilding of the Temple. May Elijah the Prophet come to us soon.

May the King Messiah spring up in our days.
May they both be glad, this one with that one!
May they both rejoice, that one with this one!
May they both prolong their days, this one with that one!
May they be vouchsafed proper sons, that one with this one!
May they build their household and prosper, this one with that one!
As they build, so may they prosper, as it is written: And the elders of the Jews builded and prospered (Ezra 6:14).
May the bridegroom rejoice with the bride,

May the bride rejoice with the bridegroom,
In sons and in daughters, in wealth and in possessions;
In sons who engage in the study of the Law
And fulfill the commandments in Israel.
Give thanks to the Lord, for He is good, for His mercy endureth for ever (Ps. 136:1).

22. THE BRIDEGROOM AND BRIDE THEN DRINK FROM THE CUP. AS THE BRIDEGROOM DRINKS, YOU ARE TO RECITE TO HIM THIS:

Drink water out of thine own cistern
And running water out of thine own well.
Let thy fountains be dispersed abroad
In the streets, as streams of water.
Let them be for thee alone,
And not for strangers with thee.
Let thy spring be blessed,
And have joy of the wife of thy youth (Prov. 5:15–18).

23. AS THE BRIDE DRINKS, RECITE TO HER THIS:

A lovely hind and a graceful doe,
Let her breasts satisfy thee at all times,
In her love take thou delight always (Prov. 5:19).
Whoso finds a wife, finds a great good,
And obtains favor from the Lord (Prov. 18:22).
A valiant woman who can find?
For her price is far above rubies (Prov. 31:10).
Grace is deceitful, and vain is beauty;
But a woman that feareth the Lord, she shall be praised (Prov. 31:30).
House and riches are the inheritance of fathers,
But a prudent wife is from the Lord (Prov. 19:14).
So shalt thou find grace and good favor in the sight of God and man (Prov. 3:4).

24. AFTER THIS, RECITE THE FOLLOWING, IN THE MELODY OF EXILE:

Ye who have escaped the sword, go ye, stand not still;

Remember the Lord from afar,
And let Jerusalem come to your mind (Jer. 51:50).
If I forget thee, O Jerusalem,
Let my right hand forget her cunning;
Let my tongue cleave to the roof of my mouth,
If I remember thee not (Ps. 137:5–6).

25. Thereupon Sprinkle Ashes upon Their Heads and Recite the Following:

If I set not Jerusalem above my chief joy (Ps. 137:6).
The joy of our hearts has ceased,
Our dance has been turned into mourning,
The crown is fallen from our head;
Woe unto us, for we have sinned.
For this our heart is faint,
For these things are our eyes dim;
For the mountain of Zion which is desolate,
And foxes walk upon it (Lam. 5:15–18).
And after all that has come upon us for our evil deeds, and our great guilt, seeing that Thou, our God, hast punished us less than our iniquities deserve, and hast given us such a remnant (Ezra 9:13).
O Lord, God of Israel, Thou art righteous, for we are left a remnant that is escaped, as it is this day. Behold, we are before Thee in our guilt, for none can stand before Thee, because of this (Ezra 9:15).
Howbeit Thou art just in all that is come upon us,
For Thou hast dealt truly,
But we have done wickedly (Neh. 9:33).
Turn from Thy fierce wrath,
And repent of this evil against Thy people (Exod. 32:12).
Turn back for the sake of Thy servants,
The tribes of Thine inheritance (Isa. 63:17).
Turn Thou us to Thee, O Lord, and we shall be turned,
Renew our days as of old (Lam. 5:21).
And forgive our sin and our transgression,

And take us for Thine inheritance (Exod. 34:9).
Blessed be the Lord into eternity. Amen, and again amen!

26. Then Change the Melody and Recite the Following:

Therefore thus says the Lord: I return to Jerusalem in mercy;
My House shall be built therein, says the Lord of Hosts,
And a line shall be stretched forth over Jerusalem.
Again proclaim, saying: Thus says the Lord of Hosts:
My cities shall again overflow with prosperity,
And the Lord shall yet console Zion,
And shall yet choose Jerusalem (Zech. 1:16–17).
Thus says the Lord of Hosts: If it be marvelous in the eyes of the remnant of this people in those days,
Should it also be marvelous in Mine eyes? says the Lord of Hosts.
Thus says the Lord of Hosts: Behold, I will save My people from the country of the east, and from the country of the west;
And I will bring them back, and they shall dwell within Jerusalem,
And they shall be My people,
And I will be their God in truth and in righteousness (Zech. 8:6–8).
Thus says the Lord of Hosts: I am jealous for Zion with great jealousy,
And I am jealous for her with great wrath.
Thus says the Lord: I return unto Zion,
And I will dwell within Jerusalem,
And Jerusalem shall be called the city of truth,
And the mountain of the Lord of Hosts the holy mountain (Zech. 8:2–3).
Thus says the Lord: The people who were left of the sword have found grace in the wilderness,
Even Israel, when I go to cause him to rest.
From afar did the Lord appear to me:

Yea, I have loved thee with a love eternal,
Therefore did I draw thee unto Me with affection.
Again will I build thee, and thou shalt be built, O virgin of Israel;
Thou shalt yet adorn thyself with thy tambourines,
And shalt step out in the dance of the merrymakers.
Thou shalt yet plant vineyards in the mountains of Samaria;
Planters shall plant, and eat the fruits thereof.
For there shall be a day when watchmen upon the mountain of Ephraim shall cry,
Arise ye, and let us go up to Zion, to the Lord, our God (Jer. 31:1–6).
For God will save Zion,
And will rebuild the cities of Judah,
And they shall dwell there, and have possession of it.
And the seed of His servants shall inherit it,
And those who love His Name shall reside therein (Ps. 69:36–37).

27. Then Bless the Bridegroom Thus:
And thou, our dear brother, the bridegroom, may the Lord, God of Israel, give thee thy heart's desire in the way of good things.
Mayest thou spend thy days and thy years in pleasantness.
While thy beginning is small, may thy ending be very great (Job. 8:7).
May He grant thee sons, and sons' sons, studying the Law.
Blessed be thou in thy coming, and blessed be thou in thy going (Deut. 28:6).
Blessed be thou more than all nations, and may there be no childless man or woman with thee, nor any unfruitful animal with thy cattle.
The Lord guard thee from all evil; may He guard thy soul.

The Lord guard thy going and thy coming, from now and into eternity (Ps. 121:6 f.).

When thou goest, may thy footstep not be narrow, and if thou runnest, mayest thou not stumble (Prov. 4:12).

28. Then Bless the Bride also, Saying:

And thou, our sister, the bride, mayest thou become a thousand times ten thousand descendants, and may thy seed inherit the gate of their enemies (Gen. 24:60).

Blessed be thou unto the Lord, blessed be thou, and blessed be thy reputation.

Blessed be ye both unto the Lord, the Maker of heaven and earth.

29. This Is to Be Followed By the Following Prayer:

Our God and God of our fathers, fulfill for us Thy good word which Thou hast spoken, to wit:

Thus says the Lord: There shall yet be heard in this place, of which ye say that it is desolate, devoid of man, and devoid of beast, even in the cities of Judah and in the streets of Jerusalem, which are abandoned, devoid of man, and devoid of inhabitant, and devoid of beast—

The voice of joy, and the voice of gladness, the voice of the bridegroom and the voice of the bride, the voice of them that say, Give thanks to the Lord of Hosts, for the Lord is good, for His mercy endureth for ever, even of them that bring offerings of thanksgiving into the House of the Lord. For I will cause the captivity of the Land to return, as at the first, says the Lord (Jer. 33:10–11).

A song of ascents (Ps. 126):

When the Lord brought back those who returned to Zion,
We were like dreamers.

Then was our mouth filled with laughter, and our tongue with song.
Then said they among the nations,
Great things has the Lord done with these people.
Great things has the Lord done with us, and we were gladdened.
Turn our captivity, O Lord, as the streams in the dry land.
Those who sow in tears shall reap with song;
Though he goes on his way weeping that bears the measure of seed,
He shall surely come home with song, carrying his sheaves.
Blessed be the Lord into eternity. Amen, and again amen!

30. As They Come Out of the Door of the Synagogue, Recite This:

Refrain: For ye shall go out with joy,
And be led forth with peace.

The mountains and the hills shall burst forth before you into song,
And all the trees of the field shall clap their hands (Isa. 55:12). (*Refrain.*)
For ye shall not go out in haste, neither shall ye go by flight;
For the Lord will go before you, and your rear guard shall be the God of Israel (Isa. 52:12). (*Refrain.*)
A palanquin did King Solomon make for himself, out of the wood of Lebanon. (*Refrain.*)
Its pillars he made of silver, its top of gold, its seat of purple, its interior lined with love, from the daughters of Jerusalem. (*Refrain.*)
Go out and gaze, O daughters of Zion, upon King Solomon and upon the crown wherewith his mother has crowned him on the day of his espousals, and

on the day of the gladness of his heart (Song 3:9–11).

31. *Refrain:* The voice of joy, and the voice of gladness, the voice of the bridegroom, and the voice of the bride (Jer. 7:34).

Adam was the handsomest among men,
And Eve was the most beautiful among women;
This one the handsomest among men,
And that one the most beautiful among women.
(*Refrain.*)

Abraham was the handsomest among men,
And Sarah was the most beautiful among women;
This one the handsomest among men,
And that one the most beautiful among women.
(*Refrain.*)

Isaac was the handsomest among men,
And Rebekah was the most beautiful among women;
This one the handsomest among men,
And that one the most beautiful among women.
(*Refrain.*)

Jacob was the handsomest among men,
And Rachel was the most beautiful among women;
This one the handsomest among men,
And that one the most beautiful among women.
(*Refrain.*)

Joseph was the handsomest among men,
And Asenath was the most beautiful among women;
This one the handsomest among men,
And that one the most beautiful among women.
(*Refrain.*)

Moses was the handsomest among men,
And Zipporah was the most beautiful among women;
This one the handsomest among men,
And that one the most beautiful among women.
(*Refrain.*)

Aaron was the handsomest among men,
And Elisheba was the most beautiful among women;
This one the handsomest among men,
And that one the most beautiful among women.
(*Refrain.*)

The bridegroom is the handsomest among men,
And the bride is the most beautiful among women;
This one the handsomest among men,
And that one the most beautiful among women.
(*Refrain.*)

32. As the Bridegroom Enters the Bridal Canopy, Recite for Him This:

Refrain: May he rise, may he rise!
May he rise, may he rise, may he rise!

May the bridegroom rise to the top, as Adam and Eve have risen to the top. (*Refrain.*)
May the bridegroom rise to the top, as Abraham and Sarah have risen to the top. (*Refrain.*)
May the bridegroom rise to the top, as Isaac and Rebekah have risen to the top. (*Refrain.*)
May the bridegroom rise to the top, as Jacob and Rachel have risen to the top. (*Refrain.*)
May the bridegroom rise to the top, as Joseph and Asenath have risen to the top. (*Refrain.*)
May the bridegroom rise to the top, as Moses and Zipporah have risen to the top. (*Refrain.*)
May the bridegroom rise to the top, as Aaron and Elisheba have risen to the top. (*Refrain.*)
May the bridegroom rise to the top, as every past bridegroom and bride have risen to the top. (*Refrain.*)
And he said, Come in, thou blessed of the Lord (Gen. 24:31).
Blessed be he who comes in the Name of the Lord;
We bless you from the House of the Lord (Ps. 118:26).

33. Give Thanks to the Lord, for He Is Good, for His Mercy Endureth for Ever. Give Thanks to the God of Gods, for His Mercy Endureth for Ever. Give Thanks to the Lord of Lords, for His Mercy Endureth for Ever (Ps. 136:1–3).

May joys be many in Israel!
May consolations be many in Israel!
May salvations be many in Israel!
May good tidings be many in Israel!
May miracles be many in Israel!
May love multiply in Israel!
May blessing multiply in Israel!
May rejoicing multiply in Israel!
May joy multiply in Israel!
May splendor multiply in Israel!
May counsel multiply in Israel!
May merit multiply in Israel!
May bridegrooms be many in Israel!
May brides be many in Israel!

34. As of This Day, and in Jerusalem, May They Rejoice and Be Glad in the Rebuilding of the Temple. May Elijah the Prophet Come to Us Soon. May the King Messiah Spring Up in Our Days.

May they both be glad, this one with that one!
May they both prolong their days, that one with this one!
May they be vouchsafed proper sons, this one with that one!
May they build their household and prosper, that one with this one!
As they build, so may they prosper,
As it is written: And the elders of the Jews builded and prospered (Ezra 6:14).
May the bridegroom rejoice with the bride,
May the bride rejoice with the groom,
In sons and in daughters, in wealth and in possessions;
In sons who engage in the study of the Law

And fulfill the commandments in Israel.
Give thanks to the Lord, for He is good, for His mercy endureth for ever (Ps. 136:1).

35. A Song of Ascents (Ps. 128)

Happy is every one who fears the Lord,
Who walks in His ways.
When thou eatest of the labor of thy hands,
Happy shalt thou be, and it shall be well with thee.
Thy wife shall be as a fruitful vine within thy house,
Thy children like olive plants round about thy table.
Behold, surely thus shall the man be blessed who fears the Lord.
The Lord bless thee out of Zion,
And see thou the good of Jerusalem, all the days of thy life;
And see thy children's children; peace be upon Israel.

36. If You Wish to Lengthen the Prayer Some More, Add This Also:

Refrain: May He bless, may He bless, may He bless, even the Lord!

May the Lord bless, bless, bless, the bridegroom and the bride, as He has blessed Adam and Eve. (*Refrain.*)
May the Lord bless, bless, bless, the bridegroom and the bride, as He has blessed Abraham and Sarah. (*Refrain.*)
May the Lord bless, bless, bless, the bridegroom and the bride, as He has blessed Isaac and Rebekah. (*Refrain*).
May the Lord bless, bless, bless, the bridegroom and the bride, as He has blessed Jacob and Rachel and Leah. (*Refrain.*)
May the Lord bless, bless, bless, the bridegroom and the

bride, as He has blessed Joseph and Asenath. (*Refrain.*)

May the Lord bless, bless, bless, the bridegroom and the bride, as He has blessed Moses and Zipporah. (*Refrain.*)

May the Lord bless, bless, bless, the bridegroom and the bride, as He has blessed Aaron and Elisheba. (*Refrain.*)

May the Lord bless, bless, bless, the bridegroom and the bride, as He has blessed all our righteous fathers. (*Refrain.*)

As it is written: The Lord bless thee out of Zion, and see thou the good of Jerusalem, all the days of thy life; and see thy children's children; peace be upon Israel (Ps. 128:5–6).

37. After All These Prayers, Turn and Bless the Congregation, Saying:

And you, O holy congregation, people of the Lord, who proclaim the oneness of God, precious possession of the living God, who have gathered together to accompany the bridegroom and the bride, and have done this kindness unto them;

May the God of Israel bless you, and guard you, and watch over you, and help you, and fulfill upon you the written blessing, to wit:

May the Lord, God of your fathers, add unto you as many as ye are, a thousand times, and may He bless you, as He has spoken to you (Deut. 1:11).

The smallest shall become a thousand,
And the least a mighty nation;
I, the Lord, will hasten it in its time (Isa. 60:22).
The Lord does build up Jerusalem,
He gathers together the dispersed of Israel (Ps. 147:2).
Peace, peace, to him that is far off and to him that is near,

Says the Lord that creates the fruit of the lips,
And I will heal him (Isa. 57:19).
Dominion and awe are with Him,
He makes peace in His high places (Job 25:2).
The Lord will give strength to His people,
The Lord will bless His people with peace (Ps. 29:11).
Blessed be the Lord in eternity. Amen, and again amen!

38. Thereupon the Congregation Is to Sit Down to a Meal with the Bridegroom. Before the Meal, the Benediction Over the Wine Is to Be Recited as Follows:

Give thanks to the Lord, for He is good, for His mercy endureth for ever.
Give thanks to the God of gods, for His mercy endureth for ever.
Give thanks to the Lord of lords, for His mercy endureth for ever. (Ps. 136:1–3).
And blessed be our God, King of the universe, who has created the vine, and gladdens with its wine the hearts of the children of man, as it is written: And wine which gladdens the heart of man, causing his face to shine more than with oil, and bread which sustains man's heart (Ps. 104:15).
Blessed art Thou, O Lord, our God, King of the universe, who givest us rejoicing and gladness and createst the fruit of the vine. Amen!

39. Those Who Sit at the Table Are then to Taste the Wine, and After This, Pronounce the Benediction Over the Bread, Saying:

Blessed art Thou, O Lord, our God, King of the universe, who bringest forth bread out of the earth. Amen!

40. They Are then to Eat and Drink of What the Lord Has Appointed to Them Out of His Hidden Bounty. And Accord-

ING TO THE ANCIENT CUSTOM, THEY ARE TO GIVE PRAISE TO THE MASTER OF ALL THINGS OVER EACH CUP OF WINE.

OVER THE FIRST CUP THE PRECENTOR SAYS:
Praise be to His great Name!
AND THE PEOPLE RESPOND:
Blessed be He, and blessed be His Name!
OVER THE SECOND CUP:
Praise be to the Name of our God!
RESPONSE:
Blessed be the Name of our God!
OVER THE THIRD CUP:
Praise be to Him who spoke, and the world came into being!
RESPONSE:
Blessed be He who spoke, and the world came into being!
OVER THE FOURTH CUP:
For the greatness of the Law of our God!
RESPONSE:
May God make it great!
OVER THE FIFTH CUP:
For the revelation of our master Elijah!
RESPONSE:
May God reveal him!
OVER THE SIXTH CUP:
For the coming of our King, the Messiah!
RESPONSE:
He shall come home with joy, bearing his sheaves! (Ps. 126:6).
OVER THE SEVENTH CUP:
For the rebuilding of Zion and Jerusalem!
RESPONSE:
The Lord does build up Jerusalem,
He gathers together the dispersed of Israel! (Ps. 147:2).
OVER THE EIGHTH CUP:
For the rebuilding of the Temple!

RESPONSE:

May it soon be renewed!

41. AFTER THIS, ALL WHO WISH TO SING HYMNS AND SONGS TO ENTERTAIN THE BRIDEGROOM AND THE BRIDE MAY DO SO. AFTER THEY HAVE EATEN THEIR FILL THEY ARE TO DRINK A CUP OF WINE TO THE JOY OF THE PARENTS-IN-LAW, SAYING:

With the joy of all who fear God,
May God gladden them;
With the joy of the parents-in-law,
May God gladden them.

THEN A CUP TO THE GROOMSMEN:

With the joy of all pious and perfect men,
May God gladden them;
With the joy of the groomsmen,
May God gladden them.

THEN A CUP TO THE USHERS:

With the joy of all desirable young men,
May God gladden them;
With the joy of the ushers at the banquet,
May God gladden them.

THEN THE LAST CUP TO THE JOY OF THE BRIDEGROOM AND THE BRIDE:

With the coming of the King Messiah,
May God bring him soon;
With the joy of the bridegroom and the bride,
May God gladden them.

42. AFTER THIS THEY ARE TO GIVE PRAISE TO HIM WHO FEEDS AND SUSTAINS ALL CREATURES, AND ADD SUCH SCRIPTURAL VERSES AS ARE APPROPRIATE TO THE REJOICING OF THE BRIDEGROOM AND THE BRIDE:

The Lord is good to all, and His mercy is upon all His works (Ps. 145:9).

What we have eaten, may it be for satiety;
What we have drunk, may it be for a healing;
What we have left, may it be for a blessing.
In our low estate He has remembered us,
For His mercy endureth for ever.
And He has redeemed us from our enemies,
For His mercy endureth for ever.
Who gives bread to all flesh,
For His mercy endureth for ever.
Give thanks to the God of heaven,
For His mercy endureth for ever (Ps. 136:23).
May Thy kindness, O Lord, be upon us,
As we have waited for Thee (Ps. 33:22).

43. Blessed Be the Lord

Blessed be Thou, O Lord, God of Israel, our Father, for ever and ever.
Thine, O Lord, is the greatness, and the power, and the glory, and the victory, and the majesty, for all things in heaven and upon earth are Thine;
Thine, O Lord, is the kingdom, and Thou art exalted as head above all.
Wealth and honor are from Thee, and Thou rulest over all, and in Thy hand is power and might, and in Thy hand is the power to exalt and to strengthen all.
And now, our God, we give Thee thanks and we praise Thy glorious Name (I Chron. 29:10–13).
And we will bless the Lord from this time forth and for ever.
Praise ye the Lord! (Ps. 115:18).
The eyes of all wait for Thee,
And Thou givest them their food in its due time.
Thou openest Thy hand,
And satisfiest with good will every living thing (Ps. 145:15–16).

Mayest Thou fill us with Thy good will,
And remove leanness from us.
Grant us our appointed measure of bread, for Thy table is spread for all creatures.
By the length of Thy patience and the bounty of Thy kindness do we live and exist, and by the openness of Thy hand.
For Thou art the one who feeds and sustains and supports all, and prepares food and sustenance for all Thy creatures, which Thou hast created.
Blessed art Thou, O Lord, who feedest all creatures.

All Those Who Are Seated at the Table Are in Duty Bound to Respond: Amen!

44. A Psalm of David (Ps. 23)
The Lord is my shepherd,
I shall not want.
He makes me to lie down in green pastures,
He leads me beside the still waters.
He restores my soul,
He guides me in straight paths for His Name's sake.
Yea, though I walk through the valley of the shadow of death,
I will fear no evil, for Thou art with me,
Thy rod and Thy staff, they comfort me.
Thou preparest a table before me, in the presence of mine enemies,
Thou hast anointed my head with oil, my cup runs over.
Surely goodness and mercy shall follow me all the days of my life,
And I shall dwell in the House of the Lord for ever.

45. With long life will I satisfy him,
And I will show him My salvation (Ps. 91:16).
I hope for Thy salvation, O Lord! (Gen. 49:18).

Consider and see that the Lord is good,
Blessed is the man who takes refuge in Him.
Fear the Lord, O ye His holy ones,
For there is no want for those who fear Him.
Young lions do lack, and suffer hunger,
But those who seek the Lord shall not want any good thing (Ps. 34:9–11).
Let the meek eat and be satiated,
Let those who seek the Lord praise Him,
May your heart be quickened for ever.
All the ends of the earth shall remember, and turn unto the Lord,
All the families of nations shall bow down before Thee.
For the kingdom belongs to the Lord,
And He is the ruler over the nations.
All the fat ones of the earth shall eat and worship,
Before Him shall kneel all those who go down to the dust,
Even he who cannot keep alive his own soul.
A seed shall serve Him,
It shall be told of the Lord unto the next generation;
They shall come and shall declare His righteousness,
Unto a people that shall be born, that He had done this (Ps. 22:27–32).
If I forget thee, O Jerusalem,
Let my right hand forget her cunning.
Let my tongue cleave to the roof of my mouth,
If I remember thee not,
If I set not Jerusalem above my chief joy (Ps. 137:5–6).
Rejoice with Jerusalem, and be joyful with her, all ye who love her;
Rejoice with her in joy, all ye who mourn for her;
That ye may suck and be satisfied with the breast of her consolations,
That ye may drink deeply with delight of the abundance of her glory (Isa. 66:10).

46. Then Recite Again From

Thou hast put gladness into my heart (above, p. 287).

To

So shalt thou find grace and good favor in the eyes of God and man (above, p. 294).

47. Then Recite This:

They that strive with the Lord shall be broken to pieces.
Against them will He thunder in heaven;
The Lord will judge the ends of the earth,
And He will give strength to His king,
And will exalt the horn of His anointed (I Sam. 2:10).
He gives great deliverances to His king,
And does kindness to His anointed,
To David and to his seed, for evermore (Ps. 18:51).
The Lord has remembered us; He will bless,
He will bless the house of Israel,
He will bless the house of Aaron,
He will bless those who fear the Lord,
The little with the great.
May the Lord add unto you,
Unto you, and unto your children.
Blessed be ye unto the Lord,
Maker of heaven and earth (Ps. 115:12–15).
The smallest shall become a thousand,
And the least a mighty nation;
I, the Lord, will hasten it in its time (Isa. 60:22).
The Lord is the rebuilder of Jerusalem,
He will gather together the dispersed of Israel (Ps. 147:2).
Peace, peace, to him that is far off and to him that is near,
Says the Lord that creates the fruit of the lips,
And I will heal him (Isa. 57:19).
Dominion and awe are with Him,
He who makes peace in His high places (Job 25:2).
The Lord will give strength to His people,

The Lord will bless His people with peace (Ps. 29:11).
Blessed be the Lord into eternity. Amen, and again amen!

II. HYMN OF SUPPLICATION

1 We pray Thee, our God, God of the spirits of all flesh, do not be angry with us, for our soul is at its extremity, and our spirit is exhausted.

Because of the multitude of our sins did all these misfortunes befall us, and because of the greatness of our guilt did all this calamity overtake us.

Our might is gone, and our hands are powerless, for help and refuge have been lost to us.

Thou art a truthful judge, and it is for Thee to conduct our trial, for Thou art the one to sit in judgment upon us and to examine our souls.

5 Are not the secrets of the heart and of the kidneys revealed before Thee? And Thou dost understand man's innermost thoughts.

It is known since eternity, O God of forgiveness, that we are doers of evil, yet Thou dost forgive us.

Pure and upright art Thou, and dost not hold a grudge into eternity, for thus hast Thou assured us through Thy seers.

Thou art living and everlasting. Have pity and mercy upon our remnant.

Thou art good, and Thou dost good. For Thee does our soul wait; we know, O our Rock, that Thou wilt not forsake us.

10 We are the creatures of Thy hand, and the work of Thy fingers.

Pray let us not perish, for what profit be there in the spilling of our blood?

We are like dry grass, and our years are like the passing shadow, which is here today, and tomorrow is no more.

There is no reckoning to Thy days, and no number to Thy years, for all things shall perish, but Thou wilt live into eternity.

Hasten and answer us, O God of our salvation, for we have been exceedingly humbled, and have gone down into the dust.

Thou hast spoken in behalf of the humble, at the time when his hand has dropped helplessly, to show him mercy and grace, and to give him strength.

O Upholder of those who are falling, be our Helper, for enemies have devoured and overwhelmed us with all their wide-open mouths.

They have stood over us at the time when our hands dropped helplessly, until they have exhausted our strength, and they gave us no respite.

We turned to the right, but no one recognized us; we looked out to the left, but no one upheld our hand.

Many misfortunes have surrounded us, and many evils have encompassed us, and pains like the pains of a woman in childbirth have taken hold of us.

Draw Thou near, and hear our voice, and hearken to our supplication.

Remember the covenant which Thou hast made with the Father of the multitude, O God who rememberest covenants; O Thou who keepest covenants, look at that covenant;

And do not break the covenant, but fulfill the oath given to mortals.

Mayest Thou remember the love of the Wholehearted One, and preserve our remnant, and may Thy mercy grow warm for our remnant,

Even though we have come to implore Thee without being worthy of Thy kindness, and without having earned merit.

III. PENITENTIAL HYMN

1 Today, may it please Thee, O God All-high, my Rock and my King, to receive my request, and my supplication, and my prayer; for this is the Day of Atonement. And be gracious unto me, O Lord, for unto Thee do I call all day.

Today, pray tear up the writ of my debt to Thee, and hearken to my cry, and purify me with hyssop, so that I may become clean. And may my sin not be counted, nor be remembered any longer, for the sake of Thy mercy, and because of the merit of him who sat at the door of the tent during the heat of the day.

Today, take notice of the confession of my lips, O Rider of the heavens, and forgive all transgression and guilt, and fulfill Thy good promises made to us, as it is written in the words of Thy Prophet: But ye who did cleave to the Lord, your God, are alive, every one of you, this day (Deut. 4:4).

Today, I have forsaken the way of evil, and I have drawn near unto Thee, my Refuge and my Shepherd, with a perfect heart, to pray for pardon, for the atonement of my evil deeds. Look down therefore upon me from Thy holy abode and hear my prayer, O God of my salvation. In Thee I place my hope all day.

5 Today, I have raised my voice before Thee in proclaiming the goodness of Thy grace, from morning until evening, and in praying for forgiveness, and amidst the supplication of the recipients of Thy mercy, who are eager to obey Thy words, and who desire to fear Thy Name. Grant therefore, I pray Thee, prosperity to Thy servant, today.

Today, I have drawn near unto Thee to confess the sin of our wickedness, for which we owe a trespass offering before Thee, our holy Creator; and the sin for which we owe a guilt offering. Be pleased and willing to accept them from us, for the day has turned toward evening.

Today, we wait for Thy mercy and kindness. Grant us Thy pity and mercy. Wipe out and remove our trespasses and vouchsafe us Thy goodness. Mayest Thou turn about to grant us Thy mercy, and mayest Thou suppress our sins, as Thou hast done day before yesterday, and yesterday, and today.

Today, Thou wilt fortify our hearts with fear of Thee, and wilt erase our trespasses from Thy book of sins which Thou hast written, and wilt decree that we be transferred to the book of life, on the tenth day of this seventh month, which Thou hast made a rule and a law in Israel, to be observed as a fast, even until today.

Today, may the cry and prayer of Thy people be acceptable before Thee, like the rams and oxen which the priest used to sacrifice in their behalf on this very day. And accept their prayer and supplication, for they have eaten no bread today.

10 Today, we hope for Thy good tidings; cause them to come to pass, therefore, do not delay. Hasten and bring near salvation and prosperity to Thy chosen people. The children of Israel, Thy holy people, have devoted themselves to Thy desolate Temple, to venerate it and to invoke a blessing upon its name, until this very day.

Today, may Thy salvation come near to us, O Awesome of deeds; and throw upon us clean water to purify us, and remove all our misdeeds and trespasses. And mayest Thou from the heavens hear the song and the prayer which Thy servant is praying before Thee, today.

IV. PENITENTIAL HYMN

1 We have come before Thee with bent heads, because of the sin of our rapacity. Trembling has seized us, and fire has been kindled in our ribs, for we are drowning in the bottomless mire of our trespasses. We know, O Lord, our wickedness, the sin of our fathers; for we have sinned. Yea, we have sinned.

Behold, Thy people are in fear of Thy Day of Judgment, because of the enormity of their disobedience. They are drawing repentance with the bucket of supplication, because of the greatness of their destitution. They bend their knee to Thee and supplicate Thee in the land of their captivity, saying, We have sinned. Yea, we have sinned.

The hosts of my sins pursue me—how then can I cheer my heart? I am imprisoned in their dungeon, and I walk softly in dread of them all my years. I am clad in trembling as in a cloak, submissive and confessing the sins of the children of Israel, which we have sinned. Yea, we have sinned.

We have been exhausted and oppressed exceedingly, we are lowly and despised. We have doffed the mantle of esteem, and have been left empty and slighted. Who has delivered Jacob to spoliation, and Israel to despoilers? Was it not the Lord, against whom we have sinned? Yea, we have sinned.

5 I am ashamed and embarrassed to raise mine eyes unto Thee. I said, I will guard my lips and refrain from multiplying talk with my tongue. I know my trespasses are many, as are the sins of my people, for I and the whole house of my father have sinned. Yea, we have sinned.

We who are swamped by the evil deeds of enemies pray in our exile, but there is none to extricate us. The gates of mercy have been locked against us because of the hardness of our hardened heart. For we have ceased to observe every commandment written in the Law of Moses, the servant of God, for we have sinned. Yea, we have sinned.

Indeed, the Lord has chastised us, and has cast us into the dust of death, for we have scorned His Law. What then can we say, after we have committed our trespass? Righteousness is Thine, O Lord, but for us a shamed face, as well as for our kings, our nobles, and our fathers, all of us who have sinned. Yea, we have sinned.

Now behold, we are fervent before Thee in confessing our debts to Thee, like a pauper begging at a door, and in tearing open the innermost part of our hearts. Pardon the evil of our deeds, for our misdeeds are many. We have sinned against Thee. Yea, we have sinned.

Pardon, we pray Thee, sins both evident and hidden, and have mercy upon my multitudes; and remember in our favor the covenant made with my great ones, and the consolations promised in my Prophets' visions. Thy comfortings will delight our souls, even though we have sinned against the Lord, our God. Yea, we have sinned.

10 Turn to the cry of Thy poor ones, and sprinkle upon us the water of purification. Consider our penitent meditation as a burnt offering and as a sin offering. Raise unto us the light of Thy countenance, and do not charge us permanently with sin, according as we have been unwise and sinful. Yea, we have sinned.

V. HYMN TO THE SABBATH

Refrain: The Sabbath day, there is none like it;
God blessed it and sanctified it.

1 From Sunday till Friday my soul longs for the Sabbath, because on the Sabbath I gain freedom, and because I call it a day of rest. God blessed it and sanctified it. (*Refrain.*)

Let us be joyful and rejoice, for it is good to give thanks and to sing praises to the All-Highest about everything of His goodness, for on the Sabbath there are desirable blessings for us; only an ignorant man knows it not. God blessed it and sanctified it. (*Refrain.*)

The Sabbath must be observed according to its regulations, it being a commandment prepared out of Mount Sinai. Yea, it is a royal crown for him who observes it, and it crowns him with honor and splendor. God blessed it and sanctified it. (*Refrain.*)

Those who love it prolong their life, likewise those who taste of it gain life, and they walk in the path of uprightness. Those who guard His testaments search for it with all their hearts. God blessed it and sanctified it. (*Refrain.*)

5 It has pleased the Lord to choose us and to set us apart from every tongue, and He endowed us with the sanctity of the Sabbath. O ye, all the seed of Jacob, do honor unto it! God blessed it and sanctified it. (*Refrain.*)

As it is written: Wherefore the Lord blessed the Sabbath day and hallowed it (Exod. 20:11).

VI. DIRGE

1 For the palace that has been forsaken,
We sit alone and weep.

For the Temple that has been demolished,
We sit alone and weep.
For fences that have been breached,
We sit alone and weep.
For my sanctuary that has been burned,
We sit alone and weep.
For the roads to the Temple that have been uprooted,
We sit alone and weep.
For bolts that have been snapped,
We sit alone and weep.
For malefactors who have prevailed,
We sit alone and weep.
For the shame that has grown great,
We sit alone and weep.
For stone colonnades that have been scorched,
We sit alone and weep.
For friends who have been dispersed,
We sit alone and weep.
For priests who have stumbled,
We sit alone and weep.
For sacred studies that have been prevented,
We sit alone and weep.
For kings who have been scorned by God,
We sit alone and weep.
For nobles who have been humiliated,
We sit alone and weep.
For the humble ones who have been reduced,
We sit alone and weep.
For the redeemed ones who have been abducted,
We sit alone and weep.
For the united ones who have been scattered,
We sit alone and weep.
For the holy ones who have been besmirched,
We sit alone and weep.
For the rains that have been abolished,
We sit alone and weep.

20 For peace offerings that have been discontinued,
We sit alone and weep.
For continual offerings that have been discontinued,
We sit alone and weep.

VII. PRIVATE PRAYER

1 May it please Thee, O Lord, my God and God of my fathers, to purify my thoughts and to set aright the utterance of my tongue and the reflections of my heart. And be Thou with my heart when my heart is thinking, and with my hands when I am at work, and with my feet when I am upon my way. And let me not say before Thee anything that is improper or against Thy wish. And do Thou rebuke Satan, and let not bad dreams frighten me, nor the evil genius gain mastery over me.

O Master of the worlds, it is open and known unto Thee that my desire is to do Thy will, save that the leaven in the dough prevents it.

May it please Thee, O my God and God of my fathers, to destroy and subdue the evil genius, and chase him away from me, and keep him away from the two hundred and forty-eight members of my body; and let him not lead me astray from Thy good paths. Rather place Thou the good genius in my heart, to make me observe Thy laws and do Thy will, and serve Thee with a perfect heart.

And accept this, my prayer, as it is written: Hear my prayer, O Lord, and give ear unto my cry; keep not silence at my tear. For I am a stranger with Thee, a sojourner, as were all my fathers (Ps. 39:13).

5 But as for me, let my prayer be unto Thee, O Lord, in an acceptable time. O God, in the abundance of

Thy mercy, answer me with the truth of Thy salvation (Ps. 69: 14).

And hear my prayer, for Thou hearest the prayer of every mouth.

Blessed art Thou, O Lord, who hearest all prayer.

VIII. PRIVATE PRAYER

1 May it please Thee, O Lord, my God and God of my fathers, that Thy Law should be my daily occupation.

And give me a good heart, and a good portion in life, and a good friend, and a humble soul, and a lowly spirit.

And let not Thy Name be profaned because of me, nor make me a byword in the mouths of Thy creatures.

And let my end be not one of being cut off, nor let my hope turn into soul's despair.

5 And let me not be in need of the charity of creatures of flesh and blood, for their charity is small, while their humiliation is great; rather let me depend upon Thy bountiful hand.

And make my portion in Thy Law together with those who do Thy will with a perfect heart.

And rebuild Thy Temple, Thy city, Thy palace, and Thy sanctuary, soon and in our own days.

And hasten to answer me, and redeem me from all hard and evil decrees.

And save me in Thy abundant mercy from all afflictions and trials.

10 For Thou hearest the prayer of every mouth.

Blessed art Thou, O Lord, who hearest all prayer.

NOTES

ANAN BEN DAVID

I. Harkavy's edition, pp. 12 ff.

I.1. *"'eṯ"*—i.e., the Hebrew particle which serves to introduce a direct complement. Anan believed that since the Bible occasionally introduces a direct complement without it, this particle must have a significance of its own and must, when used, add something new to the meaning of the entire sentence. For a talmudic interpretation of 'eṯ as an "inclusive" particle cf. B. Pĕsaḥim 22b.

I.2. *"Whosoever curses."* The Hebrew words discussed in this passage are forms of the stem *ḳallel* (from *ḳal,* "to be light"), "to curse."Anan however applies to this stem its Aramaic meaning, "to make light," i.e., to treat with neglect and contempt.

"made themselves accursed." Anan interprets this sentence as "made light of them (= God's precepts)"; the verse is addressed to the High Priest Eli and refers to his leniency toward his sons, in spite of their sacrilegious conduct (cf. I Sam. 2: 22 ff.).

I.3. "and yet he does not cease observing it"—i.e., he continues observing Rabbanite laws, even after he has been told by a Karaite scholar that they are, in Karaite opinion, contrary to the Law.

"A false witness." Actually, this verse does not speak of the punishment for false testimony, which is mentioned elsewhere in the Bible, e.g., Ps. 12: 4, Prov. 19: 9.

I.4. "Who is God?"—i.e., "I do not recognize His existence or my obligation to obey Him"; the phrase is taken from Exod. 5: 2.

"blasphemes"—Hebrew *wĕ-noḳeḇ;* the root means also "to designate, to specify."

"designated"—Hebrew *niḳḳĕḇu.*

"in a light manner"—i.e., disrespectfully or contemptuously.

"and that he incurs the death penalty." Anan means to say that the conjunction *and* preceding the word *blasphemes* connects it with the foregoing *curses,* which means, in Anan's opinion, "makes light of."

"he who speaks lightly of the Law incurs the death penalty." Anan applies here another of his exegetical principles, namely, that there is no such thing as a superfluous word or sentence in the Law. Since the clause *For his blaspheming of the name he shall be put to death* is seemingly a mere repetition of the preceding clause *And he who blasphemes the name of the Lord shall surely be put to death,* it must, according to Anan, have a different meaning, which he establishes by interpreting the second *name* as signifying the Law. For the Rabbanite interpretation of Lev. 24: 16, see B. Sanhedrin 56a.

II.1. "we . . . no longer issue death sentences." Anan thus agrees with Rabbanite law which holds that the Jewish courts can no longer pass judgment in cases involving the death penalty, and that the settlement of such cases must be left to divine justice (cf. B. Sanhedrin 37b; 41a).

II.2. For the Rabbanite law on this whole subject cf. B. Baḇa ḳamma 83b ff.

II.3. *"smiting and wounding."* Harkavy's involved explanation of this definition seems unnecessary. Anan's limitation of the term *wound* to head wounds is presumably based on the biblical context: *And a certain man of the sons of the prophets said to his fellow, by the word of the Lord, Smite me, I pray thee; but the man refused to smite him . . . Then he found another man and said, Smite me, I pray thee; and the man smote him, smiting and wounding* (I Kings 20:35–37). The implication seems to be that the smiting, being unpremeditated, was done not with any cutting or piercing weapon but with a stick or stone that might have been near at hand, and the natural part of the body to be hit would be the head and face, rather than any other limb. Moreover, since Anan interpreted *welt* as signifying body wound, he consistently had to limit *wound* to the region of the head.

II.4. *"it broke all my bones"—it* referring to "my suffering"; the translation of this difficult verse is conjectural, and the phrase may be interpreted in various ways.

II.5. *"and there should be no mischief"*—in which case the Bible prescribes the imposition of a fine; the other alternative, where mischief is caused and the principle of *life for life* (Exod. 21:23) is involved, is covered by Anan's preceding ruling regarding the abolition of capital punishment in the Dispersion.

"and he shall pay"—i.e., the guilty person.

"the word *judges."* The Hebrew word, the precise meaning of which is uncertain, is *pĕlilim.*

"should puzzle thee"—Hebrew *yippale;* this is an illustration of another of Anan's exegetical principles, namely, the drawing of inferences from biblical use of similar-sounding words, even though the words may not be cognate. In this instance, Anan assumes that pĕlilim means "judges" because it sounds similar to yippale, which is used on one occasion in a sentence dealing with judges.

"who engage in the work of God"—i.e., in the clarification and enforcement of God's precepts and ordinances.

"and thou shalt be unto him as God"—i.e., *God* means here "leader, preceptor."

"before." Once again Anan endeavors to explain away the repetition of the same statement by suggesting that the use of different prepositions (*to*—Hebrew *'el,* and *before*—Hebrew *'aḏ*) indicates different meanings.

"to the judges at the Temple in Jerusalem"—the implication being that since the judges and priests who functioned in Palestine while the Temple was yet standing are no longer in existence, such cases are no longer subject to the jurisdiction of Jewish courts.

II.7. "who refuses to submit to it"—and cannot be compelled to submit by physical means (since Jewish courts are no longer able to threaten the culprit with capital or corporal punishment for contempt of court).

"contemn God"—God meaning here also the judges of the court of law, according to Anan's interpretation. For post-talmudic Rabbanite views on the subject of this section see B. M. Lewin, *Oṣar hag-gĕ'onim* (Haifa, 1928–) Baḇa ḳamma, pp. 56 ff.

II.8. "we do not accept his repentance." In other words, murder cannot be atoned for through payment of money or other quasi-restitution, even when the relatives of the murdered person are willing to accept it. The biblical authority for this view is the verse: *And no expiation can be made for the land for the blood that is shed therein, but by the blood of him that shed it* (Num. 35: 33); cf. *KA*, III, 687–688. In this Anan is in agreement with Rabbanite law (Harkavy's remarks, *op. cit.*, p. 199, are therefore not pertinent, since repentance in this context does not seem to refer to spiritual contrition). In Mohammedan law, on the other hand, the ancient Arab custom of payment of blood money (Arabic *diya*) has been legalized.

"those other offenses"—i.e., cases of injury to limb or property.

"we may accept his repentance."—This, then, for all practical purposes, although not in theory, amounts to agreement with the Rabbanite view that the principle of *eye for eye* signifies restitution in the form of money or goods. Harkavy's statement to the contrary (*op. cit.*, p. 198), is therefore incorrect.

III. Harkavy, *op. cit.*, pp. 37 f. For the Rabbanite view on this subject cf. B. Bĕrakoṯ 54.

III.2. "before the Merciful One"—i.e., addressing the Merciful One.

III.3. *"He has not done unto us according to our sins"*—i.e., "He has saved us from deadly peril, notwithstanding that our sins had made us unworthy of His mercy."

III.4. *"in thy truth"*—meaning, according to Anan, "in Thy Law."

III.5. "it should be recited on this occasion"—i.e., the former verse *O magnify ye . . .* should be recited on this occasion because it speaks of exalting the Lord's Name.

"he shall confess." Anan bases this inference on the fact that in Hebrew the words "thanksgiving," *toḏah,* and "confess one's sins," *hiṯwaḏe,* are derived from the same root.

IV. Harkavy, *op. cit.*, pp. 67 f. Cf. above, pp. 31 ff., Daniel al-Ḳūmisī's discussion of the same subject. For the Rabbanite law in this matter cf. Mish. Ḥullin 3: 6.

V. Harkavy, *op. cit.*, pp. 69 f.

V.1. *"upon their shoulders."* For the Rabbanite law in this matter cf. Mish. Šabbaṯ 10: 3 and the Palestinian Talmud, *ad loc.* The later Karaite authorities did not accept Anan's definition.

V.3. "the letter *taw.*" The respective Hebrew words are *tĕḇa'ăru* and *ta'ăśe,* both beginning with the letter taw. As the following argument shows, Anan used this pedantic bit of proof as a sort of anchor to establish his more reasonable thesis that as far as the Sabbath is concerned, kindling fire and performing work are analogous actions subject to the same restrictive laws. For the Rabbanite view cf. Mish. Šabbaṯ, chap. 2.

V.4. For the Rabbanite law in this matter cf. Mish. Šabbaṯ 16: 8; B. Šabbaṯ 122a.

VI. Harkavy, *op. cit.*, pp. 98 f.

VI.1. "and not his father." The latter two variations are, of course, half-sisters.

VI.2. *"thy home."* Anan's inference is that the word *home* in such a context implies lawful matrimony; an illicit alliance does not result in the establishment of a proper home.

"Now she is outside." This whole seventh chapter of the Book of Proverbs describes the evil ways of the harlot. Anan's inference is that the word *outside* in such a context implies fornication. For the Rabbanite view cf. B. Yĕḇamoṯ 23a.

VI.4. "high or low degree"—i.e., the laws of consanguinity apply equally to all persons, be they freemen, of either high or low social position, or slaves. In Rabbanite law they apply to freemen only (cf. B. Yĕḇamoṯ 22b).

VI.5. For the Rabbanite law in this matter cf. Sifra to Lev. 18: 6.

VII. Harkavy, *op. cit.*, pp. 118 f.

VII.1. "or because she does not want him." This equal right of the wife to initiate divorce proceedings (providing she has legal grounds for them) is clearly not implied in the biblical ordinance, unless indeed it follows from Anan's theory that husband and wife are "one flesh," subject to the same positive and negative regulations. Later Karaite jurists upheld Anan's view on this subject. For the Rabbanite view cf. Mish. Giṭṭin 9: 10 (the husband's initiative only; he may, however, under certain conditions, be compelled to divorce his wife).

VII.2. *"a writ of cutting off"*—Hebrew *kĕriṯuṯ;* what is meant, of course, is the *geṭ* or "bill of divorcement." For the Rabbanite law in this matter cf. B. Giṭṭin 21b.

VII.3. "until he is certain that there is no offspring of his within her"—i.e., *cutting off* implies a complete break between the husband and the wife, and therefore cannot take place so long as the wife is carrying the husband's unborn child. In Rabbanite law the divorced woman must wait three months before remarrying (cf. Mish. Yĕḇamoṯ 4: 10).

"If she is not pregnant"—i.e., if no symptoms of pregnancy are observed.

"after which"—i.e., if no pregnancy develops.

VII.4. *"and he shall place it"*—i.e., the deed of divorce. For the Rabbanite view cf. B. Giṭṭin 77a; P. Giṭṭin 9: 1; Sifre to Deut. 24: 1.

VII.5. "he writes it for her thus." In the original the deed of divorce is worded completely in Hebrew. In Rabbanite practice the document is written in Aramaic or mixed Aramaic and Hebrew (cf. Mish. Giṭṭin 9: 3).

VIII. Harkavy, *op. cit.*, p. 78.

VIII.1. *"ye shall be circumcised"*—Hebrew *u-nĕmaltem,* the prefix *nĕ* indicating the passive. The whole paragraph refers, of course, to adult converts, and not to newborn infants who could not possibly operate upon themselves. For the Rabbanite view cf. B. 'Āḇoḏah zarah 10b, and Rabbanite commentaries to Gen. 17: 26.

VIII.2. " 'foreskin of the heart.' " A biblical figure of speech signifying evil thoughts and actions.

"Ye shall circumcise"—Hebrew *u-maltem,* without the passive prefix nĕ.

BENJAMIN AL-NAHĀWANDĪ

I. *Maś'aṯ Binyamin,* fol. 1b, col. 2.

I.1. "Benjamin son of Moses." The author uses his own name as an example.

"would render a deed invalid"—by causing doubts as to the precise identity of the witnesses certifying the deed.

"the names of their shops"—i.e., the sign by which each shop was known, mostly representing by way of a picture the trade or the line of merchandise to which it was devoted.

"shops"—Hebrew *duḳan,* Arabic *duḳḳān;* used in the Talmud for "place, stand," etc.

"the names of their mothers." The likelihood is that even if their fathers' names are identical, their mothers' names would not be the same.

"tall or short." The following *'o gaḇoah* is virtually a duplicate of the preceding *'o 'aroḵ*, and is presumably a reader's gloss.

"of medium build"—*yafe*, lierally: "well proportioned," i.e., neither too thin nor too fat. For the Rabbanite law on this matter cf. Maimonides, *Hilḵoṯ malwe we-lowe* 24: 8; Yale Judaica Series, II, 171.

II. *Maś'at Binyamin*, fol. 2b, col. 2.

II.1. "his master's commands"—in which case the master is responsible for the consequences of the servant's executing his orders. For the Rabbanite law in this matter cf. Mish. Baḇa mĕṣi'a 8: 3, and the commentaries thereto.

III. *Maś'aṯ Binyamin*, fol. 3a, col. 1.

III.1. "The wife's property." The text appears to be defective here, and some words (forming the end of the preceding paragraph) must have dropped out. For the Rabbanite law in this matter cf. B. Yĕḇamoṯ 66b.

"of the tribe." The verse deals with the landed inheritance of the daughters of Zelaphehad and its disposition in the event of their marriage to men of a tribe other than their own.

"to whomsoever he wishes"—i.e., without his wife's consent.

III.2. "the income"—literally: "fruits" (*peroṯ*). For the Rabbanite law in this matter cf. Mish. Kĕṯubboṯ 4: 4.

"to whomsoever she chooses"—subject, however, to the limitations set forth further on.

"their parting"—i.e., their divorce.

"it does not represent an obligation on his part"—i.e., the use of the income is the husband's vested right so long as the marriage endures, and such income is not repayable at the dissolution of the marriage.

"the husband inherits . . . her property." In this right of the husband to inherit his wife's property Benjamin followed the Rabbanite practice (cf. Mish. Baḇa baṯra 8: 1); other Karaite jurists (e.g., Daniel al-Ḳūmisī), however, denied it (cf. *KA*, XIII, ix).

III.3. *Maś'aṯ Binyamin*, fol. 5a, col. 1.

"elsewhere"—i.e., not through her husband's efforts as manager of her possessions; e.g., property inherited by the wife from her own parents. For the Rabbanite law in this matter cf. B. Kĕṯubboṯ 50a.

"subject to her disposal at will"—barring the limitations set forth further on.

"both kinds of property." A second *wĕ-'elu* seems to have dropped out.

"since she and her property belong to him." The implication seems to be that the husband cannot repossess such property during the wife's lifetime, inasmuch as while she is living she is the primary owner, and he is only the manager of it. Only after her death, when as her heir he comes (according to Benjamin) into full possession of her property, can he reclaim it from the holder. The latter presumably has no redress, on the principle of *caveat emptor*.

III.4. *"Blessed be thou . . ."* In the biblical text the two clauses are in reverse order. Abigail did all this without consulting her husband (cf. I Sam. 25: 19). For the Rabbanite view cf. B. Baḇa ḳamma 119a.

III.5. Read *u-bĕnaḵ* for *u-banayiḵ;* the biblical text reads *u-ḇeṯeḵ, "thy house,"* i.e., thy family.

"was then dead"—read *la* for *lo*.

"Restore all that was hers . . ." Benjamin evidently means to say that where a widow is left with minor children, at least part of the deceased husband's property must remain inalienable in order to provide for the children's support until they come of age and can provide for themselves. Claims against this property must presumably remain dormant until the children have grown into adulthood and are able to assume their father's debts. This is the rule in Rabbanite law also; cf. B. 'Ărakin 22a; B. Giṭṭin 50a, 52a.

IV. *Maś'at Binyamin,* fol. 3a, col. 1.

IV.1. "in his possession"—read *lo* for *bo*. For the Rabbanite law cf. Mish. Baba batra 9: 6.

IV.2. For the Rabbanite law in this matter cf. B. Baba batra 152b.

V.1. *Maś'at Binjamin,* fol. 3b, col. 1.

"regardless of the amount"—i.e., the will is valid if it contains some bequest in favor of the lawful heir, however small it may be. In other words, a man cannot cut off his lawful heir entirely, but must leave him at least a small part of his property as a token bequest, even if he chooses to bequeathe the bulk of it to someone else who has no statutory claim to it. For the Rabbanite law in this matter cf. Mish. Baba batra 8: 5.

V.2. *Maś'at Binyamin,* fol. 4a, col. 1.

"his command is void"—*lo 'amar kĕlum,* literally: "he has said nothing (that has any standing in law)."

"do ye emancipate this slave"—i.e., the bill of emancipation must be made out by the heirs acting on the deceased's wishes. The deceased himself, after his demise, cannot act as a legal person, and any document written by the deceased but not duly delivered to its proper recipient, i.e., not duly put into force, becomes null and void at the moment of his death. Morally, of course, the heirs are bound to fulfil the testator's instructions, even though there is no law to compel them to do so. For the Rabbanite view cf. Mish. Giṭṭin 1: 6.

V.3. "chastisement"—*mak'ob,* literally: "pain"; i.e., will cause him to lose his property.

"or grant him sons or daughters"—all of which may necessitate a revision of his will to provide for his lawful heirs. In other words, a will in favor of a person who is not heir in law cannot be made operative in perpetuity, regardless of any possible circumstances which may arise to affect it and irrespective of the possible appearance of lawful heirs as yet unborn at the time when the will was drawn up.

VI. *Maś'at Binyamin,* fol. 4b, col. 2.

VI.1. For the Rabbanite view in this matter cf. Mish. Yĕbamot 6: 6; B. ibid., 64a.

VI.2. "and pay her"—*wĕ-koteb* seems to be a misprint for *wĕ-noten*. For the Rabbanite law in this matter cf. B. Kĕtubbot 63a, 77a.

VI.3. "incapable of cohabiting"—i.e., impotent. For the Rabbanite view cf. Tosafot to B. Yĕbamot 65b, and RaN to B. Nĕdarim 91a.

"living with him"—literally: "sitting under his wing."

VI.4. "full support"—i.e., insufficient support, too, constitutes legal grounds for divorce.

VI.6. "morality"—*musar,* i.e., ethical conduct of life.

"partakes of her father's loaf . . ." The meaning is, of course, figurative, in the sense that she has a lawful share in his necessities of life. For the Rabbanite view cf. B. Kĕṯubboṯ 65b; B. Ḳiddušin 29a.

VI.7. "has no legal standing whatever"—literally: "no one should listen to him at all."

VII. *Maś'aṯ Binyamin,* fol. 5a, col. 1.

VII.1. "If testimony is given"—by witnesses other than the husband.

"even if no intercourse had actually occurred,"—since it was evidently their intent to commit adultery, even if they were not able to execute their plans. Benjamin based his view on the fact that the biblical verse here quoted uses the general term *lain,* without adding *carnally* (as in Lev. 18: 20), to indicate actual intercourse. For the Rabbanite view in this matter cf. Sifre to Deut. 22: 22; B. Sanheḏrin 66b.

VII.3. "had any carnal knowledge of her"—i.e., if the husband had consummated the marriage before he accused his wife of adultery, he cannot affect a reconciliation with her, since it would be the same as if he were remarrying her after she had been married to another man, which is expressly forbidden in the Law (Deut. 24: 4). If the husband has brought the charge of adultery before the consummation of the marriage, he may, if he wishes, affect a reconciliation, or, if he divorces her, she may lawfully marry her paramour, since the aforementioned biblical prohibition would not apply in such a case. For the Rabbanite law in this matter cf. Sifre to Num. 5: 13; B. Soṭah 24a, 28b.

VIII. *Maś'aṯ Binyamin,* fol. 5a, col. 2–fol. 5b, col. 1.

VIII.1. "she must therefore be separated from both"—i.e., she is forbidden to her first husband because she had cohabited with another man; and she is forbidden to her second husband because her marriage with him was in reality adulterous or bigamous.

"betrothal, wedding, and consummation of marriage"—i.e., the three statutory steps in lawful marriage. In other words, the woman's second marriage is null and void and requires no formal divorce on the part of the second husband; he is merely forbidden ever to marry her again, inasmuch as he has already lived with her. For the Rabbanite view cf. Mish. Yĕḇamoṯ 10: 1.

IX. *Maś'aṯ Binyamin,* fol. 6b.

IX.1. "his memory"—i.e., of Moses, his father.

DANIEL AL-ḲŪMISĪ

I. From the *Book of Precepts* ed. A. Harkavy, *Studien und Mittheilungen,* VIII, 187–189.

I.1. "by their legs above their feet"—cf. Lev. 11: 2 ff.

I.3. *"mur'ah* and *noṣah"*—"crop" and "feather," respectively, referred to in Lev. 1: 16 (quoted later on in this paragraph); this verse deals with birds offered for sacrifice which must of necessity belong to a clean species. For the Rabbanite view cf. Sifra (ed. Weiss) 9a on Lev. 1: 16; B. Zĕḇaḥim 65a; and Rashi and Naḥmanides to Lev. 1: 16.

"two parts"—i.e., two separate organs of the bird's body.

"its mur'ah with its noṣah." Daniel interpreted the preposition *with* (Hebrew *bĕ-*) as meaning "within."

I.4. "the gizzard." The sentence is, as Harkavy notes, corrupt, but his emendation, too, makes a rather awkward phrase. I assume that *zefeḳ* (*zĕfaḳ*) is a misplaced reader's gloss explaining mur'ah; the impossible *sagiyanah* is presumably a misreading of mur'ah. The correct wording would then be: *wĕ-'ašer hem 'omĕrim mur'ah zefeḳ ḳāniṣā.*

I.5. "until we shall have learned . . ."—i.e., until we know the precise meaning of the names of forbidden birds, we cannot be sure of the cleanness of any species of birds whatsoever. For the Rabbanite view cf. Mish. Ḥullin 3:6; B. Ḥullin 60b–63.

"with fair certainty"—i.e., from the context in which these birds' names occur.

"the *peres,* the *'ozniyah,* the *taḥmas*"—the osprey, the kite, and the night-hawk, respectively (Lev. 11:13 and 16); this translation of these terms is uncertain.

I.7. "cocks and chickens." This was the interpretation favored by the sectarian leader Malik al-Ramlī (see above, p. 53).

"have no definite time of arrival"—i.e., are not migratory birds.

"the *tor*"—singular of *torim;* the translation of the next two species of birds is uncertain.

I.8. "a sacrifice"—referring to the sacrifice of turtle doves or pigeons prescribed for a woman delivered of a child (Lev. 12:6 ff.). As Harkavy remarks, Daniel presumably thought that the ordinance concerned a widow only, otherwise the sacrifice would have been made the business of her husband; in Rabbanite law the husband is obligated to supply his wife with the sacrifices incumbent upon her.

I.9. "*śeḵwi*"—a term of uncertain meaning (Job 38:36), interpreted in the Talmud (B. Roš haš-šanah 26a) as signifying the domestic cock.

"the list of unclean birds"—Lev. 11:13 ff.

"representative of it"—literally: "father and principal of it."

I.10. 'except turtledoves and young pigeons." Daniel thus agreed, in practice, though not in theory, with Anan in this matter.

" 'until such time as the teacher of righteousness shall have come' "— paraphrased from Hos. 10:12; meaning the Prophet Elijah.

"camel"—the camel, too, being expressly forbidden in the Bible (Lev. 11:4).

II. Published by J. Mann, *JQR,* XII (1921–22), 257–298. Daniel's authorship is conjectural.

II.1. "different clothing"—i.e., old and torn vestments, as a mark of sorrow and repentance.

"Is it not for him, too"—i.e., presumably for the disgraced official.

"and His wrath has been mollified." The lacuna is presumably to be read something like *wĕ-ya 'ăḇor haḳ-ḳeṣef.*

II.2. "men and women soiled . . ." In Jewish law such defiled persons are forbidden to approach anything holy and clean.

II.4. "the scoundrels"—meaning presumably the Rabbanites, or perhaps, rather recalcitrant Karaites who were opposed to emigration to Palestine.

"until He"—i.e., God.

"it is written also in Jeremiah"—Jer. 31:17 ff.; the biblical text is interwoven piecemeal into the following exposition.

"An ordinance of men learned by rote"—a favorite Karaite term for the Rabbanite legislation which in their opinion has no basis in God's word.

II.5. "signposts." The lacuna is presumably to be read *'alāmāt.*

"bitterness"—Hebrew *tamrurim;* in this verse the word is generally presumed to have not its usual meaning, "bitterness," but rather "roadmarks."

II.7. "since the well of all godly learning is in Jerusalem"—i.e., by devoting their lives in Jerusalem not only to prayer but also to the study of God's word they turn the city into the center of all godly learning, as it was meant to be.

II.8. "nations other than Israel"—referring to the Christian and Moslem pilgrims to Jerusalem.

"and worshiped their god." This is evidently the way Daniel interpreted this sentence; the correct translation is rather: *yet they worshiped also their own gods.*

"since Israel observes"—Israel signifying here the Rabbanites.

II.9. "valid excuse"—literally: "opening of the mouth."

"the Magians." The following *parsiyyim* is presumably a reader's explanatory gloss. The Magians are, of course, the Persian followers of Zoroastrianism.

"those who sought the Law"—meaning the Karaites.

"were [ruling over them]." The lacuna should probably be read something like *hayu mošělim bahem.*

"the kingdom of Ishmael"—i.e., the Mohammedan Empire founded by the Arab conquest.

II.10. "by direct observation"—reading *bir'iyah* for *bě-yareaḥ* (cf. Mann, p. 75, n. 9). This method is used also in the Mohammedan calendar, whereas the Rabbanite calendar employs astronomical calculation (*'ibbur*) instead, which the Karaites reject as heretical.

"broke the staff"—i.e., broke the power.

III. Published by J. Mann, *JQR,* XII (1921–22), 519–521, 524–526. Daniel's authorship is conjectural.

III.1. "inasmuch as he was early"—meaning that this being so, one need not submit to Anan's authority.

"they shall be purified and whitened"—i.e., the true belief has been developed by the later Karaite theologians who purified it from the errors committed by Anan. "Men of understanding" (Hebrew *maśkilim*) is one of the terms used by the Karaites to designate themselves, as against their benighted Rabbanite cousins. Daniel al-Ḳūmisī's contemptuous appraisal of Anan and his violent opposition to much of Anan's teaching is recorded by al-Ḳirḳisānī (*KA,* I, 5), in these terms: "Daniel al-Ḳūmisī had an extreme contempt for the Ananites and opposed them with bitter enmity. At first he respected Anan greatly and frequently referred to him in his own works as 'the First of the Men of Understanding' [Hebrew *roš ham-maśkilim*]; but later he dubbed him 'the First of the Fools' [Hebrew *roš hak-kěsilim*]. Coming from a man of Daniel's learning and piety, it is a shameful procedure withal."

III.2. "the king of Ishmael"—i.e., the Prophet Mohammed and his successors in the caliphate.

"the kingdom of the Persians." The following *kol Xurāsān,* "all of the province of Xurāsān," seems to be a reader's gloss.

"the kingdom of the Romans"—i.e., the Byzantine (Romaic) Empire; the author refers to the victories of the Arabs over the Persians and Byzantines during the conquest of the vast territory which became the Arab Empire. The following *wĕ-ḳol ḳesar,* "and every Caesar," is presumably another reader's gloss.

"Samarkand . . ." All these are provinces on the eastern wing of the Mohammedan Empire, eastward from its political center, Iraq. Samarkand, Šaš (Tashkend), and Farġāna are within the modern province of Turkestan; Hinduwān is a region in the province of Fārs (Persia proper); Xawlān is presumably the region of Mosul (Mawṣil—Mosul was called Xawlān in ancient times). See Guy Le Strange, *The Lands of the Eastern Caliphate* (Cambridge, 1905), map I (facing p. 1).

III.3. *"wondrous"*—i.e., unheard of, dreadful, blasphemous.

"since he said"—i.e., Mohammed.

"'the messenger of God'"—Hebrew *šĕluaḥ 'Ĕlohim,* an exact translation of Mohammed's Arabic title, *rasūl Allāh,* "messenger (prophet) of God."

"of these kings"—i.e., the Mohammedan caliphs, according to the author.

III.4. *"he shall not regard them"*—i.e., shall not honor them.

"his permission"—i.e., Mohammed's.

"the uncircumcised"—i.e., the Christians.

"Some say"—read *wĕ-'amĕru* for *wĕ-'amar.*

"the Jewish ordinance"—rather, the Karaite; in Rabbanite law, marriage with one's niece is permitted (P. Yĕḇamoṯ 13c, ed. Krotoschin).

III.5. "al-Lāt and al-'Uzzā"—two female divinities worshiped by the pagan Arabs prior to the advent of Mohammed.

"his advent"—i.e., Mohammed's.

"fortresses meaning the same thing as provinces"—using the figure of speech called *pars pro toto,* the fortress city being the most important part of each province.

"he left [him] there"—*'oṯo* seems to have dropped out before *šam.*

"fine vestments"—presumably referring to the richly embroidered curtains used to adorn the sacred stone (*Ka'ba*) in Mecca. For *'ăśoṯ* read *'aśu.*

III.6. "Brahmins"—i.e., followers of the Brahmin religion, men of India.

"Ṭabaristān . . . Daylam"—provinces in the eastern wing of the Mohammedan Empire.

III.7. "in every direction"—i.e., without any limitation of its authority.

"tax farmers"—Hebrew *nogĕśim,* literally: "drivers, hard taskmasters"; a well-earned appellation of the financiers who bought the tax revenue of a province from the caliph for a lump sum paid in advance, and then proceeded to squeeze as much as the traffic would bear from the unfortunate inhabitants of that province.

JACOB AL-ḲIRḲISĀNĪ

I. *Book of Lights,* Discourse I, chap. ii (*KA,* I, 6–14). The English translation by L. Nemoy, *HUCA,* VII (1930), 317–397, is based on Harkavy's imperfect text, which has been superseded by the complete edition of the work.

I.1. "Jeroboam"—the first king of the northern kingdom, after its separation from the kingdom of Judah (10th century B.C.).

"the two Cherubim"—which adorned the Ark of the covenant (Exod. 25:18 ff.).

"a leap year"—which, in the Jewish calendar, has an additional month, making the seventh month (Tishri) of the next year actually the eighth.

I.2. "Jehu"—king of Israel (9th century B.C.).

"and in another verse: *to burn incense . . .*" There is no such verse; this is probably an error due to quotation from memory. Jeroboam's burning of incense upon the altar which he had built is mentioned in the next two verses, I Kings 12:33 and 13:1.

"And there ye shall worship"—i.e., in exile.

"by idolaters." In the Arabic original there follow here several examples of such metaphorical use of the terms "to sacrifice to" and "to burn incense to" in the Bible.

I.3. "Could anyone not bereft of reason say such a thing"—i.e., from this it is clear that the children of Israel requested Aaron to make for them not an actual idol but rather a symbol, as it were, of the one and true God, whom they did not for one moment intend to forsake.

"and the face of an ox"—referring to one of the angels in Ezekiel's vision.

I.4. "King Hezekiah"—in the last quarter of the 8th century B.C.

"but they walked in all the sins"—the massoretic text has *in the statutes.*

I.5. "Sanballat the Horanite"—mentioned several times in the Book of Nehemiah for his opposition to this Jewish leader.

"who was a chieftain among them." The teaching of the Samaritans is described in Disc. I, chap. 5: they acknowledge no prophets save Moses and Joshua, and no sacred books except the Law and the Book of Joshua; their holy city is Shechem, and they still offer animal sacrifices; they made some changes in the text of the Law (e.g., in Gen. 4:8 they read: *And Cain said to his brother Abel, Come, let us go out in the field,* although the second clause is not found in the massoretic text); they fix the beginnings of months according to a calendar (*'ibbur*) supposedly instituted by Jeroboam; etc.

I.6. "Simeon the Righteous"—who lived in the 3d century B.C.; his identity is not quite certain, as there were two individuals of this name in that period.

"the Great Synagogue"—the legislative body said to have been established upon the return of Jewry from the Babylonian Exile; the "Men of the Great Synagogue" are frequently mentioned in the Talmud.

"in the time of Ezra and Nehemiah"—5th century B.C.

"Gamaliel"—i.e., Gamaliel II, president of the Sanhedrin of Jabneh and spiritual head of the Palestinian Jewry (end of the 1st and beginning of the 2d century after Christ). His rulings on the calendar and other legal matters involved him in serious disputes with various scholars, and he freely used his disciplinary authority to compel their obedience. He was finally deposed from his high office, but was soon reinstated. His difficulties were, of course, due to his dictatorial procedure, and not to his views on the calendar, as al-Ḳirḳisānī implies.

"miraculous proofs of the truth of his opinion." The talmudic account of this controversy (B. Baḇa mĕṣi'a 59b) is given by al-Ḳirḳisānī in Disc. I, chap. 4. Eliezer ben Hyrcanus was a brother-in-law of Gamaliel II.

I.7. "Antigonus"—i.e., Antigonus of Socho, who flourished in the 3d century B.C. The historical existence of Zadok and Boethus and their connection with Antigonus are open to doubt; the whole story may be a later invention to explain the origin of the sect's name.

"in the manner of an assertion"—or "tradition" (Arabic *al-xabar*).

"which is also the view of the Ananites . . ." The Sadducee teaching is described in Disc. I, chap. 6: they prohibited divorce; they made all months consist uniformly of thirty days (on the basis of Gen. 7: 11, 24; 8: 3–4, from which it appears that five months made 150 days); etc.

I.8. "the Alexandrian"—Arabic, al-Iskandarānī; this is supposed to be the Judeo-Arabic name for Philo, the Hellenistic philosopher who lived at the time of Jesus; he wrote, of course, more than one book. On Philo in medieval Judeo-Arabic literature see S. Poznanski, "Philon dans l'ancienne littérature judéo-arabe," *REJ,* L (1905), 10–31.

"the Book of Yaddu'a"—an otherwise unknown work; Yaddu'a is presumably a personal name, and if so, identical with Jaddua (Neh. 10: 21).

"most of them merely resemble idle tales." Disc. I, chap. 7 treats of the teaching of the Magarians: they believed that the universe was created by one of the angels, and not by God Himself (a device intended to make it possible to apply the anthropomorphic passages in the Bible to this angel, rather than to the person of the Deity); some of them prohibited laughter, probably as incompatible with the duty to grieve for the destruction of the Temple in Jerusalem; etc.

I.9. "Pandera"—an obscure appellation found in the Talmud and in later literature. On the subject, see R. Travers Herford, *Christianity in Talmud and Midrash* (London, 1903): for some modifications of Herford's views, see his later article, "Jesus in Rabbinical Literature," *UJE,* Vol. VI.

"Jesus, the son of Mary"—Arabic, 'Īsā ibn Maryam.

"Joshua, the son of Peraḥiah." This eminent Jewish scholar lived in the 2d century before Christ, and could therefore have no connection with Jesus. The error is seemingly based on the Talmud (B. Sanhedrin 107b), where a certain Yešu (the Hebrew form of the name Jesus) is said to have been a pupil of Joshua and to have eventually become a heretic. This Yešu is commonly regarded as identical with Jesus.

"crucifixion." Al-Ḳirḳisānī knew very little about Jesus. His knowledge of Christian history and theology, on the other hand, was considerable. In Disc. I, chap. 8 the Christian teaching is described in greater detail, but the only bits of information given about Jesus himself are that he prohibited divorce; that he issued no new religious ordinances, but said that religion consisted solely of humility; and that he permitted the eating of the flesh of all animals, "from the gnat to the elephant." Al-Ḳirḳisānī adds that it was St. Paul who invested Jesus with a divine nature.

I.10. "parasangs"—the Arab parasang (Arabic, *farsax*) was equal to slightly over 5¾ kilometers.

"al-Fusṭāṭ"—the Arab name for Old Cairo.

"Johanan, the son of Kareah"—a high military officer at the time of the destruction of Jerusalem by Nebuchadnezzar (II Kings 25: 23). The teaching of the Kar'ites is described in Disc. I, chap. 9: they were said to do their own planting and harvesting (meaning that they regarded crops planted and harvested by non-Kar'ites as unclean), and to observe both Saturday and Sunday as days of rest.

I.11. "Syria"—including Palestine.

"Shemaiah and Abṭalion"—Jewish scholars who lived in the 1st century before Christ.

"a number of adherents of each school were slain." On the alleged bloody clash between the adherents of the two rival schools, see pp. 80, 343. A list of the differences in law and ritual practice between Palestinian and Babylonian Jews is given in Disc. I, chap. 10. On the subject see, M. Margulies, *Ḥillukim šebben 'anše Mizraḥ ubne Ereṣ Yiśra'el* (Jerusalem, 1938); B. M. Lewin, *'Oṣar ḥilluf minhaǧim* (Jerusalem, 1942).

I.12. "'Abd al-Malik ibn Marwān"—who reigned in the years 685–705.

"he planned to come out against the Moslem government"—i.e., planned an armed revolt against the Moslem authorities.

"Isunians." Obadiah's teaching is discussed in Disc. I, chap. 11: he prohibited divorce; he required seven daily prayers and prohibited all meat and wine; he acknowledged the prophetic mission of both Jesus and Mohammed; and he recommended the study of the New Testament and the Koran; etc.

I.13. "His partisans say that he was the Messiah." The teaching of the Yudganites is described in Disc. I, chap. 12: they believed that Yūdġān never died and that he will eventually return to earth; they forbade meat and wine, observed many prayers and fasts, and thought that the observance of Sabbaths and holidays was no longer obligatory.

I.14. "the Chief of the Dispersion"—Arabic *ra's al-ǧālūt,* from the Aramaic *reš galuṭa,* the title borne by the Rabbanite exilarchs of Babylonia and applied by the Karaites to Anan.

"Abū Ǧa'far al-Manṣūr"—the second caliph of the 'Abbāsid dynasty, who reigned in the years 754–775.

"A great deal of the truth." Note that al-Ḳirḳisānī does not say "the (whole) truth," which is consistent with his critical attitude toward a number of Anan's views.

"Hay"—variously identified with Hay ben Naḥšon, Gaon at Sura in A.D. 886–896; or more likely, Hay ben David, Gaon at Pumbeditha in A.D. 890–898.

"the book of Anan"—presumably his *Book of Precepts;* no such translation has so far been brought to light. The term "translated" is perhaps to be understood in the sense that they made Hebrew excerpts and notes from Anan's work for their own use in polemics with Karaites; such excerpting from the works of various writers was a common custom among Mohammedan scholars of that time. Even so, the statement is of rather doubtful veracity.

"while its mother was owned by a Gentile"—i.e., the first male young conceived by the mother animal while it was in the possession of a Jew was to be offered as a sacrifice, in conformity with the ordinance in Deut. 15:19. If the mother was previously owned by a Gentile and was pregnant at the time of her sale to the Jew the resulting young could not be regarded as a firstling; cf. *KA,* III, 669.

"Yannay"—one of the earliest known Jewish liturgical poets who lived not later than the 7th century. The hymn referred to is presumably the one beginning: *'One piṭre raḥămaṭayim* (cf. *Piyyuṭe Yannay,* ed. M. Zulay (Berlin, 1938), pp. 88–94).

"prevented them from doing so." A long summary of Anan's ordinances is given in Disc. I, chap. 13; e.g.: he permitted praying only in a special place which he called "court" (*ḥaṣer*); he forbade the making of Passover bread (*maṣṣoṯ*) out of wheat flour, presumably because he considered it to be too luxurious a variety of food to symbolize the *bread of poverty* (Deut. 16: 3); he instituted a fast of 70 days (from the 13th of Nisan to the 23d of Siwan), the fasting evidently to be done during daytime only, in the manner of the Mohammedan fast throughout the month of Ramaḍān; he is said to have believed in the transmigration of souls and to have composed a work on it. In Disc. VI, chap. 12, al-Ḳirḳisānī discusses in detail Anan's prohibition of the practice of medicine as incompatible with implicit faith in the healing power of God.

I.15. "al-Mu'taṣim Billāh"—who reigned in the years 833–842.

"The chariot of Israel . . ."—the epithet applied by the Prophet Elisha to his master Elijah. The summary of Ismā'īl's teaching in Disc. I, chap. 15 is entitled—in line with al-Ḳirḳisānī's profound antipathy toward this sectarian leader—"Account of the Evil Doings [*Masāwi'*] of Ismā'īl al-'Ukbarī." Ismā'īl introduced many alleged corrections into the text of Scripture; he permitted the eating on the Sabbath of food prepared by non-Jews on the same day (i.e., food prepared in violation of the Sabbath rest); and he held "many other views indicative of extreme corruption, turpitude, and ignorance."

I.16. "to the biblical text." Benjamin's teaching is summarized in Disc. I, chap. 14: he taught that God created only one angel, and that this angel created everything else in the universe—a device to explain away the anthropomorphic passages in the Bible; he forbade the surrender of fugitive slaves to their masters, whether the latter were Jews or Gentiles; he thought that the first-born son of the less favored wife should take precedence in the right of primogeniture over the first-born son of the more favored wife; etc.

I.17. "he had emigrated to Tiflis"—one of the earliest evidences of a Jewish settlement in the Caucasus.

I.18. "al-Ramla"—in Palestine, 25 miles east-northeast of Jerusalem; it was an important administrative and military center in al-Ḳirḳisānī's time.

"Malikites." The teachings of Mūsā and Malik are briefly summarized in Disc. I, chap. 16: both adopted the usual Karaite customs of celebrating Pentecost on a Sunday only, outlawing the eating of the fat tail (*'alyah*) and the marrying of one's niece, etc. Neither of the two wrote any code of law, but Mūsā composed a treatise in refutation of the schismatic Ḥayyawayh al-Balxī and an essay on the permissibility of eating meat.

I.19. " 'Ukbara"—in Iraq, a few miles' distance from Bagdad.

"there is not a single man skilled in knowledge . . ." The teaching of Mīšawayh, "another one of those dissenting fools," as al-Ḳirḳisānī chooses to call him, is described in Disc. I, chap. 17: the Day of Atonement, according to him, is to be observed always on a Sabbath, on the basis of Lev. 23: 32, where he interpreted the words *šabbaṯ šabbaṯon* (*a Sabbath of rest*), as "a double Sabbath," and during prayer one is to face always toward the west, instead of the east. As for the involved problem of the calendar and the determination of the dates of festivals, he is said to have advised his followers to follow the Rabbanites, because, as he cynically phrased it, "all coins are clipped anyway, so you might as well use the counterfeit that is at hand."

I.20. "Daniel al-Dāmaġānī" Daniel's teaching is summarized in Disc. I, chap. 18: he did not believe in the existence of angels and thought that they were mere symbols of natural forces, such as fire and wind; in some ritual matters he displayed greater rigor than other sectarians, yet he accepted the testimony of Moslems in matters pertaining to the Jewish calendar; etc.

I.21. "These are the well-known sects." The condition of these sects in al-Ḳirḳisānī's time is described in Disc. I, chap. 18: "Some of these sects have ceased to exist, for example, the Magarians and the Sadducees, nor is there left any adherent of Ismā'īl al-'Ukbarī. . . . The remaining Ananites are very few and they are constantly diminishing in number. Of the followers of Abū 'Īsā al-Iṣfahānī only about twenty souls are left in Damascus, and only a few Yudganites remain in Iṣfahān."

II. From the introduction to the *Book of Gardens,* Hirschfeld's edition (unfortunately, swarming with errors), pp. 39 ff., omitting the preliminary pious invocation. The title *Tafsīr Bĕrešit,* "Commentary on Genesis," taken by Hirschfeld from the British Museum MS Or. 2557, where it was supplied by the copyist, is patently false: the introductory paragraph characterizes the present work as a commentary on the nonlegal parts of the entire Pentateuch, which is the precise description of the *Book of Gardens.* Besides, the real *Tafsīr Bĕrešiṯ* was completed some time before the *Book of Lights,* since it is repeatedly referred to in the latter (see *KA,* V, 043, where a list of these references is given). Since the *Book of Lights* was written as an introduction to the *Book of Gardens,* the latter was even further removed in point of time from the *Tafsīr Bĕrešiṯ*. See also below, note to II, 5.

II.1. "in a separate work"—i.e., in the *Book of Lights.*

"the Mannāniyya sect." "The Mannāniyya deny the ultimate punishment altogether and assert that the punisher who confers no benefit by his punishment upon the punished or upon anyone else, and does not even punish to soothe his own anger, is guilty of a wrong, since he uses punishment where it has no proper place. Now since God by His punishment would confer no benefit upon the punished or upon anyone else, nor would He punish to soothe His own wrath, it follows that there could be no wisdom in punishment after death." (*KA,* II, 251).

"I intend [not to leave anything]"—read *'an lā 'ada['a šay'an min al-'ašyā']*.

"[without mentioning and explaining it]"—read *'illā ḏaḳar[tuhu wa-ḏaḳartu] al-ğawāba 'anhu.*

"of general import"—read *ğalla* for *ṣağura* (both look much the same in hasty cursive *nasxī*).

"an expert scholar"—read *al-ḥāḏiḳ*.

"ignorant and unlearned"—literally: "barren and unseeing."

"he attempts a reply thereto"—or, "is at a loss to reply thereto"; *fa-yaḳifu fī ğawābihī* may be translated either way.

"is covered with shame"—read *wa-yaxğalu.*

II.2. "Let us therefore begin"—read *wal-nabtadi'*.

"thorough"—point *šāfin.*

"possessing skill"—read *ḥaḏāḳa.*

"the principles of philosophy"—reading *al-ḳawānīn* for Hirschfeld's *al-tawābīn,* which makes no sense.

II.3. "al-Muḳammiṣ"—so read, instead of al-Miḳmāṣ; an eminent Jewish philosopher and theologian, who lived about A.D. 900.

"has written"—read *dawwana.*

"commentaries"—read *tafāsīr;* Dā'ūd's commentary on Genesis is mentioned also in the *Book of Lights* (*KA,* I, 44, l. 15); it was entitled *Book of Creation* (Arabic *Kitāb al-xalīḳa*). The whole paragraph is devoted to Dā'ūd's life and activity.

"the Syrians"—i.e., the Syriac-speaking Christians.

"the intended meaning of"—read *'ilayhī.*

"for which there was no need"—expunge the second *'akṯara.*

"Another scholar." Hirschfeld (p. 9) identifies him with the Gaon Sa'adiah. This seems questionable to me. Sa'adiah could hardly be said to have commented upon Genesis in a manner similar to that of a work translated from the commentaries of the Syrian Christians.

"we shall add"—read *nuḍīfu.*

"have failed to explain adequately"—read *wa-ḳaṣurā.*

II.4. "point and lead"—read *ya'ūlu.*

"We shall do"—read *naf'alu.*

"interspersed"—read *yumāziǧuhu.*

"pertaining to"—read *min* for *fī* (both look the same in cursive *nasxī*).

II.5. "the seventh chapter"—read *al-bāb.*

"our book on the biblical laws"—i.e., the *Book of Lights* (*KA,* I, 72–77). There is here another bit of evidence that Hirschfeld's text is not identical with the *Tafsīr Běrešiṯ* (cf. above p. 336), since in this chapter of the *Book of Lights* al-Ḳirḳisānī thrice uses the statement, "we have already explained this in the Commentary on Genesis" *KA,* I, p. 76, l. 15; p. 77, ll. 1 and 9.

"the hyssop"—*al-'izāb* = *ha-'ezoḇ* (I Kings 5: 13).

"other philosophers quote"—read *naḳalathu.*

"A similar thing"—read *wa-nāẓiru.*

"wisdom and understanding"—the massoretic text reads *wisdom of understanding.*

"scholars skilled"—read *ḥuḏḏāḳ.*

II.6. "Scripture mentions"—probably read *yaḏkuru* for *yaktubu.*

"we have quoted there"—i.e., in the aforementioned chapter of the *Book of Lights.*

II.7. "it is inseparable"—read *lā yaxlū.*

"without end"—referring also to the next verse: *Declaring the end from the beginning, and from ancient times the things that are not yet done.* The meaning is, of course, that matter is not eternal, else it would be coeternal with God, who alone is eternal.

"the dependence of all existent things." The reading *nafāḳuhu,* as Hirschfeld himself indicates by the question mark, makes no sense; the correct word is probably *bi-ḥāǧati*—the two groups of letters look about the same in hasty unpointed nasxī.

"refer to the validity of reasoning"—some word like *ta'ḳīd* or *išāra* (the latter, however, would require *ilā* for *li-*) has dropped out before *li-'amr al-ma'ḳūl.*

II.8. "sense perception"—read *al-ḥiss.*

"perception"—read *wal-ḥiss.*

"all five of these principles"—of which only four have been enumerated above; unless this is al-Ḳirḳiṣānī's own error, Hirschfeld's text lacks a sentence expounding the second half of Ps. 19: 8: *The testimony of the Lord is sure, making wise the simple.*

II.9. "reached the height of insolence." Hirschfeld's *hal ta'āfā al-kihata ġāyatan* is patently impossible; read *hal bākā (bakkā) lil-kihati ġāyatan;* this phrase, one of al-Kirkisānī's favorites, occurs frequently in the *Book of Lights.*

"inaccessible to the senses"—read *al-ḥiss.*

"this wisdom is merely"—read *innamā.*

"the wisdom of choice"—i.e., the wisdom of using his intelligence to sift from the mass of available facts those which, by proper combination and arrangement, enable him to achieve his purpose or attain the knowledge he seeks.

"to compel him"—read *ġaṣabahu.*

"acted wrongfully"—read *ǧā'iran.* The apodosis is understood: God, too, in His unlimited power, might have imposed upon mankind tasks beyond their ability to perform, or might have obliged them to believe in His omnipotence without giving them convincing proof of it; but being perfectly just, as well as all-powerful, He did not do so.

"as explained above"—read *wa-ḏālika.*

"confirm the validity of reasoning"—read *tu'akkidu 'amr al-ma'kūl.*

"of similar purport"—read *wali-ḏālika.*

II.10. "reason and analogy"—read *wal-kiyāsiyya.*

"its seeming ambiguities"—read *mutašābihihi.*

"the perfection of the whole of Scripture"—referring to the earlier quotation: *The Law of the Lord is perfect* (Ps. 19: 8).

II.11. "handed down"—read *dafa'a.*

"concerning it"—read *fīhā.*

II.12. "except where literal interpretation"—read *'illā.*

"a contradiction"—read *fasādun 'aw 'īhāmu munākadatin.*

"out of its literal meaning"—add *min* before *al-ẓāhir.*

"out of the literal sense"—read *min* for *'an.*

"for us to take"—read *naǧī'a.*

"out of its literal meaning"—read *min* for *'an.*

"Thus we are compelled"—probably read *fa-'innā* for Hirschfeld's *wa-'innahā,* which is patently impossible; *wa-ḏālika 'annā* would have been better Arabic.

"when Jacob heard this news"—that Joseph was alive and in good circumstances.

"the gift of prophecy came back to him"—it is said to have deserted him during the time of his mourning for Joseph; cf. Targum Onkelos and Rashi, *ad loc.*

"influenced by the moon"—read *al-kamar* and add *miṯla.*

"which [are formed]"—*tan'akidu* should be supplied here.

"the Messiah"—read *al-masīḥ.*

"when crops and fruits will ripen"—read *allaḏī ta'tī bihā al-ġallātu wal-ṯimāru.*

II.13. "the Aramaic language"—literally: "Syriac."

"built upon the order of the letters of the alphabet"—i.e., chapters in which the initial letters of verses, or groups of verses, follow the order of the Hebrew alphabet; this alphabetical order would be violated if the text were rendered in Aramaic.

"a silencer"—probably read *wa-saḳtatun* for Hirschfeld's meaningless *wa-saḳbat.*

"derived from the earth"—Hebrew *'ădamah.*

Woman—Hebrew *'iššah.*

"from man's own name"—Hebrew *'īš.*

"she was taken out of him"—i.e., was fashioned out of a rib from Adam's body.

"I have acquired"—Hebrew *ḳaniti.*

"the Arabic 'I have acquired' "—that is, *iḳtanaytu.*

"We do not say"—read *naḳul* (literally: "we did not say").

"to remove all possible doubts"—about the primordial character of the Hebrew language; al-Ḳirḳisānī presumably means to say that he introduced this example from the Arabic merely as an illustration of his point for the benefit of those who may be unfamiliar with Aramaic and may not understand the preceding examples.

"has appointed"—Hebrew *šaṯ.*

"the Arabic 'God has appointed me' "—Arabic *ğa'ala lī Allāh.*

"was divided"—Hebrew *niflĕğa.*

"[and many others.]" Other examples are given in detail in the Arabic text, but are omitted here.

"until there occurred . . ."—i.e., until the building of the tower of Babel.

"this single language"—read *tilḳa.*

"the Savior"—*al-fārūḳ* (Aramaic *paroḳa*), i.e., the Messiah.

II.14. "that its seat"—insert *'annahu* before *'innamā.*

"is the member"—read *bi-ğāriḥati.*

"with bodily members"—read *ğāriḥātin.*

ğurr—literally: "pull!"

ḳišš—literally: "scat!"

'axx, 'axš—exclamation of disgust.

"to signal other species of animals." On the Arab calls to animals see F. Schulthess, "Zurufe an Tiere im Arabischen," *Abhandlungen der Preuss. Akademie der Wissenschaften, Philos.-hist. Klasse* (Berlin, 1912); corrections were supplied by T. Noeldeke, *ZDMG,* LXVI (1912), 735 ff.

"begged to be excused"—read *ista'fū.* The purpose of this fourth principle is, of course, to condemn anthropomorphic description of God's person—one of the major items on the Karaite list of charges against the Rabbanites.

II.15. "and in doing so"—probably read *fa-ḳaunuhu* for the awkward *fa-ḳaunun;* both forms look the same in hasty nasxī.

"we would have been unable to distinguish . . ."—presumably read *lā na'rifu al-'axbār al-muḥaḳḳat min al-'axbār al-bāṭilat.*

"by making him the actual speaker"—i.e., by quoting it verbatim, in the first person; the Bible thus indicates, according to al-Ḳirḳisānī, that the man's version of the circumstances of Saul's death may not have been truthful.

"Gehazi"—the servant of the Prophet Elisha.

"Sarah having laughed"—referring to Sarah's laughter at the prediction that she was to bear a child (i.e., her son Isaac), despite her advanced age (Gen. 18: 12 ff.); the Bible thus indicates that Sarah had told a lie.

"it is all a tale"—i.e., if the story of Balaam's she-ass were a mere fairy tale, the Bible would have said so expressly or else would have quoted it verbatim under some person's name, whereas in fact the Bible relates the story in the manner of a straightforward narrative (Num. 22: 28 ff.).

II.16. "the story of the heap of stones"—Gen. 31: 46 ff.

"gal 'ed"—"heap is witness," whence the name of Gilead is supposed to have originated.

"each one naming it"—read *fa-'innamā 'asmāhu.*

"whereupon Scripture quotes"—*mā* evidently being an error for *ṯumma.*

"those in exile in Iraq"—i.e., the exiles in Babylonia.

"The gods that have not created . . ." In the Hebrew text of the Bible this verse is written entirely in Aramaic, all the rest of the Book of Jeremiah being in Hebrew.

II.17. "King Hiram's words in his letter to King Solomon." The first of the two biblical quotations in Hirschfeld's text should be moved two lines down under the heading of the Queen of Sheba, where it properly belongs.

"My servants shall bring . . ."—referring to the timber for the construction of the Temple in Jerusalem.

"or the words of the Queen of Sheba"—read *wa-ḳaulu.*

"Ben Hadad"—king of Aram.

"his letters to King Ahab"—I Kings 20: 2 ff.

"the conversation between David and Goliath"—I Sam. 17: 43 ff.

"This is impossible"—probably read *hāḏā mā lā yumḳinu bal 'innamā ḳāna.*

II.18. *"in its own writing"*—the next words in Hirschfeld's text, *that every man should bear rule in his own house* (Esth. 1: 22), are evidently the result of a scribe's confusion, since they break the continuity of the biblical quotation.

"they were skilled"—i.e., the Persian royal scribes.

II.19. "that the kings of the Arabs"—read *bi-'anna* for *ḳāla* (both look much the same in hasty nasxī).

II.20. "one [or two] persons"—the lacuna is undoubtedly to be read *waṯnayni.*

II.21. "and how she obeyed"—read *wamtiṯāluhā.*

"she speaking to him . . ."—read *tuḳallimuhu wa-yuḳallimuhā.*

"repeated twice"—the "twice" refers rather to the following *whatever thy request,* which is repeated in Esth. 7: 2.

"in which Scripture was composed"—principles 7–24 are of purely exegetical and philological nature, and are here omitted; principles 25–37 have been lost.

SALMON BEN JEROHAM

I–III. Davidson's edition, p. 35 ff.

I.2. "When I was at the age of vanity"—i.e., when I was a young man.

I.3. "a foreign land"—presumably Egypt.

"A man"—i.e., Sa'adiah.

I.4. "in all languages"—i.e., in both Hebrew and Arabic.

I.6. "Lest His wrath should burn with anger"—if Sa'adiah's activity were to remain unchecked.

"Eber . . . Dumah." Eber was the progenitor of the Hebrew nation (Gen.

10: 24); Dumah was one of the sons of Ishmael, the progenitor of the Arab nation (Gen. 25: 14). Salmon means that he planned to compose two versions of this epistle, one in Hebrew and the other in Arabic.

I.8. "He stated"—i.e., Sa'adiah.

I.9. "kept upon the tongue"—i.e., preserved orally.

"the seed of the perfect ones"—i.e., the people of Israel.

I.11. "by what is hidden from them"—i.e., by Sa'adiah's ungodly teaching, the wickedness of which would remain hidden from the congregation unless I exposed it.

I.12. "congregation of the Lily"—a self-laudatory epithet used by the Karaites in reference to themselves (cf. Song 2: 1, where Solomon's beloved—allegorically, the synagogue of Israel—is likened to a rose and a lily). Here apparently the term embraces the people of Israel in general, as shown by the next stanza.

"Who are scattered in every land"—and therefore could not possibly all have agreed to utter a testimony that is contrary to the truth.

I.15. "They remember"—i.e., all Jews, everywhere in the Dispersion.

"the splitting asunder of the Red Sea"—Exod. 14: 21 ff.

I.16. "as they say"—i.e., Sa'adiah and his partisans.

"the Fayyumite"—i.e., the native of Fayyūm, meaning Sa'adiah.

"his tongue has been silenced." The meaning is: since the Jews are not all united in acknowledging the sanctity of the oral tradition, this tradition cannot be genuine. The word *Sĕ'aḏyah* is presumably a reader's gloss, as it stretches the verse far out of meter.

I.19. "Why, then, did you write it down in ornate script?" —i.e., if God had actually revealed the mishnaic tradition and ordered Israel to preserve it orally, why did you write it down, thus flagrantly disobeying His explicit command?

I.22. "Where, then, is the oral Law?" Since this alleged oral Law has been committed to writing and has ceased being oral, where is the genuine oral Law, if there be such a one?

"they have drawn God's wrath upon themselves"—Davidson's emendation seems unnecessary.

II.2. "the words of modern men"—and not of ancient Patriarchs and Prophets known to have been inspired by God.

II.5. "And you"—meaning Salmon's Karaite colleagues.

"Had not the blackguard"—*haz-zeh* and *Sĕ'aḏyah* are glosses, but *haz-zeḏ* cannot very well be removed, as suggested by Fuerst and Davidson, without making the whole sentence meaningless; cf. the same phrase further on, in l. 60 of Davidson's text. The "blackguard" is, of course, Sa'adiah.

"intruded among the scholars"—i.e., had he not presumed to claim himself a scholar.

II.7. "contradictory"—literally: "broken."

"in content." Davidson's emendations in these two lines seem unnecessary; the suffix in *bĕ-'inyanay,* as in several rhyme words further on, was added for the sake of the rhyme only.

II.8. "in it"—i.e., in the Mishnah.

"Law of logic"—i.e., teaching based upon pure reason.

II.9. "the two"—i.e., the aforementioned two mishnaic scholars.

II.10. "they say"—i.e., the text of the Mishnah.

"Others say." A formula introducing a third view, without indicating explicitly which of the three views is to be preferred.

"issue a decision"—explicitly rejecting the views of the aforementioned two scholars.

II.11. "I would not have accepted . . ." Davidson's note is not at all clear; Salmon means that had he been living at the time of the scholars of the Mishnah, he would have challenged the right of these "others" and "scholars" to act as arbiters and to issue final decisions. The text of the Bible, according to Salmon, is the only proper place wherein one may seek a decision in matters of law; the views of scholars, even of a majority of them, are in themselves devoid of authority unless they are based on incontrovertible biblical evidence.

"the word of the Lord"—meaning the pertinent biblical ordinances; i.e., I would have weighed or compared the pertinent biblical passages against their opinions.

"judged"—literally: "called to mind" (*hizkarti*); Fuerst's and Davidson's emendations seem unnecessary. The meaning is: I would have examined their views in the light of the pertinent biblical passages and rejected everything which did not agree with the Bible.

II.12. "Gird thyself"—addressing Sa'adiah.

II.13. "between them"—i.e., the scholars of the Mishnah.

" 'I, too, am the learned So-and-so' "—i.e., I have as much right to issue decisions as Rabbi So-and-so, if it comes to issuing decisions unsupported by the biblical text.

II.14. "His heart"—i.e., Sa'adiah's.

"his written scroll"—i.e., Sa'adiah's polemical work entitled *Sefer hag-galuy*.

"his loins"—the traditional seat of man's physical courage and strength.

II.15. "He has written." The text of Sa'adiah's arguments for the validity of the oral Law (of which the following stanzas are Salmon's criticism) is given in al-Ḳirḳisānī's *Book of Lights* (*KA*, I, 123–128).

"And that they wrote it"—i.e., the later scholars.

"unanswerable"—literally: "hard."

II.18. " 'This took place' "—i.e., the composition of the oral Law.

II.20. " 'another view.' " A formula introducing a dissenting view of another mishnaic scholar.

II.21. "Now in this one thing . . ." Davidson's emendation seems unnecessary; the line refers to the following, not the preceding, quatrain, the meaning being: this one thing alone, i.e., the fact that the Mishnah records several contradictory views concerning the same legal problem is sufficient to prove that Sa'adiah is utterly wrong.

III.3. "the School of Shammay . . . the School of Hillel"—the two rival schools of mishnaic scholars, the former renowned for its rigoristic tendency, the latter for its preference for leniency.

III.5. "Then this Mishnah cannot be the Law"—i.e., the views of both schools cannot possibly be correct at the same time, and we must therefore depend on the assistance of later scholars to decide which of the two contradictory views we should accept. This being so, it is clear that the Mishnah is not God's word, for God never sets down His commandments in such a contradictory manner.

III.6. "why do they not say, 'Thus said the Lord'?"—instead of saying, "Rabbi So-and-so said," which is the actual mishnaic usage.

III.7. "Remember that many fell slain"—i.e., remember that far from being peaceful and pious discussions, these mishnaic controversies actually resulted in bloodshed. The tradition referred to goes back to the statement in the Palestinian Talmud (Šabbaṯ 1: 4; M. Higger, *Oṣar hab-bĕrayṯoṯ* [New York, 1938–48], IV, 369): "Rabbi Joshua [son of?] 'Uniya taught: the disciples of the School of Shammay stood on guard below the schoolhouse and were slaying [or perhaps rather: were threatening to slay] the disciples of the School of Hillel. It is taught further: six of the Hillelites went up into the schoolhouse, while the rest were attacked with swords and spears." The passage is an addendum (*barayṯa*) and its precise meaning is not quite clear. If the meaning is that some Hillelites were actually slain, it is the only known record of such extremist action between the two schools; there is reason to believe that the clash was of a political nature between the moderate and extremist (zealot) factions.

III.8. "I will refute thee"—i.e., Sa'adiah.

III.9. "written arguments"—in favor of the authority of the oral tradition.

"commentary on Genesis"—in the longer version, of which only fragments have so far been discovered.

"they will become like spears"—i.e., I will so thoroughly refute them that they will actually serve to confound thee.

III.10. "the ritual fringe, the *lulaḇ,* and the booth"—the fringes worn on men's garments, and the bouquet of palm fronds and festal booth used in the ritual of the Feast of Tabernacles.

"they arranged it"—i.e., the sections of the Mishnah dealing with these matters.

III.11. "the length"—Davidson's emendation seems unnecessary.

"how wilt thou distinguish?"—i.e., since not all ordinances specify definite measurements, there is no reason why one cannot assume that the fringe, too, is one of these unspecified ordinances and that God did not intend to prescribe any definite length for the fringe. This being so, how wilt thou be able to show that the opposite is true?

III.12. "heave offering"—a required offering made to the priests from the produce of the land (Num. 18: 8 ff.).

"what part of what amount"—i.e., what percentage.

III.13. "specified for it"—i.e., for the heave offering.

III.14. "three, five, and six." The interpretation of Poznanski and Davidson seems much too fanciful, and Davidson himself was doubtful about it. It seems simpler to interpret the numbers literally. The meaning is: Sa'adiah said that were it not for the talmudic mathematical calendar, we would have been unable to distinguish Sabbaths from workdays. This argument, replies Salmon, is nonsense; men simply do know which day is a Sabbath and which is not, and need no mishnaic calendar with its mathematics to tell them so.

III.16. "Yet the prayers"—i.e., the duty of praying, the daily number of prayers, and their precise content.

III.17. "Thy mouth"—in the sense of "thy mind as revealed by the utterances of thy mouth."

"the prayer of Daniel"—Dan. 9: 4 ff.

III.19. "the Dread Gathering"—i.e., the Day of Judgment and of the gathering of the exiled remnants of Israel.

JAPHETH BEN ELI

I. Edited by N. Schorstein, *Der Commentar des Karaeers Jephet ben 'Alī zum Buche Rûth* (Berlin, 1903) Heidelberg dissertation. Some corrections were supplied by S. Poznanski, *ZfHB,* VII (1903), 133–135. A Hebrew version, wrongly ascribed to Salmon ben Jeroham, was published by I. Markon; see above, p. 71.

I.1. "Blessed be the Lord"—the alternate reading is to be preferred.

"of the angels"—read *walil-malā'iḵa* (Poznanski).

"His presence"—read *li-saḵīnatihi* (Poznanski); the author has in mind the Hebrew term *šĕḵinah,* the invisible presence of the divine glory all over the earth.

I.2. "nobility of descent"—*al-ḥasab wal-nasab;* both words here mean the same thing, rather than "der Adel des eigenen Wertes und der edlen Abstammung," as Schorstein translates.

"our Sages"—*'a'immatunā,* literally: "our imams," the Arabic term for the person who leads the congregation in prayer at the mosque.

I.3. "Jethro"—the father-in-law of Moses.

I.4. "Jael"—the woman who slew Sisera (Judg. 4: 17 ff.).

"It will thus be shown"—read *yabīnu;* the variant should be read *fa-bāna.*

"Render ye sincere homage." The Hebrew text of this clause may be corrupt, and the translation is uncertain.

I.5. "purposes"—i.e., lessons.

"this scroll." The Book of Ruth is one of the five so-called "scrolls" (Song of Songs, Ruth, Lamentations, Ecclesiastes, and Esther).

"We have already set forth"—in the prefatory statement above.

"And he"—i.e., Ruth's son, Obed, grandfather of King David.

"a well-meaning person"—i.e., one worshiping the true God.

"while she expected to obtain thereby something she desired"—referring to the possibility of Naomi's remarriage, in which case Orpah might be married to a son who might be born to Naomi; cf. below, commentary to v. 11–12.

"which we have mentioned"—preferring the reading *ḏaḵarnāhā* (Poznanski).

I.6. "we shall proceed"—prefer *fal-nabtadi'.*

I.7. "placing it first." This was so in Japheth's time; in the present Hebrew canon the Book of Ruth is placed second, after the Song of Songs.

"King Solomon"—the traditional author of the Song of Songs.

I.9. "when they exercised the supreme command"—referring to the fact that the Judges did not form a continuous line of rulers succeeding one another but came into power whenever a national emergency required a single capable and energetic ruler. "In the days of the Judges" would thus have embraced also the periods when the office was vacant.

I.10. "yet Scripture does not explain." The construction here is, as Schorstein remarks, rather stilted, but his emendation seems unnecessary; the meaning is clear enough.

"Now most scholars"—read *fa-'inna* for *li-'anna.*

"and they left no sustenance for Israel"—meaning the Midianites; Japheth takes this as an allusion to the famine in the time of Elimelech.

"they would have returned"—i.e., Naomi and her family.

I.11. "Jair"—Judg. 10: 3 ff.; "Ibzan"—Judg. 12: 8 ff.; "Tola"— Judg. 10: 1 f.; 'Jephthah"—Judg. 11–12.

"David belonged to the fourth generation after Boaz"—according to the genealogy in Ruth 4: 18 ff.

"four hundred and some years"—i.e., six generations, at approximately threescore and ten years each.

"in the middle of these four hundred years." In other words, the events recounted in the Book of Ruth must have taken place less than 200 years before David, which, according to Japheth, places them at the time of Tola. The chronology of the period is very uncertain, and Japheth's figure is probably too high.

I.13. *"a land"*—the word is not found in the massoretic text.

I.14. "[depended upon him]"—the lacuna presumably contained some phrase like *yaḥtājūna 'ilā;* Poznanski's emendation requires the awkward repetition of *yalzamuhu.*

I.15. "another Bethlehem"—i.e., another town named Bethlehem, situated in another district of Palestine; this (northern) town is mentioned in Josh. 19: 15.

I.18. "blameworthy"—preferring the reading *ḏammahu* (Poznanski).

"as a punishment"—this view is found already in the Talmud (B. Baḇa baṯra 91a), but Japheth evidently learned of it indirectly from a contemporary Rabbanite scholar.

"we find the Prophet Elisha saying. . ."—i.e., Elisha would not have given this advice if it were sinful to leave Palestine in times of famine.

I.19. "and the narrator"—read *wa-ḳāna* for *'au ḳāna.*

"the continuation of this story"—i.e., Naomi's words in v. 11, *Have I yet sons in my womb, that they may become your husbands?;* the implied answer is no.

I.20. "his high station"—as an indirect ancestor of King David.

"her own merit"—her excellent character and her steadfastness in the face of hard trials, as mentioned before.

"their marriages"—add *min* before *nisbatihim.*

I.21. "Elkanah"—the father of the Prophet Samuel.

an Ephrathite—referring to the first half of this verse, *Now there was a certain man of Ramathaim Zophim, of the hill country of Ephraim, and his name was Elḳanah.*

I.25. "nor married any other women"—in addition to Naomi, although polygamy was permissible at that time.

"protector"—*sitruhā,* literally: "veil, cover."

I.26. "before his two sons were married"—otherwise their wives would have been mentioned here also.

"Naomi's sons"—and not stepsons, i.e., sons of Elimelech by a previous marriage.

"their mother"—accepting Schorstein's emendation of the obviously corrupt original. Japheth draws these conclusions from the pronouns *her* and *his.*

I.27. *"about ten years"*—preferring the reading *naḥwa* (Poznanski).

"Moabite women"—whom Naomi might conceivably have disliked as idolaters.

"had come of age"—and were no longer subject to their mother's authority in this matter.

I.29. "was married before his elder brother"—i.e., since Ruth is mentioned after Orpah, the marriage of the latter must have taken place before Ruth's marriage.

I.30. "that one of the daughters-in-law"—add *'anna* before *wāḥida* (Poznanski).

I.31. "A was left of B." Japheth means to say that *was left of* is a drastically abbreviated figure of speech, since the word *bereft* is not represented in the Hebrew text of this verse.

I.35. "to which she had moved"—presumably after Elimelech's death.

I.37. "It is a token"—reading *'inna* for *'iḏ* (both look the same in hasty nasxī); Schorstein's emendation to *'iḏā* is hardly an improvement.

I.38. "the scriptural law." This law refers, however, solely to a Jewish widow of priestly descent.

I.39. "who now were dead"—i.e., at the time when Naomi spoke thus to her daughters-in-law.

I.41. *"to thy people"*—using the reading *'ilā ša'biḵ* (Poznanski) rejected by Schorstein; since it is the exact rendering of the Hebrew *lĕ-'ammeḵ*, it must be the original one, while the reading accepted by Schorstein, *wa-nakūnu fī ǧumlati ša'biḵ*, is more of a paraphrase and is clearly influenced by the same phrase in the commentary immediately following.

I.42. *"If I should say"*—preferring the reading *'in ḵultu* (omit *'an*) *'īs lī*, rejected by Schorstein, since it reproduces exactly the Hebrew text; *'īs* is the affirmative counterpart of *laysa*, formed by Japheth on the analogy of the Hebrew *yeš* and the Aramaic *'iṯ*.

I.45. "[one of] two things"—add *'aḥada*.

I.46. "levirate marriage." The Karaite view is that levirate marriage, as commonly understood, is illegal, and that the term "brother," as used in the Bible (Deut. 25: 5 ff.) in reference to it, denotes a brother by faith and nationality, i.e., a fellow Israelite, and not a blood brother.

"but only when the other brother"—reading *yūǧibūnahu* (the subject being the Rabbanites).

"is on hand." The Talmud (B. Yĕḇamot 17a), expressly exempts an as yet unborn brother from the duty of marrying his deceased brother's widow, inasmuch as an unborn child cannot be regarded as a brother in a legal sense.

"lawfully designated"—reading *lanṭalakū* for the impossible *lam yanṭaliḵū*.

"it is thus clear"—reading *bāna* (or *bayyanat*) for the impossible *banat*.

I.47. "because she had already"—reading *li-'annahā* for the impossible *'ilayhā*; both look nearly the same in hasty nasxī.

I.48. "a reproach to Orpah"—for her relapse into idolatry and her repudiation of her adopted people.

"Do not confront me with the like of such advice"—the Hebrew word for *confront* means literally: "meet." *Bi-miṯli hāḏā al-kalām*, which has no counterpart in the Hebrew text, is clearly a gloss, taken from Japheth's commentary immediately following.

I.49. "of a child toward its parent"—the context seems to require *al-walad lil-wālid* for Schorstein's *al-wālid lil-walad*.

I.50. " 'Painful.' " Schorstein's *al-faǧǧ*, "unripe," clearly makes no sense in this context, and his explanation, "unreif = hart, unfreundlich," is much too strained. The word is presumably a misreading of *al-faǧiʿ* (= *al-fāǧiʿ*), "painful, distressing"; both look nearly the same in hurried nasxī. This is particularly probable because *al-faǧiʿ* and the Hebrew *tifgĕʿi* go back to the same root.

I.51. "since man does not know when he will die or where." Japheth points out two things: 1) when Ruth said, *Where thou wilt die, I will die,* she spoke of death because that was more probable, in the ordinary course of human affairs, than captivity or any similar calamity, although her words included them as well, i.e., that she would follow Naomi into captivity; 2) Ruth promised to remain with Naomi for the duration of her own life, because that was a matter subject to her choice; she did not promise to remain with her in death as well, because the place and time of her death were not up to her but rather up to God's decree.

I.52. "a curse oath"—i.e., a formula invoking a curse upon a person if that person should commit or omit a certain specified act.

"determined"—literally: "fortified."

I.54. *"all the city."* The preceding *niswān* has no equivalent in the Hebrew text and is presumably a gloss taken from the immediately following commentary.

"and they said." In the Hebrew text *they* is expressed by a feminine suffix.

"ten years must have gone by"—which would explain their hesitation in recognizing her.

"Naomi . . . Marah"—the former signifying "sweet" or "pleasant" in Hebrew, the latter meaning "bitter."

I.55. "was changed." The word *naḵl* seems redundant and is presumably a reader's gloss.

I.57. *of barley*—reading *al-šaʿīr* (Poznanski).

I.58. "they indeed found food"—i.e., the rumor about the cessation of the famine referred to in v. 6 was true.

"an acquaintance"—*maʿrifa* = the Hebrew *moḏaʿ,* which however is usually translated "kinsman".

I.59. "since he was an important man." The reading rejected by Schorstein, *li-'annahu ḵāna raǧulan ǧalīlan,* seems preferable to the awkward *li-'annahu maḏḵūr ǧalīl.*

I.61. "who are not honest"—read *ṯiḵāt;* meaning that Ruth did her gleaning openly, in full sight of the reapers, and not furtively.

"her own intention concerning this matter"—*ʿalā 'aṣlin ʿindahā min ḏāliḵa* is awkward, but yields fair sense, and Schorstein's remark that "die Worte *min ḏāliḵa* geben hier keinen Sinn" seems unjustified. But perhaps read *ʿalā ḵaṣdin ʿindahā* (or *minhā*) *fī ḏāliḵa* (*'aṣlin—ḵaṣdin, ʿindahā—minhā,* and *min—fī* are, respectively, almost indistinguishable in hurried nasxī), which yields the same meaning, but constitutes better grammar.

"he loves"—i.e., God.

I.62. "upon their work"—*maʿāšihim,* literally: "their livelihood."

" 'Peace be upon you' "—the kind of Hebrew and Arabic greeting commonly used in the Middle Ages and down to the present day.

"who was afraid of them"—i.e., of the warriors who had come to David's aid.

I.63. *"this is what she had gathered . . . it is but little."* The Hebrew text is presumably corrupt and has been variously emended.

I.64. "she was slow in gleaning"—i.e., inexperienced and unaccustomed to such a manner of obtaining food.

I.68. "as we shall see further on"—cf. v. 14 and the commentary thereto.

" 'water flask' "—read *ķurāz*.

I.69. "would upbraid them loudly"—literally: "would shout."

"refers to his maidservants"—because *them* is expressed by a feminine suffix in the Hebrew text.

I.70. *"neḡa' "* literally:—"affliction, wound," derived in Hebrew from the same root as the verb "to touch."

I.71. "just as the manservant of the Patriarch Abraham had done"—Gen. 24: 26: *And the man bowed his head and prostrated himself before the Lord,* in gratitude for having found Rebekah. Ruth's bow was meant for God, and not for Boaz, since God is the prime source of all favors.

I.72. "just as the Patriarch Abraham did"—cf. Gen. 12: 1 ff.

I.73. *"under whose wings thou hast come."* Schorstein's text (p. xxviii, l. 2–3) seems to be badly confused: the words in l. 2, *wa-ķāla 'ăšer baṯ la-ḥăsoṯ taḥaṯ ķĕnafaw,* belong after *'ĕlohe Yiśra'el* in l. 3.

I.74. " 'is acceptable to God.' " Since a blessing is essentially a request to God to reward the recipient of the blessing, it must be acceptable to Him to be effective.

I.75. " 'for I am inferior to them' "—since she was a stranger receiving what amounted to charity, whereas Boaz's maidservants had earned his good will by their work for him.

I.77. "it was improper for her to sit with them"—because of her chastity.

I.79. "the rightful due"—referring to the scriptural injunction to leave the gleaning to the poor and the stranger (Lev. 19: 9–10, 23: 22; Deut. 24: 19), where the term covers mostly grain and fruit growing on the edges and corners of the field or left after the harvest. Boaz therefore showed Ruth exceptional favor by letting her glean among sheaves not yet removed from the field.

"wayba"—an Arab measure of grain, equal to about five bushels.

I.82. " 'with whom hast thou worked?' "—i.e., in whose field?

I.83. "having acted with kindness . . . toward Elimelech and his sons"—by being generous to their womenfolk.

I.84. "the father's family"—i.e., Elimelech's; the father's side takes precedence in matters of inheritance.

II. Edited by Mann, pp. 31–32.

II.3. "Kiss ye the commandments"—i.e., kiss reverently, in the sense of worshiping and obeying them.

II.4. "Rock of Eternity"—i.e., God.

II.5. "noble ones among the nations"—meaning Israel, the chosen people.

"God"—reading *'Ĕlohe*.

II.9. "mourners for Zion"—the name for a group of ascetic individuals who spent their time mourning for the destruction of Zion and the dispersion of Israel and praying for their restoration. Many Karaites belonged to it.

"your Mother"—i.e., Zion.

II.11. "Your Holy House"—i.e., the Temple in Jerusalem or the city as a whole.

"strangers"—i.e., the Moslem conquerors.

II.12. "enemies of God"—i.e., the Moslem conquerors.

II.13. "to appear before Him"—i.e., to make the pilgrimage to Jerusalem, or settle permanently in the Holy City.

SAHL BEN MAṢLIAḤ

1. *LḲ*, II, 24–43 (some corrections were supplied by A. Geiger, *'Oṣar neḥmaḏ* IV [1864], 22–27); the introductory poem, the prefatory paragraph, and a number of paragraphs within the text are here omitted. It may well be questioned whether the large and involved legal excursuses (*LḲ*, II, 28–30 and 37–42), were included in the epistle as it was first written down; they may well have been added by Sahl later on.

"from Jerusalem"—*Beṯ ham-Miḳdaš*, in agreement with the use of Arabic Bayt al-Maḳdis (= al-Ḳuds).

"except the Karaites." Sahl's implication seems to be that he had come to preach to dilatory Karaites only, and not to seduce any Rabbanites from their faith, although this is not consistent with what follows.

"foods prepared by Gentiles." These were forbidden in Karaite law from the time of Anan, who prohibited the use of all food which underwent any sort of transformation or change at the hands of Gentiles; the foods listed in the next lines all come under this classification. See also further on, regarding the alleged laxity in safeguarding the ritual cleanness of Jewish meats. Such laxity is, to be sure, equally prohibited in Rabbanite law.

"who have recently been confined"—this being forbidden on biblical grounds in both Karaite and Rabbanite law, until a certain purification period has elapsed; the Karaite regulations on this point are more severe (cf. *AE*, fol. 130b), hence Sahl's accusation.

"made out of camels' hides"—i.e., vessels doubly unclean, since the camel is classified as an unclean animal (Lev. 11:4).

"mice droppings"—read *uṣfi'e* (Geiger).

4. "admonition"—read *bĕ-ṯoḳaḥtam*.

"have assembled"—read *ḳibbĕṣu;* Sahl refers to the ceaseless Karaite endeavors to maintain a representative community of their sect in the Holy City. This touching perseverance, maintained in the face of frequent overwhelming material difficulties, runs through the entire Karaite history down to modern times (cf. Mann, pp. 3 ff., 321 ff.).

"this loveliest of all women." Geiger's variant, *ha-'eḏah haḳ-ḳĕḏošah hay-yafah,* seems to be a reader's gloss.

"crying"—*wĕ-'omereṯ* seems to be a dittography of the same word in the next line.

"and saying." What follows is a regular penitential prayer (*sĕliḥah*) in poetic form.

5. "zeal for Thy House"—i.e., "zeal for my return to Thy rebuilt Temple and city."

"graves"—referring to Moslem cemeteries in the Holy City.

"all kinds of uncleanness"—i.e., the Moslem and Christian houses of worship and their rites.

"demolished my city"—reading *'iri* for the awkward *beṯi,* which is repeated in the next line.

"Ishmael"—i.e., the Arabs, and Mohammedans in general.

"Edom"—i.e., the Roman and Byzantine empires.

6. "forsook not their goal"—*pěnehem,* literally: "their faces," i.e., the purpose toward which their faces were turned.

"ashes . . . splendor"—play of words upon the Hebrew *'efer,* "ashes," and *pě'er,* "splendor."

7. "your companions"—read *ḥăḇereḵa* (Geiger).

"shooting off sparks"—i.e., "empty and false accusations against me."

"and what is my life worth"—i.e., "I possess no qualifications to make me fit to teach others, and I do so only to repel your wanton attack."

8. "two wicked women"—metaphorically refers to the two Babylonian Rabbanite academies at Sura and Pumbeditha.

"because of their leaders"—referring to Rabbanite leaders and officials. *Bě-haḵel minhağehem* obviously yields no satisfactory sense; *minhağehem* must be an error for *manhiğehem,* while *bě-haḵel* remains obscure; presumably read *bě-haḵše* (in lieu of the grammatically correct *be-haḵšoṯ*).

"forcing them to borrow"—in order to pay the various taxes and assessments.

"They vaunt their holiness and purity"—Pinsker's *miṯḵadděšim u-miṭṭahărim* seems to be preferable to the variants supplied by Geiger.

9. "the Palestinian academy of the Sanhedrin"—cf. Mann, p. 55, n. 102.

10. " 'Jose the Galilean' "—Jewish scholar, member of the Academy at Jabneh, who lived at the beginning of the 2d century and whose piety became proverbial. His (reputed) tomb was located at Daltha in Galilee (cf. Mann, p. 88).

"bowknots"—*'ăḵaḏim;* Geiger's variant, *'iḵḵarim,* "roots," seems hardly suitable.

"They perform pilgrimage rites"—*wě-ḥoněğim* (or *wě-ḥoğěğim* = the Arabic *wa-yaḥuğğūna,* Poznanski, p. 37, n. 2); strictly speaking, though, this would require the preposition *'el,* instead of *'al.* Perhaps a better interpretation would be "they walk in circles around the tombs," in imitation of the well-known Mohammedan ceremony called *ṭawāf,* "circumambulation," at Mecca.

11. "pieces of apparel"—*ḵěru'e* (Geiger, *ḵěra'e*) *běğaḏim;* the literal meaning, "tatters of garments," obviously does not fit the context; what is meant is probably minor accessories, such as kerchiefs or shawls, the use of which is a luxury, and not an absolute necessity. All these, in the Karaite view, come under the definition of "burden," the carrying of which is forbidden on the Sabbath.

"so do they also on the Sabbath"—in violation of the required Sabbath rest and limitation of travel.

12. "Jewish notables"—literally: "judges."

"the judgment place"—figuratively for places where public business is transacted and justice is dispensed.

"their saliva is blown between the flesh and the hide"—to facilitate the skinning, apparently.

"and the same butchering block . . ."—using Geiger's variant, *'ăšer yiḵrěṯu winattěḥu 'alaw běśar hab-běhemah haš-šěḥuṭah bě-yaḏ Yiśra'el yiḵrěṯu gam šěḥiṭaṯ hag-goy.*

"flesh . . . is forbidden for consumption in the Dispersion." The prohibition of eating meat in the Dispersion dates back to Anan, who was joined in this view by several of his eminent successors (Benjamin al-Nahāwandī, Daniel al-Ḳūmisī, and Ismā'īl al-'Ukbarī; cf. *KA,* V, 1241–1249), on the basis of their interpretation of several biblical verses. Other eminent authorities (Mūsā al-Za'farānī, al-Ḳirḳisānī) opposed it. This burdensome prohibition was later limited to the city of Jerusalem, but even this concession met with opposition from some later Karaite divines (extracts from a 14th-century [?] tract advocating the total abolition of this prohibition were published by Mann, pp. 71–72, 108–110). Nevertheless, the general Karaite practice remained to refrain from eating meat in the Holy City. Sahl, as was to be expected from his missionary zeal, belonged to the rigoristic party on this question.

15. "Ramla"—reading *bĕ-Ramlah* (Mann) for *bĕ-Karmĕlah;* al-Ramla was an important administrative and military center at that time.

"by those who fear God"—i.e., by their Karaite neighbors.

18. "the light is burning and the sun is shining"—meaning the true faith of Karaism, according to Sahl's view.

"the land that is desolate . . ."—i.e., the false Rabbanite persuasion, as Sahl saw it.

19. "And now you"—addressing Jacob ben Samuel.

"hold your hand over your mouth"—i.e., "be silent."

20. "or wage war"—in the sense of polemics.

"hold an assembly with him on the Sabbath"—when Sa'adiah would have had to come out of his hiding to attend public worship. The whole story of his hiding from the Karaites is, so far as known, pure fiction and psychologically inconsistent with Sa'adiah's known personal characteristics.

"because of the lamps burning in the synagogue"—since Rabbanite law permits the burning of lamps or candles on the Sabbath, provided they had been lighted before its arrival. Karaite law, on the other hand, forbids all fire, of whatever origin, on the Sabbath.

"Ben Mašiaḥ"—al-Ḥasan, or al-Ḥusayn, ben Mašiaḥ (probably more correctly ibn Masīḥ [originally ibn 'Abd al-Masīḥ?]), Karaite polemicist at Bagdad and younger contemporary of Sa'adiah; see Poznanski, pp. 15–16.

"to follow Sa'adiah to his innermost chamber." The wording here is very awkward: *wĕ-heḇi 'oṯo* does not fit the situation very well—who brought whom? Since Sa'adiah was allegedly hiding, he certainly would not have led an outspoken Karaite into his hiding place, nor would Ben Mašiaḥ have led Sa'adiah into the innermost chamber of the latter's own home. The sense seems to require *way-yaḇo 'aḥăraw,* which could easily have been misread as *wĕ-heḇi 'oṯo.*

"had written against the Karaites." As Mann (p. 25) correctly indicates, the words *'al bĕne miḳra* belong right after *ḳaṯaḇ.*

"a refutation in Hebrew"—meaning the *Book of the Wars of the Lord.*

"Sa'adiah's tract beginning with the words . . ."—read *'al 'ăšer ḳaṯab 'Eśśa mĕšali wĕ-'aḥuḏ;* the fragments of this tract, so far discovered, have been brought together by B. Lewin, "Eśśa mĕšali," *Raḇ Sĕ'aḏyah ga'on,* ed. J. L. Fischmann (Jerusalem, 1943), pp. 481–532.

"Abū al-Ṭayyib, known as al-Ğibālī." His Hebrew name was Samuel ben Asher ben Manṣūr. For the spelling al-Ǧibālī (instead of Pinsker's and Poznanski's al-Ǧabalī), see Mann, p. 25. On this 10th-century Karaite author see Poznanski, pp. 16–17.

" 'Alī ibn al-Ḥusayn"—an otherwise little-known Karaite writer; cf. Poznanski, p. 17.

"Abū 'Alī al-Ḥasan al-Baṣrī"—i.e., the great Karaite exegete Japheth ben Eli (end of the 10th century).

"search in them and you will know"—read *dĕroš wĕ-ṯeḏa'* (Geiger).

21. "wearing rings upon your fingers"—this, too, being regarded in Karaite law as carrying a burden on the Sabbath.

"then they will come"—*wĕ-hu* seems out of place and is presumably an error, the scribe having written the correct *wĕ-hem* next, without crossing out the wrong *wĕ-hu*.

22. "the two women"—see above, p. 350.

24. "Do we not direct our prayer . . ."—i.e., the Karaites pray not only for themselves but for all Israel.

25. "Remove the foreskin of your hearts"—i.e., purge your hearts of your sinful errors.

"the cutting off of the external foreskin avails nothing"—i.e., physical circumcision does not automatically make us righteous; our hearts, too, must be purified of evil ways and intentions.

27. "and upon you"—*wĕ-'al ḵol ma'ăṯiḵ has-sefer haz-ze* is obviously a gloss.

JESHUAH BEN JUDAH

I. Ed. I. Markon, *Das Buch von den verbotenen Verwandschaftsgraden des Jeschû'a ben Jehuda* (St. Petersburg, 1908), pp. 57–59. For the Rabbanite law on this subject, see, in general, Sifra to Lev. 18; B. Yĕḇamoṯ 22b–23a.

I.1. "They say"—i.e., those who defend the validity of the catenary theory of incest.

"begotten"—Hebrew *moleḏeṯ,* literally: "the giving of birth."

"Scripture would have related her to him"—i.e., would have called her "the daughter of thy father," instead of *the daughter of thy father's wife.*

"his father's daughter"—read *lo* for *li* (*ben* is used here in the general sense of "child," either male or female).

"her mother's marriage"—Hebrew *dibbuḵ,* literally: "adherence."

"and if her mother's marriage." Markon's text here makes no sense, and the variant rejected by him is really the correct one: read *ḵi 'em zu hab-baṯ* for *ḵi 'im ze haḵ-ḵaṯ*[*uḇ*].

I.2. "is not correct." Markon's rejection of *'eno* is unjustified.

"in more ways than one"—*ḥuṣ miz-ze had-dereḵ* is, I take it, a rendering of the Arabic *'alā ġayri ǧihatin.*

"their aforementioned conclusion"—preferring the reading *'amruhu* rejected by Markon.

I.3. "Now from their reasoning"—read *'ăšer* for the senseless *'KR.*

"the one husband and the other"—*ha-'iš wĕha-'iššah* is clearly impossible; probably read *ha-'iš wĕha-'iš*(?)

I.4. "This being proven." The second *ze* is to be expunged.

"had another husband"—read *'aḥer* for *'eḥad̲*.

I.5. "The mother's new husband"—i.e., the stepfather.

"by marrying"—add *lĕ* before *hiṯdabbĕḵo*.

"These two fathers alone are fathers"—i.e., these two, the real father and the step-father, are the only ones who can logically be designated as fathers; the other three "fathers" required by the catenary theory have no genuine claim to fatherhood.

"if one of them is the father of A"—add *'im* after *ḵi*.

"Now if the husband of the mother is the father"—read *ha-'em* for *ha-'aḇ*.

"and if he"—add the conjunction *wĕ* before *hu*.

"she and he had become one individual"—read *hu* for *hi*.

I.6. "And so forth, in this same manner"—i.e., the same would apply to a seventh person, and so forth, ad infinitum.

"they will at least have followed their principle—although it leads to absurdity, as just shown.

"will have violated"—reading *ḵĕḥid̲ah* for the unintelligible *bĕḥid̲ah*.

"it is highly improbable"—because of the very remote degree of relationship.

"if the principle . . . be sound"—therefore, the principle itself must be unsound.

I.7. *"begotten"*—i.e., interpreting this word in the sense of adoption, by virtue of marriage to her mother.

"the other wife of her father"—read *'aḇiha* for *'aḇi*.

"the other man"—i.e., the third husband in the case.

"[is her father]"—add a second *'aḇiha* after *'aḇiha*.

"must also be the daughter's father." The involved situation here is this: the girl's father, A, took a second wife, X (who thus became the girl's stepmother), who was formerly married to another man, B. B and A are, therefore, *one flesh,* and B consequently also becomes the girl's "father." B, having been divorced by X, took another wife, Y, who in her turn was formerly married to another man, C; C and B thus become *one flesh.* Since B and A are *one flesh,* C and A are likewise *one flesh;* therefore C, too, becomes the girl's "father."

I.8. "applies here also"—i.e., their reasoning applies equally well to a fifth, sixth, person, ad infinitum.

I.9. "the son of her mother's husband"—i.e., the son of her stepfather, by a previous marriage.

I.10. "They say also that as there are"—read *ḵĕ-'omram* for *bĕ-'omram*.

"The son of the wife"—read *u-ḇen* for *u-min*.

I.11. "and most of the rules thereof are derived from it." Since the foregoing conclusions which result from their interpretation of this verse are absurd, the theory itself must be false.

II. Markon, *op. cit.,* pp. 98–99.

II.2. "not wicked"—i.e., not illegal and incestuous.

"A becomes his brother"—since their common wife makes them *one flesh,* according to the catenary theory.

"X becomes B's mother as well"—i.e., she becomes automatically forbidden to B.

II.3. "is . . . forbidden to marry the daughter of his father's wife"—who, through her mother's marriage, becomes the mother's husband's stepdaughter and his son's stepsister.

II.4. "on this same principle"—since X would then be forbidden to marry a blood relative of her son's wife.

MOSES BEN ABRAHAM DAR'Ī

I. *LK,* I, 73. I am obliged to Dr. Simon Bernstein for help in some difficult passages in this and the following poems.

I.10. "that day turned my robe of splendor"—pointing *śam;* Pinsker's emendation (*LK,* II, 217), *tafarti* for *tif'arti,* seems unnecessary.

I.11. "caused by it"—i.e., by the city.

I.13. "upon it"—i.e., upon the city.

II. *LK,* I, 74.

II.5. "the Rock"—i.e., God.

"these false things"—i.e., the oral tradition of the Rabbanites.

II.6. "His own people"—i.e., Israel.

II.7. "no second." In Hebrew "Mishnah" and "second" are derived from the same root.

III. *LK,* I, 81.

IV. *LK,* I, 81.

IV.2. "poor"—literally: "weary."

V. *LK,* I, 81.

V.6. "his inwards"—literally: "the members of his body."

VIA *LK, I,* 83.

VI.2. "friends"—literally: "brethren."

VI.8. "justly"—i.e., truthfully.

VI.13. "my hands were helpless"—to repay my false friends for their perfidy.

VI.15. " 'divest yourselves of it!' "—"or you, too, will be cultivated by your false friends solely for the sake of your gold, and they will turn against you eventually."

VIB. *LK,* I, 85.

VI.23. " 'wilt' "—during a drought, but will bloom again after the drought is past.

VII. *LK,* I, 84.

VII.2. "laugh"—or "jest."

VIII. *LK,* I, 84.

IX. *LK,* I, 84.

IX.2. " 'A woman more bitter than wormwood!' " The conclusion, "So I divorced her," seems to be implied.

X. *LK,* I, 86.

X.6. "more than I could wish for"—i.e., "if I had not sinned against God, my prosperity would have been greater than anything I could ever have wished for."

XI. *LK,* I, 86.

XI.4. "until it is burned with fire"—when its fragrant odor is released.

XII. *LK,* I, 87.

XIII. *LḲ*, I, 88.

XIII.10. "He feels much distressed"—literally: "he is very much in sore straits."

XIII.13. "his wealth and riches"—literally: "his ability and strength," in a material sense.

XIII.19. "women . . . creditors"—an untranslatable play on words (Hebrew *našim* and *nošim*).

XIV. *LḲ*, I, 89.

XV. *LḲ*, I, 91.

XV.6. "to Thy satisfaction"—i.e., "make me as satisfactory to Thee as a servant, as Thou art satisfactory to me as a master."

XVI. *LḲ*, I, 91.

XVI.7. "barren"—literally: "empty."

XVI.16. "to dwell in bitterness"—owing to reverses of fortune.

XVI.19. "hastening to travel"—yet knowing not the perils of their journey.

XVI.20. "who go down to sea in a skiff"—and are unaware of the danger of storms.

XVI.21. "at an inn of desire"—i.e., amidst the carnal pleasures of a brothel.

XVI.22. "depart for the pit"—i.e., the pit of death.

XVII. *LḲ*, I, 93.

XVII.2. "vice"—literally: "shame;" i.e., the fool who disregards his friend's virtues and points only at his vices.

XVIII. *LḲ*, I, 93.

XIXA. *LḲ*, I, 99.

XIXA.6. "Jetur and Dishon"—descendants, respectively, of Ishmael and Esau (Gen. 25: 15, 36: 21), i.e., Moslems and Christians.

XIXA.8. "a man of violence"—i.e., lest the Holy Land should be permanently settled by non-Jews, men of blasphemy and violence.

XIXA.23. "their shepherd . . . will pass judgment"—i.e., the Messiah.

XIXB. *LḲ*, I, 98–99.

XIXB.12. "write their names"—in the heavenly record.

XIXB.15. "fire offerings"—reading *'iššim* for *'išim*.

XIXB.22. "the House of the Beloved City"—i.e., the Temple in Jerusalem.

XIXB.28. "the scapegoat"—used for the atonement of sins (Lev. 16).

XIXB.30. "the dismal land"—i.e., the desert.

XIXB.34. "the Land of Beauty"—i.e., Palestine.

XIXC. *LḲ*, I, 101.

XIXC.2. "Name"—literally: "mention."

XIXC.5. "Thy Name is I-Am-That-I-Am"—referring to Exod. 3: 13 f.

XIXC.6. "Thy Sacred Hall"—i.e., the Temple in Jerusalem.

XIXC.7. "the fools"—i.e., their foolish persecutors.

XIXC.12. "the Prince of its tent"—i.e., the Messiah.

XIXC.13. "the Offspring of David"—i.e., the Messiah.

XIXD. *LḲ*, I, 100–101.

XIXD.6. "coarse"—literally: "poor."

XIXD.33. "Esau and Ishmael"—i.e., the Christians and the Mohammedans.

XIXD.35. "the Redeemer"—i.e., the Messiah.

XIXD.42. "the House of my Sanctuary"—i.e., the Temple and the city of Jerusalem.

MOSES BEN SAMUEL OF DAMASCUS

I. Mann, pp. 213–232 (Hebrew text only); published in part with English translation in *JRAS* (1919), 155–184; additions by S. Poznanski, *ibid.* (1920), pp. 97–99.

I.1. "kidneys." Cf. Ps. 7: 10, etc.

I.6. "in the year seven hundred/And fifty and five of the reign of the Ishmaelites"—i.e., the year 755 of the Arab reckoning (of the Hegirah) or A.D. 1354.

"in full force"—*bĕ-ḳol ham-ma'ăśim,* literally: "in all actions."

I.7. "the maidservant"—i.e., Hagar, the maidservant of Sarah and Abraham and mother of Ishmael, the forefather of the Arabs.

I.8. *"I shall be safe"*—literally: "I shall have peace."

I.9. "the people of the tribute"—i.e., the Jews and the Christians who were subject to special taxation payable to the Moslem state.

I.14. " 'documents' "—i.e., decrees.

I.17. *"plans"*—literally: "thoughts."

I.19. "He called the judges"—i.e., the king called the ḳāḍis, or judges, of the Mohammedan courts of law.

" 'true believers' "—i.e., Moslems.

I.20. " 'What did the Prophet Mohammed have to say concerning them?' "—i.e., concerning the people of the tribute; the king was seeking traditional support for his decision to oppress the people of the tribute.

I.21. " 'Hear' "—in the sense of "listen to the words of our leader, the viceroy," meaning the vezier.

I.22. " 'The soul of the king will be enclosed/In the receptacle of life' "—i.e., "your soul will live forever." Cf. I Sam. 25: 29. The formula is generally applied only to deceased persons, but Mann's rendering, "May the king die, if he (Mohammed) be a help to them (the people of the tribute)," seems hardly appropriate. The vezier would not have dared to use such threatening and disrespectful language in addressing his sovereign; his purpose rather was to induce the king to consent to the decree against the Jews and Christians, and he speaks here of both the king and himself in the third person as a mark of reverence and humility, respectively.

" 'Attend' "—literally: "stand."

II.1. "He said"—i.e., the vezier.

" 'authority' "—*'emah,* literally: "awe."

II.2. " 'false religion.' " The adjective is, of course, an aside by Moses ben Samuel himself.

"I would bind it"—i.e., the Moslem faith.

II.3. " 'Let them make . . . tokens for use in the public bathhouses.' " The Moslem custom is to wear a plain loin towel in the public bathhouse, for reasons of public decency and modesty; there was thus, without special tokens, no way to distinguish between Moslems and unbelievers. The plotters, therefore, desired that Jews and Christians should be plainly recognizable even when bathing, although unlike the modern racists they evidently saw nothing objectionable in "people of the tribute" using the same bathing establishments as those frequented by Moslems. It must be borne in mind that in the Mohammedan countries public bathhouses are not only centers of sanitation and hygiene, but also places of social intercourse and friendly gathering, for women as well as for men; the construction of such establishments and the donation of funds for their upkeep are regarded as highly meritorious acts of religious piety and public benefaction.

"Whosoever of them has sinned against me"—i.e., all unbelievers are sinners in so far as they do not acknowledge the prophetic mission of Mohammed.

II.4. " 'let them strip their married women of their jewels.' " The translation given here is that of Mann, although the law was clearly meant to apply to all non-Moslem women, married and unmarried alike. Possibly *šey-yiwwaḏě'u* should be emended into *šel-lo yiwwaḏě'u,* and the verse should be translated: "And let them strip their women of their jewels, so that they may not be conspicuous in public." Resentment over the wearing of extra fine jewelry in public places by Jewish women has been manifested on many other occasions, both in the East and in Europe, for the alleged reasons that it was a provoking display of wealth and that the enhanced good looks of Jewish women constituted a temptation for Moslem or Christian men. Eminent Jewish leaders likewise were repeatedly moved to condemn the public wearing of jewels and silks by Jewish women, as a habit likely to excite Gentile indignation and cupidity and to endanger the safety of the entire Jewish community.

"If I have erred . . . do ye explain it." The implied question, "Have I erred in anything that I have said?" is no doubt meant to be rhetorical, since the speaker clearly has no doubts of the propriety and wisdom of his proposals; the meaning, therefore, is: "Do you not think that our proposals are wise?"

II.5. "And he came to a decision"—*wě-gamar;* the translation given here is that of Mann. But perhaps the word connects with the preceding, and the whole line should be rendered, "And he became like a man who had drunk until totally intoxicated."

II.6. " 'And their offspring is known' "—for their nonconformity with the ruling Moslem religion.

II.7. "the aforementioned things"—i.e., the aforementioned restrictions.

II.8. "the confidential secretary"—i.e., the chief secretary or chief clerk, who personally attended the sultan.

"instigator"—*yěsoḏ,* literally: "foundation."

II.10. "the fifth month"—the month of Ab (= July/August), the same month in which the Temple in Jerusalem was reputedly destroyed.

"For I am the unloved one"—meaning the people of Israel.

II.13. "as he had been instructed"—literally: "as he had heard."

II.14. "the Egyptians"—i.e., the Egyptian conspirators.

II.15. "the sixth month"—the month of Elul (= August/September).

II.16. "They set the date"—i.e., the Moslem authorities.

"hear . . . and observe." In the original the two verbs stand in reverse order, "observe . . . and hear," both for the sake of the rhyme and in imitation of the pledge of the Jews on Mount Sinai: *We shall observe and hear* (Exod. 24:7).

III.2. "To apportion the administration"—preferring the reading *la-ḥăloḳ* (cf. Mann, p. 231, l. 30). The meaning is to inspect the estates, collect their revenue, and reappoint or replace, as the circumstances may warrant, their overseers.

" 'my revenues' "—*šel-li,* literally: "that which belongs to me," i.e., the taxes and other imposts payable to me.

III.3. *"Curse not the king . . ."*—i.e., "when you shall receive the royal command to embrace Islam, in order to be retained in your secretarial post, obey it without saying a word against the Sultan, and without expressing your true feelings in the hearing of others."

III.4. "I apportioned them"—*ḥalaḵti* clearly refers to the foregoing *la-ḥălok̠* (cf. note to III, 2). Mann's interpretation, "And I spoke smooth words," is therefore unwarranted.

III.5. "I was like them"—i.e., they treated me in a friendly manner, as if they considered me their equal.

III.6. "The seventh month"—the month of Tishri (= September/October).

"My beloved and my friend"—referring to David Hakkohen, who is mentioned in the next quatrain.

III.7. "they told me." Moses ben Samuel was on that day in Nāblus (the ancient Shechem), according to the second version (Mann, p. 235, line 41).

"David Hakkohen"—a leading Karaite in Cairo who, together with his sons, was forcibly converted to Islam (cf. Mann, p. 235).

III.8. "Plowers"—i.e., these bad tidings.

"And the fear of Isaac was with me"—i.e., I felt as fearful as the Patriarch Isaac had felt when he was led forth to be offered as a sacrifice (Gen. 22).

III.10. "the rumor"—of the coming repressions against the people of the tribute.

III.11. "I hid myself." According to the second version (Mann, p. 236, ll. 52 ff.), Moses ben Samuel was joined by his father-in-law.

III.14. " 'open Thine eyes to my prayer.' " Prayer is being pictured as written words ascending to heaven and perceived by God's eye.

III.16. "until the night of *Šĕmini 'Ăṣeret̠"*—i.e., until the eve of the eighth day of the Feast of Tabernacles (22d of Tishri).

"I had not the understanding of a wise man"—i.e., I was not resourceful enough to escape arrest.

III.18. "Anxiety and oppression"—figuratively: the emir's police officers.

IV.1. "He oppressed me"—i.e., the emir's brother, presumably.

"and caused me great pain"—presumably meaning that Moses ben Samuel was subjected to torture.

IV.2. "he removed the crown which was upon my head"—i.e., "he forced me to renounce my ancestral faith."

IV.5. "I asked my Rock to receive my repentance"—believing himself on the verge of death.

"do thus"—i.e., "accept my repentance."

IV.6. "painful"—literally: "evil."

"my brother"—*'aḥi;* the correctness of this vocalization (not the plural *aḥay,* "my brethren") is proven by the occurrence of the same word in IV, 9, below, where aḥay would destroy the rhyme.

IV.7. "bitter"—literally: "evil."

"May the Lord consider it in my favor"—as a partial expiation of my sins.

IV.8. *"a pure heart"*—i.e., a heart submissive to God's will.

IV.12. " 'Come back to me' "—i.e., "turn back Thy countenance toward me as a mark of forgiveness."

IV.13. " 'from the sin' "—*me-'awel;* the word may also be read *me-'ol,* "from the yoke."

IV.16. " 'How did I reject wisdom?' "—i.e., "why did I behave so unwisely as to submit to forced conversion?"

"all this"—i.e., his escape from death by accepting conversion.

IV.17. "not for my own good"—*šel-lo bĕ-ṭoḇaṯi;* perhaps rather, "And not with my consent."

IV.19. "Mecca"—*Makkoṯ,* literally: "afflictions," a pun on the name of the holy city of the Moslems, frequently used in medieval Jewish literature.

"to pray"—literally: "to weep."

IV.20. "entourage"—literally: "army," probably meaning the emir's family and court.

IV.22. "on his way"—"but I asked to be excused from going along because of my illness" is to be understood at this point.

IV.23. *"If thou wilt not, hearken unto me"*—i.e., "if you will not obey my order to go with me, then listen to me as I will tell you about the punishment which I shall inflict upon you."

IV.27. " 'and say to him' "—i.e., to the emir.

IV.29. "I reached him"—i.e., the emir.

IV.30. " 'to reach thy desires' "—i.e., to remain in Damascus.

"Lest they make thee sin against me"—i.e., "lest your family should influence you to persist in your disobedience to my orders."

IV.33. "except against mine own heart." The conclusion, "But I was forced to go along, after all," is understood.

IV.34. "Mount Seir"—in the land of Edom; here meaning Arabia.

IV.35. "the city of their prophet"—i.e., Medina, or by its full name, Madīnat al-Nabī, "the City of the Prophet Mohammed."

"they pronounce a blessing upon him"—i.e., the Moslems; the custom is still in use.

IV.36. "The pilgrims"—*ha-ḥoḡĕḡim,* literally: "the festival makers."

"a light"—a heavenly light which, according to Moslem tradition, serves as a beacon for pilgrims traveling to Medina.

"of his congregation"—i.e., the emir's.

"Art thou envious of me?"—i.e., "do you envy us because of such a sign of heavenly favor vouchsafed to us?

IV.38. *"they will not believe me"*—i.e., "the real heavenly halo of the prophet is indeed capable of turning night into day, but this light which shines upon the minaret is not this true heavenly light, although my fellow Moslems would not believe me if I told them so."

IV.39. "encircling this place"—i.e., encircling the tomb.

"so as to make the light shine . . ."—i.e., the light shining upon the minaret is a reflection of the illumination supplied by these torches.

IV.40. *"Strangers yield feigned obedience to me"*—i.e., although they grudgingly admitted the truth of his explanation, they did not cease to believe in the heavenly origin of this light.

IV.41. "to cleanse my hand"—i.e., presumably, "to keep me from imagining that this light was really a miracle."

IV.42. "his words"—i.e., "this man's."

"heavy"—literally: "hard."

"And I said . . ."—i.e., "I was strengthened in my devotion to my ancestral faith."

IV.43. "there"—i.e., in Medina.

"barefoot and naked." On approaching the sacred precinct of Mecca, Moslem pilgrims are required to divest themselves of their clothing and to don the pilgrim's garb (Arabic *'iḥrām*), consisting of two sheets of white material in which the pilgrim may wrap the upper and lower parts of his body, but must leave his arm exposed up to the shoulder. For foot gear only open sandals are permitted, and the only head covering allowed is a corner of the upper sheet which may be used to shield the head against the sun or the nocturnal chill.

"twelve days"—the time required by a slow caravan to traverse the distance between Medina and Mecca.

IV.44. "the house of their worship"—i.e., the Kaaba, containing the sacred black stone.

"To which they turn their faces in their prayer." Moslems are required, when praying, to turn their faces in the direction of Mecca.

IV.45. "they walked around it." The pilgrim is required to walk or run around the Kaaba seven times (the so-called *ṭawāf* ceremony).

"May the divine king not account it a sin on my part"—i.e., "may God not regard it as a sin that I have taken part in this worship of the Kaaba, for I was forced to do it."

IV.48. "Thine own House"—i.e., the Temple in Jerusalem.

IV.50. "I am caught in my sin"—i.e., in my involuntary apostasy.

V.1. "Mount Paran"—a mountain in the upper Sinaitic peninsula; here presumably referring to Mount 'Arafat, near Mecca, a visit to which forms part of the pilgrimage ceremonies.

"Egypt." The *duran* or *diran,* which puzzled Mann, is presumably a misspelled word, and the preceding *'ăšer* would seem to indicate that it is probably not a proper name; the corresponding word in the second version (Mann, p. 237, l. 77) is *Miṣrayim,* "Egypt."

"Ishmael and Haran"—i.e., eastern Syria (the second version, Mann, p. 237, l. 77, has here Damascus) and Upper Mesopotamia.

"Their guilt offering, which they rendered unto me"—i.e., "their religious ceremony, in which they forced me to participate."

V.3. "my secret"—that his acceptance of Islam was for appearance's sake only.

V.4. "merit"—in the shape of the heavenly reward for the pilgrimage to Mecca and Medina.

"worn out"—by the rigors of the pilgrimage.

V.5. "When I shall pay what I have vowed"—i.e., "when I shall once more openly return to my ancestral faith."

V.6. *"according to the cleanness of my hands"*—i.e., "according to my innocence, since my apostasy was forced upon me."

V.7. "my seed"—i.e., "my descendants."

V.8. "Aleppo"—the second largest city in Syria and like Damascus a very ancient one; it is situated in the far north of the country.

V.10. "his own land"—i.e., Egypt.

"our land"—i.e., Syria.

"His end had come to the hostile prince"—"so I thought" is to be understood; i.e., "I thought that the emir, my tormentor, would now be permanently dismissed by the sultan."

V.11. "before him"—i.e., before the sultan.

V.12. "the Synagogue of Elijah the Prophet"—a famous ancient synagogue located at Ğawbar, near Damascus; it had a subterranean chamber in which Elijah was said to have hidden at one time.

V.13. *"I would hasten"—'aḥiša;* the author was probably thinking of *haḥiša,* "pray hasten."

V.14. "the letter"—i.e., the written petition containing his supplication.

"the Holy Ark"—i.e., the cabinet containing the scrolls of the Law.

V.16. "my heart was submissive"—to whatever dire results his refusal might involve.

" 'knows' "—reading *yoḏea'* for *yoḏia'.*

"at the tomb of the prophet"—in Medina.

V.17. " 'To multiply upon him the harshness of my deeds' "—i.e., to punish him severely.

V.20. "the lamb"—i.e., Moses ben Samuel himself.

"the lambs"—i.e., the rest of Israel.

AARON BEN ELIJAH

I. *Gan 'eḏen,* (Eupatoria, 1866), fols. 58a ff.

I.1. *"the day of trumpeting"*—i.e., the Rabbanite New Year's Day.

I.2. *"for the people"*—read *ḳi* for *wĕ-ḳol.*

I.3. "trumpeting signifies the sound of a horn." This is the Rabbanite interpretation. Cf. Mish. Roš haš-šanah 3:2 f.; B. *ibid.,* 33b–34a.

I.5. "it really means the raising of the voice"—i.e., the expression "trumpeting."

"the sound of the horn, the trumpeting of war"—i.e., *horn* and *trumpeting* are here mentioned separately, meaning, according to Aaron, that they signify two separate things.

"a thing which is obligatory every year"—i.e., the Day of Trumpeting, which is celebrated every year.

I.6. "fast these ten days"—meaning in the daytime only. For similar Rabbanite practices cf. Ṭur Oraḥ ḥayyim 581.

I.8. "The Rabbanites . . . add"—cf. B. Roš haš-šanah 11a.

I.9. "when the world was conceived"—referring to the hymn beginning "today is the day of the conception of the world" (Hebrew *hay-yom haraṯ 'olam*), forming part of the supplementary prayer (*musaf*) on New Year's Day, and recited immediately after the blowing of the horn.

"when the deeds of all men are brought up for review"—cf. B. Roš haš-šanah 16b.

I.10. "as it is written of the Sabbath"—Lev. 23:3.

"Whatsoever soul . . ."—inexact quotation. For the Rabbanite view of this matter cf. Mish. Meğillah 1:5.

I.11. For the Rabbanite view cf. B. Šabbaṯ 114b–115a.

I.14. *"with fasting"*—Hebrew *baṣ-ṣom,* literally: "in the fasting."

"which they knew of"—meaning the contemporaries of the psalmist.

"the definite article makes such an interpretation impossible"—i.e., if the meaning were "on a day of fasting," the Hebrew would have read *bĕ-ṣom* (or *bĕ-yom ṣom*), rather than *baṣ-ṣom.*

I.16. "wearing sandals." Taking off one's shoes is a mark of respect toward an honored person or a holy place, as well as one of the marks of mourning and sorrow. The prohibitions are listed in Mish. Yoma 8: 1, and in B. *ibid.,* 76a ff.

I.18. "upon adults only." Minors are not subject to the "extermination" penalty, nor are they considered capable of deliberately committing sins, and hence cannot be held responsible for them. For the Rabbanite custom in this matter cf. Maimonides, *Hilkot šĕbitat 'aśor* 2: 10–11.

I.19. "our own souls are broken with pity"—and we are thus reminded that we ourselves have caused it by our sins, a realization which should make us all the more eager to atone for them and not sin again.

I.20. "both ends of the Day of Atonement"—i.e., the concluding part of the day preceding the Day of Atonement, and the initial part of the day following it. For the Rabbanite law in this matter cf. B. Roš haš-šanah 9a.

I.21. "they were wont"—i.e., the Jews.

I.22. "Rabbi Joseph"—presumably Joseph ha-Ro'e. For the Rabbanite view cf. Tosafot to B. Sukkah 46a, at top.

I.23. "in the Book of Ezra"—rather, Nehemiah; at that time the books of Ezra and Nehemiah were regarded as one.

"the oil tree"—read *'eṣ šemen* for *gefen.*

"they shall take"—referring to the lamb, to be taken in preparation for the Passover sacrifice.

I.24. "'What is the meaning of *the fruit of goodly trees?"*—since one cannot very well build a booth out of fruits.

"shot forth sprigs"—Hebrew *porot,* supposedly from the same root as *pĕri,* "fruit," showing, according to them, that pĕri also must mean "branches," and not "fruit." The next quotation from Gen. 1: 12 indicates, according to them, that pĕri is used with reference to trees which bear no fruit.

I.30. "Rabbi Benjamin"—al-Nahāwandī.

"while we shall fetch"—referring to Ezra and his companions.

I.31. "does not fit"—reading *lo* for *ma.*

I.34. "baskets"—*'aggudot,* literally: "clusters."

I.35. "actual taking"—and not the use of them in building the booth (cf. Ibn Ezra's commentary to Lev. 23: 40).

"which remains . . ."—cf. B. Sukkah 35a.

"lulab"—the festive bouquet of palm fronds used, together with the citron fruit, in the Rabbanite ritual of the Feast of Tabernacles (cf. B. Sukkah 34b, 41b).

I.36. Cf. Mish. Sukkah 3: 12.

I.37. "in any case"—i.e., setting aside the unsolved problem whether the building of the booth is or is not obligatory. For the Rabbanite view on this matter cf. B. Sukkah 36b; Sifra (ed. Weiss) 103a.

"nut trees"—i.e., trees bearing nuts which yield oil.

I.38. "days complete both at their beginning and at their end"—which implies that the booth is to be ready prior to the arrival of the first day of the festival.

I.39. "the preposition 'on' "—Hebrew *bĕ-*, "on, at," etc.; the same preposition is used in the next quotation from Josh. 5: 13.

" 'in the vicinity of Jericho' "——the city itself having not yet been conquered by Joshua at that time.

I.40. "the ritual fringe"—worn with men's clothing (cf. Num. 15: 38 ff.).

"the rinsing of vessels"—for ritual cleansing (cf. Lev. 15: 12). For the Rabbanite view cf. B. Sukkah 8b.

I.41. "some people limit"—presumably read *šey-yeš* for *še-'im*.

"the Chosen Place"—i.e., Jerusalem or Palestine.

"jointly with the celebration of the festival at Jerusalem"—referring to the ordinance *And ye shall keep it a feast unto the Lord* (Lev. 23: 41), which precedes the command *In booths shall ye dwell seven days* (Lev. 23: 42).

"we find other things"—e.g., the ritual of Passover, the Sabbath.

I.42. "if one of them"—i.e., one of a group or family.

"one of the ordinances involving mere fulfillment"—irrespective of which persons, or how many, execute it. For the Rabbanite view cf. B. Sukkah 27b.

I.43. "Passover has been made obligatory for strangers as well"—cf. Exod. 12: 19.

"the Holy Name gave His protection during the Passover in Egypt"—by sparing them from the plague upon the first-born sons.

"the cloud in the wilderness"—cf. Exod. 13: 21 f.

"is caused only by the cloud"—i.e., is a symbol of the cloud.

"strangers dwell in booths at all times"—since they have no permanent homes of their own, having no landed property upon which to erect such homes, as explained further on.

"on the basis of the people's ability to perform them"—i.e., no scriptural ordinance demands of a man that he do something which is physically impossible. For the Rabbanite view on this whole subject cf. B. Sukkah 11b, 28b; Sifra 103a.

I.44. "This 'sitting.' " The Hebrew word for "dwelling" and "sitting" is one and the same. For the Rabbanite view on this matter cf. B. Sukkah 28b.

I.45. "in the open"—literally: "under the sky," i.e., not within a house.

I.47. "Sukkoth"—"Booths," a camping place on the route of the Exodus (Exod. 12: 37; 13: 20). For the Rabbanite view on this matter cf. Sifra 103b; B. Sukkah 11b.

I.48. "so soon after their exodus from Egypt." The Exodus took place in the first month, Nisan.

"might exhaust the joy"—literally: "despair."

"which is the first month in the reckoning of sabbatical and Jubilee years"—cf. Lev. 25: 1 ff., especially v. 9.

"winter"—the chilly rainy season in Palestine and adjacent countries. For the Rabbanite view cf. Ṭur Oraḥ ḥayyim 625, and Ibn Ezra to Lev. 23: 43.

I.49. "the Sabians"—the name assumed by a pagan sect of star-worshipers in the province of Ḥarrān, Mesopotamia; this sect is not to be confused with the true Sabians (or Mandeans), a semi-Christian sect, also in Mesopotamia.

"the time of the sun's entrance into the sign of Libra"—corresponding to September/October, or the month of Tishri in the Jewish calendar.

"whose leaves are ever fresh"—literally: "standing."

"mistaken belief"—literally: "ugly."

I.50. "the word 'assembly' "—Hebrew *'ăṣereṯ.*

" 'detention' "—Hebrew *'ăṣirah,* from the same root.

"the seventh day of the Festival of Unleavened Bread is likewise designated as a day of assembly"—Deut. 16: 8: *Six days shalt thou eat unleavened bread, and on the seventh day shall be a solemn assembly to the Lord, thy God.* For the Rabbanite view on this subject cf. B. Sukkah 47b ff.

I.51. "four periods"—reckoning by the phases of the moon.

"the last period"—the moon being then in its last quarter, or "dying," as it were.

"they used to make"—meaning the Sabians.

II. *'Eṣ ḥayyim,* ed. Franz Delitzsch (Leipzig, 1841), pp. 204–207; ed. Śimḥah Isaac Lutzki, with commentary (Eupatoria, 1847), fols. 130–131.

For a summary of the Rabbanite views on this subject cf. Maimonides, *Hilḵoṯ těšuḇah.*

II.1. "no other category"—i.e., no third category.

II.2. "by his loss"—i.e., by the punishment due him.

"by their size"—i.e., weight or gravity.

"shall be remembered"—referring to a grievous sin committed by a righteous person.

"For he found her"—i.e., the man who forcibly ravished her. The merit of her desperate, though unsuccessful, attempt to save her honor cancels her formal sin of submitting to adultery.

II.3. "This seemingly contradicts the weighing on the scales"—i.e., according to the theory of weighing on the scales, the sin committed on the single third day should have canceled the merit acquired on only one of the two preceding days, not the entire sum of merits acquired on both days together.

"the last part of the sacrifice"—i.e., only to the part eaten on the third day; *'ella* seems to have dropped out after *yěḥaššeḇ.*

II.4. "Where, then, would be the reward for his merits?"—i.e., the argument that his merits have been exhausted in canceling a portion of his sins is really immaterial, since he becomes subject to eternal punishment anyway; the final result would have been practically the same if he had had no merits at all.

"if a man has an equal share of both merits and sins"—in which case, if he is to be assigned to one of the two categories, either his merits or his sins would have to be totally annulled.

II.5. "[The Rabbanites say that] man's [deeds] are calculated." The text here appears to be defective; something like *wě-'aměru ba'ăle haḵ-ḵabbalah ḵi ham-ma-'ăśim* seems to have dropped out before *šel 'aḏam.* Cf. B. Roš haš-šanah 16b.

"They thus divide them"—i.e., all mankind.

"perfectly righteous . . . absolutely wicked"—these two groups being automatically assigned, respectively, to Paradise and to Hell.

"it implies that God does not repay"—inasmuch as He is presumed to overlook the few sins of the righteous and the few merits of the wicked.

II.6. *"in a just balance"*—for *šeḵel* read *ṣeḏeḵ* (so in the 1847 edition).

"would not be doing justice." In the biblical text this phrase is a question: *shall he not . . . do justly?*

II.8. "subject to cancellation by the Almighty." This refers particularly to transgressions solely against God (such as profanation of the Sabbath), which do not involve injury or damage to one's fellow men. Since God is exalted far above being injured or hurt by such transgressions, it would not be unjust on his part to remit the punishment for such transgressions in any case. It is not so, of course, with sins involving injury to one's fellow men (such as murder, mayhem, fraud), where forgiveness must be preceded by restitution or repair of the damage caused.

II.9. "an absolute kindness." It would be an absolute kindness on God's part if the punishment of the sinner for trespasses against Him were mandatory. However, as has been stated above, this punishment is subject to cancellation, if God so pleases, since trespasses against Him do not really involve any injury to Him.

"Therefore it is just . . ."—i.e., since the evil side of man's character leads him to do evil deeds, it is simple justice, as well as a kindness, on God's part to give him the opportunity to repent; to have withheld this opportunity would have been gross injustice on the part of the Almighty. This explains God's patience in bearing with evildoers, so as to give them ample time to repent.

II.10. "so evil as to involve punishment"—since punishment in a way frustrates the free will of the sinner in his resolve to commit a sinful deed.

"since repentance is one of the duties"—read *še-hi* for *še-hem*.

II.11. "and not a matter of necessity for Him"—i.e., God's frequent admonitions to men to repent are a matter of absolute kindness on His part, since mere justice does not require Him to do so.

II.12. "may be a manifestation of God's love for him"—in order to test his rectitude and increase his future reward, as, for example, in the case of the sufferings inflicted upon Job.

II.13. "according to the scholar"—presumably Jeshuah ben Judah.

"not a frequent occurrence"—but is done by God only in exceptional cases for good and sufficient reasons. The moral is that as soon as a man realizes that he has sinned, he ought to repent immediately, since the probability is that God will not delay his punishment.

II.14. "the utterance of our lips"—i.e., penitential prayer.

"'I will sin now, and repent later'"—such a person, of course, deliberately sins while fully realizing the wickedness of his deed. His promise to repent is therefore hypocritical, and his eventual act of repentance really insincere.

"circumstances beyond his control"—e.g., grave illness.

"for the sake of its very vileness"—and not solely out of fear of punishment for it.

II.15. "He alone knows the . . . human heart." Human courts cannot consider repentance as canceling a misdemeanor or felony, except perhaps when the penitent makes complete restitution of damages, which is not always physically possible; besides, restitution in itself partakes of the nature of punishment.

II.16. "a positive ordinance"—i.e., the ordinance to repent one's sins.

"men are divided into categories"—depending on whether the sin was committed unwittingly and because of ignorance or deliberately and with malice aforethought.

II.17. "[prompt]." Some word like *zariz* has dropped out after *šey-yihye*.

II.19. "for evil deeds"—which are bound to result from indulging these desires.

SAMUEL BEN MOSES AL-MAĠRIBĪ

I-XVII. *Al-Muršid,* Discourse IV, *Die karaeischen Fest- und Fasttage,* ed. J. Junowitsch (Berlin, 1904) Strassburg dissertation; some corrections (in part unsatisfactory) were supplied by S. Poznanski, *JQR,* XVII (1905), 594–597.

I.1. For the Rabbanite view cf. Mish. Pĕsaḥim 9: 5.

I.2. "applied both to them"—i.e., to the Jews who were in Egypt.

"the first part of the first day"—i.e., the evening of the preceding day, since the Jewish twenty-four hours begin at sunset.

For the Rabbanite law on leaven cf. Mish. Pĕsaḥim, 3; Maimonides, *Hilkot ḥameṣ u-maṣṣah* 1: 1 ff.

I.3. "whatever grease and juices are contained within them"—i.e., which have soaked into the wood.

"not to be used until after the holiday." This ritual cleansing of vessels for Passover use, coinciding with the Rabbanite custom (Maimonides, *Hilkot ḥameṣ u-maṣṣah* 5: 21 ff.; Šulḥan 'aruk, Oraḥ ḥayyim 451), is not prescribed by other Karaite authorities.

I.4. "derived from it"—read *'anhu* for *'annā.*

For the Rabbanite law on "mixed leaven" cf. Mish. Pĕsaḥim 3: 1; Maimonides, *Hilkot ḥameṣ u-maṣṣah* 1: 6; Šulḥan 'aruk, Oraḥ ḥayyim 442.

I.5. "antimony powders"—for darkening the eyelids, in order to enhance the brilliance of the eyes; a widely used cosmetic in the Near East.

"compounding and preparation"—read *tarkībihā* for *tarbībihā.*

"all these we need not remove"—the possible amount of leaven in these things being presumably so minute as to be of no account.

I.6. For the Rabbanite law prohibiting ownership and usufruct of leaven cf. B. Pĕsaḥim 28a ff.; Maimonides, *Hilkot ḥameṣ u-maṣṣah* 1: 2 ff.; Šulḥan 'aruk, Oraḥ ḥayyim 448: 3.

I.9. "in conjunction with it." The second *wa-'akl* is to be deleted.

II.1. "the regular calendar"—*al-xalīkī,* literally: "of the Creation," i.e., using the term "day" as it is employed in the account of the Creation (Gen. 1), meaning from darkness to darkness. For the Rabbanite rules on the Passover sacrifice cf. Maimonides, *Hilkot korban Pesaḥ, passim;* Yale Judaica Series, IV, 8–45.

II.3. "the legal day"—i.e., the day as reckoned for the purpose of the observance of the biblical ordinances.

"the sinking of twilight"—i.e., its complete disappearance. The precise meaning of twilight and the exact length of the day were the subject of much controversy between Karaites and Rabbanites, and among various Karaite authorities themselves. The Rabbanite view that twilight begins when the sun commences its downward course toward the west (i.e., some time after midday; cf. B. Pĕsaḥim 58a), was rejected by the Karaites who thought that twilight does not begin until after the actual setting of the sun; but they disagreed among themselves as to the relation of the twilight to the preceding and the following days. The view set forth here by Samuel is reputedly that of Anan (*KA,* VIII, xi-xv = IV, 878–885). For the Rabbanite view of the time of the Passover sacrifice cf. Maimonides, *Hilkot korban Pesaḥ* 1: 4; Yale Judaica Series, IV, 8.

II.5. "peace offerings"—the flesh of which may be eaten by women and children as well. For the Rabbanite interpretation of Deut. 16:2 cf. Sifre, *ad loc.;* Rashi and Ibn Ezra, *ad loc.*

II.6. "that they prepared the Passover sacrifices." Landauer's emendation ("they roasted") seems unnecessary.

III.1. "the House of God"—i.e., the sanctuary in Jerusalem; cf. below.

III.3. "This cannot refer to Jerusalem"—i.e., the term "House of the Lord" must mean here only the sanctuary proper, and not the whole city of Jerusalem.

III.4. "raw"—meaning, presumably, our term "rare," i.e., roasted only on the surface, and not throughout. For the Rabbanite rule cf. Maimonides, *Hilk̲ot̲ k̲orban Pesaḥ* 8:4 ff.; Yale Judaica Series, IV, 36–38.

III.5. "Nor may any bone of it be broken"—to extract the marrow, which was considered a delicacy; the rule is another allusion to the symbolically hurried manner of the meal, commemorative of the haste which attended the original Passover in Egypt.

III.6. "In all these things"—read *hād̲ihī* for *hād̲ā.*

"the blood . . . was applied to the lintels and to the side doorposts"—cf. Exod. 12:7. The clause *k̲amā tak̲addama d̲ik̲ru d̲ālik̲a* appears to be a gloss; the fact was not mentioned before in this discourse, except in the biblical quotation in I.1.

III.7. *"when a feast is hallowed"*—i.e., according to Samuel, the Feast of Passover. The "prayer of glorification" is the so-called "Hallel."

IV.1. "supplementary sacrifices"—offered at the Temple in Jerusalem on Sabbath and feast days (cf. Num. 28–29).

"each day upon its day"—implying that sacrifices must be performed at the prescribed times, whether they happen to fall on weekdays or Sabbaths.

IV.3. "Passover was handed down prior to . . . Sabbath"—the Passover ordinance being contained in Exod. 12, while the Sabbath is first mentioned in the Ten Commandments (Exod. 20:8 ff.).

"circumcision"—which was first imposed upon Abraham (Gen. 17:10 ff.), long before the promulgation of the Sabbath.

"Passover is not a sacrifice involving any revenue to the priest"—as distinct from other sacrifices, part of the meat of which was given to the officiating priest as his fee.

"individual sacrifice"—offered by an individual to mark an occasion in his private life; the Passover, on the other hand, is a duty imposed upon the entire community. This view of the precedence of the Passover over the prohibition of slaughtering and cooking on the Sabbath was accepted also by most other Karaite authorities, although not without some controversy. Anan taught that the Passover must be postponed to the next Sunday (i.e., Saturday night), while some early Karaites postponed the sacrifice, though not the eating of unleavened bread, to the fourteenth day of the next month, Iyyar (cf. *KA,* IX, x-xi = IV, 906–913). For the Rabbanite view on this matter cf. Mish. Pĕsaḥim 6:1–2; B. Pĕsaḥim 65b ff.

V.1. "persons afflicted with flux and leprosy"—who are ritually unclean by reason of their affliction. For the Rabbanite view on the Second Passover cf. Mish. Pĕsaḥim 9:1 ff.; Maimonides, *Hilk̲ot̲ k̲orban Pesaḥ,* 5 ff.; Yale Judaica Series, IV, 24 ff.

VII.1. "of the wilderness"—following the exodus from Egypt.

VII.2. "and had no uncircumcised person in their possession"—i.e., had no uncircumcised relative or slave in their household.

VII.3. "'Whereof, then, did they make the unleavened bread?'"—since there were no crops in the wilderness to supply grain and flour for unleavened bread.

"the showbread"—the sacrificial bread placed on the table in the sanctuary.

"the meal offerings"—made of flour, to accompany the animal sacrifices.

VII.4. "over the four corners of the earth"—*'āfāḳ*, literally: "over the horizons."

VIII.1. For the Rabbanite custom cf. Maimonides, *Hilḵoṯ ḥameṣ u-maṣṣah* 7: 1 ff.

VIII.3. "to recount to our children"—add *'alā* after *naḳuṣṣu.*

"guests"—*man yalūḏu binā,* literally: "those who seek refuge with us," meaning strangers temporarily living with us, under our protection, for one reason or another.

VIII.4. "the first of the seven days"—add *'awwal* before *al-sab'a 'ayyām,* and expunge the following *min 'awwalihi.*

"the section of Phinehas"—comprising Num. 25: 10–30: 1.

VIII.10. *"festival"*—Hebrew *ḥaḡ,* from the root *ḥaḡaḡ,* meaning "to make a pilgrimage to a holy place of worship"; the Arabic *ḥajja* has the same meaning, especially referring to the pilgrimage to Mecca.

VIII.11. "the circumambulation of the sanctuary"—an interpretation influenced by the Moslem ceremony of walking or running several times around the Kaaba in Mecca (Arabic *ṭawāf*).

"They reeled"—yaḥoggu, from the same root *ḥaḡaḡ,* the idea being that of going around and around.

"circuit"—ḥuḡ, from the root *ḥuḡ,* akin to *ḥaḡaḡ.*

VIII.12. "the people of the time of Israel's kingdom"—i.e., those who lived while the Hebrew kingdom was yet extant.

IX.1. "the two days"—i.e., the first and the seventh days. For the Rabbanite law on this whole subject cf. Mish. Beṣah, *passim;* Maimonides, *Hilḵoṯ šeḇiṯaṯ yom ṭoḇ, passim.*

"are these"—read *hiya* for *huwa.*

IX.2. "permitted us"—read *'abāḥahu* for *'abāḥa.*

IX.3. "since slaughtering . . . eating"—i.e., slaughtering is too far removed from the actual cooking of the meat for eating to be regarded as a necessary adjunct of the preparation of food; it cannot therefore be ruled permissible upon the holiday.

"the state of life"—literally: "the house (*bayt*) of life."

"cutting . . . grapes"—read *wa-ḳaṭf* for *wa-ḳunūf.* Samuel means to say that from a legal point of view there is no difference between cutting an animal's throat and cutting a vegetable or a fruit from its vine or tree.

IX.4. "or anything else"—like leaves, flowers, etc.

IX.5. "that have dropped"—from exhaustion; or such as have been caught in a natural obstruction located on our property.

IX.6. "a mortar." Why Poznanski condemned *al-hāwan* as "falsch" is a mystery to me.

IX.7. "since we have to leave it burning"—in contrast to the Sabbath, on which all the older Karaite authorities forbade having any fire, whatever its use, purpose, or origin might be.

"we may use it for lighting"—on the additional ground that the light may be needed for the preparation of food.

IX.9. "the principal varieties of work"—which are forbidden on the Sabbath (Mish. Šabbaṯ 7: 2). In Rabbanite law, however, carrying things is permitted on holidays, the issue against which Samuel is taking a stand.

"As for what they claim"—i.e., the Rabbanites; one would have expected *yaḳūlūna* for *yuḳālu.*

"and send portions . . ."—referring to the festival celebrated by the Jews in Jerusalem under Ezra's leadership and showing that they did carry their donations upon the holiday.

IX.10. "handclapping"—as accompaniment to secular music or singing.

IX.13. "is repeated with reference to all the other holidays"—i.e., Pentecost (Num. 28: 26); New Year's Day (Num. 29: 1); Day of Atonement (Num. 29: 7); Tabernacles (Num. 29: 12, 35).

IX.15. "and others who are like us." Poznanski's emendation *wali-ġayrihi* seems unsuitable, since the suffix *hi* would have no antecedent; read *wali-ġayriḳa.*

IX.16. "as a matter of duty and not as a voluntary matter." In Rabbanite law (B. Pĕsaḥim 120a), the eating of unleavened bread is obligatory only on the first eve of Passover; during the remaining days one may eat it or not, as he may choose, providing he does not eat any leaven.

"at their end." Junowitsch's emendation of *wa-min* into *wa-ilā* is unnecessary; the meaning is that nothing may be cut off at either end from this period of seven days.

X. For the Rabbanite rules on this subject cf. Maimonides, *Hilḳoṯ ḥameṣ u-maṣṣah,* 5; Šulḥan 'aruḳ, Oraḥ ḥayyim 453 ff.

X.3. "wheat . . . barley . . . spelt . . . oats . . . rye"—thus agreeing with the Rabbanite regulation (B. Pĕsaḥim 35a). Anan, on the other hand, permitted the making of unleavened bread from barley only, on the ground that the resulting coarse bread is the only exact equivalent of the *bread of poverty.* Al-Ḳirḳisānī thought that since the Bible mentions bread made of wheat and barley only, these two species alone were to be used for unleavened bread, but he admitted that any other grain subject to leavening might be employed (*KA,* IV, 896). To these five species Bašyatchi added millet, making six in all.

X.6. "thin cakes"—the usual form of bread in Near Eastern countries.

"lest a part of some of them remain heated"—i.e., the innermost part, which in a thick cake might not be thoroughly baked, and would not cool off quickly enough after the cake has left the oven to prevent fermentation. Presumably read *yasxun* for *yasxunū.*

X.7. "[and even then]"—*wa-ḏāliḳa* seems to have dropped out after *ḏāliḳa.*

"to watch over him"—to see that the dough and bread do not become contaminated with leaven.

X.8. "and pour it out"—i.e., the first container of water, which has become heated.

"will quickly scatter"—i.e., will quickly flow over the ground and be absorbed by it.

X.9. "seven hundred and twenty drams." The Arab dram (Arabic *dirham*) equals approximately 3.15 grams; 720 drams thus make about 2¼ kilograms or 5½ pounds.

X.11. "unleavened cakes"—*mallāt,* a term applied to thin bread-cakes baked in the ashes of a fire.

"they have most often"—i.e., they are usually too famished to let the bread rise, but bake it for immediate consumption.

"Others say . . ." The clause placed by Junowitsch in the footnote is, as the mark *ṣaḥīḥ* indicates, to be restored in the text, where it was omitted by oversight; for *al-sağad* read *al-ğasad* (cf. *mĕʿanne hag-guf* in Bašyatchi, AE, fol. 64d).

"Hardship"—Hebrew *ʿinnuy,* from the same root as *ʿoni,* "poverty."

"act in haste"—reading *naḥtafiz* for *naḥtariz.*

"anything harmful'—i.e., fermentation.

X.12. " 'workdays of the holiday' "—Hebrew *ḥol ham-moʿeḏ.*

XI. For the Rabbanite law relating to the workdays of the holiday cf. Mish. Moʿeḏ ḳaṭan, *passim;* Maimonides, *Hilḵoṯ šeḇiṯaṯ yom ṭoḇ,* 7–8.

XI.2. "press fruits"—to extract their oil or juice.

XI.3. "before it becomes damaged"—by the dyeing chemicals.

XI.4. "remarrying a divorced wife"—which is, in a sense, merely a renewal of a former marriage, dissolved in a fit of anger and in great haste. It is understood, however, that the wife had not been married in the meantime to another man, in which case she can never remarry her first husband, in accordance with the biblical ordinance (Deut. 24: 4).

XI.5. "the section of Phinehas"—cf. Num. 28: 16–25.

XII.1. "in the sense in which the word is used in the story of Creation"—Gen. 2: 1 ff.; i.e., in the sense of the seventh day of the week.

"a day of abstention from work"—from Hebrew *šaḇaṯ,* "to rest from doing something," or "to abstain from doing it."

XII.2. "which Sabbath this is"—read *hāḏihī* for *hāḏa.*

"This can be done . . ." The clause placed by Junowitsch in the footnote belongs into the text, from which it must have been omitted by oversight.

XII.3. "since this extra sacrifice is mentioned . . ."—i.e., if this extra sacrifice were to refer to a holiday prior to Passover, that holiday would have been mentioned first in this chapter of Leviticus.

"eighteen days"—seven days of Passover, eight days of Tabernacles, and one day each of Pentecost, New Year's, and Atonement total 18.

XII.4. "if the first . . . fell on a Sunday"—in which case the following Sabbath would be the last of the seven days.

"the preceding Sabbath"—i.e., the Sabbath preceding the Passover.

XII.5. "All this confirms . . ." In other words, *the morrow after the sabbath* (Lev. 23: 11), and *the morrow after the Passover* (Num. 33: 3), fell in that year on the same day; since this day is stated to have been the 15th of Nisan (Num. 33: 3), it follows that the 14th was a Sabbath, hence the 15th must have been a Sunday. This shows (according to Karaite law) that *sabbath* in Lev. 23: 11 means the Sabbath day proper, and that the waving of the sheaf must always be done on a Sunday, with the result that the Feast of Pentecost, 50 days hence, would also invariably fall on a Sunday. In Rabbanite law *the sabbath* is interpreted in the sense of "day of rest," *the morrow after the sabbath* thus being the day after the first day of Passover, i.e., the 16th of Nisan, whatever day of the week it may happen to be (cf. B. Mĕnaḥoṯ 65; Ibn Ezra to Lev. 23: 11).

XII.7. "the sequence of the seven days of Creation"—which ran from Sunday to Sabbath.

"the decisive proof"—i.e., the proof that the count of 50 days must begin on a Sunday, and that consequently the Feast of Pentecost must also invariably fall on a Sunday, and not on any other day of the week.

"seekers of the truth"—one of the self-complimentary epithets of which the Karaites were very fond.

"the dissidents"—i.e., the Rabbanites, for the most part.

XII.8. "Scripture mentions *sabbaths* before *days*"—referring to the foregoing quotation from Lev. 23: 15 f., where *seven sabbaths* comes first, and *fifty days* only afterward.

XII.10. "The first and the last Sabbaths"—"the last" signifying the seventh.

"should be included in it"—i.e., the 50 days include both the first Sunday, when the count is to begin (according to Karaite law), and the last Sunday, which (again, according to Karaite law) is the Day of Pentecost.

XIII.1. "just one man or two men or even three men"—i.e., the first man, or the first few men, to bring an offering.

"all the people had brought"—*'iǧābatuhum* is evidently meant to be derived from the colloquial *ǧāba,* "to bring, to fetch," and not from the regular *'aǧāba,* "to answer."

XIII.2. "leap years"—which in the Jewish calendar are a whole (13th) month longer than regular years.

XIII.3. "it shall be waved"—*tarǧīḥihi* seems somewhat awkward, but apparently the word is used here in a wider sense.

XIII.4. "at the beginning of the daytime." In Rabbanite law the count takes place at the legal beginning of the day, i.e., on the preceding evening (cf. Alfasi, Pĕsaḥim, end; Maimonides, *Hilḵoṯ tĕmiḏin u-musafim* 7: 22).

"immediately after the sacrifice"—the special sacrifice prescribed for the day of the waving of the sheaf (Lev. 23: 12 f.).

XIII.5. "both in the plural"—i.e., Scripture does not say "thou shalt count," which might have been interpreted to mean that one person may do the counting for the entire congregation or community.

XIII.6. "the Sabbath concluding"—*hiya* seems to have dropped out after *allatī.*

"then the number of the week third"—i.e., we are to say, for example, at the conclusion of the first week, "one Sabbath, seven days, the first week after the waving of the sheaf," and so on, to the end of the seventh week.

XIII.7. "is not a legal prohibition"—but merely a matter of general custom.

"These days are characterized by frequent changes in the weather"—this being early spring, when rain or lack of rain affect the state of the crops and the salubriousness of the air.

"the bounties"—read *bi-ni'amihi* for *bi-ni'mati.*

"the dissenters' "—i.e., the Rabbanites'.

"the ten martyrs"—the ten Jewish scholars who suffered martyrdom during the persecution following the unsuccessful revolt under Bar Kokhba (A.D. 135) against Roman rule. The reference is incorrect, since the customary mourning during the days of counting (Hebrew *sĕfirah*) is generally connected with the death of the disciples of Rabbi 'Aḳiḇa, who were said to have numbered 24,000 (B. Yĕḇamoṯ 62b). The Karaite adoption of this custom is thus older than Mann (p. 685) had thought. The Rabbanite prohibition of marrying extends, however, only through the 32d day of the count. On the Rabbanite customs during the days of counting cf. Šulḥan 'aruḳ, Oraḥ ḥayyim 493.

XIV.2. "the term *holy convocation*"—read *miḳra* for *miḳra'e.*

XIV.3. "*With the coming . . . With the completion*"—meaning "after."

XIV.4. "a kid of goats"—*ḳahr* is not the equivalent of *ḳahran* ("= unbedingt" [sic]), as Junowitsch remarks; *ḳahr mā'iz* is rather a literal rendering of the Hebrew *śĕ'ir 'izzim* (Lev. 23: 19).

XIV.6. "private peace offerings are not permitted"—since they involve slaughtering, skinning, etc.; these types of work are permitted only in the preparation of public sacrifices prescribed on each holiday.

"the dissenters"—i.e., the Rabbanites.

"it must fall always"—read *dā'iman* for *dā'imuhu.*

XIV.7. "If they should fall back upon the faulty principle"—meaning the Rabbanites. On this principle see E. Mahler, *Handbuch der jüdischen chronologie* (Leipzig, 1916), p. 497.

"a violent misinterpretation"—read *ḳābarū* for *xābarū.*

"All such deferments"—of the first day of Passover when it happens to fall on one of the aforementioned days of the week.

XIV.10. "the prohibition of eating the fat and the blood of animals"—which is in force at all times and in all places.

XIV.11. "to observe all the ordinances that we can"—read *mā* for *mah.*

XV.1. "the new wheat crop"—which ripens about the time of Pentecost.

"on the analogy"—read *ḳiyāsan* for *ḳiyāsuhu.*

"applicable only to crops"—read *'alā* for *'ilā.*

XV.2. "the array of Israel before Mount Sinai"—to receive the revelation of the Ten Commandments.

XV. 3. "the Rabbanites' claim." Cf. B. Šabbaṯ 86b.

XVI.1. "the king was blinded"—*'uḳḥila,* "to be blinded by the application of the stylus" (ordinarily used in applying collyrium to enhance the brilliancy of the eyes), after it had been heated in the fire, to the inside of the eyelids.

XVI.2. "slew them at Antioch"—on the coast of northern Syria; the biblical account names the Syrian city of Riblah (II Kings 25: 21), inland and to the south.

XVI.3. "on the day mentioned there"—i.e., on the 7th of Ab.

XVII.1. "the region of the stomach"—in the larger sense of the digestive apparatus. For the Rabbanite rules on fasting cf. Maimonides, *Hilḳoṯ ta'ăniyoṯ, passim;* Šulḥan 'aruḳ, Oraḥ ḥayyim 564 ff.

"that of the mouth"—i.e., in a wider sense, the oral region.

"it is unavoidable that"—*mā* must be an abbreviation of *min 'an.*

"of forbidden food or drink"—i.e., ritually unclean.

XVII.2. "on the night of the fast"—i.e., the eve of it.

XVIII.3. "like the one consumed by Moslem fasters"—literally: "Gentiles," referring to the Mohammedan fast during the holy month of Ramaḍān, when eating and drinking are permitted throughout the night, from sunset to sunrise.

"the third watch of the night." The Jewish night is divided into three parts or "watches": the first, the middle, and the last.

"he may not do so . . ." In other words, one may eat and drink on the eve of a fast only as much as is normally required at the time to satisfy one's hunger and thirst. One may not eat and drink excessively in order to forestall hunger and thirst throughout the ensuing fast day, as do the Moslems, since that would defeat the purpose of the fast as a day of mortification of the flesh (cf. *Ye shall afflict your souls* [Lev. 23: 32], speaking of the Fast of Atonement).

XVII.4. "On these days"—i.e., from the 1st to the 10th of Ab.

XVII.6. "these four fasts." The two mentioned above (the 9th of Tammuz and the 7th [and 10th] of Ab), the 23d (24th) of Tishri (Neh. 9: 1), and the 10th of Tebet (Jer. 52: 4). All four fasts are mentioned in Zech. 8: 19: *Thus said the Lord of hosts, The fast of the fourth month, and the fast of the fifth, and the fast of the seventh, and the fast of the tenth, shall be to the house of Judah joy and gladness and cheerful seasons.* For a list of Rabbanite fasts cf. Maimonides, *Hilḵoṯ ta'aniyoṯ* 5: 1 ff.; Šulḥan 'aruḵ, Oraḥ ḥayyim 580.

"the promise"—contained in the verse quoted in the preceding note.

"the destruction"—read *xarb* for *xabar*.

"this is not true with regard to the first Temple"—referring to the aforementioned verse (II Kings 25: 8), where the date is given as the 7th of Ab.

IBN AL-HĪTĪ

1–27. Published, with English translation, by G. Margoliouth, *JQR,* IX (1897), 429 ff. Reviewed by S. Poznanski, *ZfHB,* II (1897), 78–80.

2. "he exposed his life to the danger of death"—referring to the alleged persecution of Anan by the Rabbanites.

"It is said that he lived . . ." The uncertainty implied in this formula has been dispelled by al-Ḳirḳisānī's positive statement to the same effect; see above, p. 52.

"year 136 of the Hegira"—A.D. 754.

"exilarch of all Israel"—so the Karaites called him.

3. "Daniel al-Ḳūmisī"—see above, p. 30.

"David al-Muḳammiṣ." Dā'ūd ibn Marwān al-Muḳammiṣ, a native of al-Raḳḳa, on the Euphrates, theologian and philosopher, flourished about A.D. 900 (Steinschneider, p. 37).

"a work on the principles of faith"—entitled *Twenty Discourses* (Arabic *'Išrūn maḳālāt*); it is the earliest known medieval philosophical work written by a Jewish author.

"al-Ḳirḳisānī"—see above, p. 42.

"Book of Lights"—Arabic *Kitāb al-anwār.*

"Ismā'īl [al-'Ukbarī]"—see above, p. 52.

"as well as the scholars of . . ." There is clearly a lacuna here in the Arabic text; the correct reading probably was *wa-hum Ismā'īl al-'Uḵbarī wa-*[several further names] *wal-'ulamā' al-'Uḵbariyyīn* . . .

" 'Ukbara"—see above, p. 335.

"Tustar"—the Persian form is Šustar; a large city in the Persian province of 'Arabistān.

"Basra"—the well-known commercial center near the entrance of the Tigris and the Euphrates into the Persian Gulf.

3. "Fārs"—Persia proper.

"Xurāsān"—the vast province to the east of Iran.

"Ğibāl"—the ancient Media; the name signifies "the mountains," and describes accurately the nature of most of its territory.

4. "the year 1278 of the Seleucid era"—the era beginning with the battle of Gaza in 312 B.C. The two dates do not agree: A. SELEUC. 1278 = A.D. 967, whereas A.H. 315 = A.D. 927; the error is probably the fault of a copyist, and not of Ibn al-Hītī himself. The correct date is A. SELEUC. 1248 = A.H. 325 = A.D. 937 (Poznanski, pp. 8–9, n. 4).

5. "David ben Boaz"—the fifth descendant of Anan as exilarch of the Karaites (Poznanski, pp. 18–20; Steinschneider, p. 76; Mann, pp. 132–134).

"year 383 of the Hegira"—A.D. 993; this again appears to be a scribal error, since David flourished in al-Ḳirḳisānī's time, some 50 years earlier, unless indeed he lived to a very advanced age.

6. "Abū al-Surrī"—i.e., Sahl ben Maṣliaḥ; see above, p. 109.

"in his commentary"—i.e., Abū al-Surrī's.

"Sa'adiah . . . lived before al-Ḳirḳisānī"—i.e., rather, he was al-Ḳirḳisānī's older contemporary.

"Israel ben Daniel"—a Karaite jurist of this name flourished in the year 1062 (Poznanski, pp. 60–61; Steinschneider, pp. 113–114), which is much too late for this context; presumably read: "Daniel al-Ḳūmisī."

"the prince Solomon"—the sixth descendant of Anan as exilarch of the Karaites, flourished in 1004–1016 (Mann, pp. 134–135).

"Book of Incest"—the title is in mixed Arabic and Hebrew, *Kitāb al-'ărayoṯ*.

"Benjamin"—al-Nahāwandī; see above, p. 21.

"Abū 'Alī al-Baṣrī"—i.e., Japheth ben Eli; see above, p. 83.

"and his son"—Levi ben Japheth, who flourished in 1007 (Steinschneider, pp. 85–86; Poznanski, pp. 42–46; Mann, pp. 32–33), author of an extensive work entitled *Book of Precepts.*

"the learned doctor Abū 'Alī"—the identity of this scholar is uncertain.

7. "Abū Ya'ḳūb Yūsuf ibn Nūḥ"—Joseph ibn Nūḥ, a highly esteemed Karaite scholar in Jerusalem who flourished about the year 1000 (Mann, pp. 33–34; *JQR,* XVIII (1927–28), 4–11).

"the search for fresh ears"—necessary in order to determine the date of the Feast of Passover and the nature of the current year, whether it is to be a regular year of 12 months or a leap year of 13 months. The logic is not quite convincing, since one scholar need not necessarily be the contemporary of another in order to dispute his views.

"Abū Ya'ḳūb al-Baṣīr"—i.e., Joseph ha-Ro'e, eminent Karaite theologian and philosopher of the first half of the 11th century, author of an important code of law entitled *Book of Investigation*—i.e., into the biblical ordinances—Arabic *Kitāb al-istibṣār* (Steinschneider, pp. 89–91; Poznanski, pp. 46–48). Cf. above, p. 123.

"Abū al-Farağ Hārūn"—Aaron ben Jeshuah (?), Karaite grammarian and exegete at Jerusalem in the first half of the 11th century (Steinschneider, pp. 86–88; *JQR,* XVIII (1927–28), 11–27).

"year 393 of the Hegira"—A.D. 1002–03.

8. "whom he calls warriors"—read *'asmāhum* for the awkward *ḏakarnāhum;*

"warriors" is, of course, meant in the sense of theological defenders of the true faith.

"Abū Isḥāḳ Abraham ibn . . . al-Iṣfahānī"—a name seems to have dropped out here.

"Salmon ben Jeroham"—see above, p. 69.

" 'May God have mercy upon them . . .' "—a formula used with reference to deceased persons.

10. "Abū Sa'īd, son of . . . Abū 'Alī"—i.e., Levi, son of Japheth ben Eli; see note to Sec. 6.

"Abū al-Farağ Furḳān ibn 'Asad"—i.e., Jeshuah ben Judah; see above, p. 123.

"quotes some views of his"—*ḏaḳara 'anhu* (the complement, something like *'aḳāwīl,* is understood). Margoliouth's translation, "in mentioning him," would have required *ḏaḳarahu.*

"He lived"—i.e., Abū Sa'īd.

"since he made"—i.e., Abū Sa'īd.

"his commentary"—on the Pentateuch.

"in his *Book of Precepts*"—i.e., Abū Sa'īd's.

"Al-'Arīšī"—an otherwise unknown scholar (or perhaps a misspelling of another name?).

11. "those who went on with their studies"—presumably meaning that Abū al-Farağ Hārūn and his colleagues managed the college after their teacher's demise.

"the Karaite synagogue at Damascus"—an old and venerated synagogue which remained in Karaite hands until the beginning of the 19th century, when, the local Karaite community having become extinct, it was sold and was replaced by a Greek church (Mann, p. 202).

"I have seen"—reading *ra'aytu* for *ra'au.*

"he says that he had been living . . ."—*'anna* must have dropped out before *lahu.* "He had been" and "said he" presumably refer to Ibn Nūḥ. Margoliouth, who mistook the *mā* for the relative pronoun, could make no sense out of this clause; the following *fa-kayfa,* however, clearly indicates that *mā* here is the negative particle. Still, the style is awkward, and the text was presumably corrupted by the copyist. The precise nature of "fresh ears" has been the subject of much controversy among Karaite scholars.

"that he continued"—i.e., presumably, Ibn Nūḥ.

12. "in their works"—read *taṣānīfihimā* for *taṣnīfihimā.*

" 'May God be gracious unto him' "—a formula used with reference to deceased persons.

"the year 428"—A.D. 1036–37.

"in which the author refers to him"—i.e., to Abū al-Farağ Hārūn.

" 'May God prolong his dignity' "—a formula used with reference to living persons; showing that both were among the living in that year.

"a tract of his"—i.e., of Abū al-Farağ Hārūn.

"both opinions"—presumably referring to the differing opinions of Abū al-Surrī and Ibn Nūḥ regarding fresh ears.

"the year 458"—A.D. 1065–66.

"saying of each of them"—*'anhum* seems to have dropped out after *ḳāla.*

"It is said that he used to attend"—i.e., Abū al-Farağ Furḳān.

"the month of Rabī' the First of the year 446"—June/July, 1054.

"the composition and copying of which took seven months." Margoliouth's text here is patently corrupt; presumably read: *muddat taṣnīfihimā wa-naḳlihimā sab'a 'ašhur*. Ibn al-Hītī presumably means that he saw this autograph manuscript of the Exodus part.

13. "al-Ṭawīl"—"the Tall One."

14. "The prince Solomon"—the tenth descendant of Anan (Steinschneider, pp. 94–95; Mann, pp. 140–142).

"to the east, to the west, and into Syria"—probably meaning, respectively, Iraq and Persia, North Africa, and Syria, including Palestine.

"Book of Incest"—see above, note to Sec. 6.

"the year 600"—A.D. 1203–04.

15. "Abū al-Ḥasan ben Mašiaḥ"—rather al-Ḥasan (Hebrew Japheth) ben Mašiaḥ; see above, p. 351.

"Salmon ben Jeroham"—see above, p. 69.

"clad in torn garments . . . ."—in token of deep mourning.

"When he was reproved"—by his fellow Rabbanites; the whole story, however, is probably fictitious; see above, p. 69.

"Gentiles and others"—i.e., Mohammedans and non-Moslems (Christians, etc.).

"they make vows to it"—in supplication for favors.

16. "Abū ['Alī] 'Īsā ibn Zar'a"—Christian physician, died in 1008.

"Ibn Šu'ayb"—Bišr ibn Finḥās ibn Šu'ayb, a Jewish scholar and mathematician (Steinschneider, pp. 106–107). The puzzling *'altama* (or *'iltām,* as Margoliouth suggests) *sab'īn* can, pending the discovery of a better manuscript of the Chronicle, be only tentatively emended into the logical and simple *'ilā Ibn Šu'ayb;* a short tract like this need not have had any special title, anyway, beyond the name of the addressee.

"the year 387"—A.D. 997.

17. "Abraham al-Harzalānī"—mentioned also by Mordecai ben Nisan, *Notitia Karaeorum* (Hamburg and Leipzig, 1714), p. 116.

"Ṣabtiyya"—perhaps a mutilation of the Hebrew name Shabbethai.

18. "Samiyya"—or Sumayya.

"the year 459"—A.D. 1066–67.

"and the other by Ṣadaḳa." Margoliouth's translation would require *wa-'an Ṣadaḳa,* whereas the text has *wali-Ṣadaḳa,* going back to *kitābayn;* moreover, the singular pronoun in *ta'rīxuhu* and *kātibuhu* shows that only one of the *kitābayn* was by 'Alī ben Joseph.

19. "[in] theological research"—*fī* seems to have dropped out before *al-taṣaffuḥ,* and *'asmāhu* before *kitāb.*

"Book of Secrets"—Arabic *Kitāb al-'asrār.*

"an [outstanding] scholar"—*fāḳa* seems to have dropped out after *'annahu.*

"It is said that he was"—presumably meaning Hananiah ben Jacob, and not his father.

20. "Ibn Sāḳawayh"—an early Karaite writer of the first half of the 10th century (Steinschneider, p. 45; Poznanski, pp. 4–8).

"the observation of the New Moon"—necessary for the fixing of the calendar and of the dates of holidays.

"the date of Pentecost"—which according to Karaite law must always fall on a Sunday.

"eating the fat tail and other fat"—forbidden by Karaite law.

"the authority of the Rabbanite tradition"—which the Karaites do not recognize.

21. "Abū Anan Isaac ben 'Alī ben Isaac"—flourished in the middle of the 10th century (Poznanski, p. 16).

"Book of the Lamp"—Arabic *Kitāb al-sirāğ* (so read, instead of *bil-sirāğ*).

"the equinox"—i.e., the vernal equinox, the date of which is of importance in determining the date of Passover.

22. "Abū al-Ṭayyib al-Ğabalī"—read al-Ğibālī; 10th-century Karaite scholar (Steinschneider, p. 79; Poznanski, pp. 16–17).

"lived in the time of Abū al-Farağ Hārūn." The statement is erroneous, since Hārūn lived in the first half of the 11th century.

"the legal year"—which begins in the month of Tishri.

"Abū 'Alī"—i.e., Japheth ben Eli.

"the Rabbanite cycle"—the nineteen-year cycle (12 regular years and 7 leap years) upon which the Rabbanite calendar is based, and which harmonizes the lunar year with the solar.

"Menahem"—Rabbanite scholar of the first half of the 10th century; his precise identity is uncertain.

"Abu Ṯābit"—an otherwise unknown scholar.

23. "Abū Sa'īd"—it is not clear which of several scholars so named is meant here.

24. "Yašar ben Ḥesed ben Yašar al-Tustarī"—Karaite scholar of the end of the 11th century; his Arabic name was Sahl ibn Faḍl (Steinschneider, p. 113; Poznanski, pp. 53–55; Mann, pp. 39–40).

"Book of Clarification"—Arabic *Kitāb al-talwīḥ.*

"its terminology and evidences"—read *'alfāḍ(ẓ)ihi wa-barāhīnihi.*

"many works on law, and the *Book of Introduction.*" Margoliouth's text is clearly corrupt, and *al-fiḳh al-mudxal* yields no good sense (nor does Margoliouth's rendering, "foreign law," there being no such thing in Karaite jurisprudence). Presumably read *wa-kutub kaṯīra fī al-fiḳh wa-Kitāb al-mudxal.* What the work might have been an introduction to is of course uncertain. Professor Obermann suggests that *al-fiḳh al-mudxal* may mean "practical (exoteric) law," as distinguished from *al-fiḳh al-bāṭin,* "esoteric law."

25. *"Book of Facilitation"*—Arabic *Kitāb al-taysīr,* a Hebrew-Arabic lexicon.

"Abridged Lexicon"—in mixed Hebrew and Arabic *al-'Agron al-muxtaṣar,* an abridgment of the great Hebrew-Arabic lexicon (Arabic *Ğāmi' al-'alfāẓ*) of David ben Abraham al-Fāsī (10th century). On 'Alī ben Solomon (end of the 11th century) see Steinschneider, pp. 241–242; Mann, pp. 41–42.

"Aaron ben Elijah al-Ḳisṭanṭīnī"—"the Constantinopolitan," i.e., Aaron ben Elijah of Nicomedia, or Aaron the Younger; see above, p. 170.

"Judah ben Elijah Hadasi, the Mourner"—eminent author of the 12th century (Poznanski, pp. 68–72); the appellation "the Mourner" (Hebrew *ha-'abel*) identifies him as a member of an ascetic confraternity known as "Mourners for Zion" (Hebrew *'ăbele Ṣiyyon*).

"Israel, the Judge"—lived in the 14th century (Steinschneider, pp. 243-244; Poznanski, p. 78).

"Japheth ben Ṣaġīr"—lived in the 14th century (Steinschneider, pp. 244-245; Mann, p. 211).

"Samuel ben Moses al-Maġribī"—see above, p. 196.

"Book of Question and Answer"—Arabic *Kitāb al-mas'ala wal-ǧawāb.*

"Book of Precepts"—meaning his *Guide* (Arabic *al-Muršid*).

"Prefaces to the Pentateuch"—a homiletic commentary on the Pentateuch; read: *Mukaddimāt 'alā al-Tawrāt;* Margoliouth's *'alā al-mas'ala wal-ǧawāb* is evidently a scribe's error induced by the same two words in the preceding line. Samuel's authorship of it is uncertain, the work being ascribed also to Samuel al-Sinnī.

ELIJAH BEN MOSES BAŠYATCHI

I. *AE,* preliminary leaves v–vi. For the Rabbanite view of these principles cf. Maimonides, *Hilkot yĕsode Torah* and *Hilkot de'ot.*

I.2. For the Rabbanite view cf. Naḥmanides' introduction to his commentary on the Pentateuch.

I.3. "the Giver of the Law"—i.e., God.

I.4. "the three Patriarchs"—Abraham, Isaac, and Jacob.

I.5. "which is constantly subject to change." Consequently the irritability of a person and his proneness to anger or joy being matters of individual psychology, do not remain constant, but change with advancing age. In other words, what would anger or gladden the soul of a boy of 16, may have a vastly different effect upon a man of 60, and vice versa. Hence any definite ordinance regarding anger or joy would have been capable of being fully observed only during a very short part of a man's life span, when his mind and his body are in an optimum state relative to this ordinance; at other times man would be physically unable to conform fully to the ordinance, no matter how eager he might be to do so.

"matters of this kind are not suitable for being prescribed." In other words, moral qualities cannot be legislated, but must be a voluntary manifestation of man's own belief in a just and merciful divinity, and his own desire to come as near as possible to God's righteousness, in thought and deed.

I.6. "would . . . assuredly flog him"—no matter how large a portion of the tasks imposed upon him he may manage to perform.

I.7. *"unclean"*—since they cannot obtain perfectly clean bread, like the bread they had eaten in Palestine.

I.9. *"Ye shall surely destroy all the places"*—devoted to the worship of idols.

"the excellence of the ordinances"—*yofyam,* literally: "beauty."

"the incipience of the world"—i.e., that the world had a beginning, having been created by God out of nothing, and is not everlasting; only God is eternal and without a beginning.

"which also teaches us the existence of the Lord . . ."—i.e., the fact itself of the Exodus is evidence of God's existence and of His principle of rescuing the oppressed from their oppressors.

"for in the image of God did he make man"—bloodshed being outlawed by

reason of the sacredness of human life, since man was made in the divine image.

I.11. "as we shall explain in another place." This is explained, somewhat unconvincingly, in the foreword to the discussion of the laws governing the Sabbath (*AE,* fol. 37b): as we meditate upon the reason for our resting on the Sabbath, our intellect cannot but tell us that it is a memorial of God's resting after the six days of Creation; inasmuch as this reason was, in effect, existent since the very first Sabbath on earth, it obviously antedates the revelation of the Law.

I.12. "by way of example from the deeds of the biblical personages"—i.e., by way of meditating upon the deeds of biblical personages and deducing the moral lessons contained in them.

"until he shall have learned its causes and beginnings." In other words, man should not insist on examining all the theoretical and practical aspects of a divine commandment, before he pledges submission to it. All divine commandments, being perfect, are firmly rooted in reason and moral perfection. For man to investigate them, however, requires time and effort, and such investigation should follow submission, not precede it.

I.15. "the word *fear*"—meaning fear of punishment for doing something one was commanded not to do.

I.16. "resting is not action, but lack of action"—i.e., what this ordinance amounts to is "And the children of Israel shall not do any work on the Sabbath"; in other words, although worded as a positive ordinance, it goes back to a prohibitive, i.e., negative, command.

I.17. "which are outwardly commands, while inwardly they are admonitions"—i.e., they are outwardly positive and inwardly negative.

I.18. "the violator of which draws the punishment of being cut off"—for circumcision, Gen. 17:14; for Passover, Exod. 12:15.

I.19. "are committed in secret"—and are therefore for the most part not amenable to human disposal in courts of law. Cf. Naḥmanides' commentary to this verse.

I.22. *"the utterance of thy lips"*—referring to vows.

"And thou shalt teach them"—i.e., the ordinances of the Law.

I.24. "once a week . . . once in fifty years"—referring, respectively, to the ordinances governing the Sabbath, the New Moon, the yearly cycle of festivals and fasts, the sabbatical year, and the Jubilee year.

I.26. "brothers by common family"—in the larger sense of tribe or nation.

"the Law forbids the application of this ordinance to brothers by blood"—referring to the verse *Thou shalt not uncover the nakedness of thy brother's wife, it is thy brother's nakedness* (Lev. 18:16).

"to refer only to brothers by family"—contrary to Rabbanite law which interprets *brethren* as brothers by blood and exempts the levirate duty from the general prohibition of marrying the wife of one's brother.

I.26. "refers to sisters by religion, and not by blood." The latter view is that of the Rabbanites, who apply the ordinance to two brothers who married two sisters; if one of the brothers dies, the other may not marry the widow and is exempt from the duty of the levirate (cf. B. Yeḇamoṯ 3b).

I.27. "one of which is clean and the other unclean"—the flesh of the ox may be eaten, whereas the flesh of the ass may not.

"as is well known to practitioners of medicine." This is doubtful zoology, but true enough in the sense that the unclean animals (the camel, the horse, the mule, the ass, the swine, and the beasts of prey) are generally capable of greater short bursts of strength and speed than domestic cattle and the various species of antelopes, whose flesh may be used for food. The explanation of the prohibition of eating the flesh of these unclean animals because of hygienic reasons, is probably based on the ancient theory of humors, the strong and virulent humors of the unclean beasts having been thought to be incapable of assimilation by the human organism.

I.29. *"thy daughter's daughter"*—i.e., one's granddaughter, whom one may not marry.

I.30. *"she is thine own mother"*—implying that the grandmother, the great-grandmother, etc., are also forbidden, since they, too, are one's "mothers."

"the word *month"*—Hebrew *ḥodeš,* from the root *ḥadaš,* "to be new."

"the renewal of the visibility of the moon"—i.e., the appearance of the New Moon; meaning that just as the appearance of the New Moon marks the beginning of the new month, so the coming of the month of Nisan marks the beginning of the new civil year (as distinguished from the legal year, which begins with the 7th month of Tishri).

I.31. "preference demanded by both reason and common knowledge"—since stepuncles are generally held to be as close relatives as blood uncles.

"as will be explained in the proper place." The Bible itself contains only a few rules relating to inheritance and succession. The *'Adderet 'Eliyahu* has no section dealing with the law of inheritance.

I.33. "These are the varieties of analogy." These 7 Karaite principles of construction and interpretation of law agree in number, but only partly in content, with the seven original Rabbanite hermeneutic rules formulated by Hillel (about the time of Jesus), and extended to 13 by R. Ishmael (2d century), and to 32 by R. Eliezer ben Jose (2d century). Several of these Rabbanite rules were, in fact, severely criticised by Karaite scholars (e.g., al-Ḳirḳisānī), as contrary to both the spirit of the Law and strict logic.

"this latter may be derived also by analogy"—by a rather forced interpretation of some biblical verses. This problem was one of the major points of disagreement between Karaites and Rabbanites.

I.34. "Rabbi Tobiah"—i.e., Tobiah ben Moses, the great translator of Karaite works from the Arabic into Hebrew; he lived in the second half of the 11th century (Poznanski, pp. 61–65).

I.35. "they say that the meaning is forty less one." This is derived by connecting *forty stripes* with the last words, *by number,* of the preceding verse, and interpreting the result as "approximately 40 stripes," i.e., 39, at most. The alleged reason is that if the person counting the stripes should make a mistake of one, the culprit would actually receive 41 stripes, which would constitute a violation of the immediately following *He shall not exceed* (cf. B. Makkot 22a). The real reason, however, is clearly purely humanitarian and reflects the general distaste felt by the Sages toward capital and corporal punishment.

"he shall inherit her"—Hebrew *'otah,* i.e., "he shall inherit the landed property"; the Hebrew word for landed property, *naḥălah,* is feminine.

"this is a matter of mere assumption"—i.e., the husband's right to inherit his wife's property is, according to these few, merely a matter of public custom.

The right of the husband to his wife's estate is not expressly formulated in the Bible, and the talmudic controversy regarding it is set forth in B. Baḇa baṭra 111b; this right, however, has been generally accepted in Rabbanite law.

"hereditary landed property"—i.e., the parcels of land distributed to the Israelites at the time of the conquest of Canaan, and mostly held in hereditary possession by the same families. Bašyatchi means to say that the pronoun *her* cannot possibly refer to the deceased wife.

"Rabbi Nissi ben Noah"—an eminent Karaite divine who lived presumably in the 11th century (Steinschneider, p. 75).

"our people"—i.e., the Karaites. The pertinent passage is quoted by Pinsker, *LḲ*, I, 41.

II–III. *AE*, fols. 78b ff.

II.10. "forsaken"—*ma'as*, literally: "become disgusted with."

"the descendant of King David." These ten articles of the Karaite creed invite comparison with the 13 articles of the Rabbanite creed as formulated in the 12th century by Maimonides (which gained general acceptance, in spite of some criticism by later authorities): 1. the existence of God (= Bašyatchi's 1 and 2); 2. the oneness of God (= 3, second half); 3. God's spirituality and uncorporeality (= 3, first half); 4. God's eternity (= 2); 5. the duty to worship Him alone (implied in 2); 6. the divine inspiration of true prophecy (= 4 and 7); 7. Moses' supremacy as a Prophet (= 4); 8. the divine inspiration of the Law (= 5 and, in a sense, 6); 9. the immutability of the Law (implied in 5); 10. God's omniscience (implied in 2): 11. the certainty of reward and punishment in this world and the next (= 9); 12. the certainty of the advent of the Messiah (= 10); 13. the resurrection of the dead (= 8). Cf. Maimonides' commentary to Mish. Sanhedrin 10.

III.1. "Eber"—one of the descendants of Shem and the forefather of the Hebrew people (Gen. 10:24 ff.).

"the tongue of Eber"—i.e., the Hebrew tongue.

III.2. "because it does not include words . . ."—i.e., because it contains no coarse terms, such as are used only by foul-mouthed persons. The explanation is, of course, of doubtful linguistic validity: that the ancient Hebrew literary documents contain no (rather, few) such terms is hardly proof that they did not exist in the spoken everyday language of the people, particularly of the lower classes.

"yišgalennah"—meaning *shall lie with her;* the word is presumed to be a coarse one, since the Massoretes have ruled that a more polite word was to be substituted for it in reading aloud; there are other instances of this kind in the Hebrew biblical text.

III.3. "the holy tongue was submerged under the local secular languages"—i.e., it ceased to be the spoken language of the Jews and was replaced by the local tongue of each country to which the Jews were exiled.

"were borrowed from other languages"—i.e., from Aramaic, Greek, and Latin.

III.4. "the proper names in the Law cannot be translated"—i.e., their derivation and meaning can be understood only by those who know Hebrew.

"many obscurities have crept into these translations"—i.e., they contain doubtful passages, due to inexact or ambiguous rendering of the Greek originals.

"but had to leave some of them in the original Hebrew"—i.e., they had to incorporate these Hebrew words into their own language.

" 'If you cannot do that which would satisfy you . . .' "—i.e., our older scholars would have preferred to write their works in Hebrew, but were constrained to use Arabic in order to reach a wider circle of readers. The explanation is historically rather lame.

III.6. "merely for his training"—i.e., merely to observe the older boys and to become acquainted with the procedure.

III.7. "lenient"—*šafal,* literally: "humble," i.e., patient.

"else his pupils will grow weary of him"—meaning, presumably, that if he is too lenient, the children will pay no attention to his orders, and if he is too strict they will despair of ever pleasing him; in either case, they are bound to neglect their studies.

III.8. "sections . . . some closed and others open"—referring to the blank spaces which divide the sections of the text of the Pentateuch in the Hebrew Bible. The "closed" ones are in the middle of a line, while the "open" ones are at the end of a line. Bašyatchi means to say that instruction should be dispensed in well-rounded and well-explained units, and should not be given piecemeal and without thorough explanation.

III.9. "in writing"—presumably, copying the biblical text as an exercise for memorizing it, as well as for teaching penmanship.

"the greater moisture of their humors." This is the ancient conception of the bodily humors becoming progressively drier with advancing age.

III.10. "a book that is handsome." The author has in mind handwritten books, i.e., manuscripts.

"Books . . . should be given to indigent students"—i.e., should be lent to them.

III.11. "draw the attention of the cells of his mind"—literally: "awaken the tools of his heart."

"scholars call the words of sacred prophecy 'Recitation' "—Hebrew *miḳra,* the regular rabbinic term for the text of the Bible.

"the musical accents"—i.e., the scheme of musical notation (Hebrew *ṭĕʿamim*) indicating the singsong *recitativo* in which the Sacred Text is read in the service of the synagogue.

"the Jerusalemite exiles of Spain"—meaning the Sephardic Jews exiled from Spain and settled in the Balkan Peninsula and in Asia Minor under Turkish rule, and their descendants.

"mĕnaṣṣeaḥ"—"chief musician" or "conductor," from the root meaning "to overcome, to overpower." The word occurs in the superscriptions of several psalms.

"music . . . gains mastery over a nature which is uneven . . ."—the idea being that anger or sorrow or any other mental disturbance disarranges the balance of humors, while pleasant music restores it.

"practical singing"—as distinguished from the theoretical (mathematical) branch of musicology.

III.12. "repetition translates his potentialities into action"—i.e., it brings out in the form of spoken words that which one has memorized, and thereby strengthens one's hold upon it.

"I have gained more understanding than all my teachers." The verse goes

on, *for thy testimonies are my meditation;* i.e., "by meditating upon them, over and over, I have learned them better than my teachers." Possibly the author means that meditating here signifies teaching the Law to others.

III.15. *"teach them"*—meaning the Lord's commandments. In Hebrew "to teach" (*šinnen*) and "to repeat" (*šinna*) come from etymologically closely related roots.

IV–VI. *AE,* fols. 99b ff.

IV.3."imitate him"—*yitharu,* literally: "vie with him."

IV.5. " 'change his clothes' "—i.e., renounce his faith and become an apostate. In other words, if there is danger of his renouncing Karaism, it is permissible to withhold the ban, in the hope that eventually he will be moved by public disapproval and his own better sense to repent and mend his ways.

IV.9. Cf. Maimonides' commentary to Mish. 'Abot 1: 18.

IV.10. "silver coins"—*lĕbanim,* literally: "white ones," Turkish silver coins.

"accepts the latter's apology"—meaning a verbal apology, which does not necessarily imply the eventual granting of the loan; in the meantime the need for the loan may have passed or the money may have been borrowed from someone else; the apology is thus merely for the distress caused by the original refusal to grant the loan. For the Rabbanite view cf. B. Yoma 23a.

IV.11. "Rabbi Japheth"—Japheth ben Eli, the famous Karaite commentator on the Bible; see above, p. 83.

"King David held his grudge against Shimei"—cf. I Kings 2: 8 f.

IV.12. "one sixth being the fixed market increase"—i.e., one sixth, or approximately 16½ per cent, over and above par value, is the maximum surcharge customarily allowed in commercial transactions on the market. For the Rabbanite rule in this matter cf. Mish. Gittin 4: 6; B. *ibid.,* 45a.

IV.13. "by way of admonition"—i.e., admonition not to exercise the opposite of charity.

IV.14. *"But there was no reckoning made with them . . ."*—referring to the doorkeepers of the Temple in Jerusalem who collected the donations brought by the people. For the Rabbanite view cf. B. Baba batra 8a ff.

IV.15. "our Sages have said . . ."—cf. B. Baba batra 9a.

V.2. For the Rabbanite views on this subject cf. B. Kiddušin 31a ff.; B. Kĕtubbot 103a; B. Yebamot 5b; Mĕkilta (ed. Weiss) 77a ff.

V.3. "building up their burial place so that it may be recognizable"—meaning the erection of gravestones over their graves.

"King Solomon fulfilled the testament of his father"—cf. I Kings 2.

"one's father's orphans"—i.e., of one's stepbrothers and stepsisters, as well as one's blood brothers and blood sisters.

V.4. "Scripture sometimes mentions the mother before the father"—e.g., in the foregoing quotation from Lev. 19: 3.

"the brothers of the father and the brothers of the mother"—i.e., one's uncles.

"but make them known"—meaning the commandments of the Law. The author means to say that the words *and thy children's children* indicate that the grandfathers, too, are to take part in the religious instruction of the children, and must therefore be honored in an equal degree with the father.

V.5. "deviate from the proper line of conduct"—owing to senile weakness of mind or body or both.

V.6. "these evil attributes cause one another." The text of this whole paragraph seems to be corrupt, and the translation given here is, therefore, in part conjectural. The meaning seems to be that the son could not claim that he inherited his waywardness and gluttony from his parents; rather, it was assumed that in most cases the son begins by disobeying his parents of his own accord and is then led naturally from one bad habit to another.

V.7. "they are now a burden upon him"—in the sense that they depend upon him for care and support. Cf. on the subject, Rašbam to Deut. 27: 15.

V.8. "while he is yet living"—so that the son might make a start in business for himself and be able to have the benefit of his father's advice during the first few years of his independence. For the Rabbanite view cf. B. Ḳiddušin 29 f.

V.9. *"teach them"*—i.e., the precepts of the Law. For the Rabbanite view cf. Maimonides, *Hilḵoṯ talmuḏ Torah* 1: 3.

VI.1. "Rabbi Joseph al-Ḳirḳisānī"—an error for Jacob al-Ḳirḳisānī. For the Rabbanite views on this subject cf. B. Ḳiddušin 32b ff.

"Honoring is greater than rising"—i.e., is more comprehensive, and involves marks of respect other than rising.

"whiteness of the beard"—which may occur early in life and does not necessarily indicate advanced age.

VI.4. "do him honor"—i.e., address him respectfully.

VI.5. "has weak sight"—and is unable to notice any lack of respect.

"on their left side"—as a mark of acknowledgment of their superior rank, the custom being for the inferior person to be placed on the left side, and the superior on the right.

VI.6. "Rabbi Levi"—son of Japheth ben Eli; see above, p. 374.

"Rabbi Jeshuah"—Jeshuah ben Judah; see above, p. 123.

"possessed of both wisdom and piety"—*ba'al din; din* is used here in the sense of the Arabic *dīn,* "religion, piety."

"will be devastated and . . . perish." Flagrant disrespect toward old age is said to be one of the marks of the dissolute times which will immediately precede the advent of the Messiah (cf. Mish. Soṭah 9: 15).

VI.7. "twice only each day"—i.e., when they come in and again when they leave.

"in order that they might not be reproached . . ."—i.e., if only these newly arrived men were to rise, while the others were to remain seated, the impression would be created that the latter were deliberately discourteous.

VI.8. "excepting when other men have entered . . . "—in which case all should rise, including the son, for the same reason as before.

VI.9. "it would have been permissible for a father to forgive his rebellious . . . son"—which is impossible, as it would run counter to a direct biblical command (Deut. 21: 18 ff.).

"all the people stood up respectfully before Moses"—cf. Exod. 33: 8: *And it came to pass, when Moses went out unto the tent, that all the people rose up and stood, every man at his tent door, and looked after Moses until he was gone into the tent.*

"nevertheless he did not prevent them"—i.e., although Moses, being an exceedingly modest man, would have preferred to forbid these manifestations of respect toward him, he could not do so, as it would have been a violation on his part of a direct biblical command.

VI.11. "in order not to . . . lose their respect"—i.e., scholars should not unnecessarily pass to and fro in the midst of ordinary people, nor engage them in unnecessary conversation, for the sole purpose of causing them to rise and show similar marks of deference; people are likely to resent such vanity and to lose respect for scholars in general, even for those who are modest and humble in demeanor.

VII. *AE,* fols. 121b–122a. The verse referred to is the biblical authority for the Rabbanite prohibition of eating meat and milk products together, forming the basic principle of Rabbanite dietary law (Hebrew *ḳašruṯ*).

VII.1. "Just as in the case of the dictum . . ." For the Rabbanite view on this matter cf. Sifra to this verse.

"the general is better known than the special"—i.e., all biblical ordinances are meant to be general rules, even if, for the sake of clarity, they are sometimes set forth in the biblical text in application only to a particular case; except when there is some decisive evidence restricting the application of the ordinance, which is not so in this instance, according to Bašyatchi.

VII.2. "joining"—i.e., physical contact of any sort.

VII.3. "the usufruct of them"—i.e., the usufruct of those already extant or made by non-Jews.

"mixed breeding . . . is forbidden"—cf. Lev. 19: 19.

"King David and King Solomon rode mules"—I Kings 1: 32–33: *And King David said . . . Cause Solomon my son to ride upon mine own mule.*

VII.4. "or vice versa"—i.e., the mother's flesh in the milk of her offspring.

"no matter what meat it may be"—i.e., no matter what the relationship may have been between the two animals from whom the milk and the meat have been obtained.

VII.5. For the Rabbanite view of this matter cf. B. Ḥullin 113b, 115b.

VIII. *AE,* fols. 53a–b.

VIII.1. "in so far as they come under the heading of work"—i.e., in so far as they are the regular duties forming part of the profession of midwifery, by the performance of which a midwife earns her wages. For the Rabbanite view on this subject cf. B. Yoma 85b.

"that he may live by them"—i.e., by the ordinances of the Bible; showing that they are meant to safeguard life, and not to expose it to danger.

"unless he is pulled out"—although the exertion attending the rescue comes, strictly speaking, under the heading of work forbidden on the Sabbath.

"Goliath . . . stood for forty days"—cf. I Sam. 17: 16.

VIII.2. "Rabbi Joseph ha-Ro'e"—see above, p. 123.

VIII.3. " 'shedding of blood' "—i.e., murder; a discussion of this principle is found in B. Sanhedrin 74a; cf. B. Nĕḏarim 27a.

"who delivered themselves to be put to death"—rather than consent to worship idols; cf. Dan. 3.

"she should have been slain"—because she did not resist the assault to the extent of letting herself be slain rather than submit to her assailant.

"no blood shall be spilled for him"—i.e., his slaying is not punishable by the execution of his slayer.

"you may strike first . . ." In other words, manslaughter in self-defense is justifiable and unpunishable. The assumption is that a burglar surprised in the act of breaking in is a desperate man and would not hesitate to murder his captor.

VIII.5. " 'Perhaps we shall have no need for them' "—i.e., for the medicines, etc.

"The ordinances . . . are not meant to exact vengeance . . ."—i.e., the biblical ordinances are not meant to serve solely as a pretext to enable God to punish men for violating any one of them, regardless of the circumstances attending the violation.

VIII.6."the Rabbanites say"—cf. Maimonides, *Hilkot Šabbat* 2:3.

KARAITE LITURGY

I. *Karaite Liturgy* (Wilno, 1890–92), IV, 51 ff. I am obliged to Dr. Simon Bernstein for help in several difficult passages.

I.1. "From His abode." The hymn was written by Mordecai Comtino, who lived at Constantinople in the 15th century. A Rabbanite scholar himself, he counted many Karaites among his pupils, and was in turn highly esteemed by them.

"Restitution for Zion"—*rib,* literally: "contest, quarrel."

"the year of recompense"—reading *šillum* for *šalom.*

"the stream of His gardens"—i.e., the stream which waters Paradise (Gen. 2:10).

"until the moon shall shine no more"—i.e., until the end of time.

"as fruitful as Manasseh and Ephraim"—i.e., the two sons of the Patriarch Joseph, who were the ancestors of two large Hebrew tribes, the great number of whose members became proverbial (Gen. 48:20).

"He has planted thee by the side of streams of water"—water being of utmost importance for cultivation in the warm and dry climate of the Near East.

I.3. "As the Bridegroom Enters the Synagogue"—i.e., if the wedding is to take place in the synagogue.

I.4. "by way of bridal gift. . ." For the Rabbanite Law on this point cf. Mish. Ḳiddušin 1:1.

I.7. "I will betroth thee unto me." In the biblical context God Himself is the speaker.

I.8. "The ornament of my bridegrooms." The author of this hymn was a certain physician named Judah ben Elijah Tišbi, of whom nothing further is known.

"those who stand"—in prayer.

"With . . . humility"—literally: "with bended knee."

"Multiply, so that thou mayest live/Forever"—in the person of thy descendants (Gottlober's emendation—*Bikkoret lĕ-tolĕdot hak-kara'im* [Wilno, 1865], p. 43—seems unnecessary).

"The fruit which/The Lord loves"—in the sense of human fruit, i.e., progeny.

I.9. "If They Do Not Reach the Aforementioned Place"—by the time this hymn is finished.

"God is in her midst"—i.e., the city's midst.

I.10. "For all her household are clad in scarlet"—i.e., in well-knit, warm robes.

"Her husband is known in the gates." The city gates were the customary place where the elders held court and dispensed justice and counsel and where the people gathered together.

"And delivers girdles to the merchant"—i.e., girdles adorned with her embroidery.

"And she laughs at the time to come"—i.e., she has no fear of it.

I.11. "THE FOLLOWING MARRIAGE CONTRACT." This form of the marriage contract differs in some minor respects from older forms, although the basic features remained the same in all periods. One of the most conspicuous earmarks of Karaite marital documents is that they are written wholly in Hebrew, whereas the Rabbanite are worded in Aramaic or mixed Aramaic and Hebrew. Cf., in general, L. M. Epstein, *The Jewish Marriage Contract* (New York, 1927).

I.11A. "in the year so-and-so since the creation of the world"—the era being B.C. 3760; in older Karaite documents the Seleucid era (B.C. 312) is mostly used (cf. Mann, pp. 158–159, n. 8; p. 164, n. 14).

"in the domain of the lord So-and-so"—meaning the Gentile sovereign or local noble landowner.

I.11C. "to the extent that I can afford"—literally: "according to the reach of my hand."

"as prescribed in the Law"—cf. Exod. 21:10.

I.11F. "by the covenant . . ."—i.e., under oath.

"if they can find them"—i.e., if they can find the fresh ears in Palestine personally or procure information of their having been found in time to celebrate the Karaite Passover accordingly.

I.12. "OR IF SHE BE A WIDOW." The blessing reflects the popular attitude of uneasiness toward the state of widowhood and the silent assumption that the loss of a husband by death may imply God's punishment for some hidden transgression. In part this feeling was nurtured by economic conditions, which made the widow a rather helpless individual, more or less dependent for her very livelihood upon the good will of others, since in ancient society the wife's social position and security were bound up with that of her husband. Jewish law, accordingly, treats the widow with unswerving solicitude, provides as far as possible for her protection, and holds care for, and charity toward, widows and their orphaned children to be a sublime virtue.

"OR IF SHE BE A DIVORCÉE." Here again is a reflection of ancient society where the male occupied a ruling position; the initiative in divorce actions was most commonly taken by the husband, and it was usually the wife who was "forsaken" by her husband, and not vice versa.

I.13. "THE CURTAIN"—read *hap-paroḵeṯ;* one of the curtains hung in front of the Ark containing the scrolls of the Law.

"like Rachel and like Leah"—the wives of the Patriarch Jacob.

"Perez, whom Tamar bore unto Judah"—cf. Gen. 38:27 ff. The whole quotation is in part inexact.

I.14. The hymn was composed by a certain Judah, tentatively identified with Judah ben Aaron Ḳilṭi, a Rabbanite poet who lived in Greece, probably in the 15th century.

"And give thee the benediction bestowed upon Abraham"—referring to Gen. 13:16: *And I will make thy seed as the dust of the earth.*

"the congregation of/Who is this"—referring to Song 3:6: *Who is this that comes up out of the wilderness like pillars of smoke?*—i.e., allegorically, the synagogue of Israel. The meaning of the sentence is, mayest thou live to see thy sons out of this girl grow into pious and devout men.

I.15. "Seven Benedictions." For the Rabbanite rule cf. B. Ketubbot 7b ff.

I.18. "Two are better than one"—i.e., a married couple are better than a single person.

I.21. "May Elijah the Prophet come to us soon"—as the forerunner of the Messiah.

"this one with that one"—masculine (i.e., the groom) and feminine (i.e., the bride), respectively.

I.22. "You Are to Recite"—meaning the aforementioned person who recited the benediction, the precentor.

"Drink water out of thine own cistern . . ."—i.e., be faithful to thy marriage vows.

"Let thy fountains be dispersed . . ."—i.e., may thy progeny be numerous.

"Let them be for thee alone . . ."—i.e., may all thy children be begotten in purity.

I.24. "in the Melody of Exile"—i.e., in a mournful tune; even in the midst of nuptial rejoicing, the newlyweds must not forget the plight of Israel in exile. The Rabbanite custom is also to break a glass (Šulḥan 'aruk, Oraḥ ḥayyim 560: 2).

I.25. "upon Their Heads"—i.e., upon the heads of the bridal couple. For the Rabbanite custom cf. Maimonides, *Hilkot ta'ăniyyot* 5: 13.

I.26. "Then Change the Melody"—to one of hope and reassurance.

I.28. "may thy seed inherit the gate of their enemies." A figure of speech (Gen. 24: 60) based on the military axiom that once a city's gate is forced by the conqueror, the city itself is at his mercy.

I.31. "among men . . . among women"—i.e., among the men and women of their generation.

"Asenath"—the daughter of Potiphera and wife of Joseph (Gen. 41: 45).

"Zipporah"—wife of Moses (Exod. 2: 21).

"Elisheba"—wife of Aaron (Exod. 6: 23); in the Greek form, Elizabeth, found in the New Testament.

I.32. "rise to the top"—in piety and good reputation.

I.40. "For the coming of our King, the Messiah!"—read probably *ham-mašiaḥ* for *'Eliyahu.*

I.42–43. The two hymns are part of the festival grace after meals.

II. By Aaron ben Joseph (*Karaite Liturgy,* III, 35); recited on the eve of the Day of Atonement.

II.7. "Thy seers"—i.e., the biblical Prophets.

II.21. "Remember"—literally: "see."

"the Father of the multitude"—i.e., the Patriarch Abraham; cf. Gen. 17: 4 ff.

II.22. "the oath given to mortals"—to make the progeny of Abraham numerous, Gen. 17: 2.

II.23. "the Wholehearted One"—the epithet applied to Abraham, Gen. 17: 1.

III. By Judah Tišbi (*Karaite Liturgy,* III, 184–185); recited in the morning of the Day of Atonement.

III.2. "purify me with hyssop"—i.e., by sprinkling me with a bunch of hyssop dipped in the purifying water; cf. Num. 19: 18; Ps. 51: 9.

"because of the merit of him who sat at the door of the tent during the heat of the day"—i.e., the Patriarch Abraham (Gen. 18:1 ff.).

III.6. "for the day has turned toward evening"—i.e., the time is short, and if we are not granted mercy soon, we shall be lost.

III.8. "the tenth day of this seventh month"—or the 10th of Tishri, i.e., the Day of Atonement.

III.9. "which the priest used to sacrifice"—cf. Lev. 16:3.

"they have eaten no bread"—i.e., they have fasted, "bread" being meant in the general sense of food.

III.10. "have devoted themselves"—literally: "have chosen."

IV. By Aaron ben Joseph (*Karaite Liturgy*, III, 205); recited on the first night of the "ten days of mercy" between New Year's Day and the Day of Atonement.

IV.2. "They are drawing repentance with the bucket of supplication." The supplicant is pictured as a traveler parched with thirst, straining to draw a bucket of water from the well.

IV.6. "there is none to extricate us"—*moše,* literally: "who would draw, or pull, us out," a play on *Moše,* the Hebrew form of Moses, whose name, according to popular etymology (Exod. 2:10), is supposed to signify "he who was drawn out of the water."

IV.9. "my multitudes"—i.e., Israel's multitudes.

"my great ones"—i.e., the Patriarchs.

IV.10. "the water of purification"—used in ritual purification (Num. 19:17 ff.).

V. By a certain Manṣūr (*Karaite Liturgy,* IV, 104–105).

V.1. "From Sunday till Friday"—literally: "from the first day to the sixth day," the workdays of the week having no individual names in the Hebrew language.

"I gain freedom"—from worldly cares and labors.

V.2. "knows it not"—i.e., does not know the Sabbath.

V.5. "from every tongue"—i.e., from every other people.

VI. By the Rabbanite poet Eleazar Ḳalir, who flourished presumably in the 8th and 9th centuries (*Karaite Liturgy,* IV, 250); it is to be recited by pilgrims in Jerusalem.

VII. To be recited on Tuesdays (*Karaite Liturgy,* I, 155).

VII.1. "the evil genius." The adversary of the good genius; both wage war forever in man's heart for control of his thoughts and actions.

VII.2. "save that the leaven in the dough prevents it"—figuratively for the weakness and proneness to stray from the right path present in the make-up of the human character.

VII.3. "the two hundred and forty-eight members of my body"—the traditionally accepted number, corresponding to the 248 positive ordinances in the Law; the number of sinews in the human body, 365, corresponds to the 365 negative ordinances.

VIII. To be recited on Fridays (*Karaite Liturgy,* I, 157).

VIII.1. "that Thy Law should be my daily occupation"—i.e., "that I should be able and anxious to study it as regularly as one engages in one's trade or profession."

VIII.4. "being cut off"—the biblical punishment for a grievous sin.

VIII.5. "charity"—literally: "gift."

ABBREVIATIONS

AE—Elijah Bašyatchi, *'Adderet 'Eliyahu* (Odessa, 1870)
HUCA—*Hebrew Union College Annual*
JRAS—*Journal of the Royal Asiatic Society*
JQR—*Jewish Quarterly Review*
KA—Ya'ḳūb al-Ḳirḳisānī, *Kitāb al-'anwār wal-marāḳib* (ed. L. Nemoy, New York, 1939–43), 5 vols. Quoted by volume and page, or by discourse, chapter, and paragraph.
LḲ—S. Pinsker, *Liḳḳuṭe ḳadmoniyyot* (Vienna, 1860)
Mann—J. Mann, *Texts and Studies in Jewish History and Literature* (Cincinnati, 1931–35), Vol. II: *Karaitica*
Poznanski—S. Poznanski, *The Karaite Literary Opponents of Sa'adiah Gaon* (London, 1908)
REJ—*Revue des études juives*
Russian-Jewish Encyclopedia—*Yevreyskaya entsiklopediya* (St. Petersburg, 1906–13), 16 vols.
Steinschneider—M. Steinschneider, *Die arabische Literatur der Juden* (Frankfurt a. M., 1902)
UJE—*Universal Jewish Encyclopedia* (New York, 1939–43), 10 vols.
ZDMG—*Zeitschrift der Deutschen Morgenlaendischen Gesellschaft*
ZfHB—*Zeitschrift fuer hebraeische Bibliographie*

GLOSSARY

Ark, Holy
a recess or cabinet in the synagogue in which the scrolls of the Law are kept

Ashkenazic Jews
originally a term for the German Jews, subsequently applied to their descendants in Poland, Russia, Bohemia, Hungary, etc. (cf. Sephardic Jews)

Booth (Hebrew *sukkah*)
the lightly constructed cabin built for use during the Feast of Tabernacles

Catenary theory of forbidden marriages
a theory used by the early Karaites to determine those relatives a Karaite may not lawfully marry; the forbidden degrees of relationship were deduced one from another, like links of a long chain (Latin *catena*)

Doorpost amulets (Hebrew *mĕzuzoṯ*)
strips of vellum inscribed with certain portions of the Pentateuch, enclosed in cases of metal, wood, or glass, and affixed to doorways; popularly regarded as amulets to ward off evil spirits

Exilarch
the chief magistrate of the Jewish community in Iraq (Babylonia) and its representative before the Persian kings and, later, the Moslem caliphs; they flourished from about the second through the eleventh century

Gaon ("Eminence")
the title assumed by the presidents of the two major rabbinical academies in Iraq (Babylonia), at Sura and at Pumbeditha, from the sixth to the eleventh century

Halakhah (literally: "rule")
a technical term for law, particularly postbiblical law, as set forth in the Mishnah and Talmud and later works

Ḥălīṣah
the escape ceremony used in Rabbanite legal practice by which a man may signify his refusal to marry the childless widow of his brother (cf. Levirate marriage)

Kašruṭ, Law of
the regulations in Rabbanite law governing the choice of food and the manner of its preparation

Law (Hebrew *Torah*)
in a narrow sense, the Pentateuch (the five books of Moses); in a wider sense, the Divine Law incorporated in the Old Testament

Levirate marriage
the marriage of a childless widow to her deceased husband's brother (cf. *Ḥăliṣah*)

Lulaḇ
the festive bouquet of palm fronds used in the ritual of the Feast of Tabernacles

Massoretes
Jewish scholars (active mostly during the second half of the first Christian millennium) whose principal work was the establishment of a definitive text of the Hebrew Bible; their notes bearing on this subject are called "Massora," and the Hebrew biblical text established by them is referred to as the massoretic text

Nazirite
the biblical term for a person who has made a vow to abstain from certain enjoyments, like wine, etc.

Phylacteries (Hebrew *tĕfillin*)
strips of vellum inscribed with certain passages from the Pentateuch and enclosed in leather cases with leather straps; they are affixed to the forehead and the left arm during the morning prayer.

Prophetic lessons (Hebrew *hafṭaroṯ*)
readings from the prophetic books of the Old Testament recited in the synagogue as appendices to the regular lessons from the Pentateuch.

Redemption (Hebrew *gĕ'ulah*)
the re-purchase by a kinsman of the landed property of his deceased relative which had been sold to a person outside the family (cf. Lev. 25: 25 ff.)

Redemption of the first-born son (Hebrew *piḏyon hab-ben*)
the offering prescribed in the Bible (Num. 18: 15 ff.), as a symbolic substitute for the sacrifice of the first-born son

Ritual fringes (Hebrew *ṣiṣiṯ*)
the fringes required by the Bible to be affixed to men's garments

Sadducees
a faction in Palestine (active approximately during the first century before and the first century after the birth of Christ) which was opposed to any modification of biblical law by oral tradition and custom (as postulated by the Pharisee faction)

Seleucid era
the era beginning with the Battle of Gaza in 312 B.C.; frequently used by Jews during the Middle Ages and after

Sephardic Jews
originally the term for Spanish Jews; subsequently applied to their descendants in the Balkans, the Near East, western Europe, and elsewhere (cf. Ashkenazic Jews)

Shiism
the teaching of the Shiite sect of Islam (as opposed to the orthodox Sunnites)

Targum (pl. Targumim)
the Aramaic translations of the Old Testament prepared for use among Jews at the time when Aramaic had become their spoken tongue

BIBLIOGRAPHY

(for works cited by author's name only see List of Abbreviations)

A properly documented history of the Karaites and of their literature, particularly in the period before A.D. 1500, does not exist, nor could it be written at the present embryonic stage of Karaite research. The older works of W. H. Rule (*History of the Karaite Jews* [London, 1870]), and of J. Fuerst (*Geschichte des Karaeertums* [Leipzig, 1862–69], 3 vols.), are now antiquated and unreliable. Z. Cahn's *The Rise of the Karaite Sect,* New York, 1937, is a sorry performance unworthy of consideration. The only available short sketches are those by A. Harkavy in the *Jewish Encyclopedia* (VII, 438–446), and in the Russian-Jewish Encyclopedia (IX, 268–290); by S. Poznanski in Hastings' *Encyclopedia of Religion and Ethics* (VII, 662–672); and by I. Markon in the *Encyclopedia Judaica* (IX, 923–945). S. Pinsker, *Liḳḳuṭe ḳaḏmoniyyoṯ* (Vienna, 1860), while antiquated, is still valuable for the early documents published there for the first time. J. Mann, *Texts and Studies in Jewish History and Literature, II: Karaitica* (Philadelphia, 1935), is a veritable thesaurus of new and highly important documents and studies relating to Karaism, but the major portion of it is devoted to the period after A.D. 1500.

The history of Karaite criticism of Sa'adiah from the tenth to the ninteeenth century is briefly but ably sketched, with copious bibliographical references, by S. Poznanski, *The Karaite Literary Opponents of Sa'adiah Gaon* (London, 1908).

A bibliographical survey of the Karaite literature written in Arabic is included in M. Steinschneider, *Die arabische Literatur der Juden* (Frankfurt a.M., 1902). Additions to it were supplied by S. Poznanski, *Orientalistische Literaturzeitung,* VII (1904), 257–274, 304–315, 345–359.

A critical survey of Karaite law was undertaken by B. Revel, *The Karaite Halaḳah, Part I* (Philadelphia, 1913); unfortunately, the remainder of the work was never published.

The social and economic factors in early Karaism are discussed in detail in a highly interesting Yiddish study by R. Mahler, *Karaimer, a Yidishe geuleh-bawegung in mitlalter* (New York, 1947). His main thesis, however, that Karaism was essentially a movement for political and social reform which assumed a religious garb for reasons of a purely practical nature seems rather premature and lacks sufficient documentary evidence. Cf. L. Nemoy, "Early Karaism (the Need for a New Approach)," *JQR,* XL (1950), 307–315.

For the background of Islamic history and civilization, see P. Hitti, *History of the Arabs* (3d rev. ed., London, 1946).

ANAN BEN DAVID

Fragments of Anan's *Book of Precepts* have been published in A. Harkavy, *Studien und Mittheilungen aus der K. Oeffentlichen Bibliothek zu St. Petersburg* (St. Petersburg, 1903), Vol. VIII (with Hebrew translation); S. Schechter, *Documents of Jewish Sectaries* (Cambridge, 1910), Vol. II; J. Mann, "Anan's Liturgy," *Journal of Jewish Lore and Philosophy,* I (1919), 329–353; M. Sokolov, "A Fragment of the Book of Precepts of Anan," *Bulletin (Izvestiya) of the Russian Academy of Sciences, Section of Humanistic Studies,* VII (1928), 243–253 (in Russian); and J. Epstein, "New Fragments of Anan's Book of Precepts," *Tarbiṣ,* VII (1935–36), 283–290 (in Hebrew).

S. Poznanski, "Anan et ses écrits," *REJ,* XLIV (1902), 161–187; XLV (1902), 50–69, 176–203.

L. Nemoy, "Anan ben David, a Re-appraisal of the Historical Data," *Semitic Studies in Memory of Immanuel Loew* (Budapest, 1947), pp. 239–248.

AL-NAHĀWANDĪ

The best available comprehensive essay on Benjamin al-Nahāwandī is by S. Poznanski in the Russian-Jewish Encyclopedia, V, 483–490.

AL-ḲŪMISĪ

I. Markon, *Korrespondenzblatt der Akademie fuer die Wissenschaft des Judentums,* VIII (1927), 18–30.

S. Poznanski in the Russian-Jewish Encyclopedia, VI, 945–950.

Mann, pp. 8–18.

AL-ḲIRḲISĀNĪ

Steinschneider, pp. 79–81.

Poznanski, pp. 8–11.

H. Hirschfeld, *Qirqisānī Studies,* "Jews' College Publication" (London, 1918), No. 6, contains the introductory chapter of the *Book of Gardens.*

SALMON BEN JEROHAM
Steinschneider, pp. 76–78.
Poznanski, pp. 12–14.
Mann, p. 18–22, 1469–1470.

JAPHETH BEN ELI
Steinschneider, pp. 81–84.
Poznanski, pp. 20–30.
Mann, pp. 26–28, 30–33.

SAHL BEN MAṢLIAḤ
Poznanski, pp. 30–41.
Mann, pp. 22–29.

JESHUAH BEN JUDAH
M. Schreiner, *Studien ueber Jeshu'a ben Jehuda* (Berlin, 1900).
Steinschneider, pp. 91–94.
Poznanski, pp. 48–53.
Mann, pp. 34–40.
I. Husik, *A History of Medieval Jewish Philosophy* (New York, 1916), pp. 55–58.

MOSES BEN SAMUEL OF DAMASCUS
Mann, pp. 201–255.

AARON BEN ELIJAH
Poznanski, pp. 79–81.
I. Husik, *A History of Medieval Jewish Philosophy* (New York, 1916), pp. 362–387.

AL-MAĠRIBĪ
Steinschneider, pp. 250–251.
Poznanski, pp. 81–82.

IBN AL-HĪTĪ

Steinschneider, p. 251.

Poznanski, p. 82.

BAŠYATCHI

The best characteristic of Elijah Bašyatchi is by S. Poznanski in the Russian-Jewish Encyclopedia.

Poznanski, pp. 82–83.

KARAITE LITURGY

J. Mann, "Anan's Liturgy," *Journal of Jewish Lore and Philosophy,* I (1919), 329–353, which includes the pertinent portions of Anan's *Book of Precepts.*

INDEX

(The proper names in biblical quotations and in book titles have not been indexed here.)

YALE JUDAICA SERIES

Saadia Gaon: The Book of Beliefs and Opinions. Translated by Samuel Rosenblatt

The Book of Civil Laws (*The Code of Maimonides, Book 13*). Translated by Jacob J. Rabinowitz

The Book of Judges (*The Code of Maimonides, Book 14*). Translated by Abraham M. Hershman

The Book of Offerings (*The Code of Maimonides, Book 9*). Translated by Herbert Danby

The Book of Acquisition (*The Code of Maimonides, Book 12*). Translated by Isaac Klein

Falasha Anthology. Translated by Wolf Leslau